# Globalization and Self-Determination

Is the nation-state under siege? A common answer is that globalization poses two fundamental threats to state sovereignty. The first threat concerns the unleashing of centrifugal and centripetal forces such as increasing market integration and the activities of institutions like the IMF, World Bank, and WTO that imperil state sovereignty from "outside" the nation-state. The second threat emanates from self-determination movements that jeopardize state sovereignty from "inside" the nation-state.

This book rigorously analyzes popular hypotheses regarding globalization's effect on state sovereignty from a broad social scientific perspective. Using empirical evidence the authors suggest that globalization's multi-level threats to state sovereignty have been overestimated. In most instances globalization is likely to generate pressure for increased government spending while only one form of market integration – foreign direct investment by multinational enterprises – appears to increase any feeling of economic insecurity.

Also contrary to popular perception, the net effect of IMF conditionality may be positive, limits on state sovereignty by multilateral development banks are not inevitable, and the WTO is not necessarily a threat to state sovereignty. Furthermore, globalization is likely to increase the risk of secessionism only in very specific conditions. And while some self-determination movements may find globalization useful, on the whole countries with more open economies appear less likely to house self-determination movements and are more likely to implement policies of fiscal centralization.

**David R. Cameron** is Professor of Political Science and Director of the Yale Program in European Union Studies at Yale University. **Gustav Ranis** is the Frank Altschul Professor Emeritus of International Economics at Yale University. **Annalisa Zinn** is a Ph.D. candidate in Political Science at Yale University.

## Routledge studies in the modern world economy

1 **Interest Rates and Budget Deficits**
A study of the advanced economies
*Kanhaya L. Gupta and Bakhtiar Moazzami*

2 **World Trade after the Uruguay Round**
Prospects and policy options for the twenty-first century
*Edited by Harald Sander and András Inotai*

3 **The Flow Analysis of Labour Markets**
*Edited by Ronald Schettkat*

4 **Inflation and Unemployment**
Contributions to a new macroeconomic approach
*Edited by Alvaro Cencini and Mauro Baranzini*

5 **Macroeconomic Dimensions of Public Finance**
Essays in honour of Vito Tanzi
*Edited by Mario I. Blejer and Teresa M. Ter-Minassian*

6 **Fiscal Policy and Economic Reforms**
Essays in honour of Vito Tanzi
*Edited by Mario I. Blejer and Teresa M. Ter-Minassian*

7 **Competition Policy in the Global Economy**
Modalities for co-operation
*Edited by Leonard Waverman, William S. Comanor and Akira Goto*

8 **Working in the Macro Economy**
A study of the US labor market
*Martin F. J. Prachowny*

9 **How Does Privatization Work?**
*Edited by Anthony Bennett*

10 **The Economics and Politics of International Trade**
Freedom and trade: Volume II
*Edited by Gary Cook*

11 **The Legal and Moral Aspects of International Trade**
Freedom and trade: Volume III
*Edited by Asif Qureshi, Hillel Steiner and Geraint Parry*

12 **Capital Markets and Corporate Governance in Japan, Germany and the United States**
Organizational response to market inefficiencies
*Helmut M. Dietl*

13 **Competition and Trade Policies**
Coherence or conflict
*Edited by Einar Hope*

14 **Rice**
The primary commodity
*A. J. H. Latham*

15 **Trade, Theory and Econometrics**
Essays in honour of John S. Chipman
*Edited by James C. Moore, Raymond Riezman and James R. Melvin*

16 **Who benefits from Privatisation?**
*Edited by Moazzem Hossain and Justin Malbon*

17 **Towards a Fair Global Labour Market**
Avoiding the new slave trade
*Ozay Mehmet, Errol Mendes and Robert Sinding*

18 **Models of Futures Markets**
*Edited by Barry Goss*

19 **Venture Capital Investment**
An agency analysis of UK practice
*Gavin C. Reid*

20 **Macroeconomic Forecasting**
A sociological appraisal
*Robert Evans*

21 **Multimedia and Regional Economic Restructuring**
*Edited by Hans-Joachim Braczyk, Gerhard Fuchs and Hans-Georg Wolf*

22 **The New Industrial Geography**
Regions, regulation and institutions
*Edited by Trevor J. Barnes and Meric S. Gertler*

23 **The Employment Impact of Innovation**
Evidence and policy
*Edited by Marco Vivarelli and Mario Pianta*

24 **International Health Care Reform**
A legal, economic and political analysis
*Colleen Flood*

25 **Competition Policy Analysis**
*Edited by Einar Hope*

26 **Culture and Enterprise**
The development, representation and morality of business
*Don Lavoie and Emily Chamlee-Wright*

27 **Global Financial Crises and Reforms**
Cases and caveats
*B. N. Ghosh*

28 **Geography of Production and Economic Integration**
*Miroslav N. Jovanović*

29 **Technology, Trade and Growth in OECD Countries**
Does specialisation matter?
*Valentina Meliciani*

30 **Post-Industrial Labour Markets**
Profiles of North America and Scandinavia
*Edited by Thomas P. Boje and Bengt Furaker*

31 **Capital Flows without Crisis**
Reconciling capital mobility and economic stability
*Edited by Dipak Dasgupta, Marc Uzan and Dominic Wilson*

32 **International Trade and National Welfare**
*Murray C. Kemp*

33 **Global Trading Systems at Crossroads**
A post-Seattle perspective
*Dilip K. Das*

34 **The Economics and Management of Technological Diversification**
*Edited by John Cantwell, Alfonso Gambardella and Ove Granstrand*

35 **Before and Beyond EMU**
Historical lessons and future prospects
*Edited by Patrick Crowley*

36 **Fiscal Decentralization**
*Ehtisham Ahmad and Vito Tanzi*

37 **Regionalisation of Globalised Innovation**
Locations for advanced industrial development and disparities in participation
*Edited by Ulrich Hilpert*

38 **Gold and the Modern World Economy**
*Edited by MoonJoong Tcha*

39 **Global Economic Institutions**
*Willem Molle*

40 **Global Governance and Financial Crises**
*Edited by Meghnad Desai and Yahia Said*

41 **Linking Local and Global Economies**
The ties that bind
*Edited by Carlo Pietrobelli and Arni Sverrisson*

42 **Tax Systems and Tax Reforms in Europe**
*Edited by Luigi Bernardi and Paola Profeta*

43 **Trade Liberalization and APEC**
*Edited by Jiro Okamoto*

44 **Fiscal Deficits in the Pacific Region**
*Edited by Akira Kohsaka*

45 **Financial Globalization and the Emerging Market Economies**
*Dilip K. Das*

46 **International Labor Mobility**
Unemployment and increasing returns to scale
*Bharati Basu*

47 **Good Governance in the Era of Global Neoliberalism**
Conflict and depolitization in Latin America, Eastern Europe, Asia and Africa
*Edited by Jolle Demmers, Alex E. Fernández Jilberto and Barbara Hogenboom*

48 **The International Trade System**
*Alice Landau*

49 **International Perspectives on Temporary Work and Workers**
*Edited by John Burgess and Julia Connell*

50 **Working Time and Workers' Preferences in Industrialized Countries**
Finding the balance
*Edited by Jon C. Messenger*

51 **Tax Systems and Tax Reforms in New EU Members**
*Edited by Luigi Bernardi, Mark Chandler and Luca Gandullia*

52 **Globalization and the Nation State**
The impact of the IMF and the World Bank
*Edited by Gustav Ranis, James Vreeland and Stephen Kosack*

53 **Macroeconomic Policies and Poverty Reduction**
*Edited by Ashoka Mody and Catherine Pattillo*

54 **Regional Monetary Policy**
*Carlos J. Rodríguez-Fuentez*

55 **Trade and Migration in the Modern World**
*Carl Mosk*

56 **Globalisation and the Labour Market**
Trade, technology and less-skilled workers in Europe and the United States
*Edited by Robert Anderton, Paul Brenton and John Whalley*

57 **Financial Crises**
Socio-economic causes and institutional context
*Brenda Spotton Visano*

58 **Globalization and Self-Determination**
Is the nation-state under siege?
*Edited by David R. Cameron, Gustav Ranis and Annalisa Zinn*

# Globalization and Self-Determination

## Is the nation-state under siege?

**Edited by David R. Cameron, Gustav Ranis and Annalisa Zinn**

LONDON AND NEW YORK

First published 2006
by Routledge
2 Park Square, Milton Park, Abingdon, Oxon OX14 4RN

Simultaneously published in the USA and Canada
by Routledge
711 Third Ave, New York, NY 10017

*Routledge is an imprint of the Taylor & Francis Group, an informa business*

First issued in paperback 2011



Typeset in Baskerville by Wearset Ltd, Boldon, Tyne and Wear



*British Library Cataloguing in Publication Data*
A catalogue record for this book is available from the British Library

*Library of Congress Cataloging in Publication Data*
A catalog record for this book has been requested

ISBN13: 978-0-415-77022-4 (hbk)
ISBN13: 978-0-415-51274-9 (pbk)
ISBN13: 978-0-203-08663-6 (ebk)

# Contents

# Illustrations

## Figures



## Tables

# Contributors

**Arun Agrawal** is an Associate Professor at the University of Michigan in the School of Natural Resources and Environment. His research concerns the political economy of development and environment.

**Nancy Brune** is a Ph.D. candidate in Political Science from Yale University and is currently a Fellow at the Center for Globalization and Governance at Princeton University.

**David R. Cameron** is a Professor of Political Science at Yale University. He has written extensively on trade openness and the European Union.

**Mary C. Cooper** is an Assistant Professor in the Department of Political Science at the Ohio State University and is currently completing a book manuscript on the creation of stock exchanges in China.

**Geoffrey Garrett** is President of the Pacific Council on International Policy and a Professor of International Relations at the University of Southern California.

**Soo Yeon Kim** is an Assistant Professor in the Department of Government and Politics at the University of Maryland.

**Bruce Kogut** is the Eli Lilly Professor at INSEAD, Fontainebleau and has written about corporate governance, privatization and globalization.

**Pierre F. Landry** is an Assistant Professor of Political Science at Yale University. His research interests focus on Chinese politics, comparative local government and quantitative comparative political analysis.

**Philip I. Levy** is a member of the Policy Planning Office of the U.S. Department of State. He served until recently on the President's Council of Economic Advisers. His research focuses on international trade, political economy and economic development.

**Gustav Ranis** is the Frank Altschul Professor Emeritus of International Economics at Yale University and is currently a Carnegie Scholar. His recent publications include *Globalization and the Nation-State* (2005, co-editor with James Vreeland and Stephen Kosack).

**Jesse C. Ribot** is Senior Fellow at the World Resources Institute. His research focuses on African politics, the political economy of development and the institutional politics of decentralization reforms.

**Jonathan Rodden** is the Ford Career Development Associate Professor of Political Science at MIT. His research and teaching focus on comparative political economy, with particular attention to federalism, distributive politics and political geography.

**Nicholas Sambanis** is an Associate Professor of Political Science at Yale University. His research interests are in the area of ethnic conflict, civil violence and economic development.

**Kenneth Scheve** is a Professor of Political Science at Yale University.

**Matthew J. Slaughter** is an Associate Professor of Business Administration at the Tuck School of Business at Dartmouth and is currently a member of the President's Council of Economic Advisors.

**Meredith L. Weiss** is a research fellow at the East-West Center Washington. Previously she was an Assistant Professor in International Studies at DePaul University. She specializes in Southeast Asian politics.

**Annalisa Zinn** is a Ph.D. candidate in Political Science at Yale University. Her research focuses on the prevention of violent conflict.

# Acknowledgments

This volume is one of the results of a broad three-year project entitled Globalization and Self-Determination, supported by a grant from the Carnegie Corporation of New York, with supplementary assistance from our host, the Yale Center for International and Area Studies, as well as the Coca Cola World Fund at Yale and the Edward J. and Dorothy Clarke Kempf Fund. The project was first conceived in 2000 by Arun Agrawal, Geoffrey Garrett and Gustav Ranis. David R. Cameron later joined Gustav Ranis as a co-principal investigator. The project came to involve many of our colleagues working on related international issues at Yale University and we are indebted to these colleagues, too numerous to name individually, for their input and involvement in the project. We are especially grateful to the Carnegie Corporation and to Stephen Del Rosso, senior program officer, for his interest and support.

This volume incorporates the results of a coherent research program presented at a conference on "Globalization and Self-Determination: The Nation-State under Siege," held at Yale University on 14–15 May 2004. We are grateful to all those who presented papers, served as discussants of the various panels, as well as others who offered helpful suggestions and raised important questions from the floor. These included Keith Darden, Anna Grzymala-Busse, John Freeman, Oona Hathaway, Pauline Jones-Luong, Jack Knight, Guillermo Mondino, Mahmood Monshipouri, Victoria Murillo, Ibrahim Saif, Beth Simmons, Anand Swamy, Daniel Treisman, James Vreeland and John Williamson. For administrative support, we would like to thank Richard Kane, Peg Limbacher, Marilyn Wilkes, Lisa Brennan and Beverly Kimbro.

The quality of the conference papers exceeded our high hopes, and it was clear that they deserved wider dissemination. We therefore assembled and edited this volume during the 2004–2005 academic year and we are grateful to our editor at Routledge, Robert Langham, for his support in this endeavor. Any opinions, findings, conclusions or recommendations expressed in this publication are those of the authors and do not necessarily reflect the views of the supporting institutions.

Chapter 2 was first published in Bardhan, P., Bowles, S. and

Wallerstein, M. (eds) (2006), *Globalization and Egalitarian Redistribution*, Princeton University Press, reprinted by permission of Princeton University Press. Chapter 3 was first published as Scheve, K. and Slaughter, M. (2004) "Economic Insecurity and the Globalization of Production," *American Journal of Political Science*, 48/4: 662–74, published by, and reprinted by, permission of Blackwell Publishing. Chapter 4 was first published as Brune, N., Garrett, G. and Kogut, B. (2004) "The IMF and the Global Spread of Privatization," *IMF Staff Papers*, 51/2: 195–219. Copyright from IMF Staff Papers. Chapter 11 was first published in Kahler, M. (2003) *Governance in a Global Economy*, © 2003 Princeton University Press, reprinted by permission of Princeton University Press.

# Editors' introduction

*David R. Cameron, Gustav Ranis and Annalisa Zinn*

State sovereignty has been the key institutional support for self-determination for more than three centuries. Wars, whether civil or international, have redefined the relevant actors and their inter-relationships from time to time and more or less radically. The nature of sovereignty, whether it is understood territorially, judicially or economically, has also undergone redefinition. Nonetheless, the fundamental pillar of the Westphalian system of states – the respect for national borders and the autonomy of domestic actors within them – has endured, at least legally. The key question is whether it will continue to endure also in practice.[1]

A common answer is that globalization – defined minimally as the international integration of markets for goods, services, labor and capital – poses two fundamental threats to state sovereignty. The first threat concerns the unleashing of powerful centrifugal and centripetal forces that limit state sovereignty from "outside" the nation-state. These forces include the increasingly integrated nature of markets, the emergence of regional institutions to govern these markets, and the activities of multilateral institutions such as the International Monetary Fund (IMF), the World Bank and the World Trade Organization (WTO). But although these forces may limit the autonomy of nation-states – for example by imposing certain economic reforms or reducing control over macroeconomic policy – they do not change the form of national governments, and so are thought to represent *de facto* rather than *de jure* threats to state sovereignty.

By contrast, globalization's second threat to state sovereignty – the facilitation of attacks on existing political arrangements and boundaries from "inside" the nation-state – has both *de jure* and *de facto* dimensions. Although movements for subnational autonomy, which demand either a redefinition of national political boundaries or strive for a greater share of the national political and economic pie, have been constant features of the political landscape for centuries (Tilly *et al.* 1975; Sewell 1990), many assume that contemporary globalization processes have increased the number of such movements, as well as their bases of support and chances of success (Dragadze 1996; Marks and McAdam 1996; Sorens 2004).

As such, it has become more likely that the demand for greater subnational autonomy, also known as the demand for ethnic or regional self-determination when the demanding group is defined on the basis of an ethnic or regional identity, results in either the devolution of political power within countries – a *de facto* reduction of state sovereignty – or the creation of new states – a *de jure* redistribution of state sovereignty.

Moreover, many assume that these outside and inside threats to the nation-state are likely to be mutually reinforcing, with several causal mechanisms operative. First, the integration of markets has made it possible for subnational groups to pursue their own destinies as independent actors (Alesina and Spolaore 1997; Anderson and O'Dowd 1999). Second, globalization and the concomitant increases in communication networks and labor mobility have made it much easier for subnational groups to mobilize across national borders and also to involve diasporic populations, which may contribute to the success of these movements (McLellan and Richmond 1994; Waterman 1998; Kumar 2000). Third, globalization has provided subnational groups with additional resources, which may also make independence appear more feasible.[2] Fourth, globalization can produce popular backlash, which opportunistic political actors representing interests threatened by globalization, may utilize to shape demands for greater autonomy (Dragadze 1996).

These processes all suggest a larger causal relationship between globalization and self-determination: linkages between supranational and subnational actors that actively fuel self-determination movements by reducing the control of national government within their own borders. At the same time, however, these processes also point to the proposed central tension of globalization, namely that it increases the ability of groups to achieve political autonomy while simultaneously lessening their ability to exercise effective independence in the realm of policy choice, which calls into question the value of winning *de jure* recognition of their autonomy.

It is in this setting of ideas, assumptions and uncertainty about the relationship between globalization, self-determination and state sovereignty that this volume appears. There exist multiple common notions about how globalization is threatening state sovereignty from both the inside and the outside, but we still do not know how many of these are consistent with reality or myths that need to be debunked. The chapters in this volume help fill this significant gap in understanding by investigating the extent, over time and space, to which globalization is threatening the nation-state from both outside and inside. Their general consensus is that some of the common notions about globalization and state sovereignty are fallacious, others are only partially valid, while still others are applicable only in a specific, circumscribed context.

The volume's first part – "Threats from the outside: market integration and national autonomy" – presents three chapters that explore how greater market integration is affecting state sovereignty. In particular, the contributors to this part take a critical look at two popular hypotheses about globalization's threat to the nation-state from above: globalization has increased the power of finance and industry to put downward pressure on interventionist government and globalization increases economic insecurity within nations.

A deep conviction among critics of globalization is that the political power of finance and industry has increased dramatically with market integration. Quite simply, if capital does not approve of conditions in one country, it can credibly threaten to move its activities elsewhere. This, in turn, induces governments to seek the approval of foreign capitalists, which may create a problem for the acceptance of globalization if it enhances worker insecurity, because capital prefers that government play a smaller, not a larger, role in the economy.

The first two chapters investigate this common belief from different angles, and while they demonstrate that the situation is more complex than the simple hypothesis suggests, the overall conclusion is that globalization puts downward pressure on government only in some circumstances and for the most part encourages additional government spending.

In Chapter 1 – "Trade, political institutions and the size of government" – David R. Cameron and Soo Yeon Kim investigate the effects of economic openness and political institutions on the relative size of government in 19 developed democracies in the last three decades of the twentieth century. On the basis of pooled time-series data for the 19 countries, Cameron and Kim find the extent of trade openness has no effect on changes in government spending and revenues. Contrary to the hypothesis that increasing openness results in increased spending and revenues, large increases in openness were associated with small increases or decreases in the relative size of public expenditures and revenues. However, they argue that the balance of trade reflects much better than the aggregate volume of trade – the conventional measure of openness – the extent to which a country is likely to experience trade-related dislocations that result in increased spending. Consistent with that argument, they find that large trade deficits and deterioration of the balance of trade had significant expansionary effects on government spending across the advanced capitalist world over the three decades.

In "Public opinion, international economic integration and the welfare state," Kenneth Scheve and Matthew J. Slaughter take Cameron and Kim's study a step further by investigating whether the mechanism linking globalization to higher levels of government spending is indeed increased political support for social insurance and redistributive policies as a result of economic liberalization's cost to workers. To do so, they examine extensive data on individual policy preferences, macroeconomic conditions and individual-level characteristics such as educational attainment, occupation and industry of employment.

Scheve and Slaughter find that labor market concerns are key in accounting for both individual policy decisions and the variation in these across countries. Not only are individual opinions decidedly more liberal when liberalization is tied to support for workers, but countries with more generous labor market policies have publics with less protectionist opinions and less salient differences in opinion across more and less-skilled workers. This evidence leads Scheve and Slaughter to conclude that substantial social insurance and redistributive policies are *not* inconsistent with economic globalization because political support for liberalization itself depends in part on those very policies. Though approaching the issue from a different angle, this chapter also challenges the popular view that globalization necessarily puts downward pressure on interventionist government.

It is also widely believed that globalization, by increasing the disparities between those who benefit from market allocations of wealth and risk and those who do not (at least in the short term), has made many citizens feel much less secure about their economic futures. As a result, the demands on government to compensate market losers – through income transfer programs, the public provision of social services, subsidies and the like (i.e. the hallmark of the postwar OECD's mixed economies) – have increased as a result of globalization (Rodrik 1997).

In Chapter 3 – "Economic insecurity and the globalization of production" – Kenneth Scheve and Matthew J. Slaughter investigate whether economic integration does indeed increase worker insecurity in advanced economies. While previous research failed to find any link between international trade and worker insecurity, Scheve and Slaughter present evidence suggesting that foreign direct investment (FDI) by multinational enterprises (MNEs) is the key aspect of integration generating perceptions of risk, with the following causal mechanism operative. FDI by MNEs increases firms' elasticity of demand for labor; more elastic labor demands, in turn, raise the volatility of wages and employment, all of which tend to make workers less secure. By showing that one form of market integration increases the feeling of economic insecurity, the Scheve-Slaughter chapter qualifies, to a limited extent, aforementioned popular hypotheses on globalization and worker insecurity.

The volume's second part – "More threats from the outside: international economic institutions and national autonomy" – presents four chapters that explore how greater market integration and the increasing scope of activity by multilateral lending institutions are affecting state sovereignty. In addition to investigating the popular conception that the benefits of international financial institution (IFI) lending and policy may be outweighed by the constraints imposed by the ways capital flows and conditionality are negotiated, two of these chapters also shed light on new research questions: the domestic political impact of China's WTO membership and international economic institutions' effects on state sovereignty.

A popular notion is that the benefits of IFI lending are outweighed by the policy constraints imposed by conditionality. Not surprisingly, studies supported by the IMF and World Bank on the effects of official development assistance on recipient countries have tended to show that such assistance increases growth, lowers inflation and stabilizes economies (Bird 1996). Independent research, however, has been more skeptical and more supportive of the view that once the reason countries go to the IMF is taken into account (i.e. that they are in crisis), loans *cum* conditionality are bad for macroeconomic performance (see Przeworski and Vreeland 2000).

In Chapter 4 – "The International Monetary Fund and the global spread of privatization" – Nancy Brune, Geoffrey Garrett and Bruce Kogut, however, challenge the view that the policy constraints imposed by IMF conditionality render IFI loans on the whole more detrimental than beneficial to recipient countries. Using both cross-sectional analysis covering the 1985–1999 period and panel data, the authors find that IMF conditionality has an important indirect economic benefit. For every dollar a developing country owed the IMF in the early 1980s, it subsequently privatized state-owned assets worth roughly 50 cents. And since the increased revenues from privatization, if of the one-shot variety, represent a large capital flow to developing countries, the significance of this effect should not be underestimated.

According to Brune, Garrett and Kogut, the reason why private investors are willing to pay more for privatized assets in countries that owe the IMF money is that they view IMF conditionality as a *de facto* good housekeeping seal of approval, given that such countries are more likely to pursue market-friendly policies, such as deregulation and balanced budgets, into the future. This suggests that the primary value of the IMF may be financial market enhancement rather than the provision of capital, in which case the net effect of conditionality, contrary to the popular hypothesis, may turn out to be good. The authors are nevertheless careful to argue that the additional capital drawn into developing countries as a result of the IMF–privatization nexus does not necessarily justify the long list of policy conditions typically imposed by the IMF on recipient countries.

The next chapter – "The MDBs and the nation-state" by Gustav Ranis – addresses a modified version of the popular hypothesis that IFI lending is frequently more detrimental than beneficial to both state sovereignty and economic development. As Ranis notes, critics on the left often complain that multilateral development banks (MDBs), using their conditionality clout, have involved themselves in a neo-imperialist fashion in the most sensitive domestic policy arenas and threaten countries' self-determination efforts, while critics on the right generally point to what they see as a lack of overall development success as an indication that development should be left to private markets.

The response Ranis offers to these critics is that yes, there has been some threat to state sovereignty by MDBs, but this threat has been a choice, not an inevitable consequence. MDBs' intrusion on state sovereignty can be minimized if they adopt a more precise stance and encourage recipients to take the initiative in formulating reform packages and seeking support for their implementation. In addition, Ranis proposes that the safeguarding of self-determination by recipients would be furthered if the MDBs agreed on and implemented a more effective division of labor. For example, given the World Bank's superior analytical capability, it should focus on macro analysis and let the various regional development banks focus on microeconomic, sectoral and institutional matters, which are likely to be country-specific and require much local knowledge.

In Chapter 6 – "The political impact of WTO membership in urban China" – Mary C. Cooper and Pierre F. Landry use mass survey data collected in several Chinese cities to examine the political implication of the Chinese leadership's embrace of globalization. These surveys included residents of cities that expect large economic benefits from WTO membership, cities that expect significant economic harm from WTO membership, and cities facing more uncertainty about their prospects under the WTO. Based on a detailed socioeconomic analysis of the respondents, Cooper and Landry find that there is not necessarily congruence between citizens' cost/benefit analysis of accession and objective measures of the "WTO challenge" in their sector and region of employment. Rather, a significant determinant of support for China's WTO membership was nationalism stemming from the regime's policy of portraying WTO membership as a foreign policy accomplishment, e.g. as an expression of national self-determination rather than a curtailment of state sovereignty.

The next chapter by Philip I. Levy also investigates international economic institutions' effects on state sovereignty. As Levy notes, a popular allegation is that supranational organizations such as the WTO are undermining the sovereign rights of the nation-state by making decisions on agricultural and environmental policy that are the normal domain of elected national or subnational legislatures. While this allegation may be superficially appealing, Levy demonstrates that it does not stand up to close analysis for two main reasons. First, it is based on misunderstandings of the legal status of trade agreements and dispute settlement mechanisms. Second, once the concept of sovereignty is properly understood as freedom from compulsion, it is clear that international trade agreements do not pose a threat to the sovereign rights of nations. To amount to violations of state sovereignty, international trade agreements would have to prevent physically a country from exercising the normal functions of government within its borders or from engaging in voluntary commercial transactions with others – scenarios that simply do not arise in international trade negotiations or in the enforcement of the agreements that emerge.

In the volume's third part – "Threats from the inside: globalization, autonomy movements and political organization" – the authors turn to the question of how globalization is affecting the emergence, goals and strategies of self-determination movements, and shaping the institutional and political responses of governments to these demands for political reorganization. Popular views have been that globalization increases the frequency and intensity of culturally-based movements for regional autonomy or even independence and makes it more likely that nation-states will devolve considerable power to subnational units, thus increasing the credibility of secessionist threats.

Several studies (Dragadze 1996; Marks and McAdam 1996; Sorens 2004) have in fact found a causal link between globalization and demands for greater regional autonomy, with the international integration of domestic economies increasing both the attractiveness and economic viability of greater autonomy. Their evidence, however, is limited to a small number of countries, almost exclusively in Europe, which points to the need for research on whether globalization affects self-determination movements in other regions of the world. In addition, while these works offer explanations for their findings, they do not provide a theory of how and why globalization may affect demands for greater regional autonomy and such a theory would be the necessary starting point for further empirical research on the links between globalization and self-determination movements.

To fill in this theoretical gap, in Chapter 8 – "Globalization, decentralization and secession: a review of the literature and some conjectures" – Nicholas Sambanis addresses the three questions that a theory of globalization and subnational self-determination would need to answer: why do groups want to secede? In which regions are we most likely to observe violent self-determination movements? How does globalization influence the risk that some groups will want to secede? In doing so, he reviews the relevant theoretical and empirical literature, as well as several cases, and outlines some conjectures on the conditions under which globalization is likely to increase the risk of secession. Sambanis's main argument is that, if globalization increases the risk of external economic shocks that are unevenly distributed within and across countries, and if it increases the level of fiscal centralization as has been shown in several studies, then globalization could increase the risk of secession in countries where the central government has a poor track record of providing social insurance to peripheral regions.

In Chapter 9 – "Economic integration and political separatism: parallel trends or causally linked processes?" – Annalisa Zinn empirically investigates whether globalization has increased the frequency and intensity of demands for self-determination by stimulating the formation of movements for greater regional autonomy or independence and encouraging the persistence of existing movements. With the help of a multivariate statistical analysis of 116 countries from 1980–1999, Zinn finds that countries with open economies appear *less likely* to be places where ethnic, religious or regional groups form political organizations to demand self-determination, compared to countries with more closed economies. This finding challenges the popular view that globalization amplifies the intensity of subnational threats to state sovereignty and suggests that increases in the number of active self-determination movements are actually being curbed by the increasing level of trade between countries.

Chapter 10 – "Globalization and ethnonationalist movements: evidence from Spain and India" – by Meredith L. Weiss further investigates the links between globalization and demands for greater political autonomy by comparing and contrasting four ethnonationalist movements, two in Spain (Basque and Catalan movements) and two in India (Punjabi and Kashmiri movements). In particular, Weiss examines when and why ethnonationalist sentiments still carry weight, the significance of domestic and international support and sanctions to these movements, and what such movements reveal about the relative potency of nation-states and global forces in managing or changing their course.

While Weiss' four cases are not collectively exhaustive of possible scenarios, they effectively highlight several significant findings, all of which question a strong and direct link between globalization and the demand for greater autonomy. First, economic considerations notwithstanding, ethnic, regional and religious sentiments remain powerful motivators for political behavior, especially when local cultures, languages or religions appear to be under siege. Second, while international sanction and support clearly inform the decisions of both states and movement activists, the domestic context – how states respond when faced with ethnonationalist demands – remains more important to the course of those movements. Third, not all ethnonationalisms encounter globalization alike; movements that can call upon a large and engaged diasporic population or that invoke transnational identities may find forces of globalization more useful than movements that are truly local in scope. Fourth, the global forces at play are mercurial. Shifts in global norms and priorities in particular may (de)legitimate ethnonationalist movements, provide or diminish inspiration, or shift political opportunity structures and available resources in important ways, even if global economic forces appear relatively insignificant to activists' calculations.

Globalization is also commonly believed to render national governments more likely to devolve considerable power to subnational units. The rationale behind this proposition is that international market integration increases the credibility of secessionist threats by increasing the economic viability of independence. This, in turn, renders nation-states that are exposed to globalization forces less likely to repress political movements that demand change, especially when such demands do not require massive political transformations or the reconfiguration of state boundaries.

In Chapter 11 – "Globalization and fiscal decentralization" – Geoffrey Garrett and Jonathan Rodden tackle the above hypothesis head-on. As previously mentioned, popular speculation is that globalization has caused a downward shift in the locus of governance by reducing the economic costs of smallness and allowing localities and regions with distinct preferences to pursue their own political and economic strategies (e.g. Alesina and Spolaore 1997; Bolton and Roland 1997). Garrett and Rodden, however, find a striking relationship in the opposite direction. Using a large cross-national dataset composed of expenditure and revenue decentralization data for the 1980s and 1990s, they find that international market integration has actually been associated with fiscal centralization.

Contrary to the popular hypothesis, Garrett and Rodden's proposed explanation for the positive association between globalization and fiscal integration is that globalization actually undermines the credibility of regional exit threats by increasing perceptions of aggregate and region-specific risk within countries. These perceptions, in turn, create powerful new demands for fiscal centralization because centralized fiscal arrangements permit more macroeconomic stabilization, interregional risk sharing and redistribution, and are thus better equipped to deal with globalization's uncertainties.

Further analysis of whether globalization promotes decentralization is presented in Chapter 12 – "Recentralizing while decentralizing: how national governments re-appropriate forest resources" by Arun Agrawal and Jesse C. Ribot. In this chapter the authors investigate four countries' (Senegal, Uganda, Nepal and Indonesia) decentralization initiatives in the forestry sector, and in particular, the pressures that led central governments to yield reforms as policy concessions, and the political instruments that the same governments used to reduce the exercise of meaningful local authority.

Several insights emerge from the detailed, comparative case study analysis regarding the relationship between globalization and decentralization. First, while the globalization of ideas and resources, as represented in the common agenda of a number of international donors, played an important role in the initiation of decentralization reforms in some countries (e.g. Senegal and Nepal), in other countries (e.g. Indonesia and Uganda) decentralization was forced onto the agenda by powerful provincial actors who sought a share in decision-making or revenues. Second, even though globalization may stimulate some initial attempts at decentralization in developing countries, such attempts have rarely led to meaningful reforms. Rather, these "decentralizing" central governments have tended to create policies that restrict the ability of local governments to make meaningful decisions by limiting the kinds of powers that are transferred and the domain in which such powers can be exercised and choosing local institutions that serve and answer to central interests.

In proceeding through the volume, the reader is encouraged to keep in mind three questions of substantial importance. First, how are greater market integration and the increasing scope of activity by multilateral lending institutions affecting national sovereignty? Second, how is globalization affecting movements for subnational autonomy? Third, how can respect for the principle of self-determination be re-constituted within a new political reality that comprises overlapping jurisdictions? We offer this volume as a way to shed some light on these critical questions. The answers presented are not definitive but will hopefully stimulate further research.

## Notes

1 See Krasner (1999) for a penetrating analysis of the theory and practice of Westphalian sovereignty.
2 For example, the European Union's structural funds are given to regional units, not national member governments and the World Bank and other international development agencies often fund projects in the subnational units and through NGOs, rather than through central governments in developing countries.

## References

Alesina, A. and Spolaore, E. (1997) "On the Number and Size of Nations," *Quarterly Journal of Economics*, 112/4: 1027–56.

Anderson, J. and O'Dowd, L. (1999) "Borders, Border Regions and Territoriality: Contradictory Meanings, Changing Significance," *Regional Studies*, 33/7: 593–604.

Bird, G. (1996) "The International Monetary Fund and Developing Countries: A Review of the Evidence and Policy Options," *International Organization*, 50: 477–511.

Bolton, P. and Roland, G. (1997) "The Breakup of Nations: A Political Economy Analysis," *Quarterly Journal of Economics*, 112/4: 1057–90.

Dragadze, T. (1996) "Self-Determination and the Politics of Exclusion," *Ethnic and Racial Studies*, 19/2: 341–51.

Krasner, S. D. (1999) *Sovereignty: Organized Hypocrisy*, Princeton: Princeton University Press.

Kumar, A. (2000) *Passport Photos*, Berkeley: University of California Press.

Marks, G. and McAdam, D. (1996) "Social Movements and the Changing Structure of Political Opportunity in the European Union," *Western European Politics*, 19/2: 249–78.

McLellan, J. and Richmond, A. H. (1994) "Multiculturalism in Crisis: A Postmodern Perspective on Canada," *Ethnic and Racial Studies*, 17/4: 662–83.

Przeworski, A. and Vreeland, J. (2000) "The Effect of IMF Programs on Economic Growth," *Journal of Development Economics*, 62/2: 385–422.

Rodrik, D. (1997) *Has Globalization Gone Too Far?*, Washington: Institute for International Economics.

Sewell, W. (1990) "Collective Violence and Collective Loyalties in France: Why the French Revolution Made a Difference," *Politics and Society*, 14: 527–52.

Sorens, J. (2004) "Globalization, Secessionism, and Autonomy," *Electoral Studies*, 23: 727–52.

Tilly, C., Tilly, L. and Tilly, R. (1975) *The Rebellious Century*, Cambridge: Harvard University Press.

Waterman, P. (1998) *Globalization, Social Movements, and the New Internationalisms*, Washington, DC: Mansell.

# Part I

# Threats from the outside

## Market integration and national autonomy

# 1 Trade, political institutions and the size of government

*David R. Cameron and Soo Yeon Kim*[1]

Over the past several decades, the developed economies of North America, Europe and Asia have become increasingly open, increasingly dependent upon exports to international markets to sustain domestic production, employment and consumption, increasingly dependent upon imports to supply domestic consumption, and increasingly dependent upon direct and portfolio investment from abroad.[2] In some of the countries, citizens and governments have long been accustomed to dealing with the vagaries and uncertainties created by a high degree of dependence upon international markets, producers and investors – indeed, long before "globalization" became a part of everyday discourse. In others, the discovery that the performance of the economy depends to a considerable degree upon international actors is a more recent phenomenon. But in all – even those which are least dependent on international markets, producers and investors – openness has become a fact of contemporary economic life.

As the developed economies became increasingly open in recent decades, most if not all of their polities experienced an equally consequential increase in the relative size of government, defined in terms of spending and revenues. Six decades ago, Clark (1945) predicted that government spending as a proportion of Gross National Product would reach an upper limit at about 25 percent. Time soon rendered that vision obsolete, and year after year throughout the 1950s, 1960s and 1970s government spending and revenues relative to GNP or GDP increased and in many countries reached levels that were more than twice Clark's imagined upper limit.[3] And despite the rhetorical commitment of many political leaders to liberalization, deregulation and privatization, and efforts in some nations to roll back high levels of taxation and public expenditure, the fiscal role of government remains significant in all and continues to increase in some.

The simultaneous increases throughout much of the advanced capitalist world in recent decades in the extent of economic openness and the relative size of government in fiscal terms suggest the possible existence of a causal relationship between the two. And indeed, after finding a strong positive cross-sectional relationship between the extent of openness, measured by the ratio of exports and imports to GDP in 1960, and the magnitude of the change in the ratio of total government revenues to GDP from 1960 to 1973, Cameron (1978) suggested that openness influences the structure of an economy and, in turn, the organization of labor, partisanship of government and extent of social spending. Building on that argument and evidence of a positive relationship between the extent of openness and extent of government spending, Garrett (1998, 2001) and Rodrik (1998) suggested that openness generates pressures on government to increase spending on social programs in order to protect or compensate the individuals and economic actors who are exposed to, and adversely affected by, the competitive pressures emanating from the international marketplace.

As plausible as the trade-related compensation hypothesis may be, several studies have concluded that, rather than having an expansionary effect on year-to-year changes in spending, openness has had a negligible or even *contractionary* effect on spending. In a pooled cross-sectional time-series analysis, Cameron and McDermott (1995) found that once a variety of controls, including the level of spending in the previous year, were introduced, the extent of trade openness had a negligible relationship with the magnitude of year-to-year changes in spending between 1960 and 1992. Likewise, Garrett (2001) reported that, while the extent of trade was closely related to several measures of public spending across a large number of countries, it had virtually no relation with the extent of change in spending once various controls were introduced. He found that a measure of change in the extent of openness was negatively and significantly associated with various measures of spending. That inverse relationship suggested that, rather than causing governments to spend more in order to compensate those adversely affected by globalization, increasing openness forces governments to reduce spending and taxes in order to compete with other governments for mobile capital. Similarly, Garrett and Mitchell (2001) found, in a pooled cross-sectional time-series analysis of annual fluctuations in spending in 18 countries between 1961 and 1993, a consistently significant negative relationship between the extent of openness and the extent of increase in several measures of government spending. And in an analysis of annual changes in spending in 18 countries between 1961 and 1994, Burgoon (2001) found that the extent of openness had a consistently significant negative impact on a variety of measures of spending, suggesting that high and increasing openness constrains public spending. Likewise, in an analysis of changes in spending in 14 Latin American countries between 1973 and 1997, Kaufman and Segura-Ubiergo (2001) found that trade openness – measured both in terms of the extent of openness and the yearly change in openness – had a significant negative impact on changes in spending, suggesting that high and increasing exposure to the competitive pressures of the international economy cause economic interests to put pressure on government to reduce spending.

Iversen and Cusack (2000) have presented the most forceful critique of the view that high and increasing levels of openness result in increases in the relative size of government. In a pooled cross-sectional time-series analysis of annual changes in transfer payments and public consumption expenditures in 15 countries between 1961 and 1993, they found that, whereas the extent of openness had a modest negative impact on spending – insignificant in the case of transfer payments and significant in the case of consumption expenditures – and the change in openness had a significant positive impact on spending on transfers, the increases in both types of expenditure were much more strongly associated with the extent and year-to-year change in "deindustrialization."[4] They concluded that the most powerful influence on the expansion of welfare spending in the postwar era did not come from the international economy but, rather, from within the countries – in particular, from dislocations in their labor markets caused by technologically-driven changes in the sectoral occupational structures of their economies.

How – if at all – does trade openness affect the size of the public economy? In view of the significant negative relationships reported by Garrett, Garrett and Mitchell, Burgoon, Kaufman and Segura-Ubiergo, and Iversen and Cusack between the extent of openness or change in openness and year-to-year changes in government spending, should the hypothesis that increasing openness results in increased trade-related compensation be set aside in favor of one that sees high and increasing levels of openness as forcing governments to reduce spending and taxes in order to compete for mobile capital? Or, following Iversen and Cusack, should the hypothesis that openness influences the size of government be abandoned altogether in favor of one that locates the expansionary impulse for government spending in the transformations that take place within a country's occupational structure? But if the trade-compensation hypothesis is set aside in favor of one that emphasizes the need for governments to reduce spending and taxes in order to compete for capital as they become increasingly exposed to the global economy, why is it that, in a period marked by a substantial increase in the extent of openness, the relative size of government has increased rather than decreased? And if the trade-compensation hypothesis is set aside in favor of one that locates the expansionary impulse for government spending in the sectoral and labor market changes associated with "deindustrialization," why is it that some countries that have experienced "deindustrialization" in recent years have experienced substantial *de*creases in the relative size of government?

This chapter seeks to answer these questions by examining the change in the relative size of government, defined in fiscal terms, in 19 countries over the past three decades. In doing so, it addresses several analytic shortcomings that characterize many of the studies that have examined the relationship between trade openness and the relative size of government. In most, the explanatory models are haphazardly specified, often with idiosyncratic and incomplete specifications of the variables that may account for variations across time and space in government spending. For example, although "Wagner's Law" (1877, 1893) is a staple of public economics, most studies do not consider whether spending (or taxing) varies with the affluence of a country.[5] Similarly, while most of the studies take into account the effects on spending and taxes associated with change in the "real" or constant-price GDP and the size of the dependent population, several fail to include measures of the level of unemployment, changes in unemployment and changes in prices, all of which may influence changes in the relative size of government.

Most of the studies that have examined the relationship between trade openness and the relative size of government also suffer from a failure to consider many aspects and attributes of politics and political institutions that may affect the size of government. Reflecting a long tradition in the literature, scholars routinely consider the impact of the partisan composition of government on fiscal outcomes – for example, by considering the effects associated with control of government by left-of-center, or Christian Democratic, or conservative parties.[6] But little attention has been devoted to assessing the impact on the relative size of government of other political-institutional features and attributes.[7] Thus, we know very little about the effects on the size of government of such fundamental differences as those involving federal versus unitary systems, presidential versus parliamentary government, independent versus politically subordinate central banks, plurality versus proportional systems of representation, election years versus non-election years and even democratic versus non-democratic regimes.[8]

The most important omission from the analyses considering the impact of openness on the relative size of government, however, concerns the definition of trade openness itself.[9] Surprisingly, when scholars have examined the effect of trade openness on the relative size of government they have restricted their attention to the extent and/or change over time in the relative share of GDP represented by exports and imports. As a result, they have failed to consider the effects of the *difference* between exports and imports – that is, the Balance of Trade – and changes over time in the Balance of Trade. Yet it is more plausible to think that if openness does in fact affect the size of government – for example, in inducing government to protect or compensate those who might be or in fact have been adversely affected by trade – it does so because of *imbalances* between exports and imports – specifically, a large and/or deteriorating trade deficit – rather than because of the aggregate volume of trade or change in that volume. Indeed, it is not apparent why one would expect the combined volume of exports and imports to have *any* effect at all on the fiscal role of government. That is especially true if one is concerned with identifying the forces that cause the relative size of government to change from one year to another.

This chapter examines the effects of economic openness and political institutions on the relative size of government in 19 developed democracies in the last three decades of the twentieth century.[10] Included among the 19 are three – Greece, Spain and Portugal – which are invariably omitted in pooled cross-sectional time-series analyses of the relationship between trade openness and the size of government, despite the fact that comparable data are available for the countries and the rationale for excluding them – the existence of non-democratic regimes prior to the mid-1970s – ceased to be relevant decades ago.[11]

In the first section of the chapter, some descriptive data pertaining to trade openness and the relative size of government in the 19 countries are presented. These data indicate the magnitude of the increases that have occurred in the 19 countries over the past three decades in the extent of trade openness and the relative fiscal role of government. They provide some preliminary support for the view that high and increasing levels of trade openness are not positively associated with large increases in the relative size of government.

In the second section, the results of regression analyses of various measures of the relative size of government that make use of pooled cross-sectional time-series data for the 19 countries are presented.[12] These analyses provide the basis for inferences about the effects of trade openness – defined both in terms of the level and change in the aggregate volume of trade and in the Balance of Trade – on the relative size of government. They suggest that, consistent with the trade competition hypothesis, large increases in openness are associated with small increases or decreases in the relative size of public expenditures and revenues. But they also suggest that governments experiencing large trade deficits and a deteriorating Balance of Trade provide trade-related compensation that results in large increases in public expenditures and budget deficits. The results suggest, contra Iversen and Cusack, that "deindustrialization" has no significant effect on spending once the explanatory model is more fully specified to take into account other factors that may be associated with increased spending. And they suggest that some political-institutional attributes – most notably, the nature of the political regime, the electoral calendar and the electoral system (but not the partisan composition of government) – have significant independent effects on spending and taxes.

## Openness and the size of the public economy, 1970–2000

Figure 1.1 presents the average ratios of exports, imports, and exports plus imports, of goods and services to GDP for the 19 countries from 1970 to 2000.[13] The data in Figure 1.1 demonstrate that, taken together, the 19 nations are highly dependent on international markets for the consumption

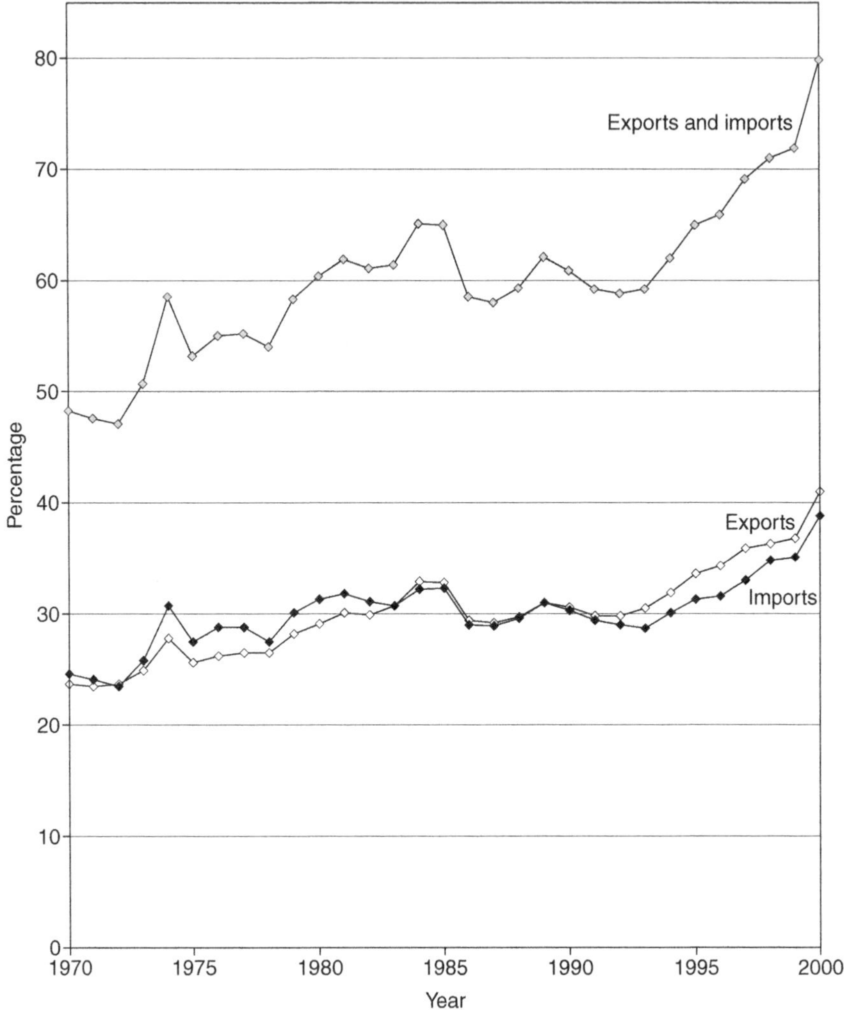


*Figure 1.1* Trade as a percentage of GDP in 19 nations, 1970–2000.

of a large portion of their domestically-produced goods and services and international producers for a large portion of the goods and services they consume, and that the extent of their dependence on international consumers and producers has increased dramatically over the past three decades. Thus, whereas exports and imports represented on average an amount equivalent to slightly less than 50 percent of GDP in the early 1970s, by the late 1990s they represented an amount equivalent to more than 70 percent of GDP, and in 2000 reached an amount equivalent to 80 percent of GDP.

While Figure 1.1 suggests a dramatic increase over the three decades in the relative importance of trade in the most developed countries, it also suggests the extent of openness did not increase at a uniform rate through time. A sharp increase driven largely by imports, reflecting the increased cost of imported oil in the wake of the Organization of Petroleum Exporting Countries' four-fold price increase after the Yom Kippur War, occurred in the early-to-mid 1970s. That was followed by a second sharp increase after the second major OPEC price increase in the wake of the Iranian Revolution in 1978–1979. A third major increase occurred in the mid-to-late 1990s. But, unlike the earlier increases, the latter increase was driven as much by exports as by imports. Figure 1.1 also suggests a sharp turnabout in the balance of trade between the 19 countries, taken as a group, and the rest of the world. In every year but one between 1970 and 1982, their imports exceeded their exports. But in every year since 1990, their exports exceeded their imports.[14]

Figure 1.2 presents the average for the 19 countries for each year between 1970 and 2000 of the total outlays and total revenues of all levels of government relative to GDP.[15] The trend lines in Figure 1.2 indicate that the relative size of government increased over the past three decades in these 19 countries, both in terms of spending and revenue. While all levels of government in the 19 countries spent, on average, an amount equivalent to about 35 percent of GDP in the early 1970s, by the early 1980s they were spending an amount equivalent to almost 50 percent of GDP. Even after having dropped for seven consecutive years after 1993, the outlays of all levels of government in the 19 countries were equivalent, on average, to about 45 percent of GDP in 2000.

The average for the 19 countries of the ratio of total outlays to GDP exhibits considerable variability over time, increasing most sharply in the three synchronized recessions of 1974–1975, 1980–1983, and 1990–1993 and increasing less rapidly, or even decreasing, in the several years of economic recovery that followed each recession. However, one observes a progressively sharper contraction of spending relative to GDP in each successive recovery. Thus, while the rate of increase in the ratio of government spending to GDP slowed slightly in the recovery of the late 1970s, it stabilized and then dropped slightly after the recession of the early 1980s and then dropped sharply after the recession of the early 1990s. As a result, while there has been a long upward trend in the average ratio of outlays to GDP, it is also the case that over the past two decades the relative size of government, defined in terms of spending, has leveled off. Indeed, except for the sharp increase during the recession years of 1990–1993, the average ratio of total spending to GDP in the 19 countries has dropped every year since 1985!

The trend over three decades in the average ratio of outlays to GDP has at least two important implications for those seeking to understand why the size of government has changed over time. It suggests that, in order to

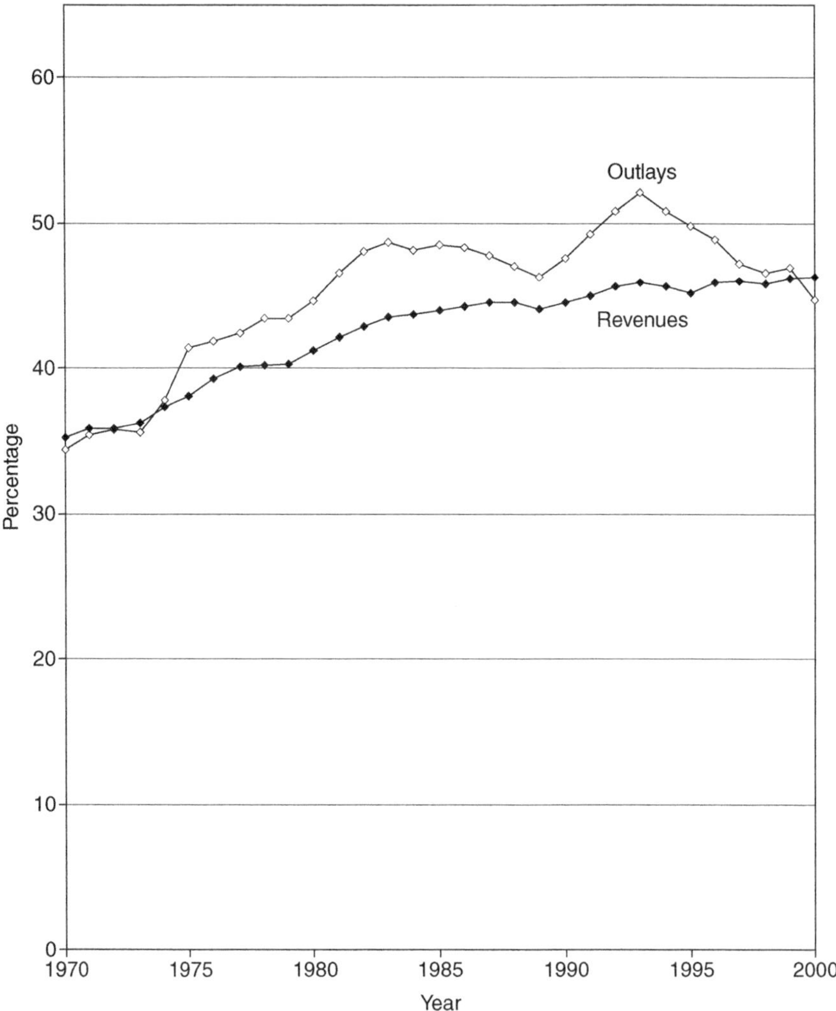


*Figure 1.2* Total outlays and revenues of all government as a percentage of GDP in 19 nations, 1970–2000.

be plausible, any explanation of the change in the size of government must be able to explain not only the *expansion* of the public economy that occurred in the 1970s and early 1980s but also its subsequent *contraction*. In addition, the fact that the decrease in spending was greatest in precisely the years – 1994–2000 – in which the extent of trade openness increased most dramatically suggests that, whatever the underlying causal mechanism in earlier decades, and even if governments do tend to compensate those adversely affected by increased trade openness, over the past decade increased trade openness did not contribute to a continued increase in the relative size of the public economy.

The trend line for the ratio of total revenues to GDP exhibits much less variability than that for outlays as it moved upward from an average of slightly more than 35 percent of GDP in the early 1970s to about 47 percent of GDP in the late 1990s. That the trend line exhibits less variability over time no doubt reflects the fact that, in addition to being pushed upward during economic recessions because of the diminution of its denominator, the ratio of revenues to GDP also tended to increase in periods of economic recovery as tax revenues increased. It should also be noted, however, that although the trend line of revenues to GDP exhibits much less variability than that for outlays, it also appears to increase at a slower rate after the early-to-mid 1980s.

Figure 1.2 also demonstrates a marked change over the three decades in the propensity of the governments in the 19 nations to incur budget deficits. Beginning with the economic recession of the mid-1970s and continuing through the late 1970s, 1980s and much of the 1990s, all levels of government in the 19 countries incurred budget deficits that were, on average, equivalent to several percentage points of GDP. Not surprisingly, the peak years of deficit financing occurred during the recessions of the early 1980s and early 1990s. But interestingly, the three decades ended as they began, with several years in which the total revenues of all levels of government were, on average, equal to or greater than total outlays.[16]

The simultaneous increases over the last three decades of the twentieth century in the relative size of the public economy, defined in terms of the total spending and revenue of government, and the extent of economic openness, defined in terms of the ratio of trade to GDP, suggest a causal relationship between the two that would be consistent with, and perhaps explained by, the trade-related compensation hypothesis. On the other hand, as noted above, with the exception of four years in the early 1990s, the ratio of outlays to GDP leveled off in the last two decades and, indeed, dropped significantly over the past decade, just as the extent of trade openness was increasing sharply to its highest levels. This might suggest that, regardless of any relationship between openness and the size of government in the past and notwithstanding the overall rising trends in both, there is in fact an *inverse* relation between them. That would suggest, in turn, that, far from generating more compensation and spending, over the past decade (if not longer) openness has contributed to a contraction in the relative size of the public economy, consistent with the hypothesis that increased exposure to the international economy has forced governments to reduce spending and taxes.

A first, and very preliminary, means of assessing the validity of these contending hypotheses is to compare the extent of covariation across the 19 nations between the extent and degree of increase in economic openness and the magnitude of increase in the relative size of government. If there is in fact a causal relationship between the two that exists in all of the countries, we should see evidence of it in the pattern of covariation between openness and the change in the fiscal role of government across the countries. That would not prove the existence of a causal relationship, of course. But it would at least suggest which hypothesis – one which attributes increased spending to the effort to compensate those adversely affected by openness or its alternative – best fits the experience of these 19 countries.

Table 1.1 presents several bivariate measures of the covariation across the 19 countries between the extent and change in openness and the magnitude of change in public outlays and revenues relative to GDP. While there is a fairly strong correlation between the extent of trade openness in 1970 and the relative size of government in terms of spending and revenues in that year, the statistical relationship is much weaker in 2000. That weakened relationship reflects the fact that, contrary to Cameron's (1978) finding of a strong positive relationship between the extent of openness in 1960 and the first-order increase in government revenues relative to GDP from 1960 to 1973, there is a modest *negative* correlation between the extent of openness in 1970 and the first-order changes in total spending relative to GDP from 1970 to 2000 ($r = -0.33$). There is a modest but

*Table 1.1* The relationship between trade openness and the total outlays and revenues of government across 19 countries, 1970–2000[a]

| | *Total outlays/GDP* | | |
|---|---|---|---|
| | *1970* | *2000* | *Increase, 1970–2000* |
| Exports and imports/GDP, 1970 | 0.57 | 0.21 | −0.33 |
| Exports and imports/GDP, 2000 | | 0.10 | −0.34 |
| Increase 1970–2000, exports and imports/GDP | | | −0.27 |
| | *Total revenues/GDP* | | |
| | *1970* | *2000* | *Increase, 1970–2000* |
| Exports and imports/GDP, 1970 | 0.49 | 0.41 | −0.09 |
| Exports and imports/GDP, 2000 | | 0.22 | −0.13 |
| Increase 1970–2000, exports and imports/GDP | | | −0.14 |

Note

a Entries are Pearsonian product-moment correlations. N = 19. The trade ratios were calculated from data reported in OECD 2004b and earlier editions. The ratios of total outlays to GDP are reported in OECD 2004c and earlier editions. There are numerous discontinuities in the ratios of outlays to GDP reported by the OECD for various countries in various years. In order to make the series comparable across time and space, the reported data for earlier years have been recalculated. The ratios of revenues to GDP were calculated from the data on outlays and data reported in OECD 2004c and earlier editions on the aggregate budget surplus or deficit.

negative correlation as well between the extent to which the economies became increasingly open between 1970 and 2000 and the extent of increase in the relative size of government over that period ($r = -0.27$).

The weakening correlation between the extent of trade openness and the levels of public spending and revenue, relative to GDP, and the consistent, albeit modest, negative correlations between both the level of openness and increase in openness and increases in the relative importance of public expenditures and revenues, suggest that the largest cumulative increases in the relative size of government tended to occur in the countries that had relatively *closed* economies and that experienced relatively *small* increases in trade openness over the three decades. The data in Table 1.2 confirm this.

Table 1.2 lists the extent of trade openness in 1970, the increase in trade openness between 1970 and 2000, and the change from 1970 to 2000 in the ratios of outlays and revenues to GDP for the 19 countries. The data indicate that the largest increases in public spending took place in Greece, Portugal, Japan and Spain, followed by Denmark, Finland and Italy. Some – Denmark, Finland and Portugal – were highly dependent upon trade in 1970. But others – Japan, Greece and Spain – had relatively

*Table 1.2* The change between 1970 and 2000 in total outlays and total revenues of all governments as a percentage of GDP[a]

| | *Exports and imports/GDP* | | *Increase, 1970–2000* | |
|---|---|---|---|---|
| | *1970* | *Increase, 1970–2000* | *Outlays/GDP* | *Revenues/GDP* |
| Greece | 24 | 36 | 25.1 | 23.2 |
| Portugal | 50 | 24 | 23.9 | 20.0 |
| Japan | 20 | 0 | 19.8 | 10.6 |
| Spain | 27 | 36 | 16.2 | 15.3 |
| Denmark | 60 | 23 | 16.1 | 15.4 |
| Finland | 53 | 24 | 15.1 | 17.9 |
| Italy | 33 | 23 | 13.8 | 17.1 |
| Sweden | 48 | 38 | 13.2 | 14.7 |
| Belgium | 100 | 68 | 13.0 | 15.2 |
| France | 31 | 25 | 13.0 | 10.5 |
| Austria | 60 | 41 | 10.4 | 7.5 |
| Australia | 29 | 17 | 9.1 | 7.1 |
| Germany | 40 | 27 | 7.9 | 9.0 |
| Canada | 43 | 43 | 5.9 | 8.1 |
| Netherlands | 89 | 41 | 2.2 | 5.5 |
| United States | 11 | 15 | 0.7 | 3.4 |
| Norway | 74 | 2 | 0.1 | 11.9 |
| United Kingdom | 45 | 15 | −2.4 | −1.4 |
| Ireland | 79 | 103 | −6.9 | 1.1 |

Note

a See Table 1.1 for sources.

closed economies in 1970. Some – most notably Greece and Spain – experienced large increases in the extent of trade openness over the three decades. But others – most notably Japan, but also Portugal, Denmark, Finland and Italy – experienced relatively small increases in trade openness over the three decades. Indeed, Japan, which experienced one of the largest increases in public spending relative to GDP, experienced no increase at all in the extent of trade openness and by 2000 its economy was the *least* open, as measured by the ratio of exports plus imports to GDP, of the 19. On the other hand, several of the countries that had unusually high levels of trade openness in 1970 or experienced unusually large increases in trade openness over the three decades experienced modest increases in the ratios of outlays and revenues to GDP. Indeed, representing the antithesis of the Japanese experience, Ireland, which was third after Belgium and the Netherlands in the extent of trade openness in 1970 and which experienced by far the largest increase in trade openness over the three decades, experienced a substantial *decrease* in the ratio of outlays to GDP.

In addition to suggesting an inverse relation between the initial extent and increase in trade openness, on one hand, and the magnitude of the increase in the relative size of government, on the other, the data in Table 1.2 contain an intriguing suggestion about the impact of democratic politics on the size of government. Three of the four countries that experienced the largest increases over the past three decades in the relative size of government, defined in terms of spending, are the southern European countries – Greece, Portugal and Spain – that threw off the shackles of authoritarian government in the mid-1970s. Consistent with Boix's (2001) analysis, the data suggest that the change from an authoritarian to a democratic regime introduced an expansionary impulse in fiscal policy in the three countries. As the data in Figure 1.3 indicate, when the authoritarian regimes were in power in the three countries in the early 1970s, all levels of government spent an amount equivalent to roughly 20 percent of GDP – less than in all of the other countries except Japan. But in the first decade after the demise of the authoritarian regimes, all three experienced unusually large increases in the relative size of government, compared with the other countries. Indeed, the relative size of government in the three countries increased to such an extent that by the early 1990s they were indistinguishable from the other countries.

The importance of the installation of democratic regimes in southern Europe in the 1970s is suggested by the data in Table 1.3. Table 1.3 presents the correlations across the 19 countries between a simple measure of whether the country did or did not have an authoritarian regime in the early-mid 1970s and the relative size of the public economy, defined in terms of spending, in 1970 and 2000 and the magnitude of change over the three decades. One observes a strong correlation between the exist-

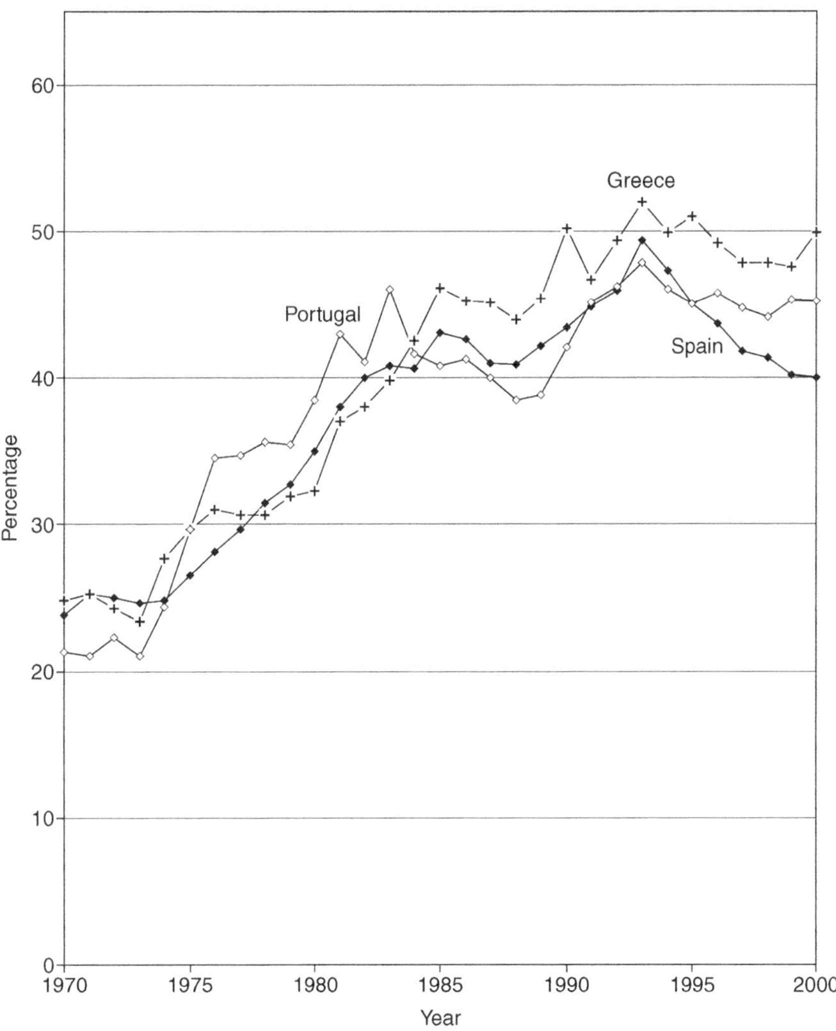


*Figure 1.3* Total outlays of government as a percentage of GDP in Spain, Portugal and Greece, 1970–2000.

ence of a non-democratic regime and a low ratio of outlays to GDP in 1970 ($r = -0.63$) and an equally strong positive correlation ($r = 0.64$) between the existence of a non-democratic regime in the 1970s and the magnitude of the increase in spending over the three decades.

*Table 1.3* The relation between democratization and the level and increase in government spending across 19 countries[a]

| | Total outlays/GDP | | |
|---|---|---|---|
| | *1970* | *2000* | *Increase, 1970–2000* |
| Non-democratic regime, early-mid 1970s | −0.63 | 0.13 | 0.64 |

Note

a Entries are Pearsonian product-moment correlations. N = 19. Greece, Portugal, and Spain have a value of 1 on the regime variable, all others a value of 0.

## Openness and the size of the public economy: pooled cross-sectional time-series analysis

Clearly, if one were simply interested in accounting for the variation across the 19 countries in the extent to which the relative size of government increased over the past three decades, the nature of the regime would appear to provide a much better explanation than either the extent of trade openness or the increase in openness over the three decades. And if we were to rely only on the cross-sectional correlations, we would conclude that the extent of openness is only faintly associated with the relative size of government and that both the extent of openness and change in openness are inversely related, albeit modestly, to the magnitude of change in the relative size of government. There would, in sum, be little support for the trade-related compensation hypothesis and, instead, some modest support for the alternative hypothesis that increased exposure to the international economy generates competitive pressures on government to reduce the relative size of government.

But cross-sectional correlations are only that – cross-sectional correlations. They do not control simultaneously for the effects of all the other factors that may influence the size of government. As a result, we can not be sure that the modestly negative cross-sectional correlations between trade openness and the magnitude of increases in the relative size of government accurately depict the true relationship between the two. In order to better assess that relationship, it is necessary to expand the number of observations so that the effects of the many other factors that influence the size of government can be taken into account. This can be done by pooling and analyzing the time-series data for the three decades for the 19 countries under consideration.

In order to assess the impact of trade openness on the relative size of government, we have conducted a series of regression analyses based on the pooled time-series data for the 19 nations for the 30 years from 1971 through 2000. Pooling the data creates a much larger set of observations – in this case, 570 – and enables us to ascertain with much greater precision and reliability than is afforded by cross-sectional analysis the extent to which (if at all) variations in the relative size of the public economy are systematically related to variations in the extent or change in openness, after taking into account the simultaneous impact of a variety of other attributes.

### *The dependent variable*

While the technique of pooling cross-sectional time-series data has been widely employed in comparative analysis, scholars have differed in their conceptualization of the objective of the analysis. Some – for example, Boix (2001), Hicks and Swank (1992), Huber *et al.* (1993) and Rodrik (1998) – have conceived of the objective as accounting for the variation in the *level* of public spending. Others – for example, Burgoon (2001), Cameron and McDermott (1995), Garrett and Mitchell (2001), Iversen and Cusack (2000) and Kaufman and Segura-Ubiergo (2001) – have conceived of the objective of the analysis as accounting for the variation in the annual change from one year to the next in spending. While either conceptualization may be appropriate, depending on the scholar's concerns, the latter provides the most appropriate basis for drawing causal inferences. Analyses that do not take into account the prior level of the dependent variable may mistake what in fact are spurious relationships between the dependent variable and one or more independent variables for causal relationships, particularly when the variables under consideration are serially correlated. In contrast, analyses that seek to account for *change* in the dependent variable and control for the previous level of the dependent variable not only eliminate the potential problem of autocorrelation but apply a rigorous standard as the basis of causal inference, by requiring that the variation over time and across the countries in the magnitude of the change in the dependent variable be systematically associated with the variation across time and across the countries in the independent variable after controlling for the covariation that exists across time and space between the dependent variable and the other independent variables.

In the analysis which follows, the dependent variable is defined in terms of the *change* from one year to the next in total government outlays (or revenues or the budget deficit) as a proportion of GDP. An obvious way to operationalize this definition is to treat the ratio of outlays to GDP in each country in each year as the dependent variable and include the lagged dependent variable as one of the independent variables. Another way is to employ an "error correction model," in which the dependent variable is the first-order difference between the outlays/GDP ratios in years $t$ and $t-1$ and the measure of outlays to GDP in the prior year is included as an independent variable. Analytically speaking, the choice of method makes no difference; the regression coefficients and standard errors for all of the independent variables other than the lagged dependent variable are identical in the two operationalizations and the only difference between the two methods, apart from the different coefficients and standard errors for the lagged dependent variable, is a significantly lower R-squared in the error correction model.[17]

### *Measuring trade openness*

Based on the data summarized in Figure 1.1, we have created four measures that capture various aspects of trade openness. The first is the standard and widely-employed measure of openness – the ratio of exports plus imports to GDP. The second is the first-order change from year $t-1$ to year $t$ in that aggregate measure of openness. The third is the Balance of Trade – the difference between exports of goods and services and imports of goods and services, measured as a proportion of GDP. The fourth is the change from year $t-1$ to year $t$ in the Balance of Trade.

All of the scholars who have searched for the effects of openness on the size of government have confined themselves to the first, and occasionally second, measures when testing the proposition that high and increasing levels of openness are associated with high and/or increasing levels of public spending. However, it is not obvious why one would expect to find a significant positive relationship between either the extent of openness or increases in the extent of openness, on one hand, and change in the relative size of government, on the other, and it is quite possible that the relationships are negligible or negative. After all, although high and increasing levels of trade, defined in terms of the aggregation of exports and imports, may well be associated with a heightened sense of dependence upon, and vulnerability to, the vicissitudes and fluctuations of international markets, they do not, in and of themselves, pose a threat to firms and/or individuals that might prompt a government response.

There is, in contrast, good reason to think that large trade *deficits* and a deteriorating Balance of Trade may have an impact on public spending. For although high and increasing levels of trade dependence, defined in terms of the sum of exports and imports, may not create economic dislocations that require public compensation, trade deficits – especially large ones – and a deterioration in the Balance of Trade may cause governments to respond in ways that cause the relative size of the public economy to increase. In both instances – when there is a trade deficit and when the trade surplus is decreasing or the deficit is increasing – the well-being of some firms in the export and import-competing sectors and the income and jobs of some individuals employed in those sectors are likely to suffer. In such circumstances, governments may find themselves providing income supplements to a variety of firms and individuals – to workers in export-dependent or import-competing firms to induce them to moderate their wage demands in order to restore competitiveness, to firms that depend on exports or compete in the domestic market with imports to enable them to compete more effectively, and/or to firms and individuals hurt by the macroeconomic adjustments put in place in order to dampen demand for imported goods and services and stimulate demand for domestically-produced goods and services in external markets.

### *Other economic variables*

In addition to the measures of openness, several other economic variables that may possibly affect the relative size of government have been included in the analysis. They are:

1 the Gross Domestic Product per capita in constant prices;
2 the annual rate of change in the constant-price GDP;
3 the annual rate of unemployment;
4 the first-order change from year $t-1$ to year $t$ in the rate of unemployment;
5 the annual rate of change in consumer prices;
6 the proportion of the population over 64;
7 the extent of "deindustrialization" as defined by Iversen and Cusack (2000);
8 the first-order change from year $t-1$ to year $t$ in "deindustrialization."[18]

Ever since Wagner (1877, 1893) first articulated his "Law" more than a century ago that government will spend more as society becomes more affluent, scholars have considered whether public spending tends to increase as the income or gross economic product of a country increases. If Wagner's "Law" remains in effect, a positive relationship should exist between Gross Domestic Product per capita and the change in government spending, indicating that, all else being equal, larger increases in spending tend to occur at higher levels of affluence.

If Wagner's "Law" is speculative and elusive in regard to the intervening causal mechanism, there can be little doubt that changes in the relative size of government are inversely associated with changes in the rate of economic growth. Indeed, virtually every analysis of the size of government that has included some measure of change in "real" or constant-price GDP has found a strong and statistically significant inverse relationship between it and the magnitude of change in public spending.[19] In part, of course, the inverse relationship reflects the fact that the denominator of the measures of outlays and revenues is the GDP, meaning that fluctuations in the GDP will affect, inversely, the ratio of outlays or revenues to GDP. But the inverse relationship may also reflect a tendency for government spending to change as well – as when spending on income supplements for the unemployed, on employment programs, subsidies for firms, and/or public works increases in bad economic times and remains stable or decreases in good times.

Measures of the rate of unemployment and the change from one year to the next in the rate of unemployment are often omitted in analyses of government spending, presumably because they are regarded as being closely associated with, and reflective of, fluctuations in the rate of growth.[20] However, while the level and change in unemployment are undoubtedly related to the rate of growth, the relationships are not so strong that the effects of unemployment can simply be inferred from the effects of growth. The most important reason for including the measures of unemployment is the possibility that, above and beyond any effects associated with the rate of growth, changes in the relative size of the public economy may vary systematically with both the level and magnitude of change in unemployment.[21] Specifically, even after controlling for the effects of growth (and other variables), high levels of unemployment and/or large increases in unemployment may be associated with large increases in the ratio of total outlays (and the aggregate deficit) to GDP.

Most scholars disregard, also, the direct effect of the rate of change in prices on the relative size of government.[22] However, it is possible that prices in the public sector may change, relative to those in other sectors, and that those relative price effects contribute to changes in the size of the public economy.[23] Those effects may be most evident in periods of high inflation, in which case we would expect to find a positive relationship between the rate of inflation and the magnitude of change in the relative size of the public economy.

Most scholars attempt to take into account the variation across time and space in the relative size of the dependent population – usually defined in terms of the proportion of the population that is elderly.[24] The assumption, of course, is that at least some of the increase in public spending over the past three decades has reflected the policy consequences – most notably, increased spending for pensions and long-term health care – of the demographic transformation that, in varying degrees in all of the countries, has resulted in the elderly constituting a larger portion of the population.

As noted above, Iversen and Cusack (2000) argue that effects on the relative size of government that have often been attributed to globalization are in fact the result of processes of large scale socioeconomic change such as "deindustrialization" that do not derive from international economic pressures. Thus, they report a strong positive association between increases in transfer payments and public consumption expenditures and the extent and increase in "deindustrialization," compared with insignificant associations between those aspects of spending and the extent and change in trade openness. To test their argument, we have included measures of both the extent and change in "deindustrialization." The extent of "deindustrialization" is measured by 100 – the sum of the proportions of the working-age population who are employed in agriculture and manufacturing. The year-to-year change in "deindustrialization" is the first-order change.

***Trade openness and the size of government: results***

Table 1.4 presents the results of three regressions that estimate the effects of trade openness and the other economic variables on year-to-year changes in the ratio of total outlays to GDP.[25] The regressions employ the error correction method, which defines the dependent variable as the

*Table 1.4* The effects of trade openness and other variables on the year-to-year change in total outlays of all government as a percentage of GDP in 19 countries, 1971–2000[a]

| *Variable* | *1* | *2* | *3* |
|---|---|---|---|
| Outlays/GDP, $t-1$ | −0.120*** | −0.126*** | −0.132*** |
| | (0.024) | (0.024) | (0.023) |
| GDP/capita, $t$ | −0.112* | −0.104** | −0.030 |
| | (0.046) | (0.044) | (0.041) |
| Change in real GDP, $t-1$ to $t$ | −0.410*** | −0.374*** | −0.373*** |
| | (0.047) | (0.045) | (0.044) |
| % unemployed, $t$ | −0.033 | −0.035 | 0.038 |
| | (0.054) | (0.053) | (0.053) |
| Change in % unemployed, $t-1$ to $t$ | 0.246** | 0.253** | 0.337*** |
| | (0.106) | (0.104) | (0.099) |
| Change in cons. prices, $t-1$ to $t$ | 0.019 | 0.035 | 0.001 |
| | (0.024) | (0.023) | (0.023) |
| % pop. over 64, $t$ | 0.132 | 0.148* | 0.050 |
| | (0.090) | (0.087) | (0.078) |
| Deindustrialization, $t$ | 0.033 | 0.059 | 0.008 |
| | (0.055) | (0.056) | (0.054) |
| Change in deindustrialization, $t-1$ to $t$ | 0.033 | 0.002 | 0.117 |
| | (0.136) | (0.136) | (0.131) |
| Exports and imports/GDP, $t$ | | −0.008 | 0.009 |
| | | (0.011) | (0.010) |
| Change, exports and imports/GDP, $t-1$ to $t$ | | −0.052** | −0.071*** |
| | | (0.020) | (0.018) |
| Exports–imports/GDP, $t$ | | | −0.105*** |
| | | | (0.028) |
| Change, exports–imports/GDP, $t-1$ to $t$ | | | −0.152*** |
| | | | (0.041) |
| No. of observations | 570 | 570 | 570 |
| $R^2$ | 0.49 | 0.51 | 0.56 |

Note

a The dependent variable is the change in the ratio of outlays to GDP from year $t$ to year $t-1$. The entries are the regression coefficients. The parentheses contain the standard errors. The coefficients and standard errors for the constants and country dummies are omitted. Asterisks indicate statistical significance: *** = $p \leq 0.01$, two-tailed test; ** = $p \leq 0.05$; * = $p \leq 0.10$.

first-order change in the outlays/GDP ratio from year $t-1$ to year $t$ and includes the lagged outlays/GDP ratio as an independent variable.[26] The results therefore show the direct and independent effect of each independent variable, controlling for the effects of the others, including the previous level of spending relative to GDP, on the annual change in the ratio of outlays to GDP. The standard errors, in parentheses, have been corrected for heteroskedasticity (differing variances) and contemporaneous correlation of the error terms across the panels.[27] Because the F-test decisively rejects the null hypothesis that the panels share a common intercept, dummy variables for the countries have been included in order to control for the fixed effects associated with each country.[28] The asterisks indicate conventional levels of statistical significance and identify the variables that are most consistently and strongly associated with the dependent variable across the 19 countries over the three decades.[29]

The first regression in Table 1.4 presents the coefficients and standard errors of the independent variables when all of the economic variables except the four pertaining to trade openness are included. The second presents the coefficients and standard errors when all of the variables included in the first regression plus the conventional measure of trade openness and the change in trade openness are included. The third presents the coefficients and standard errors when all of the variables in the second regression plus the two measures pertaining to the Balance of Trade are included.

The results presented in Table 1.4 indicate that, contrary to the findings of Burgoon (2001), Garrett and Mitchell (2001) and Kaufman and Segura-Ubiergo (2001), the *extent* of trade openness, conventionally defined, has no independent effect on the year-to-year change in outlays relative to GDP. Equations 2 and 3 indicate, on the other hand, that, as Garrett (2001) and Kaufman and Segura-Ubiergo (2001) have found, the magnitude of the year-to-year change in outlays is strongly and inversely associated with the magnitude of the year-to-year change in trade openness. As the preliminary cross-sectional correlations suggested, and contrary to the trade-related compensation hypothesis, the relative size of government tended to increase when the extent of trade openness decreased. Or put the other way, increases in the extent of trade openness were associated with *small* increases, or decreases, in the ratio of outlays to GDP.

The strong inverse relationship between changes in the extent of trade openness and the ratio of outlays to GDP would appear to offer support for the hypothesis that, far from stimulating an expansion of the public economy, increasing trade openness was associated with a *contraction* in the relative size of the public economy. Before discarding the compensation hypothesis, however, it is necessary to consider the results of the third regression presented in Table 1.4, the one which includes the magnitude and year-to-year change in the Balance of Trade. After controlling for the effects associated with the other variables, both measures are strongly and inversely associated with year-to-year changes in the ratio of outlays to GDP. The negative signs indicate that large trade deficits and a deteriorating Balance of Trade are associated with large *in*creases in the ratio of outlays to GDP. Large trade surpluses and an improving Balance of Trade, on the other hand, are associated with large *de*creases in the ratio of outlays to GDP. Both inverse relationships are precisely what one would predict on the basis of the trade-related compensation hypothesis.

The results presented in Table 1.4 suggest that several of the other variables are associated with changes in spending as anticipated. As predicted, the rate of economic growth is strongly and inversely associated with the year-to-year change in outlays relative to GDP. The ratio of outlays to GDP consistently increases as the growth rate drops and, conversely, drops as the growth rate increases. And as we suggested, even after controlling for the rate of growth, increases in the rate of unemployment were strongly associated with increases in outlays. Likewise, spending tended to increase when the elderly constituted a large portion of the population, although the effect is statistically significant in only one of the three equations.

The results in Table 1.4 do not, however, support the "deindustrialization" hypothesis put forward by Iversen and Cusack (2000). While positive, the coefficients for both the extent of "deindustrialization" and the year-to-year change in "deindustrialization" are not significant. Given the forcefulness and substantive appeal of their argument, we have sought to identify why our results differ so markedly from those of Iversen and Cusack. Given the alternative specifications presented in Table 1.4, it is obvious the difference does not derive from the inclusion of the extent and change in the Balance of Trade or the extent and change in trade openness. One possible explanation is our inclusion of the three southern European countries that were not included in Iversen and Cusack's study.[30] Another involves the different temporal periods covered by the two analyses – the fact that our analysis covers 1971 through 2000 while that of Iversen and Cusack covers 1961 through 1993.[31] Yet another involves the inclusion here of the level and change in unemployment.

Of these three possible explanations, only the inclusion of the measures of unemployment – in particular, the change in unemployment – appears to have contributed to the insignificance of "deindustrialization." When the analysis is run without the three southern European countries, the coefficients for two measures of "deindustrialization" are, although positive, far from significant. When the analysis is run for the 1971–1993 period, the coefficients for the two measures are likewise far from significant (and in the case of the measure of change wrongly signed). But when the second equation in Table 1.4 is estimated without the change in unemployment, the coefficient for the change in "deindustrialization" is positive and, although not statistically significant, is nevertheless quite strong. And when the third equation in Table 1.4 is estimated without the change in unemployment, the coefficient for the change in "deindustrialization" is positive and highly significant. Evidently, the effects on spending that Iversen and Cusack (2000) attribute to "deindustrialization" in fact derive not from sectoral changes or changes in the active labor force but to changes in the rate of unemployment, whether or not the latter changes are generated by sectoral changes or changes in labor force participation. By burying the effects of unemployment in a measure that includes two other larger components – employment in the service sector and the inactive population – and by ignoring the impact of trade deficits and a deteriorating Balance of Trade, it is perhaps not surprising they conclude that openness has little impact on spending and that there is little support for the trade compensation hypothesis.

The ratio of the total outlays of all levels of government to GDP conveys better than any other single measure the relative size of the public economy. But the relative size of the total revenues of all levels of government and the aggregate budget deficit or surplus of all levels of government – which, taken together, comprise the total outlays – are also of interest. The effects of trade openness and the other economic variables on changes in the ratios of total revenues to GDP and the aggregate budget deficit to GDP have been estimated with regressions that are identical in form (except, of course, for the dependent variable and lagged dependent variable) to the third equation in Table 1.4. The results are presented in Table 1.5. To simplify the presentation, Table 1.5 presents only the *t*-statistics – the ratio of the regression coefficient to the standard error – for the measures of trade openness and the other economic variables. The table also includes the *t*-statistics for the third equation in Table 1.4 that estimated their effects on changes in the ratio of total outlays to GDP. The sign and asterisks indicate, respectively, the nature and statistical significance of the relationships.

The data in Table 1.5 indicate that trade openness has a pervasive independent effect on the relative size of the public economy, after controlling for the effects of growth, changes in unemployment, demographic composition and "deindustrialization." The year-to-year change in the extent of trade openness is inversely and significantly associated with the magnitude of the year-to-year changes in the ratios of total revenues to GDP and the aggregate deficit to GDP as well as the year-to-year changes in outlays. The Balance of Trade is likewise inversely and significantly associated with the magnitude of the year-to-year changes in the ratios of total revenues to GDP and the aggregate deficit to GDP, indicating that a large trade deficit not only contributes to increases in the ratio of outlays to GDP, but also to increases in the ratios of revenues to GDP and the aggregate deficit to GDP. And changes in the Balance of Trade are inversely and significantly associated with the magnitude of the year-to-year changes in the ratio of the aggregate deficit to GDP as well as the year-to-year changes in outlays, suggesting that deterioration in the

*Table 1.5* The effects of trade openness and other variables on the year-to-year changes in total outlays, total revenues and the total budget deficit as a percentage of GDP in 19 nations, 1971–2000[a]

| *Variable* | *Total outlays* | *Total revenues* | *Total budget deficit* |
|---|---|---|---|
| Lagged dependent variable | −5.66*** | −5.21*** | −5.35*** |
| GDP/capita | −0.74 | −1.03 | −0.03 |
| Change in real GDP | −8.54*** | −3.54*** | −4.96*** |
| % unemployed | 0.72 | −1.52 | 2.59*** |
| Change in % unemployed | 3.40*** | 1.08 | 2.13** |
| Change in cons. prices | 0.06 | 0.98 | −0.33 |
| % pop. over 64 | 0.64 | 1.82* | −0.74 |
| Deindustrialization | 0.15 | 2.39** | −1.52 |
| Change in deindustrialization | 0.89 | −1.39 | 2.03** |
| Exports and imports/GDP | 0.90 | 0.41 | 0.49 |
| Change in exports and imports/GDP | −3.87*** | −2.39** | −1.91* |
| Exports–imports/GDP | −3.73*** | −1.73* | −2.63*** |
| Change in exports–imports/GDP | −3.73*** | −0.03 | −2.74*** |
| No. of observations | 570 | 570 | 570 |
| $R^2$ | 0.56 | 0.20 | 0.36 |

Note

a The entries for total outlays are the *t*-statistics for the coefficients in equation 3 in Table 1.4. The entries for total revenues and total budget deficit are the *t*-statistics for the coefficients in equations identical to equation 3 in Table 1.4 except for the dependent variable and lagged dependent variable. The *t*-statistics for the constants and country dummies are omitted. Asterisks indicate statistical significance: *** = $p \leq 0.01$, two-tailed test; ** = $p \leq 0.05$; * = $p \leq 0.10$.

Balance of Trade – a diminishing surplus or an increasing deficit – results in increased spending and larger deficits.

Among the other variables, only the rate of economic growth and, to a lesser degree, change in the rate of unemployment appear to have as pervasive an effect on the relative size of the public economy as trade openness. The proportion of the population that is elderly and the extent of deindustrialization are positively and significantly associated with changes in the ratio of revenues to GDP. And the level of unemployment, change in unemployment and change in deindustrialization are positively and significantly associated with changes in the ratio of the aggregate budget deficit to GDP. But only the variations across time and space in the rate of growth and two or more measures of trade openness are significantly associated with all three aspects of the public economy. Although we have analyzed total spending (and revenues and deficits), rather than spending on social programs, Iversen and Cusack (2000: 324, 334) would appear to be simply wrong when they say globalization has not "been much of a factor in the postwar expansion of the welfare state" and the effects of "domestic economic variables carry far greater weight than globalization in shaping government spending."

### *The impact of political-institutional attributes*

Several aspects of politics might conceivably have affected the size of government in the 19 countries in addition to trade openness and the other economic influences described above. They fall into two clusters. The first involves various features and attributes of the political institutions of the countries such as the nature of the regime, the existence of a federal or unitary form of government, the existence of a presidential or parliamentary system of government, and the extent to which the central bank was independent from or subordinate to the government. The second involves various aspects of electoral politics such as the electoral calendar, the use of a proportional representation or a first-past-the-post electoral system, and the extent to which parties holding distinctive views with respect to fiscal policy control government.

Regarding the political-institutional attributes, the strong cross-sectional relationship between the magnitude of the cumulative increase in spending and revenues, relative to GDP, over the three decades and the nature of the political regime (see Table 1.3) suggests that the magnitude of the year-to-year change in the relative size of government may have been influenced by the nature of the political regime – in particular, whether the country adhered to democratic rules and procedures in its formation of the government. Following Boix (2001) and Adserà and Boix (2002), we would expect that democratic regimes would, on average, experience larger year-to-year increases in outlays and revenues than non-democratic regimes.

The magnitude of year-to-year changes in spending and revenues may also be influenced by the particular institutional configuration of a polity. Although there is, as Persson and Tabellini (2004) note, a great deal of "constitutional inertia" that makes it difficult to attribute effects to institutional structures that usually do not vary across time within a polity, there is good reason to believe that, for example, the distinction between federal and unitary forms of government has an impact on spending and revenues. Thus, Rodden (2003) notes that if the subnational units of a federal polity have some degree of revenue-generating and spending autonomy, they may compete with each other for mobile sources of investment and revenue by reducing taxes.[32] In addition, compared with unitary systems, the vertical fragmentation of political authority characteristic of federalism increases the number of "veto players" involved in determining the total outlays, revenues and budget deficit of a country.[33] One result may be that budgets in federal systems are more stationary over time and less susceptible to non-incremental changes in spending and revenues than those in unitary systems. And applying the "veto players" logic to other institutional attributes, one might expect year-to-year changes in spending and revenues to be less in presidential systems than in parliamentary systems and less in systems in which the central bank is independent of government than in those in which it is subordinate to the government.

The rates of change in spending and revenues across the 19 countries over the three decades may have varied systematically also with variations in the electoral calendars of the countries, their electoral systems and the partisan composition of their governments. Following Nordhaus (1975) and Tufte (1978), one might hypothesize that fiscal policy moves over time with an electoral rhythm, resulting in relatively large increases in spending and deficits, and relatively small increases in taxes, in election years and relatively large increases in revenues and small increases in spending and deficits in non-election years.[34] Similarly, variations across time and space in the rate of change in spending and revenue generation may also depend on the nature of the electoral system. Persson and Tabellini (1999, 2000, 2003 and 2004) suggest that, because different electoral systems create different incentives for representatives to supply public goods and transfer payments, the overall level of spending may vary across countries depending on their electoral systems. In majoritarian systems, in which parties compete in key swing districts, governments may spend more on territorially-disaggregated public goods, whereas in proportional systems, where parties compete more broadly for support from large aggregations of social groups, governments may spend more on transfer payments and more overall.[35]

Perhaps no political-institutional attribute has received as much attention from scholars concerned with the size of government as the partisan composition of government. Ever since Kirschen *et al.* (1964) asserted that ideologically distinctive groupings of parties pursue distinctive macroeconomic and fiscal policies when in office, scholars have sought to ascertain whether control of government by distinctive groupings of parties – e.g. those which are left-of-center or those which are conservative – has had a discernible effect on spending or whether, as Downs (1957) suggested a half-century ago, partisan distinctions – at least in first-past-the-post electoral systems – are blurred by the pursuit of the median voter.[36] The results have varied from analysis to analysis, with some suggesting that the partisan composition of government has an independent effect on policy and others suggesting it has little or no effect. Cameron (1984), Castles (1982), Cusack (1997, 1999), Garrett (1998), Garrett and Lange (1991), Garrett and Mitchell (2001), Hibbs (1977), Hicks and Swank (1984, 1992), Huber *et al.* (1993), Iversen and Cusack (2000), Rose (1984), Swank (1988, 1992), Tufte (1978), and many others have found significant relationships between various measures of the partisan composition of government and various measures of spending. On the other hand, Cameron and McDermott (1995) with respect to total outlays and revenues, Iversen and Cusack (2000) with respect to changes in transfer payments and Garrett and Mitchell (2001) with respect to changes in transfer payments, consumption expenditures and total spending have found insignificant or negligible relationships between the extent to which distinctive groupings of parties govern and the extent of change in various aggregates of spending.

In order to assess the impact of various political-institutional attributes on the relative size of government in the 19 countries over the past three decades, we have included measures of the following attributes along with the measures of trade openness and the other economic variables in regressions of the annual change in outlays, revenues, and deficits:

1 the democratic or non-democratic status of the regime;[37]
2 the federal or unitary organization of national and subnational government;[38]
3 the presidential or parliamentary organization of the national government;[39]
4 the independence or subordination of the central bank;[40]
5 the electoral calendar;[41]
6 the electoral system, defined in terms of whether the national legislature was elected from party lists by proportional representation or from territorial districts on a first-past-the-post basis;[42]
7 the partisan composition of government, as measured by the proportion of cabinet portfolios held by left-of-center, centrist, Christian Democratic and conservative parties in the year in question.[43]

Table 1.6 presents the results of those regressions. To simplify the presentation, we present only the *t*-statistics for the political-institutional attributes.

The upper panel in Table 1.6 contains the *t*-statistics for the variable indicating the existence of a non-democratic regime when that measure is added to regressions that include all of the economic variables considered earlier. Consistent with Boix (2001) and Adserà and Boix (2002), the negative and statistically significant coefficients for the regime variable in the regressions of outlays and revenues indicate that the absence of democracy in Greece, Portugal and Spain in the early 1970s had a significant dampening effect on spending and, especially, revenues, above and beyond the combined effects of the various economic attributes.

The lower panel in Table 1.6 presents the *t*-statistics for the other political-institutional measures when they are included along with the full set of economic measures in regressions of the changes in outlays, revenues, and deficits. Since it makes little sense to test for the effects of the political-institutional and electoral attributes in countries that are under authoritarian rule, we have excluded Greece and Portugal prior to 1975 and Spain prior to 1977 from the analyses presented in the lower panel. The results presented in the lower panel suggest that, consistent with Rodden (2003) and Tsebelis (1995, 2002), both the vertical and horizontal fragmentation of authority in a polity – that is, the existence of a

*Table 1.6* The effects of political-institutional attributes on the year-to-year change in total outlays, total revenues and the total budget deficit as a percentage of GDP in 19 nations, 1971–2000[a]

| | *Total outlays* | *Total revenues* | *Total budget deficit* |
|---|---|---|---|
| N = 570, 1971–2000 all countries, all years | | | |
| Non-democratic polity | −1.82* | −2.25** | 0.06 |
| N = 555, 1971–2000 excluding Greece 1971–1974, Portugal 1971–1974, and Spain 1971–1976 | | | |
| Federal system | −0.95 | −1.57 | 0.43 |
| Presidential system | −1.32 | −1.19 | −0.52 |
| Independent central bank | 0.56 | 0.48 | −0.38 |
| Election year | 2.59*** | −0.61 | 2.82*** |
| First-past-the-post electoral system | −0.77 | 1.86* | −2.53*** |
| % of cabinet portfolios held by left parties | 0.44 | 0.48 | 0.07 |
| % of cabinet portfolios held by centrist parties | 0.55 | 0.42 | 0.20 |
| % of cabinet portfolios held by Chr. dem. parties | 0.64 | 0.26 | 0.43 |
| % of cabinet portfolios held by conserv. parties | 0.36 | 0.27 | 0.24 |

Note

a Entries are the *t*-statistics for each coefficient when the listed variables are added to equations that include the economic variables in equation 3 in Table 1.4 and those in Table 1.6. The coefficients and standard errors for the constants, lagged dependent variables, country dummies and other variables have been omitted. Asterisks indicate statistical significance: *** = $p \leq 0.01$, two-tailed test; ** = $p \leq 0.05$; * = $p \leq 0.10$.

federal system of government and the existence of a strong presidency – had a dampening effect on spending and revenues. While the effects are not so consistent across all countries and years as to be statistically significant, in some cases – most notably, as Rodden (2003) suggested, in the effect of federalism on revenues – they do approach that degree of consistency. It would appear then, that, all else being equal, countries in which the subnational jurisdictions and the executive branch have some degree of constitutionally-defined autonomy from the national government and the legislative branch, respectively, experienced smaller increases in outlays and revenues than countries which are organized as unitary and parliamentary systems. Whether the central bank was independent of the national government, however, had little effect on outlays, revenues and deficits.

The results in the lower panel of Table 1.6 indicate that both the electoral calendar and the electoral system had significant effects on fiscal policy across the 19 countries over the three decades. Perhaps the most surprising result is the very strong relationship between the electoral calendar and changes in outlays and the budget deficit. Consistent with Nordhaus (1975) and Tufte's (1978) notion of a "political business cycle," the year-to-year changes in outlays and the budget deficit, relative to GDP, were significantly larger in election years than in non-election years. Clearly, there has been an expansionary electoral rhythm present in the public economies of these 19 countries over the past three decades.

The results also suggest that, as Persson and Tabellini (1999, 2000) and Milesi-Ferretti *et al.* (2002) have argued, the type of electoral system – in particular, the distinction between the representation of territorial districts in which the representatives are chosen on a first-past-the-post basis and the representation of party lists from which representatives are chosen by proportional representation – was strongly associated with the magnitude of the increases in revenues and budget deficits. Holding all else constant and compared with PR systems, majoritarian electoral systems appear to dampen the size of year-to-year increases in outlays and, in particular, the budget deficit while producing larger increases in revenues. PR systems, on the other hand, appear to produce somewhat larger increases in spending, significantly smaller increases in revenues, and significantly larger budget deficits.

The data in Table 1.6 suggest that the partisan composition of government has, at best, only a very modest effect on fiscal policy. There are some differences in the effects associated with the distinctive groupings of parties. As Huber *et al.* (1993) argue, Christian Democratic parties appear to be considerably more expansive, in terms of spending than left-of-center parties, which are only slightly more expansive than conservative parties. Left-of-center and centrist parties appear to be more expansive, in terms of revenues, than Christian Democratic and conservative parties. And left-of-center parties typically incur smaller increases in budget deficits than centrist, conservative and, especially, Christian Democratic parties. But all of these effects are quite modest and none is so consistent across all 19 countries and three decades as to be statistically significant.

## Conclusion

In this chapter, we have considered why the relative size of government, as measured by the total outlays and revenues of all levels of government, has varied across time and space throughout the advanced capitalist world. In particular, mindful of the work of Boix (2001), Garrett (2000, 2001), Garrett and Mitchell (2001), Iversen and Cusack (2000), Rodrik (1998) and others, we have sought to understand the nature of the relationship, if any, between the long upward trend in the extent of economic openness, on one hand, and the relative size of government, on the other.

After considering the extent to which the relative size of government has changed over the last four decades in 19 countries, we sought to ascertain the extent to which the differences among the countries in magnitude of change in government spending relative to GDP were associated with differences in the extent or change over time in economic openness, defined in terms of trade. We did not find support for the proposition that the largest increases in the relative size of government occurred in countries that are highly dependent upon trade, as had been the case in the pre-OPEC era. Indeed, we found that the countries that were most dependent upon trade and those which experienced unusually large increases in trade dependence experienced relatively *modest* increases in the size of government over the past three decades. Indeed, a few of them – most notably, Ireland, by 2000 the most trade dependent of the 19 countries – experienced *contractions* in the relative size of government over that period.

With those somewhat disquieting findings as a prelude, we conducted a pooled cross-sectional time-series analysis of the change in the relative size of government over the past three decades. That analysis found that the aggregate volume of trade is quite inconsequential in accounting for the year-to-year changes in the relative size of government. But the analysis suggested that certain aspects of trade openness – specifically, the change in the aggregate volume of trade and, in particular, the Balance of Trade and the degree of deterioration in the Balance of Trade – were closely associated with changes in the size of government. While the aggregate volume of trade appears to be unrelated to changes in the size of government, large increases in that volume of trade, relative to GDP, were consistently associated with small increases, not large increases, in spending, revenues, and budget deficits. On the other hand, the existence of large trade deficits and deterioration of the Balance of Trade appear to have exerted a significant *expansionary* impulse on government spending across the advanced capitalist world. The analysis suggests that the Balance of Trade may reflect much better than the aggregate summation of exports and imports – the conventional measure of openness – the extent to which a country is likely to experience trade-related dislocations that result in increased government spending.

## Notes

1 Earlier versions were presented at the triennial meeting of the International Political Science Association, the annual meeting of the American Political Science Association, the European University Institute, Harvard University and Yale University. For their comments and suggestions, the authors thank William Clark, John Freeman, Peter Hall, Mark Hallerberg, Oona Hathaway, Torben Iversen, Jane Jenson, Anastassios Kalandrakis, T. J. Pempel, Kenneth

Scheve and James Vreeland. Kathryn McDermott provided invaluable assistance in the early stages of the research reported here.

2 For discussions of these trends see e.g. Garrett (2000, 2001), Garrett and Mitchell (2001) and Quinn and Inclán (1997).

3 For discussions of trends over the long term in the relative magnitude of government spending and taxation see e.g. Boix (2001), Burgoon (2001), Cameron (1978), Cameron and McDermott (1995), Garrett (2001), Garrett and Mitchell (2001), Hicks and Swank (1984, 1992), Huber *et al.* (1993), Iversen and Cusack (2000), O'Connor (1988), Persson and Tabellini (1999), Rice (1986), Rodrik (1998), Saunders and Klau (1985), Swank (1988, 1992), Tarschys (1975) and Taylor (1983).

4 Iversen and Cusack (2000) define deindustrialization as 100 minus the sum of the proportions of the working-age population employed in agriculture and manufacturing. In other words, "deindustrialization" consists of the sum of the proportions of the working-age population that are employed in the service sector, unemployed in all sectors, and inactive. The two largest components by far are the proportions employed in the service sector and inactive. Burgoon (2001) also finds a positive relationship between deindustrialization and increases in several measures of public spending.

5 For a discussion of Wagner's "Law," see Bird (1971).

6 See e.g. Alvarez *et al.* (1991), Blais *et al.* (1993), Cameron (1984), Cameron and McDermott (1995), Castles (1982), Cusack (1997), Garrett and Lange (1991), Garrett and Mitchell (2001), Hicks and Swank (1984, 1992), Huber *et al.* (1993), Iversen and Cusack (2000) and Swank (1988, 1992).

7 For exceptions, see Cameron and McDermott (1995), Hallerberg and Basinger (1998), Hicks and Swank (1992), Huber *et al.* (1993), Rodden (2003) and Steinmo and Tolbert (1998).

8 There are, of course, exceptions: on the impact of federalism, see Cameron and McDermott (1995) and Rodden (2003). On the impact of presidentialism and parliamentarism, as well as the type of electoral system, see Persson and Tabellini (1999, 2000). On the role of central bank independence, see Cukierman (1992, 1994). On the role of institutional fragmentation and "veto players," see Tsebelis (1995, 2002) and Tsebelis and Chang (2004). On the impact of the electoral calendar, see Cameron and McDermott (1995), Nordhaus (1975), Tufte (1978) and Rodden (2003). On the impact of democracy and non-democracy, see Adserà and Boix (2002), Boix (2001) and Cameron and McDermott (1995).

9 Obviously, there are other facets of openness in addition to trade – most notably, those involving foreign direct investment and portfolio investment. For analyses of those other aspects of openness see e.g. Garrett (1995, 2000) and Quinn and Inclán (1997).

10 The 19 countries are Australia, Austria, Belgium, Canada, Denmark, Finland, France, Germany, Greece, Ireland, Italy, Japan, the Netherlands, Norway, Portugal, Spain, Sweden, the United Kingdom and the United States.

11 For discussions which consider the impact of authoritarian regimes in southern Europe, see Adserà and Boix (2002), Boix (2001) and Cameron and McDermott (1995).

12 Pooled cross-sectional time-series analysis has become the standard mode by which scholars have investigated the relationship between openness and the size of government. For discussions of the technique and some of the issues posed by its use, see Beck and Katz (1995, 2001), Green *et al.* (2001), Sayrs (1989) and Stimson (1985).

13 The data upon which Figure 1.1 is based were calculated from data reported in OECD (2004b) and earlier editions.

14 The US, it should be noted, deviates significantly from this overall pattern.

15 The data for total outlays include the current disbursements and net capital outlays of all levels of government. The data for total revenues were calculated by adding to the ratios of total outlays to GDP the combined financial balance of all levels of government as a proportion of GDP. The data on outlays and deficits are reported in OECD (2004c) and earlier issues. For all of the countries, the time-series data reported by the OECD for the ratio of outlays to GDP have occasional discontinuities; where that is the case, the earlier data have been recalculated to make them comparable with the data reported in OECD (2004c).

16 Again, it should be noted the US deviates significantly from this pattern.

17 Why the two operationalizations yield identical results for all of the independent variables other than the lagged dependent variable is evident from simple algebraic transformation: the former is, of course, represented as $Y_t = a + bY_{t-1} + \ldots$. The latter can be represented as $Y_t - Y_{t-1} = a + bY_{t-1} + \ldots$, which can be rewritten as $Y_t = a + bY_{t-1} + Y_{t-1} + \ldots$, or $Y_t = a + (b + 1)\ Y_{t-1} + \ldots$. Thus, the only difference between the two involves the coefficient of the lagged dependent variable. In the former, *b* is generally in the range of 0.85 to 0.9 whereas in the latter it is generally in the range of −0.1 to −0.15.

18 The data on per capita GDP in constant dollars are reported in OECD (2004b) and earlier issues. Those on the annual rate of change in "real" GDP and consumer prices and the standardized rate of unemployment are reported in OECD (2004c) and earlier issues. The data on the age of the population, the working-age population and the sectoral composition of the work force are reported in OECD (2004a) and earlier issues.

19 See e.g. Burgoon (2001) and Garrett and Mitchell (2001). Iversen and Cusack (2000) make use of an alternative measure of "unexpected growth" that represents the deviation in a given year from the average rate in the preceding three years. In addition to being idiosyncratic, that measure understates the effect of growth in periods of sustained high (or low) growth lasting several years.

20 For exceptions, see Burgoon (2001), Garrett (1998), Hicks and Swank (1992) and Huber *et al.* (1993).

21 Iversen and Cusack (2000) devise a complex measure of the automatic, or nondiscretionary, component of transfer payments in place of the standard controls for unemployment and the elderly population. Their measure consists of the change in the proportion of the population that is elderly or unemployed multiplied by the replacement rates, which are estimated by the share of the GDP represented by transfer payments relative to the share of the total population that is elderly or unemployed. We prefer to use conventional measures of unemployment and the size of the dependent population and to estimate their effects separately.

22 For an exception, see Hicks and Swank (1992) which reports a significant positive effect.

23 Iversen and Cusack (2000) assert that costs, including wage costs, increase at the same rate in public services as in the rest of the economy, although productivity in the public sector lags behind that in the economy, thereby causing prices of government services to rise faster than those in the rest of the economy. To control for that effect, they use a measure of the product of the share of government consumption in GDP and the rate of growth in the price deflator for government services divided by the rate of growth in the price deflator of GDP. For the sake of simplicity, we use, instead, a measure of the annual change in consumer prices.

24 See Burgoon (2001), Garrett and Mitchell (2001) and Kaufman and Segura-Ubiergo (2001).

25 There are, of course, many interactions that could be posited among the variables. However, the specification and use of such terms in such regression analyses is often idiosyncratic and, in any event, is designed to identify effects that are conditional and depend on the presence of another attribute. Given the scope of our analysis and the number of variables already under consideration, we have limited ourselves here to simply estimating the independent and direct effects of each variable.

26 The error correction method removes the need to correct for serial correlation within the panels.

27 The regression coefficients and standard errors have been estimated with Stata 8.2's *xtpcse* program. For a discussion of the desirability of obtaining panel-corrected standard errors in analyses of pooled cross-sectional time-series data, see Beck and Katz (1995).

28 The F-test does not establish that a random effects model with a common intercept would produce biased estimates. But in view of the F-test, there is no reason to risk biasing the results by assuming random effects. For a discussion of fixed effects in pooled cross-sectional time-series data, see Green *et al.* (2001) and Beck and Katz (2001).

29 The ratio of the regression coefficient to the standard error is the *t*-statistic. The asterisks indicate the probability, *p*, based on the magnitude of the *t*-statistic, that the regression coefficient is incorrectly signed.

30 While they did not include Greece, Spain and Portugal, Iversen and Cusack (2000) included New Zealand and Switzerland. We did not include the latter two because the data reported for outlays and revenues for those countries are not comparable to those reported for the 19 countries included in our analysis.

31 In 1993, Europe was in the depths of a major recession. Subsequently, the ratio of spending to GDP dropped dramatically in countries such as Sweden, Denmark and Norway, despite the fact that the extent of "deindustrialization" continued to increase.

32 Rodden (2003) reports that the extent to which subnational units depend on their own sources of revenue, as well as the change in that reliance on own revenues, is associated negatively and significantly with the extent of change in total spending. See also Hallerberg and Basinger (1998) and Steinmo and Tolbert (1998).

33 On "veto points" and "veto players," see Tsebelis (1995, 2002).

34 Consistent with that conjecture, Rodden (2003) finds evidence of a significant electoral effect on total expenditures in a pooled analysis of total public spending in 24 countries between 1980 and 1993.

35 Persson and Tabellini (2003) find, for example, that the existence of a proportional electoral system had a significant expansionary effect on welfare spending and on total spending by central governments. Similarly, Milesi-Ferretti *et al.* (2002) find a significant relationship between the existence of a proportional electoral system and the extent of welfare spending.

36 In addition, of course, programmatic distinctions among the parties could be muted by the necessity to form coalitions, including coalitions that cross the conventional Left-Right divide, and by the institutional constraints that parties encounter when in government.

37 The military ruled in Greece between April 1967 and November 1974 and the regime is regarded as democratic after July 1975. Authoritarian rule ended in Portugal with the revolution of April 1974 and the regime is regarded as democratic after April 1975. Franco died in November 1975 and the Spanish regime is regarded as democratic after June 1977. The years in which those regimes were not democratic are assigned a value of 1. All other years, and in the other countries all years, are assigned a value of 0.

38 Federal systems are coded 1, unitary systems 0. As with most constitutional attributes, the hierarchical organization of each polity was generally unchanged throughout the three decades. Nevertheless, there were some major changes – most notably, the transformation of Belgium into a federal polity and the devolution of some powers to subnational units in Spain, Britain, France and Italy. In the latter cases, we have assigned an intermediate value.

39 Finland prior to 1982, France and Greece between 1975 and 1985, Portugal between 1976 and 1982, and the US are coded as having strong, directly-elected, presidencies. Austria and Finland after 1981 and even more so after 1992, Germany and Greece after 1986, Ireland, Italy and Portugal are coded as having weak presidencies. See Lijphart (1999).

40 Taken largely from Cukierman *et al.* (1992), the values range from 0 to 1, the latter reflecting complete independence. The values for the countries of the European Union have been adjusted to reflect the greater independence of the central bank mandated by the Treaty on European Union in the second transitional stage of EMU that began in 1994. For the countries that entered the third and final stage of EMU in 1999, the values have been further adjusted to reflect the greater political independence of the European Central Bank.

41 Years in which national elections take place are assigned a value of 1; all others are assigned a value of 0.

42 Taken largely from Lijphart (1999), the measure ranges from 0 for PR systems to 1 for first-past-the-post systems, with mixed systems receiving a value that reflects the proportion of seats in the national legislature that are filled in single-member districts.

43 To address the possibility that, as Huber *et al.* (1993) suggest, Christian Democratic parties might have expansionary or contractionary effects on spending different from those associated with left-of-center or conventional conservative parties, we have included separate measures of the extent of partisan control of government by left-of-center, centrist, Christian Democratic and conservative parties. The measures have been calculated from information on the composition of governments reported in Keesing's (2000) and earlier.

## References

Adserà, A. and Boix, C. (2002) "Trade, Democracy and the Size of the Public Sector: The Political Underpinnings of Openness," *International Organization*, 56: 229–62.

Alvarez, M., Garrett, G. and Lange, P. (1991) "Government Partisanship, Labor Organization, and Macroeconomic Performance," *American Political Science Review*, 85: 539–56.

Beck, N. and Katz, J. (1995) "What to Do (and Not to Do) with Time-Series Cross-Section Data," *American Political Science Review*, 89: 634–47.

—— (2001) "Throwing Out the Baby with the Bath Water: A Comment on Green, Kim, and Yoon," *International Organization*, 55: 487–95.

Bird, R. (1971) "Wagner's 'Law' of Expanding State Activity," *Public Finances/Finances Publiques*, 26: 1–26.

Blais, A., Blake, D. and Dion, S (1993) "Do Parties Make a Difference? Parties and the Size of Government in Liberal Democracies," *American Journal of Political Science*, 37: 40–62.

Boix, C. (2001) "Democracy, Development and the Public Sector," *American Journal of Political Science*, 45: 1–17.

Burgoon, B. (2001) "Globalization and Welfare Compensation: Disentangling the Ties that Bind," *International Organization*, 55: 509–51.

Cameron, D. (1978) "The Expansion of the Public Economy: A Comparative Analysis," *American Political Science Review*, 72: 1243–61.

—— (1984) "Social Democracy, Corporatism, Labour Quiescence, and the Representation of Economic Interest in Advanced Capitalist Society," in J. Goldthorpe (ed.) *Order and Conflict in Contemporary Capitalism*, Oxford: Oxford University Press, 143–78.

Cameron, D. and McDermott, K. (1995) "The Expansion and Contraction of the Public Economy, 1960–92," unpublished typescript, Yale University.

Castles, F. (1982) "The Impact of Parties on Public Expenditure," in F. Castles (ed.) *The Impact of Parties*, London: Sage Publications, 21–96.

Clark, C. (1945) "Public Finance and Changes in the Value of Money," *Economic Journal*, 55: 371–89.

Cukierman, A. (1992) *Central Bank Strategy, Credibility, and Independence*, Cambridge: The MIT Press.

—— (1994) "Central Bank Independence and Monetary Control," *Economic Journal*, 104: 1437–48.

Cukierman, A., Webb, S. and Neyapti, B. (1992) "Measuring the Independence of Central Banks and its Effect on Policy Outcomes," *World Bank Economic Review*, 6: 353–98.

Cusack, T. (1997) "Partisan Politics and Public Finance: Changes in Public Spending in the Industrialized Democracies, 1955–1989," *Public Choice*, 91: 375–95.

—— (1999) "Partison Politics and Fiscal Policy," *Comparative Political Studies*, 32: 464–86.

Downs, A. (1957) *An Economic Theory of Democracy*, New York: Harper and Row.

Garrett, G. (1995) "Capital Mobility, Trade, and the Domestic Politics of Economic Policy," *International Organization*, 49: 657–87.

—— (1998) *Partisan Politics in the Global Economy*, Cambridge: Cambridge University Press.

—— (2000) "The Causes of Globalization," *Comparative Political Studies*, 33: 941–91.

—— (2001) "Globalization and Government Spending Around the World," *Studies in Comparative International Development*, 35: 3–29.

Garrett, G. and Lange, P. (1991) "Political Responses to Interdependence: What's 'Left' for the Left?," *International Organization*, 45: 539–64.

Garrett, G. and Mitchell, D. (2001) "Globalization, Government Spending and Taxation in the OECD," *European Journal of Political Research*, 39: 145–77.

Green, D., Kim, S. Y. and Yoon, D. (2001) "Dirty Pool," *International Organization*, 55: 441–68.

Hallerberg, M. and Basinger, S. (1998) "Internationalization and Changes in Tax Policy in OECD Countries: The Importance of Domestic Veto Players," *Comparative Political Studies*, 31: 321–52.

Hibbs, D. (1977) "Political Parties and Macroeconomic Policy," *American Political Science Review*, 71: 467–87.

Hicks, A. and Swank, D. (1984) "On the Political Economy of Welfare Expansion: A Comparative Analysis of 18 Advanced Capitalist Democracies, 1960–71," *Comparative Political Studies*, 17: 81–119.

—— (1992) "Politics, Institutions, and Welfare Spending in Industrialized Democracies, 1960–82," *American Political Science Review*, 86: 658–74.

Hood, C. (1991) "Stabilization and Cutbacks: A Catastrophe for Government Growth Theory?," *Journal of Theoretical Politics*, 3: 37–63.

Huber, E., Ragin, C. and Stephens, J. (1993) "Social Democracy, Christian Democracy, Constitutional Structure, and the Welfare State," *American Journal of Sociology*, 99: 711–49.

Iversen, T. and Cusack, T. (2000) "The Causes of Welfare State Expansion: Deindustrialization or Globalization?," *World Politics*, 52: 313–49.

Kaufman, R. and Segura-Ubiergo, A. (2001) "Globalization, Domestic Politics and Social Spending in Latin America: A Time-Series Cross-Section Analysis, 1973–1997," *World Politics*, 53: 553–87.

Keesing's Limited (2000) *Keesing's Contemporary Archives*, London: Keesing's Limited.

Kirschen, E. S., Benard, J., Besters, H., Blackaby, F., Eckstein, O., Faaland, J., Hartog, F., Morissens, L. and Tosco, E. (1964) *Economic Policy in Our Time*, 3 vol. Amsterdam: North-Holland.

Lijphart, A. (1999) *Patterns of Democracy: Government Forms and Performance in Thirty-Six Countries*, New Haven: Yale University Press.

Milesi-Ferretti, G., Perotti, R. and Rostagno, M. (2002) "Electoral Systems and Public Spending," *Quarterly Journal of Economics*, 117: 609–57.

Nordhaus, W. (1975) "The Political Business Cycle," *Review of Economic Studies*, 42: 169–90.

O'Connor, J. (1988) "Convergence or Divergence? Change in Welfare Effort in OECD Countries 1960–1980," *European Journal of Political Research*, 16: 277–99.

O'Donnell, G., Schmitter, P. and Whitehead, L. (eds) (1986) *Transitions from Authoritarian Rule: Southern Europe*, Baltimore: Johns Hopkins.

Organization for Economic Cooperation and Development (2004a) *Labour Force Statistics 1982–2002*, Paris: OECD.

—— (2004b) *National Accounts of OECD Countries: Main Aggregates, Vol. 1, 1991–2002*, Paris: OECD.

—— (2004c) *OECD Economic Outlook 75*, Paris: OECD.

Persson, T. and Tabellini, G. (1999) "The Size and Scope of Government: Comparative Politics with Rational Politicians," *European Economic Review*, 43: 699–735.

—— (2000) *Political Economics: Explaining Economic Policy*, Cambridge: The MIT Press.

—— (2003) *The Economic Effects of Constitutions*, Cambridge: The MIT Press.

—— (2004) "Constitutional Rules and Fiscal Policy," *American Economic Review*, 94: 25–46.

Quinn, D. and Inclán, C. (1997) "The Origins of Financial Openness: A Study of Current and Capital Account Liberalization," *American Journal of Political Science*, 41: 771–813.

Rice, T. (1986) "The Determinants of Western European Government Growth 1950–1980," *Comparative Political Studies*, 19: 233–57.

Rodden, J. (2003) "Reviving Leviathan: Fiscal Federalism and the Growth of Government," *International Organization*, 57: 695–729.

Rodrik, D. (1998) "Why Do More Open Economies Have Bigger Governments?," *Journal of Political Economy*, 106: 997–1032.

Rose, R. (1984) *Do Parties Make a Difference?*, 2nd edn, Chatham: Chatham House.

Saunders, P. and Klau, F. (1985) "The Role of the Public Sector: Causes and Consequences of the Growth of Government," *OECD Economic Studies*, 4: 189–202.

Sayrs, L. (1989) *Pooled Time Series Analysis*, Beverly Hills: Sage Publications.

Steinmo, S. and Tolbert, C. (1998) "Do Institutions Really Matter? Taxation in Industrialized Democracies," *Comparative Political Studies*, 31: 165–87.

Stimson, J. (1985) "Regression in Space and Time: A Statistical Essay," *American Journal of Political Science*, 29: 914–47.

Swank, D. (1988) "The Political Economy of Government Domestic Expenditure in the Affluent Democracies, 1960–1980," *American Journal of Political Science*, 32: 1120–50.

—— (1992) "Politics and the Structural Dependence of the State in Democratic Capitalist Nations," *American Political Science Review*, 86: 38–54.

Tarschys, D. (1975) "The Growth of Government Expenditures: Nine Modes of Explanation," *Scandinavian Political Studies*, 10: 9–31.

Taylor, C. (ed.) (1983) *Why Governments Grow: Measuring Public Sector Size*, Beverly Hills: Sage Publications.

Tsebelis, G. (1995) "Decision Making in Political Systems: Veto Players in Presidentialism, Parliamentarism, Multicameralism and Multipartyism," *British Journal of Political Science*, 25: 289–325.

—— (2002) *Veto Players: How Political Institutions Work*, Princeton: Princeton University Press.

Tsebelis, G. and Chang, E. (2004) "Veto Players and the Structure of Budgets in Advanced Industrialized Countries," *European Journal of Political Research*, 43: 449–76.

Tufte, E. (1978) *Political Control of the Economy*, Princeton: Princeton University Press.

Wagner, A. (1877) *Finanzwissenschaft*, Leipzig: C. F. Winter.

—— (1893) *Grundlegung der Politischen Ökonomie*, Leipzig: C. F. Winter.

# 2 Public opinion, international economic integration and the welfare state

*Kenneth Scheve and Matthew J. Slaughter**

## Introduction

Identifying the consequences of international economic integration for social insurance and redistributive policymaking involves specifying the economic and political constraints that these policy areas generate for one another. The main questions addressed in this inquiry typically take the form of determining whether increased international flows of goods, services and factors of production raise the economic costs of the provision of social insurance and redistributive transfers such that political support for these policies is substantially diminished in democratic states. The most common answer to these questions is that yes, economic globalization reduces the capacity, or at least political resolve, of states to implement generous social insurance and redistributive policies. Dissents to this mainstream view, however, are many. These scholars point to a long tradition of egalitarian policymaking in highly open and internationally competitive economies (e.g. Cameron 1978; Rodrik 1997; Garrett 1998). At the core of most of these dissents is the idea that international economic liberalization generates costs for workers and thus may actually increase political support for social insurance and redistributive policymaking. An obvious strategy for evaluating this dissenting view regarding the supposed opposition of economic globalization and egalitarian policymaking is to evaluate how exposure to international integration may influence public support for both economic integration itself and the social insurance and redistributive policies that are the core of the modern welfare state.

In this chapter, we focus on one aspect of this research agenda and investigate the determinants of public support for the policies that govern the liberalization of flows of goods, services and factors of production. This analysis is informative for debates about the relationship between globalization and egalitarian redistribution for at least two reasons. First, as is widely recognized, global economic integration is in part determined by policy liberalization – the reduction of impediments to international trade and flows of capital and labor. Any political economy model that seeks to explain policymaking for these areas in democratic states must specify the preferences of citizens in addition to the institutions that aggregate these preferences. To understand the impact of globalization on political support for the welfare state, it is necessary to understand the political bases of support for globalization itself. Second, our analysis emphasizes the importance of labor market concerns in individuals' evaluations of international economic policies and how these concerns may be mitigated in the presence of generous adjustment, insurance, and/or training schemes. We contend that simple conclusions that substantial social insurance and redistributive policies are inconsistent with economic globalization are implausible because political support for liberalism itself depends in part on those very policies.

There are four remaining sections to the chapter. The next section describes the broad patterns of public opinion around the world about international economic integration. Given the importance of labor market concerns evident in this description, the third section briefly reviews the theoretical effects of integration on the level and volatility of wages and employment and the existing empirical evidence evaluating these theories. The fourth section is the main section of the paper, and it examines the determinants of variation across individuals and countries in policy preferences. The final section concludes with a discussion of the implications of this evidence for explanations of variation in economic policymaking, including both those policies that govern the pace of international economic integration and those social insurance and redistributive policies that may alter its consequences for the welfare of workers.

## Public attitudes about international economic integration

What do people around the world think about the forces of trade, immigration and FDI that drive international economic integration? Is there unabashed support? Or resistance? Or is there a more fundamental lack of understanding of the relevant economic issues at hand? In this section, we outline some broad patterns of public opinion around the world about globalization.

The comparative focus of this section draws on a growing body of recent research on preferences around the world over international economic policies. Our earlier work in this literature examined the United States, and others have addressed many other OECD and non-OECD countries as well.[1] The interested reader can note that commonly used cross-country data include the 1995–1997 World Values Survey (WVS), a set of surveys designed for cross-national comparisons; and the 1995 International Social Survey Programme (ISSP). US-specific data include the biennial National Election Studies surveys and the quadrennial surveys of the Chicago Council on Foreign Relations (CCFR).

In drawing upon these and other sources, our goal is not to generate an exhaustive catalog of each. Instead, we use them selectively to provide a representative overview of the salient patterns in public opinions about globalization and its constituent forces of trade, immigration and FDI. We now address each of these in turn, where throughout we enumerate a list of salient facts.

### *Public attitudes about globalization*

*Fact 1: In many countries – but not all – a plurality or majority of people thinks that globalization is good for the overall country.*

The broadest question one could ask about cross-border integration would invoke the catch-all term "globalization." CCFR (2002a, b) reports responses of seven countries to the question, "Overall do you think globalization is good or bad for the national economy?" The good-bad split ranges from 62 to 22 percent in the Netherlands to 25 to 34 percent in Poland, which is the one country among the seven sampled in which a plurality regards globalization as a net minus, not a plus.[2]

*Fact 2: People perceive an asymmetric distribution of the benefits of globalization: more for consumers and corporations but less for workers.*

The phrasing of the above question is open to a wide range of interpretations, as globalization encompasses a range of economic and non-economic topics. That said, some insight on the salient issues can be gleaned from a set of related US questions in CCFR (2002a) that asked whether globalization is good or bad for different constituencies. When given the same good-or-bad choice, majorities of Americans think globalization is good both for "consumers like you" (55 to 27 percent) and for "American companies" (55 to 30 percent).

There is much more ambivalence, however, about the labor-market impacts of globalization. Americans are evenly split (within sampling error) over whether globalization is good or bad for "creating jobs in the US" (43 to 41 percent), and a sizable majority thinks that globalization is bad for "job security of American workers" (51 to 32 percent). This widespread concern about labor markets will be seen quite clearly below when we examine the particular modes of global integration of trade, immigration and FDI. This concern also appears when placed in the context of US foreign policy. An overwhelming 85 percent of Americans state that protecting the jobs of American workers should be a "very important" goal of US foreign policy (with this percentage representing the third highest-ranking goal chosen).

*Fact 3: Some evidence suggests that in some countries, support for globalization has waned in recent years.*

It is notable that recent surveys (e.g. CCFR, 2002a) suggest that American support for globalization has been waning in recent years. For example, the 52 percent in 2002 stating that globalization is good for consumers was down from 68 percent in 2000. Similarly, the 85 percent in 2002 stating job protection should be a "very important" goal for US foreign policy was the highest response rate for this item since it was first asked by CCFR in 1974. Such trends over time might reflect many factors, such as a deepening of globalization in recent years or the deteriorating US macroeconomy and labor market since 2000.

### Public attitudes about trade

*Fact 4: In most countries around the world, a plurality to majority of individuals prefer policy options aimed at more trade restrictions, not freer trade. Thus, the "average" citizen of the world appears to be more of a protectionist than a free-trader.*

The most comprehensive comparative data on public attitudes about trade comes from the 1995–1997 WVS. For the following question, this wave of the WVS reports responses for 52 countries (or intra-national regions) around the world:

> Do you think it is better if goods made in other countries can be imported and sold here if people want to buy them, or that there should be stricter limits on selling foreign goods here, to protect the jobs of people in this country.

Of the 65,123 total respondents stating a preference for one of these two options, 64.2 percent chose stricter limits on trade. By country, a similar pattern emerges: in 42 of the 52 countries a majority of respondents stating a preference for one of these two options chose stricter trade limits. Anti-trade sentiments appear to be particularly strong in many countries of North and South America: the United States (73.0 percent), Peru (83.3 percent), Mexico (83.5 percent), Brazil (87.0 percent), Venezuela (87.9 percent), and Uruguay (92.6 percent). Most of the ten "pro-trade" countries were formerly part of the Soviet bloc (Armenia, Azerbaijan, Belarus, Bosnia, Georgia, Serbia, Ukraine), with only two from the OECD (West Germany and Japan, the country with the highest pro-trade response rate at 71.7 percent).

The WVS question frames the trade issue in an explicit labor-market context. Given the earlier evidence that an – if not the – important reservation people express about globalization is its possible labor-market damage, one might worry that the widespread anti-trade sentiment in WVS responses is sensitive to framing. An alternative frame of reference is given by the 1995 ISSP survey. Here, trade protection is considered in the context of the overall economy, rather than the labor market in particular.

> How much do you agree or disagree with the following statements: (Respondent's country) should limit the import of foreign products in order to protect its national economy.
> - Agree strongly
> - Agree
> - Neither agree nor disagree
> - Disagree
> - Disagree strongly

One can count pro-trade opinions as those responding "disagree" or "disagree strongly," and similarly anti-trade opinions as those responding "agree" or "agree strongly." Of the 29,350 total respondents stating a preference, only 22.3 percent were pro-trade while 59.5 percent were anti-trade. As with the WVS evidence, here too in the large majority of countries – 21 of 23 – a majority of respondents stating a preference for one of these two options chose stricter trade limits. The only two without such a minority are the Netherlands and Japan (with West German opinions, broadly consistent with the WVS evidence, nearly evenly split).

Even with the ISSP evidence, though, one might still worry about question framing. The ISSP question does not offer any rationale for disagreeing with protection as a policy choice. Indeed, the question could be read as though the idea that import limits somehow protect economies is indisputable fact, evidence from the economics profession notwithstanding.

Scheve and Slaughter (2001c) explore the impact of question framing for the case of the United States, thanks to their sample of hundreds of trade-policy survey questions from the 1930s forward. They document two broad categories of trade-policy questions: those that mention both benefits and costs to trade (e.g. the WVS question) and those that do not. For questions in the former category, a plurality to majority of respondents still oppose policies aimed at freer trade. Some of the latter questions elicit more pro-trade responses – especially questions that do not mention policy per se, but rather the general idea of international trade as cross-border commerce. Even with these questions, however, the evidence at best suggests the US public is split on the issue of trade. Thus, while a more systematic examination of framing issues in a cross-section of countries would be of help, for now, our reading of the evidence is that the "average" respondent across countries is skeptical about trade liberalization.

One might also wonder about whether Fact 4 has held consistently over time. US evidence indicates that the split in that country's opinions between freer and more-protected trade has existed for about a generation. Scheve and Slaughter (2001c) report time-series evidence from a *Los*

*Angeles Times* survey conducted annually since 1982. Every year, approximately two-thirds of respondents have opted for a policy of trade barriers to protect jobs over a policy of free trade to allow broader consumer variety and lower consumer prices. CCFR (2002a) reports similar time-series stability for a trade-policy question it has asked quadrennially since 1976. Every year, approximately half or slightly more of respondents have opted for a policy of trade barriers to protect jobs over a policy of free trade to lower consumer prices.

*Fact 5: Anti-trade opinions do not simply reflect ignorance about the subject. The US evidence is that large majorities of individuals acknowledge that trade generates the benefits that economic theory predicts. Similarly large majorities also worry, however, that trade generates labor-market costs in terms of job destruction and lower wages.*

Scheve and Slaughter (2001c) document evidence on both components on this fact. Gains from trade that large majorities of Americans acknowledge include lower consumer prices (especially for poor families), wider consumer variety and sharper competitive and innovative pressures for American firms. Yet a wide swatch of questions reveals deep concerns among consistent pluralities to majorities that trade destroys US jobs and pressures US wages. For detailed questions and discussion, see Scheve and Slaughter (2001c). Note how this US evidence on the perceived distribution of benefits and costs for trade parallels the perceived distribution for globalization noted earlier in Fact 2.

Facts 4 and 5 can be brought together in sharp relief by recent US questions by CCFR and the Program on International Policy Attitudes (PIPA). In 2000 and then again in 2002, PIPA and then CCFR asked the following question:

> Which of the following three positions comes closest to your point of view? A: I favor free trade, and I believe that it IS necessary for the government to have programs to help workers who lose their jobs. B: I favor free trade, and I believe that it is NOT necessary for the government to have programs to help workers who lose their jobs. C: I do not favor free trade.

In 2000 66 percent of Americans chose option A, the policy duo of free trade plus labor-market supports. In 2002 73 percent of Americans chose this option. The response to this particular trade-policy question stands in sharp contrast to the questions discussed for Fact 4. When the policy option of free trade is explicitly linked with policies aimed at ameliorating any adverse labor-market impacts, large majorities of Americans opt for free trade.

### *Public attitudes about immigration*

*Fact 6: In most countries around the world, a plurality to majority of individuals prefer policy options aimed at admitting fewer immigrants, not more. Thus, the "average" citizen of the world appears to prefer less immigration, not more.*

Public opinion about immigration broadly parallels that of trade. As with trade, for comparative evidence we start with the WVS question:

> How about people from other countries coming here to work? Which one of the following do you think the government should do?
>
> - Let anyone come who wants to.
> - Let people come as long as there are jobs available.
> - Place strict limits on the number of foreigners who can come here.
> - Prohibit people coming here from other countries.

We aggregated responses by assigning each a number one through four (in the foregoing order) and then averaging. Of the 64,369 total respondents stating a preference, the average was about 2.42 – that is, the "average" response was somewhere between allowing immigrants conditional on job availability and strictly limiting immigrants. We consider this to be lukewarm enthusiasm for immigration, at best. By country, a similar picture emerges: in 47 of the 49 countries the average response was over two.

The WVS question frames the immigration issue in an explicit labor-market context. Indeed, the question seems to presume that immigrants tend to take jobs away from natives. Given the earlier evidence that an – if not the – important reservation people express about globalization and trade are the possible labor-market damage, one might worry that the widespread anti-immigration sentiment in WVS responses is sensitive to framing. An alternative frame of reference is given by the 1995 ISSP survey. Here, respondents are asked about changes in existing immigration levels without reference to any particular economic issue.

> Do you think the number of immigrants to (respondent's country) nowadays should be reduced a lot, reduced a little, remain the same as it is, increased a little, or increased a lot?

One can count pro-immigration opinions as those responding "increased a little" or "increased a lot," and similarly anti-immigration opinions as those responding "reduced a little" or "reduced a lot." Of the 27,001 total respondents stating a preference, only 7.9 percent were pro-immigration while 61.7 percent were anti-immigration. In all 23 countries this anti-immigration group was larger than its pro-immigration counterpart, and the national fraction accounted for by this anti-immigration group was less than half in just three countries: Canada (41.3 percent), Ireland (21.6 percent) and Spain (40.0 percent).

*Fact 7: Anti-immigration opinions, like those for trade, appear to have an important labor-market component to them. People acknowledge some benefits from immigration but appear to worry more about costs such as labor-market pressures.*

Individuals do acknowledge some economic and social benefits from immigration. For example, the ISSP survey asked whether immigrants make the host country "more open to new ideas and cultures." The average response across all countries was somewhere between neutral and agree. Scheve and Slaughter (2001c) report similar US evidence: for example, 69 percent of Americans agree that "immigrants help improve our country with their different cultures and talents."

But there appears to be widespread concern that immigrants generate social and economic costs. For example, the ISSP survey asked whether immigrants "increase crime rates." The average response across all countries was somewhere between neutral and agree. In terms of economic impacts, the average response was similar to the question of whether immigrants "take jobs away from people who were born in the country." Scheve and Slaughter (2001c) report similar US evidence. Large majorities of Americans think that immigrants take jobs away from natives – with a plurality regularly stating that this outcome is either extremely or very likely. When asked questions about US immigration policy that explicitly raise the potential cost of job competition for natives, large majorities of Americans chose the option of decreasing immigration.

The balance of opinion on immigration, then, looks broadly similar to that for trade. Though people acknowledge benefits, both economic and otherwise, they appear to worry more about costs – especially labor-market costs – such that on balance they opt for policies of less immigration, not more. Consistent with this, the ISSP asked broadly whether "immigrants are generally good for the country's economy." The average response fell between neutral and disagree.

### *Public attitudes about FDI*

We are unaware of comprehensive comparative evidence on foreign direct investment (FDI) opinions. In Scheve and Slaughter (2001c), we present US evidence, which we briefly summarize. The issue of how this US evidence might be representative of other countries should be treated carefully. Our discussion in this section indicates that many US opinion patterns over trade and immigration that we documented in Scheve and Slaughter (2001c) broadly match patterns elsewhere in the world. That said, to the extent that many other countries have broader histories of inward and outward FDI flows, US opinions over FDI might not generalize as easily.

*Fact 8: A majority of Americans want restrictions on both inward and outward foreign direct investment, as Americans acknowledge some economic benefits but seem to worry more about perceived labor-market costs.*

On the one hand, a plurality of Americans acknowledge that inward FDI generates economic benefits as foreign firms help invigorate US industry via new technologies and management techniques.

On the other hand, there is significant concern about the labor-market impacts of inward and outward FDI, especially whether it reduces the number of jobs. Across a wide range of questions, a consistent plurality to majority think that FDI in both directions eliminates jobs. This opinion appears more widespread about outward FDI, with the prominent concern that outward FDI entails US firms "exporting" jobs outside the country. Over two-thirds of Americans think that "companies sending jobs overseas" is a "major reason" for "why the economy is not doing better than it is." With inward FDI, there also appears to be concern that inward FDI somehow grants foreigners excessive control over the US economy.

In light of these labor-market and security concerns, one might expect Americans not to support FDI liberalization. This is indeed the case: a majority favors restrictions on FDI.

### *Summary of findings: ambivalence and variation*

Our two-word summary of the opinions collected in this section is "ambivalence" and "variation."

In many countries, pluralities to majorities of citizens acknowledge the many economic benefits of global integration. This belies the idea that globalization is too complex for people to understand. But at the same time, these same pluralities to majorities also vocalize concerns about this process. Particularly salient appear to be concerns about labor-market pressures on wages, employment and job security. On balance, it appears that the "average" citizen in many countries supports the broad idea of globalization yet at the same time prefers policies aimed at less trade, less immigration and less FDI. At the very least, it is clear that there is division, and therefore substantial concern, about further liberalization. Thus, ambivalence is an important feature of the data.

A second important feature is the cross-country variation in opinions. The broad assessments of benefits and costs just described are not uniform in every country. Rather, countries look quite different on many basic questions. It is not the case that in every country the average citizen is against freer trade or immigration. And even within the large groups of anti-liberalization countries, countries vary substantially in how widely these attitudes are held. We examine what accounts for this cross-country variation in the fourth section. But before turning to that analysis, in the next section, we briefly outline the possible labor-market impacts of globalization.

## The labor-market impacts of globalization

In this section, we discuss linkages from global economic integration to a few key labor-market outcomes: the level of real and relative wages, and insecurity in terms of the volatility of wages and employment.[3] We have two overall messages to this section: that there are sound reasons in theory that integration can affect labor markets, and that at least some of these links have mattered empirically for some countries in recent decades. As is the case in much of the literature on globalization and labor markets, our discussion in this section presumes the benchmark of relatively flexible labor markets that clear at full employment. In reality, in less flexible labor markets the supply-and-demand forces generated by globalization can have employment as well as wage impacts. This will be considered empirically in the next section.

### *The theory of the impact of trade on wages*

Standard trade theory predicts that trade's effect on people's current income depends crucially on the degree of intersectoral factor mobility, i.e. on the degree of factor specificity. There are two main models to consider. In a Heckscher-Ohlin (HO) framework, where factors can move costlessly across sectors, factor incomes tend to vary by factor type. In contrast, in a Ricardo-Viner (RV) framework, where some or all factors cannot move to other sectors, factor incomes tend to vary by industry of employment. Because factor mobility increases over time, it is often thought the HO model better describes longer time horizons while the RV model better describes shorter ones.[4]

In both models, changes in trade policy affect factor incomes by changing the country's relative product prices. The HO assumption that factors can move costlessly across sectors means each factor earns the same return in all industries. Here, trade liberalization tends to raise/lower wages for factors employed relatively intensively in sectors whose relative prices are rising/falling (per the Stolper-Samuelson theorem of 1941).

This process works via cross-industry shifts in labor demand. Suppose international trade changes domestic product prices – for example, because of changes in a country's trade barriers (e.g. the US eliminates apparel quotas in the Multi-Fiber Arrangement) or because of changes in supply and demand in world markets (e.g. world apparel prices decline as China produces more). Whatever the case, at initial factor prices any industry enjoying a rise in its product price now earns positive profits, while any industry suffering a fall in its price now earns negative profits. Profit-maximizing firms respond by trying to expand output in profitable sectors and reduce output in unprofitable sectors. As firms do this, economy-wide demand for factors of production changes. Relative labor demand increases for the factors employed relatively intensively in expanding sectors and reduces for the factors intensive in the contracting sectors. To restore equilibrium, at fixed labor supply, relative wages must adjust in response to the demand shifts until profit opportunities are arbitraged away.

Note that in the HO framework, it is *not* just people working in traded industries who face wage pressures from international trade. Non-traded workers do too, not directly through international product-market competition, but indirectly through domestic labor-market competition. If US trade barriers in apparel are removed, it is not just American apparel workers who face wage changes. It is all workers in the American economy competing in the same labor market as these apparel workers – regardless of the industries of these other workers.

### *Empirical studies of the impact of trade on wages*

Do these linkages from trade to wages seem to matter in the real world? The short answer is, "yes." A comparative analysis of wage changes is clearly beyond the scope of this chapter. We briefly summarize the US experience, both because most academic research in recent years has focused on this case and because its changes have been paralleled in many other countries.

In recent decades, there have been sharply different wage trends for more-skilled and less-skilled Americans. First, the premium earned by more-skilled workers over less-skilled workers has been rising sharply since the late 1970s. Second, average real-wage growth in the United States has been very sluggish since the early 1970s. And when talking about less-skilled US workers, it is very important to remember that this category, as typically defined by labor economists, constitutes the majority of the US labor force. All this means that *for about 25 years less-skilled workers, the majority of the US labor force, have had close to zero or even negative real-wage growth while more-skilled workers have been enjoying real-wage gains.* These patterns differ sharply from earlier decades, when real-wage growth was both faster and enjoyed across all groups with steady and/or declining inequality.[5]

What role has international trade played in these developments? There is a very large academic literature on this subject, with a wide range of conclusions. Taken together, most studies seem to have concluded that technological change favoring skilled workers has been the major force driving up the returns to skill. This "skill-biased" technological change (SBTC), widespread across the majority of US industries, does not appear to be robustly related to various globalization forces.

Most trade economists looking at the role of international trade have organized their data analysis around the Stolper-Samuelson process outlined earlier. For trade to have driven changes in US relative wages via changes in US relative product prices, it would have done so by raising the relative price of less-skill-intensive goods during the 1970s but then lowering the relative price of less-skill-intensive goods since around 1980. Have prices actually moved in this manner? Perhaps. Changes in observed US product prices have not clearly matched up with changes in the skill premium. But when decomposing observed prices into trade-related components, some studies have found evidence of the necessary relative price changes. Most Stolper-Samuelson studies have concluded that trade may have played some role in the rising skill premium, but that it has not been the major force driving wage movements. Other studies using other methods have reached similar conclusions.[6]

Does this US experience apply to other countries? The basic issue for any country is to see if changes in a country's relative product prices related to trade policy (or to some other aspect of trade) correlate in the predicted way with changes in that country's relative wages. In many other countries, Stolper-Samuelson analyses have linked trade with wage changes. For example, Haskel and Slaughter (2001) relate changes in UK tariffs with rising UK wage inequality. Hanson and Harrison (1999) document that recent increases in Mexican wage inequality coincided with deeper cuts in Mexican tariffs in unskill-intensive industries.

Hanson and Harrison (1999) highlight that this cross-industry pattern of trade liberalization is the opposite of what one would expect if trade protection in a country simply concentrated in its industries that employ relatively intensively its relatively scarce factors *and* if Mexico is poorly endowed with more-skilled labor (i.e. not less-skilled labor) relative to the rest of the world. But while Mexico may be scarce in more-skilled labor relative to the United States, it may be abundant in this factor relative to many lower-income countries in the world such as China. Mexico's case demonstrates the general point that the expected Stolper-Samuelson cleavages from trade liberalization are likely to be linked with countries' relative endowments of factors of production. Our comparative empirical work in the fourth section returns to this important issue.

### *The theory of the impact of immigration on wages*

To make the connection between individual factor income and immigration policy, we briefly summarize three models: the HO trade model; the factor-proportions-analysis model; and the area-analysis model.[7] For simplicity we assume just two factors of production: more-skilled and less-skilled labor.

The HO trade model usually assumes interregional factor mobility (as well as intersectoral factor mobility discussed earlier), which means that there are no geographically segmented "local" labor markets. Immigration's wage effects depend on the size of the immigration shock and on whether the country is big enough to have any influence on world product prices.

In the HO framework, immigrant inflows sometimes have *no* wage effects at all. Instead, immigrants are completely absorbed via output-mix changes. With the change in factor supplies available to hire, firms have an incentive to produce more output of those products that employ relatively intensively the now more-abundant factors (per the Rybczynski theorem of 1955). Thanks to trade, these output changes can be absorbed onto world markets, and if the country is too small for this absorption to affect world prices, then its wages do not change either. The long-run nature of the HO model is crucial here, as output-mix changes take time.

In the HO framework, however, immigrant inflows sometimes do change wages. For example, if the country is sufficiently big then its output changes do alter world prices and thus wages (via the Stolper-Samuelson process). Or if the immigration shock is sufficiently big, then firms have an incentive to start up entirely new industries, which means that absorption entails changes in both outputs and wages. In either case, if the immigrant pool is predominantly made up of less-skilled workers, then less-skilled wages fall relative to more-skilled wages.

Like the HO model, the factor-proportions-analysis model also assumes a national labor market. Unlike the HO model, however, this model assumes a single aggregate output sector. This means there can be no output-mix changes to absorb immigrants. Instead, immigrants price themselves into employment via lower wages. Any immigration inflow of, let's assume, less-skilled workers, affects national wages as one might expect without output-mix changes: less-skilled immigrants accept lower less-skilled wages to induce firms to hire them. The bigger the immigrant inflow, the bigger the wage changes.

Like the previous model, the area-analysis model also assumes a single output sector. But this model assumes distinct, geographically segmented labor markets within a country. For countries like the United States with lots of internal migration, this assumption is probably inappropriate in the very long run. But it may be realistic over shorter time horizons thanks to frictions such as information and transportation costs that people must incur to move. The more important frictions like these are, the more sensible it is to treat Portland, Maine, and Portland, Oregon as two distinct labor markets. Given this, economists often analyze "local" labor markets within the United States, usually defined by states, cities or metropolitan areas (e.g. the Twin Cities of Minneapolis and St. Paul plus surrounding suburbs). Each local market has its own equilibrium wages determined by local supply and local demand.

### *Empirical studies of the impact of immigration on wages*

There is also a very large literature examining the impact of immigration on native wages in US regions. The standard area-analysis approach is to regress the change in native wages on the change in the stock of immigrants across US metropolitan areas. Most area-analysis studies find that immigration has, at most, a small negative impact on local native wages. Borjas *et al.* (1996, 1997) argue that immigration's wage effects should appear nationally rather than in local labor markets. They accordingly work from the factor-proportions perspective, and conclude that greater immigrant inflows have helped pressure the wages of high-school dropouts. Hanson and Slaughter (2002) find evidence that output-mix effects matter for absorbing US immigration flows.[8] Links from immigration to native wages at the national level have also been found outside the United States, for example, Friedberg's (2001) study of the recent immigration surge from Russia into Israel.

### *The theory of the impact of FDI on the variability of earnings and employment*

Globalization can help shape labor-market outcomes other than just the level of real and relative wages. Another important issue may be the volatility of wages and employment. The extent of labor-market volatility depends in part on the aggregate shocks influencing firms and their hiring decisions. Greater exposure to the international economy may theoretically increase or decrease these shocks. Labor-market volatility does not, however, depend just on the magnitude of these shocks. For some given level of aggregate shocks, it also depends on the elasticity of labor demand – that is, on how responsive firm's hiring decisions are to changes in wages. Standard models in international trade predict that greater FDI by multinationals can make labor demands more elastic through both the scale and substitution effects.[9] This, in turn, should boost worker insecurity via greater labor-market volatility just described. To see how this works, first consider the idea that greater FDI raises labor-demand elasticities.

Many models predict that FDI and its related international trade make product markets more competitive. Through the scale effect, this should make labor demands more elastic. For example, liberalization of FDI policies can force domestic firms to face heightened foreign competition. Or developments abroad (e.g. capital accumulation via FDI) can be communicated to domestic producers as more-intense foreign competition. In these cases more competitive product markets mean that a given increase in wages, and thus costs, translates into larger declines in output and thus demand for all factors. Different models predict different magnitudes of FDI and/or trade's impact on product-market demand.

The second way through which FDI can increase labor-demand elasticities is through the substitution effect. Suppose that a firm is vertically integrated with a number of production stages. Stages can move abroad either within firms, as multinationals establish foreign affiliates (e.g. Helpman 1984), or at arm's length, by importing the output of those stages from other firms (e.g. Feenstra and Hanson 1997). Globalization of production thus gives firms access to foreign factors of production as well as domestic ones, either directly through foreign affiliates or indirectly through intermediate inputs. This expands the set of factors that firms can substitute toward in response to higher domestic wages beyond just domestic non-labor factors to include foreign factors as well. Thus, greater FDI raises labor-demand elasticities.

How do higher labor-demand elasticities translate into greater labor-market volatility? Visualize equilibrium in a standard competitive labor market drawn as wages against employment. We introduce volatility into the labor market by assuming that the position of the demand schedule is stochastic (in accord with a wide range of empirical evidence). This position depends crucially on product prices and production technologies facing the relevant firms. Movements in prices and technologies trigger movements in labor demand and thus in equilibrium wages and/or employment.

For workers, the critical issue is that volatility in labor-market outcomes depends not just on the volatility of labor-demand shifters such as product prices and production technology. It also depends on the magnitudes of the elasticities of labor supply and demand. If elasticities are assumed to be fixed, then greater labor-market volatility arises if and only if there is greater aggregate volatility in prices or technology. But this is not the only way to generate greater labor-market volatility. It can also be generated from increasing the elasticity of demand for labor, holding fixed the amount of aggregate risk. Higher labor-demand elasticities trigger more volatile labor-market responses to price or technology shocks to labor demand.[10]

### *Empirical studies of the impact of FDI on the variability of earnings and employment*

In the literature on globalization and labor markets, there are several recent studies indicating that MNEs and FDI influence labor-demand elasticities in the ways just suggested. Using industry-level data for US manufacturing, Slaughter (2001) estimates that demand for production labor became more elastic from 1960 to the early 1990s, and that these increases were correlated with FDI outflows by US-headquartered multinationals. Using industry-level data for all UK manufacturing from 1958 to 1986, Fabbri *et al.* (2003) estimate increases in labor-demand elasticities for both production and non-production labor.

One important margin on which multinationals may affect elasticities is on the extensive margin of plant shutdowns. In response to wage increases, multinationals may be more likely than domestic firms to respond by closing entire plants. Evidence that multinational plants are more likely to close than are domestically-owned plants has now been documented for the manufacturing sectors in at least three countries. For the United Kingdom, Fabbri *et al.* (2003) estimate that multinational plants – again, both UK- and foreign-owned – are more likely to shut down than domestic plants are (conditional on a set of operational advantages enjoyed by multinationals that make them less likely to shut down, like being older and larger). Gorg and Strobl (2003) find that foreign-owned plants in Irish manufacturing are more likely to exit. For the United States, Bernard and Jensen (2002) report higher death probabilities for plants owned by firms that hold at least 10 percent of their assets outside the United States.

Does this connection between FDI and elasticities seem to relate to worker insecurity? Scheve and Slaughter (2004) provide one piece of evidence that it does. Their analysis of panel data covering individuals in Great Britain over 1991–1999 finds that individual perceptions of economic insecurity are positively correlated with FDI activity in the industries in which individuals work.

More generally, we note that there is now a large body of evidence that labor-market volatility has been rising in many countries, especially in the 1990s, in terms of greater earnings volatility, declining job tenure and self-reports. Gottschalk and Moffitt (1994) report substantial increases in year-to-year earnings volatility for the United States over the 1970s and 1980s. Looking at the 1990s as well, a symposium issue of the *Journal of Labor Economics* (1999) documented declines in US job stability, especially in the 1990s, for large groups of workers such as those with more tenure. Within that symposium issue, Schmidt's (1999) analysis of individual surveys finds that US workers in the 1990s were more pessimistic about losing their jobs than they were during the 1980s. A wide range of surveys have found evidence of rising US job insecurity over the 1990s relative to earlier decades, despite the ongoing economic expansion (e.g. Bronfenbrenner 2000).

This micro-evidence on FDI, elasticities and worker insecurity reinforces the point that labor-market volatility does not arise from just aggregate volatility in prices and/or technology. There is ongoing empirical disagreement about whether globalization has played a role in raising aggregate volatility.[11]

## Explaining policy preferences about international economic integration

The second section outlined some broad patterns of public opinion around the world about trade, immigration and FDI, emphasizing the importance of labor-market concerns in public attitudes about international economic integration. The third section suggested that there are important theoretical reasons why integration may have substantial consequences for labor-market performance but that these effects should vary across countries according to factor endowments. Further, there is some empirical evidence consistent with these theoretical predictions – though the evidence varies in strength depending on precisely what link between integration and labor-market performance is in question. In this section, we evaluate empirically the determinants of differences in public opinion about integration across individuals and across countries with particular emphasis on how the connections between international economic integration and labor-market performance help to account for this variation.

### *Theoretical determinants of policy preferences*

Why are some individuals more supportive of free trade than others? Why do some citizens prefer restrictionist immigration policies while others are less concerned with, if not welcoming of, new citizens? It is useful to place answers to these questions along a number of different dimensions.

First, some explanations emphasize the impact of policy alternatives on aggregate national welfare while others focus attention on the importance of how policy is expected to affect the individual economic welfare of citizens. In the case of trade, there is a virtual consensus among academic economists that free trade is good for national economic welfare and so if this was the only consideration, we would expect to observe nearly unanimous support in the public for liberalization.[12] As discussed in the previous section, however, it is widely recognized that while free trade may have aggregate benefits, its distributional consequences generate both winners and losers. This suggests that policy opinions should be expected to be divided along these lines. National and individual welfare considerations are not mutually exclusive and it is likely that both play a role in opinion formation. With that said, the data presented in the second section suggest substantial divisions in policy opinions that may be difficult to account for from a purely national economic welfare framework.

Second, explanations focus more or less attention on economic versus non-economic considerations that inform individual policy opinions. Economic concerns include the effects of integration on real and relative wages, the level of unemployment and the volatility of wages and employment. Further economic considerations include the possible impact of integration on the values of the assets that individuals own as well as national levels of income and growth as discussed earlier. Non-economic concerns include the possible role individual values and identities might play in informing policy opinions. Again, economic and non-economic concerns are not mutually exclusive sets of considerations, and there is substantial empirical evidence that both types of factors are important in opinion formation. We will focus attention in this section on political economy approaches that emphasize economic factors but will briefly summarize the evidence in the literature on non-economic considerations.

A simple political economy model of preference formation focuses attention on how different policy alternatives affect the earnings of individuals in the labor market. As discussed in the previous section, there are a number of different aspects of labor-market outcomes that may be affected by international economic integration. For simplicity, we focus on the real and relative income effects described above and limit our discussion to trade and immigration policy.[13]

### *Trade policy preferences*

For trade policy, recall from the previous section that standard trade theory predicts that trade's effect on people's current income depends crucially on the degree of intersectoral factor mobility, that is, on the degree of factor specificity. Moreover, it is likely that factor mobility varies across countries and across time and thus divisions in the impact of trade liberalization on factor income may vary as well with factor type and industry of employment being better predictors of how liberalization affects worker wages in some countries and at certain times than others.

To demonstrate how different links between policy alternatives and wages might account for differences among individuals in policy opinions, it is useful to start with opinion formation in a particular country – the United States. In the HO model with mobile factors, it is usually assumed that protection is received by the sectors that employ relatively intensively the factors with which the country is poorly endowed relative to the rest of the world, because in opening to trade, these factors suffer income declines. In contrast, the factors with which the country is well endowed relative to the rest of the world enjoy income gains in opening to trade. Thus a country's abundant factors support freer trade while its scarce factors oppose it.

Many studies (e.g. Leamer 1984) have documented that the United States is well endowed with more-skilled labor relative to the rest of the world. And the recent US pattern of protection accords with the model's predictions: US tariffs throughout the 1970s and 1980s were higher in less-skill-intensive industries (Haskel and Slaughter 2003). *According to the HO model, US more-skilled workers should support freer trade while less-skilled workers should oppose it.*

At the opposite extreme from the HO model, the RV model assumes that some or even all factors cannot move across sectors, thanks to mobility barriers such as industry-specific human capital gained through on-the-job experience. These immobile, that is, specific, factors need not earn the same return in all sectors. Instead, income for specific factors is linked to their sector of employment as trade-liberalization-induced changes in relative product prices redistribute income across sectors rather than factors. Sectors whose product prices fall – presumably comparative-disadvantage sectors – realize income losses for their specific factors while sectors whose product prices rise – presumably comparative-advantage sectors – realize income gains for their specific factors. In the RV model trade-policy preferences are determined by sector of employment. *Workers employed in sectors with product prices elevated by trade protection (likely comparative-disadvantage sectors) should oppose trade liberalization while workers employed in sectors with prices lowered by protection should support it.*[14]

## *Immigration policy preferences*

To make the connection between individual factor income and immigration-policy preferences, we use the three models discussed earlier – the HO trade model, the factor-proportions-analysis model, and the area-analysis model – and again focus our attention initially on the US case. For all three models, we assume US citizens know that current immigrant inflows increase the relative supply of less-skilled workers. This assumption clearly reflects the facts about US immigration in recent decades (e.g. Borjas *et al.* 1997). It implies that preferences depend on how an immigration-induced shift in US relative labor supply toward less-skilled workers affects factor incomes. For simplicity we assume just two factors of production, more-skilled and less-skilled labor.

The HO model has different predictions about the link between skills and immigration-policy preferences. *If individuals think that immigration does not alter wages, then there should be no link from skills to preferences.* In this case people evaluate immigration based on other considerations. *If individuals think that immigration affects wages, then less-skilled (more-skilled) workers nationwide should prefer policies that lower (raise) immigration inflows.*

In the factor-proportions-analysis model, recall that immigration inflow affects national wages as one might expect without output-mix changes. This model makes a single prediction about the link from skills to immigration-policy preferences. *Less-skilled (more-skilled) workers nationwide should prefer policies to lower (raise) immigration inflows.* Note this prediction can also come from the HO model.

In the area-analysis model, each local market has its own equilibrium wages determined by local supply and local demand. In this framework, how do Americans think about the labor-market impacts of immigration? Well, it depends on where immigrants settle. If there is literally no mobility among local labor markets, then immigrants pressure wages only in the "gateway" communities where they arrive. And it is well documented that in reality, immigrants are indeed concentrated in these gateway communities. In 1990, 75 percent of all immigrants living in the United States were in one of six gateway states: California, Florida, Illinois, New Jersey, New York and Texas. Borjas *et al.* (1996) report that in 1992, 60 percent of all US legal immigrants came into California or New York alone; another 20 percent entered the other four gateway states.

What does this framework predict for immigration-policy preferences? *In the area-analysis model less-skilled (more-skilled) workers in gateway communities should prefer policies to lower (raise) immigration inflows. In non-gateway communities there should be no correlation between workers' skills and their preferences.* More generally, with some labor mobility similarly skilled workers everywhere should share the same preferences, but with a stronger skills-preferences link among gateway workers.

To summarize: trade-policy preferences may cleave along skills and industry of employment; immigration-policy preferences along skills and geography. And different cleavages may hold over different time horizons, as sectoral and/or geographic labor mobility increases over time.

***Policy preferences in the United States***

Empirical studies of the determinants of individual trade and immigration policy preferences rely on the analysis of survey data that contain direct measures of individual preferences over policy alternatives. In this section, we report some of the key results of our examination of the 1992, 1994 and 1996 National Election Studies (NES) surveys (Sapiro *et al.* 1998), each of which is an extensive survey of current political opinions based on an individual-level stratified random sample of the US population. These surveys also report a wealth of respondent information such as educational attainment, occupation and industry of employment. With this information, we built datasets with several plausible measures of "exposure" to freer trade and immigration across factor types, industries and many other demographic variables such as age, gender, ideology and race. Merging this information with the NES surveys yielded individual-level datasets identifying both stated policy preferences and potential trade/immigration exposure through several channels. We then evaluated how these preferences vary with individual characteristics that the theories reviewed in the previous section predict might matter.

Here is a restatement of the NES question about trade-policy preferences.[15]

> Some people have suggested placing new limits on foreign imports in order to protect American jobs. Others say that such limits would raise consumer prices and hurt American exports. Do you favor or oppose placing new limits on imports, or haven't you thought much about this?

By coding responses 1 for those individuals favoring protection and 0 for those opposing it, we constructed the variable *Trade Opinion*. This question requires respondents to reveal their general position on the proper direction for US trade policy. Note that the question does not ask what sector(s) would receive import restrictions. We assume that respondent opinions are informed by the idea that import limits will be placed on comparative-disadvantage sectors. This seems more sensible than alternatives such as limits on comparative-advantage sectors, and it allows us to construct measures of factor and industry trade exposure that follow closely from the theory. In 1992 about 67 percent of respondents favored trade restrictions while 33 percent were opposed. In 1996, among those giving an opinion, preferences were more evenly divided, with 53 percent supporting restrictions and 47 percent opposed. These marginal rates of opinion are consistent with other survey results.[16]

Here is the NES question about immigration-policy preferences:

> Do you think the number of immigrants from foreign countries who are permitted to come to the United States to live should be increased

a little, increased a lot, decreased a little, decreased a lot, or left the same as it is now?

This question requires respondents to reveal their general position on the proper direction for US immigration policy. Note that the question does not ask what skill-mix immigrants would have relative to natives. We assume that respondent opinions are informed by the belief that immigrant inflows would increase the relative supply of less-skilled workers. As discussed in the previous section, this assumption clearly reflects the facts about US immigration in recent decades.[17] We construct the variable *Immigration Opinion* by coding responses 5 for those individuals responding "decreased a lot" down to 1 for those responding "increased a lot." Thus, higher levels of *Immigration Opinion* indicate preferences for more-restrictive policy. The "average" value for *Immigration Opinion* over the three surveys (1992, 1994, 1996) was about 3.8, between the responses "left the same as it is now" and "decreased a little."

We then merged these survey questions with measures of trade and immigration exposure, consistent with the hypotheses outlined in the previous section (see Scheve and Slaughter 2001a, b, c for details about variable construction). To test whether skill levels are a key determinant of policy preferences, for each individual-year observation we constructed two variables measuring skills. One was *Education Years*, recorded in the NES survey as years of education completed. The other was *Occupation Wage*, which was that year's average weekly wage nationwide for the three-digit Census Occupation Code occupation reported for the individual. Educational attainment is a common skills measure; *Occupation Wage* assumes that average national earnings for a given occupation are determined primarily by the skills required for that occupation. According to the HO model, US less-skilled workers are more likely to benefit from trade restrictions and thus are more likely to support new trade barriers.

To test whether sector of employment matters for trade-policy preferences, for each person we constructed two measures of industry trade exposure based on the reported industry of employment coded according to the three-digit 1980 Census Industry Code classification. The first, *Sector Net Export Share*, is the industry's 1992 net exports as a share of output. This variable follows the common assumption that an industry's comparative advantage is reflected in its net exports: industries with positive (negative) net exports are assumed to be comparative-advantage (disadvantage) industries. This variable covers manufacturing, agriculture and tradable services; for all non-tradable services sectors we set this variable equal to zero. The second measure is the industry's 1992 US tariff rate, *Sector Tariff*, constructed as tariff duties collected as a share of customs-value imports. We assume that industries with higher *Sector Tariff* have more of a comparative disadvantage. The tariff data cover all tradable industries in agriculture and manufacturing; for all other sectors we set this variable to zero. For both measures, according to the RV model, workers in industries with greater revealed comparative disadvantages are more likely to support trade protection for these industries.

For both trade policy and immigration policy, our empirical work aims to test how different types of trade and immigration exposure variously defined affect the probability that an individual supports restrictions. Although this analysis is based on the estimation of various logit and ordered probit regression models (see Scheve and Slaughter 2001a, b for details), the main results are summarized intuitively in Table 2.1 for trade and Table 2.2 for immigration.

The results of our analysis of trade policy opinions strongly support the hypothesis that individuals' skill levels determine trade-policy preferences. Little evidence is found consistent with the hypothesis that industry of employment influences policy preferences. Models 1–4 each include in the original logit model one measure of exposure to trade liberalization based on factor type – the skill level of the respondent – and one measure of exposure based on the respondent's industry of employment. Each column in Table 2.1 reports results of a different model. Within each column each row reports the estimated effect on the probability of supporting trade restrictions of increasing that row's variable from one standard deviation below its sample mean to one standard deviation above, holding fixed all other variables at their means. For example, the 1992 results from Model 1 indicate that increasing *Occupational Wage* from one standard deviation below its mean ($345 per week) to one standard deviation above its mean ($719 per week) reduces the probability of supporting trade restrictions by 0.139 on average. This change has a standard error of 0.023 and a 90 percent confidence interval of [−0.178, −0.101].

Across all models in Table 2.1, higher skills are strongly correlated with lower probabilities of supporting trade restrictions. The mean estimates of probability changes are substantively significant and much larger (in absolute value) than those for the industry measures. They are also precisely estimated: all have 90 percent confidence intervals strictly less than zero. Similar analyses of the 1996 NES data differ only in that the magnitudes of the effects are even larger.

In contrast, higher industry trade exposure has much more ambiguous effects. In unreported bivariate regressions, greater industry trade exposure is correlated with support for trade restrictions in 1992 but these estimated effects are not statistically significant. Adding the skill measures *Occupational Wage* and *Education Years* as reported in Table 4.1 for Models 1–4 produces qualitatively similar results (for the *Education Years* models, the signs are even wrong). The 1996 results are similar though the *Sector Tariff* measure in Model 1 is marginally statistically significant in the hypothesized positive direction. But even in this case, the substantive impact is quite small: a two standard deviation increase in *Sector Tariff* results in just a 0.036 increase in the probability of supporting trade

*Table 2.1* Determinants of respondent opinion in the US on international trade restrictions: 1992 factor-income models

| *Change in probability of supporting trade restrictions as a result of a two standard deviation increase in the independent variable for each model* | | | | |
|---|---|---|---|---|
| *Variables* | *Model 1* | *Model 2* | *Model 3* | *Model 4* |
| Occupation wage | −0.139<br>(0.023)<br>[−0.178, −0.101] | −0.140<br>(0.022)<br>[−0.175, −0.101] | | |
| Education years | | | −0.251<br>(0.025)<br>[−0.293, −0.211] | −0.251<br>(0.026)<br>[−0.293, −0.208] |
| Sector tariff | 0.014<br>(0.017)<br>[−0.013, 0.042] | | −0.001<br>(0.004)<br>[−0.006, 0.006] | |
| Sector net export share | | −0.016<br>(0.014)<br>[−0.039, 0.007] | | 0.000<br>(0.003)<br>[−0.005, 0.005] |

Note

For Models 1 through 4, we estimated using multiple imputation with a logit specification the effect of factor and industry exposure to international trade on individuals' trade policy opinions. The parameter estimates from this analysis are reported in Scheve and Slaughter (2001a). Here we interpret those results by presenting the impact of a two standard deviation increase in each independent variable, holding other variables constant, on the probability that the respondent supports trade restrictions. Specifically, each triple of entries in the table begins with the mean effect from 1,000 simulations of the change in probability of supporting trade restrictions due to an increase from one standard deviation below the independent variable's mean to one standard deviation above, holding all other variables constant at their means. The standard error of this estimate is reported in parentheses. Finally, a 90 percent confidence interval for the probability change is presented in brackets.

*Table 2.2* Estimated effect of increasing skill levels on the probability of supporting immigration restrictions in the US: 1992

| *Change in probability of supporting immigration restrictions as a result of a two standard deviation increase in the independent variable for each model* | | |
|---|---|---|
| *Variables* | *Model 5* | *Model 6* |
| Occupation wage | −0.049<br>(0.021)<br>[−0.083, −0.013] | |
| Education years | | −0.102<br>(0.020)<br>[−0.133, −0.069] |

Note

For Models 5 through 6, we estimated using multiple imputation with an ordered probit specification the effect of different measures of skill level on individuals' immigration policy opinions. The parameter estimates from this analysis are reported in Scheve and Slaughter (2001b). Here we interpret those results by presenting the impact of a two standard deviation increase in each independent variable, holding other variables constant, on the probability that the respondent supports trade restrictions. Specifically, we simulated the consequences of changing each skill measure from one standard deviation below its mean to one standard deviation above on the probability of supporting immigration restrictions. The mean effect is reported first, with the standard error of this estimate in parentheses followed by a 90 percent confidence interval.

restrictions. Overall, one cannot conclude with a high degree of confidence that individuals employed in relatively trade-exposed sectors are more likely to support trade restrictions, conditional on skill levels.

*The key message of the analyses presented in Table 2.1 is that in the United States an individual's skill level rather than industry of employment is strongly correlated with the probability of supporting trade restrictions.* The effects of skill trade exposure are large and precise; the effects of industry trade exposure are small and uncertain. These results suggest that individuals care about trade policy in a manner consistent with the HO model, and that there is relatively high intersectoral labor mobility in the United States over the time horizons relevant to individuals when evaluating trade policy. It is important to recall that our analysis in no way precludes individuals evaluating both short-run and long-run effects of trade liberalization, where preferences might vary by both factor type and industry of employment.

Table 2.2 reports the summary results for our analysis of this division in public opinion over immigration. The findings strongly support the hypothesis that individuals' skill levels determine immigration-policy preferences. Models 5–6 each include in the original ordered probit model a measure of skill type and a set of control variables including age, race, sex, immigrant status, and ideology. Each column in Table 2.2 reports results of a different model. Within each column each row reports the estimated effect on the probability of supporting immigration restrictions (i.e. the probability of supporting a reduction in immigration by either "a lot" or "a little") of increasing that row's variable from one standard deviation below its sample mean to one standard deviation above, holding fixed all other variables at their means. For 1992, increasing *Occupation Wage* from one standard deviation below its sample mean to one standard deviation above ($325 per week to $699 per week), holding fixed all other regressors at their means, reduces the probability of supporting immigration restrictions by 0.049 on average. This estimated change has a standard error of 0.021 and a 90 percent confidence interval of [−0.083, −0.013]. The 1992 results for *Education Years* are similar. Increasing *Education Years* by two standard deviations (about 10.1 years to 15.7 years), holding fixed all other regressors at their means, reduces the probability of supporting immigration restrictions by 0.102 on average. This estimated change has a standard error of 0.020 and a 90 percent confidence interval of [−0.133, −0.069]. The magnitude of these estimated effects are even larger in unreported results for 1994 and 1996. *Higher skills are strongly and significantly correlated with lower probabilities of supporting immigration restrictions.*

The result that skills correlate with immigration-policy preferences is consistent both with the factor-proportions-analysis model and with an HO model in which immigration affects both wages and output mix. By pooling all regions together, however, we have not tested the area-analysis model. To do this we add to our initial specification an indicator variable for whether the respondent lives in a high-immigration region (see Scheve and Slaughter 2001b for various definitions of what counts as a high-immigration region) and this variable's interaction with the skill measure in each regression. If preferences are consistent with the area-analysis model, then the correlation between skills and preferences should be stronger in gateway communities. These preferences imply a positive coefficient on the high immigration indicator variable and a negative coefficient on its interaction with skills. Our estimates of this model indicate across all years of our data that neither is the high immigration indicator variable significantly positive nor is its interaction with skills significantly negative. *Overall, people in high-immigration areas do not have a stronger correlation between skills and immigration-policy preferences than people elsewhere. This is inconsistent with the area-analysis model.*

To summarize, preferences over trade and immigration policy divide strongly across skills. There is not strong evidence of many other commonly supposed cleavages. For trade, industry of employment is not systematically related to trade-policy preferences. Those working in "trade exposed" industries (e.g. textiles and apparel) are not more likely to oppose freer trade, conditional on skill type. For immigration, people living in "immigration gateway" communities (e.g. California) are not more or less likely to oppose freer immigration. These results are all consistent with the importance of labor-market outcomes in determining policy preferences.[18]

### *Policy preferences in comparative perspective*

These findings can be put into comparative perspective by examining a growing body of research on the determinants of international economic policy preferences around the world (Balistreri 1997; Gabel 1998; Scheve 2000; O'Rourke and Sinnott 2001; Mayda 2002; Beaulieu 2002; Beaulieu *et al.* 2002; Baker 2003, 2005; Mayda and Rodrik 2005; Hays *et al.* forthcoming; Hainmueller and Hiscox forthcoming). For our purposes, the key question of interest that is addressed in many of these studies is the extent to which divisions in public opinion about policy along factor lines – specifically differences in individual skill levels – are replicated in other countries. In the interest of brevity, we limit our comparative discussion to trade policy preferences.

As discussed in the third section, it is, however, important to be clear that our theoretical expectation under the HO model is that the direction and magnitude of the skills cleavage vary across countries according to national skill or human capital endowments.

The most straightforward way to evaluate these predictions is to reproduce a figure presented in O'Rourke and Sinnott (2001) and Mayda and Rodrik (2005). Figure 2.1 plots the marginal effect of skill type on trade opinions in a cross-section of countries around the world against national skill endowments as measured by the natural log of per capita GDP.[19]

To construct this figure, we used data from the 1995–1997 World Values Survey (WVS) (Inglehart 2000), a set of surveys designed for cross-national comparisons. The first step in the analysis was to construct the dependent variable similar to the trade opinion measure employed in the US analysis described earlier. As noted in the second section, the World Values Survey includes the following question that measures trade-policy preferences:

> Do you think it is better if (1) goods made in other countries can be imported and sold here if people want to buy them or that (2) there should be stricter limits on selling foreign goods here, to protect the jobs of people in this country?

By coding responses 1 for those individuals favoring stricter limits and 0 for those who gave the response supportive of trade, we constructed the variable *Trade Opinion*. We then constructed a measure of the skill type of each individual in the surveys. The variable *Occupational Skill* is an 11–point skill measure based on the occupation of each respondent.[20]

Then for each country in our dataset, we regressed the trade measure on the variable *Occupational Skill*.[21] The regression coefficient on the skill measure is an estimate of the marginal effect of skill type on trade-policy opinion. The vertical axis in Figure 2.1 is the marginal effect of *Occupational Skill* on trade-policy opinions while the horizontal axis is the natural

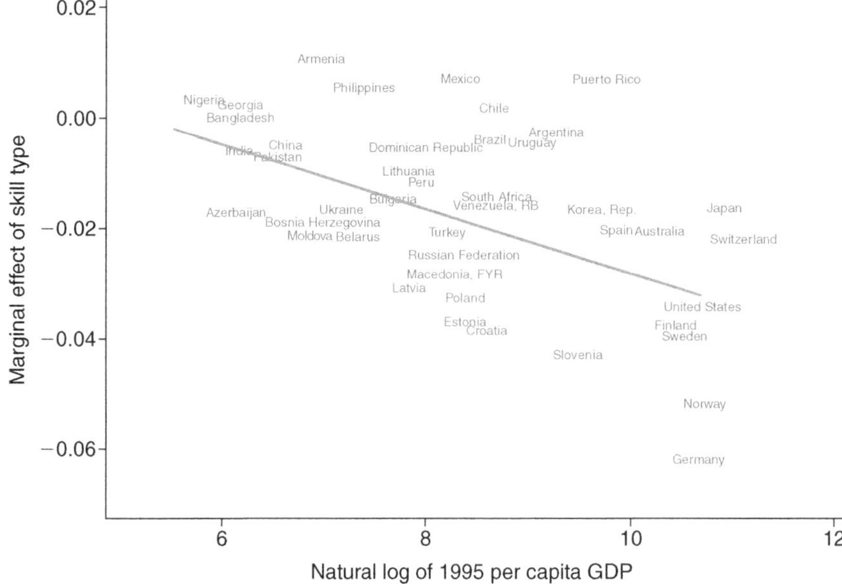


*Figure 2.1* Marginal effect of skill on trade preferences versus national endowment of human capital.

log of 1995 per capita gross domestic product. This variable is a commonly used measure of each country's relative human capital or skill endowment.[22]

The key result is that the direction and magnitude of the skill-policy preferences correlation varies across countries in a manner generally consistent with the predictions of the HO model. The downward-sloping regression line indicates that as per capita GDP increases, the absolute value of the negative correlation between individual skills and protectionist trade opinion also increases. Consequently, for all the countries in which GDP per capita is roughly equivalent to that in the United States, there is a negative and statistically significant correlation between skills and trade-policy opinions. In contrast, at lower levels of per capita GDP, the correlation is sometimes positive and sometimes negative and generally small in magnitude.

To evaluate further the relationship between the marginal effect of skill type on policy opinions and per capita GDP, we regressed the marginal effect measure on the natural log of per capita GDP. The estimated slope coefficient is equal to −0.0058 with a standard error of 0.0014, a statistically significant relationship.[23] Moreover, the natural log of per capita GDP explains nearly 30 percent of the variation in the marginal effect of skill type on trade-policy opinions.

For our purposes, the key point in Figure 2.1 is that the skills-policy preferences correlation of the United States is also evident in other similarly endowed countries. This is consistent with the claim that individual opinions about international economic policies are substantially influenced by how policy alternatives are expected to affect workers' earnings. At the same time, the evidence in these figures indicates that the magnitude of the skill cleavage in public opinion decreases in countries with lower levels of GDP per capita. This result is again roughly consistent with the prediction of the HO model in that policy liberalization is not expected to benefit skilled workers in countries that are not relatively well endowed with human capital.

The evidence presented in Figure 2.1 does raise important questions for how the distributive consequences of trade liberalization in the labor market may influence policy-opinion formation. For example, the HO model predicts that in those countries relatively well endowed with less-skilled workers, the skills-trade-policy-opinion correlation should be in the opposite direction of that observed for countries well endowed with skilled workers. In these countries, the expectation is that less-skilled workers will have more liberal policy preferences than more-skilled workers. In terms of Figure 2.1, the theoretical expectation is that in countries with relatively low levels of per capita GDP, the estimated marginal effect of skill type on policy opinions should be positive. In Figure 2.1 we do observe an estimated positive effect for some low-income countries, but these estimates are generally not significantly different from zero. While there are a number of possible explanations for this anomaly implicit in the literature (see, for example, Gabel 1998; Beaulieu *et al.* 2002; Hiscox 2003; Hainmuller and Hiscox forthcoming), it is not clear that any of these accounts are likely to be complete replacements for the HO framework, because they do not predict the cross-country variation by national skill endowments in Figure 2.1.

### *Policy context and individual opinion formation*

The previous two sections focused attention on the importance of the impact of policy liberalization on real and relative wages for explaining individual and country variation in trade and immigration policy opinions. In this section, we consider other factors that may influence the links that individuals make between policy alternatives and their individual economic welfare. We focus on the role of two different sets of national-level characteristics that may influence how individuals form opinions about trade policy and thus account for country differences in both the level of and divisions in public support for liberalization: macroeconomic conditions and labor-market policies and institutions.

To evaluate these potential explanations for variation in public opinion about trade, we turn our attention to the 1995 International Social Survey

Program (ISSP) dataset, which, like the WVS, is a comparative dataset that elicits individual opinions on trade and immigration policy. To evaluate various arguments about the possible effect of macroeconomic conditions and labor-market policies and institutions, we employ data that is primarily available for relatively wealthy countries – specifically, OECD members. We use the ISSP data in this analysis because it includes more OECD countries than does the WVS data.[24]

In the second section, we noted that public concern about globalization generally and trade liberalization in particular seems to be closely tied to labor-market concerns. Our analysis of the determinants of individual and cross-country variation has so far focused attention on the links among policy alternatives, wage effects and individual opinion formation. It is these links that are most salient in the academic political economy literature. Nonetheless, given that the public seems attentive to possible links between unemployment and trade liberalization, macroeconomic conditions may influence individuals' overall evaluation of the desirability of trade liberalization or trade protection. Specifically, high levels of unemployment may heighten individual concerns about the employment risks associated with liberal trade policies. This possibility is buttressed by a number of studies that suggest that variation in levels of protection over time and/or regions may be related to variation over time and across regions in macroeconomic conditions, particularly the level of unemployment (Takacs 1981; Cassing *et al.* 1986; Rama 1994; Epstein and O'Halloran 1996).[25]

To assess whether macroeconomic conditions are an important determinant of public opinion about trade, we constructed the variable *Trade Opinion* for the respondents in the ISSP survey.[26] This variable is again a dichotomous variable with individuals giving protectionist responses coded 1 and non-protectionist responses coded 0. We then calculated the average values for each country, *Average Trade Opinion*, to determine an estimate of the level of protectionist opinion. Figure 2.2 plots this variable against unemployment as a percent of the labor force, *Unemployment*, in each country. For the 23 countries in the ISSP sample, *Average Trade Opinion* is positively correlated with *Unemployment*.[27] The levels of protectionist opinion are higher in those countries with a greater proportion of their work force unemployed. A bivariate regression of *Average Trade Opinion* on *Unemployment* generates a slope estimate of 0.018 with a standard error of 0.005, thus the positive estimate is significantly different than zero at conventional levels of statistical significance.[28] *The key result is that cross-country variation in trade opinion seems in part a function of the aggregate performance of the labor market as measured by unemployment.* This is consistent both with arguments about the importance of macroeconomic conditions in accounting for trade policies and with the main claim of this chapter that public attitudes toward international economic integration are tightly connected to labor-market concerns.

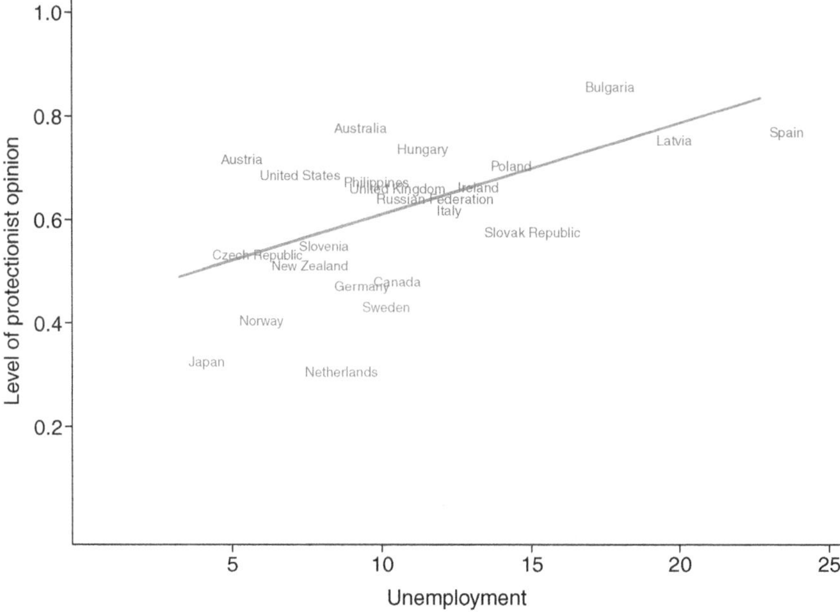


*Figure 2.2* Level of protectionist opinion versus unemployment.

In the second section, we pointed out that public opinion over trade policy is decidedly less protectionist when policy liberalization is explicitly linked to government adjustment policies for workers (see also Scheve and Slaughter 2001c: 94–6). This characteristic of public opinion resonates with a large literature that links the growth of government to integration with the world economy (Cameron 1978; Katzenstein 1985; Rodrik 1998; Boix forthcoming). In Rodrik's account, the general argument is that openness to the world economy generates greater risks to workers, which leads them to demand greater levels of public social insurance. Consequently, depending on the supply side of policymaking, including perhaps the impact of economic integration on the state's capacity to provide social insurance, more open economies may have larger public sectors, particularly policies that insure workers against labor-market risks, than less open economies.

An interesting implication of this argument for explaining cross-country variation in public opinion about international economic integration is that the level of public support for workers may have a substantial effect on how individuals view trade. If the risks that workers perceive from integration are largely insured risks or if the adjustment costs that workers perceive from integration are largely subsidized, then individuals are more likely to favor liberalization. Moreover, to the extent that social insurance policies redistribute some of the risks and rewards of integration with the world economy, more generous social insurance policies may mitigate the skill divisions in public opinion over policy liberalization (see Scheve 2000; Scheve and Slaughter 2001c; and Hays *et al.* forthcoming for previous empirical evidence on these arguments).[29]

Figure 2.3 provides evidence on the first question of whether generous labor-market policies reduce support for protectionism. Since we have already suggested that the evidence is consistent with the idea that increased levels of unemployment raise protectionist sentiments, we control for *Unemployment* in the data presented in Figure 2.3. The vertical axis is then composed of residuals from the regression of *Average Trade Opinion* on *Unemployment* and the horizontal axis shows the residuals from the regression of total national spending on labor-market programs (unemployment compensation, training, etc.) as percent of GDP, *Labor Spending*, on *Unemployment*. The source for the labor spending data is the OECD, and so the analysis in Figure 2.3 includes only 16 of the original 23 countries in the ISSP data.[30]

It is first worth noting that *Unemployment* remains significantly positively correlated with protectionist opinion with the introduction of the *Labor Spending* measure (with or without the natural log of per capita GDP and trade openness). The data in Figure 2.3 also offer some modest support for the hypothesis that more generous labor-market policies increase support for freer trade. The partial regression line is downward sloping

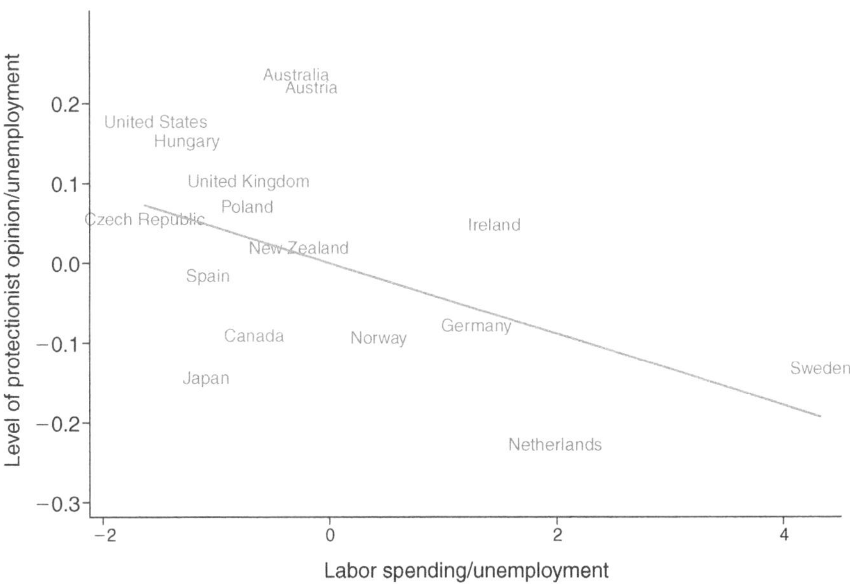


*Figure 2.3* Level of protectionist opinion versus labor spending.

and the estimated partial regression coefficient on *Labor Spending* is −0.044 with a standard error of 0.015. The observation for Sweden is obviously influential, but, excluding it, the partial regression coefficient is statistically significant at the 0.10 level. The result is also robust to including the natural log of per capita GDP and trade openness as additional control variables.

Given this modest but suggestive evidence for the hypothesis of a link between labor-market policies and protectionist sentiment, we examined a number of other observable implications of the general argument. First, we examined the relationship between the level of protectionist opinion in the WVS and a more-aggregated measure of social insurance spending available for a larger sample of countries (28). In this analysis, both the bivariate and partial correlation between spending and protectionist sentiment was negative and statistically significant. Second, returning to the ISSP data, we found a negative and statistically significant bivariate and partial correlation between the OECD's measures of employment protection and the level of protectionist opinion. Employment protection is a very different policy instrument for protecting the welfare of workers from the potential risks of economic openness, but it may have a similar effect of reducing workers' assessments of the risks associated with liberalization. In total, there is much evidence consistent with the claim that the labor-market policies of governments have a substantial influence on how individuals view the costs and benefits of trade liberalization.

Figure 2.4 provides evidence on our second hypothesized effect of generous labor-market policies: do they mitigate the differences between more- and less-skilled workers in their opinions about trade policy? Since we have already established that the skills-policy preferences correlation varies across countries according to their human capital endowments, the analysis in Figure 2.4 controls for the natural log of per capita GDP. The vertical axis in Figure 2.4 is equal to the residuals from the regression of the marginal effect of skill type on trade policy opinions on the natural log of per capita GDP. The horizontal axis comprises the residuals from the regression of *Labor Spending* on the natural log of per capita GDP. The positive relationship in this figure between *Labor Spending*, controlling for skill endowments, and the marginal effect of skill type, controlling for endowments, is consistent with the argument that social spending decreases the differences in opinion about trade policy among more- and less-skilled workers. The estimate of the partial regression coefficient for labor spending from the regression of the marginal effect of skill type on trade policy opinions on *Labor Spending* and the natural log of per capita GDP is 0.012 with a standard error of 0.004. This positive estimate is robust to dropping obvious outliers (e.g. United Kingdom or Sweden), and also to adding control variables such as *Unemployment*.[31]

One final national-level characteristic of labor markets that may influence individual opinion formation is the extent of centralized wage bar-

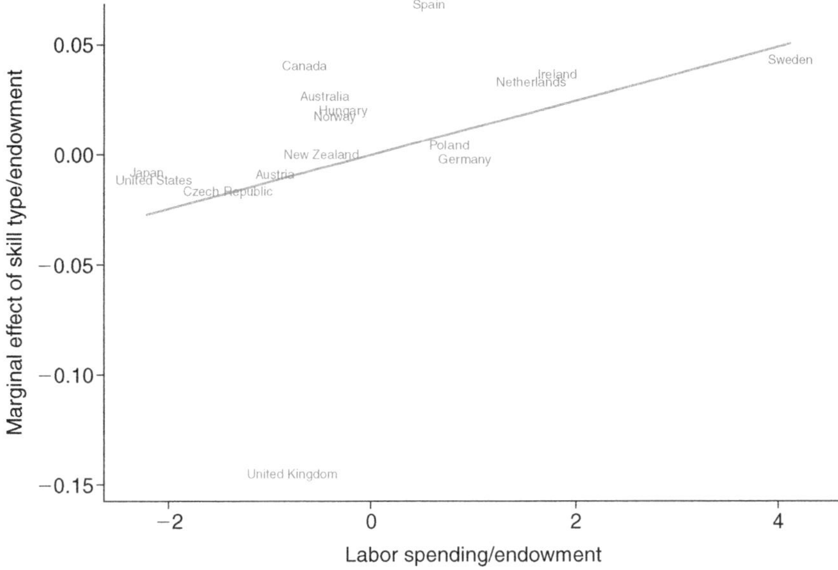


*Figure 2.4* Marginal effect of skill on trade preferences versus labor spending.

gaining and, more generally, corporatist institutions. Scheve (2000) investigates the argument that because centralized wage bargaining tends to reduce wage inequality (OECD 1997; Wallerstein 1999), the actual distributive consequences of international economic integration will be mitigated in countries with greater centralization, and so skill divisions in public opinion will be lessened as well. This argument resonates with original claims in the comparative political economy literature on the relationship between openness and the welfare state (Cameron 1978; Katzenstein 1985). Scheve (2000) presents evidence consistent with this argument for opinion formation over European regional economic integration using 148 surveys in the 1990s for 15 member states of the European Union. An increase in centralization from the United Kingdom's score to the value for Denmark is estimated to decrease the magnitude of skill-integration opinion regression coefficient by 40 percent.

Because comparable measures of wage bargaining centralization are available for a relatively small set of advanced countries, investigating this relationship in the ISSP and WVS data limits the number of observations to between nine and 12.[32] Not surprisingly, it is not clear in these data that the centralization of wage bargaining significantly attenuates skill divisions in trade-policy opinions. This question, as well as that of the possible influence of other dimensions of corporatism on opinion formation, remains an important question for future research.

One line of this future research might also examine cross-country differences in the endowment of skills, above and beyond measures based on national-level averages. It is well documented that less-skilled workers (e.g. at the 5th or 25th percentile) within each country can differ quite substantially across countries with similar mean levels of skills. The evidence suggests, for example, that the less-skilled are relatively more-skilled in Nordic countries compared to Anglo-American countries. More-complex measures of national skill endowments might yield additional insight on policy preferences: for example, perhaps less-skilled workers in Nordic countries are less protectionist than their American counterparts because they do not face direct international product-market competition from freer trade with low-wage countries.[33]

### *Additional determinants of policy preferences*

While labor-market concerns broadly defined are central to understanding opinion formation, there is also evidence in the literature that non-economic factors may also play important roles.[34]

For trade policy, both O'Rourke and Sinnott (2001) and Mayda and Rodrik (2005) employ evidence from the ISSP surveys to consider the possible roles of ideas and identities on the formation of individual policy opinions. O'Rourke and Sinnott focus their analysis on evaluating the impact that strong feelings of nationalist identity have on opinions about trade policy. They present evidence that protectionist attitudes are strongly related to nationalist feelings as measured by a group of survey questions identified as measuring patriotism – preference for one's own country – and a group of survey questions identified as measuring chauvinism – an exclusive sense of nationality. They also present strong evidence consistent with the HO model, even when a range of cultural, ideological and demographic factors are taken into account. Their interpretation is that both nationalist ideologies and economic concerns inform opinions.

As these authors point out, the interpretation of the correlation between nationalist attitudes and policy opinions is problematic. The determinants of nationalist feeling most likely include economic considerations, and so it would be incorrect to attribute all the estimated effect of the nationalism variables to non-economic considerations. We view this as a reasonable interpretation, but point out that it implies that empirical research posed in the "do economic or non-economic determinants matter more?" framework may be hopelessly misspecified without serious models of the determinants of nationalist ideologies and other non-economic factors.[35]

For immigration policy, the starting point of most analyses is non-economic considerations such as values, identities and perceptions of the impact of immigration on largely non-economic issues such as crime or risks of terrorism. Mayda (2002) reports results for the non-economic determinants of immigration that are representative of the key findings. Individuals with stronger attachments to their national identities, individuals less tolerant of other racial groups and individuals that value a homogenous culture have more restrictionist immigration opinions.

### *Summary and future research*

There is substantial evidence of important links between individual opinions about trade and immigration policy and the likely distributive consequences in the labor market of different policy alternatives. This research raises a number of questions that merit further investigation. First, we noted little evidence that sector of employment is a strong predictor of US opinions about trade. As has been emphasized in the endogenous trade policy literature (e.g. Alt and Gilligan 1994; Hiscox 2001), factor specificity may vary across individuals, occupations, sectors, time and countries. Future research that develops measures of intersectoral factor mobility may substantially improve our understanding of variation in opinion formation.[36]

Second, the importance of labor-market institutions for how individuals connect policy alternatives to their interests is not completely clear. For example, by better matching survey data with data on labor-market institutions, it would be possible to evaluate whether the centralization of wage bargaining and other corporatist institutions may mitigate divisions in opinion via redistribution of gains from international economic integration. Finally, only limited attention has been paid to the role of information and elites in influencing how individuals evaluate policy alternatives and their interests. Again, significant cross-country differences in the amount and direction of information regarding the impact of trade on welfare may be important in explaining cross-country variation in opinion.[37]

## Conclusion

This analysis of public preferences about the policies that regulate international economic integration is essential for constructing explanatory models of policymaking in these issue areas. Political economy models must specify the preferences of all relevant actors as well as the institutions that aggregate these preferences (Rodrik 1995). Characterizing the public's views is an essential element of the task. Only once this specification is made is it possible to identify the importance of many other factors – costs of collective action, properties of electoral systems – that are widely thought to be important determinants of policymaking.

This chapter highlights the importance of labor-market concerns in accounting for individual policy opinions. We contend that this pattern of opinion is informative for debates about the supposed opposition between economic globalization and the modern welfare state. It has long been recognized that protectionism and other restrictionist international economic policies are inefficient instruments for redistributing income and risk. Given that the distributional consequences in the labor market of policy alternatives seem so important in individuals' policy opinions, there is at least the possibility that greater economic openness generates greater demand for social insurance and redistributive spending. If non-economic considerations dominate opinion formation, then the possibility of side payments to facilitate liberalization is greatly reduced. Our review suggests that the scope for such payments may be quite substantial.

Moreover, there is explicit evidence that political support for international economic liberalization depends on many key features of the modern welfare state. Individual opinions are decidedly more liberal when liberalization is tied to support for workers. Further, countries with more generous labor-market policies have publics with less protectionist opinions and less salient differences in opinion across more- and less-skilled workers. This again suggests that more economic openness generates more demand for social insurance and redistributive spending.

While definitive conclusions, of course, require analyses of opinion formation about welfare state policies and their interaction with the international economic policies discussed here, the evidence presented in this chapter certainly suggests that simple conclusions that substantial social insurance and redistributive policies are inconsistent with economic globalization are implausible because it seems that political support for liberalism itself depends in part on those very policies.

## Notes

* This chapter originally appeared in Bardhan, P., Bowles, S. and Wallerstein, M. (eds) (2006) *Globalization and Egalitarian Redistribution.* For financial support, we thank the National Science Foundation and the Carnegie Corporation's Globalization and Self-Determination Project at the Yale Center for International and Area Studies.

1 Our US studies appear in Scheve and Slaughter (2001a, b, c). Other studies include Balistreri (1997); Gabel (1998); Scheve (2000); O'Rourke and Sinnott (2001); Beaulieu (2002); Beaulieu *et al.* (2002); Mayda (2002); Baker (2003, 2005); Hiscox (2003); Mayda and Rodrik (2005); Hainmueller and Hiscox (forthcoming) and Hays *et al.* (forthcoming).

2 The other splits were 52 to 30 percent in the United States, 51 to 30 percent in the United Kingdom, 51 to 31 percent in Italy, 43 to 37 percent in Germany, and 45 to 44 percent in France.

3 The literature on how globalization affects labor markets is far too vast to cover systematically in this section. More thoroughly comprehensive overviews can be found in Johnson and Slaughter (2001) for trade; Hanson *et al.* (2002) for immigration; and Scheve and Slaughter (2004) for FDI. The discussion in this section draws heavily on these earlier works, as well as on the work in Scheve and Slaughter (2001a, b, c).

4 Many studies have examined how an RV short-run equilibrium transforms over time into an HO long-run equilibrium. See, for example, Mussa (1978) and Neary (1978).

5 Obviously, the exact timing and magnitude of wage changes vary somewhat with the data series used. But all series show the same major changes. For more discussion, see, for example, the 1997 and 2000 *Economic Report of the President*, each of which devotes substantial space to labor markets and inequality. Inequality has risen across education, experience, and occupational groups as well as within these groups. These trends also hold even when accounting for the relatively robust wage gains of the late 1990s.

6 Leamer (1998) and Baldwin and Cain (1997) find that US relative product prices fell, not rose, for less-skill-intensive sectors during the 1970s. And these two studies plus Lawrence and Slaughter (1993) and Bhagwati (1991) find no clear trend in US relative product prices during the 1980s. Feenstra and Hanson (1999) decompose US price changes into input-trade-related components and find a non-trivial role for trade in raising inequality. Haskel and Slaughter (2003) apply a similar methodology but decompose US price changes into tariff- and transport cost-related components; they find no strong link from trade-barrier-related price changes to US wages. See Slaughter (2000) for a survey of these product-price studies. And despite the ambiguous product-price evidence, Leamer (1998) argues greater international trade has played a role. Borjas *et al.* (1997) calculates trade's role in rising inequality by calculating changes in US labor supplies "embodied" in flows of US exports and imports. This is a very different methodology from the product-price studies, but they also find only a small role for trade. Surveys of methods and results also appear in Freeman (1995), Richardson (1995) and Johnson and Slaughter (2001).

7 The terms "area analysis" and "factor-proportions analysis" come from Borjas *et al.* (1996).

8 Recent immigration papers include Card (2001) from the area-analysis perspective and Borjas *et al.* (1996, 1997) from the factor-proportions perspective. For surveys see Borjas (1999a, b) and Hanson *et al.* (2002).

9 This elasticity consists of two parts. One is the substitution effect. It tells, for a given level of output, how much the firm substitutes away from labor toward other factors of production when wages rise. The second is the scale effect. It tells how much labor demand is altered after a wage change thanks to the change in the firm's output. Higher wages imply higher costs and thus, moving along the product-market demand schedule, lower firm output. When wages rise, both the substitution and scale effects reduce the quantity of labor demanded. The firm substitutes away from labor toward other factors, and with higher costs the firm produces less such that it demands less of all factors, including labor.

10 See Scheve and Slaughter (2004) for a mathematical derivation of this point.

11 For example, Rodrik (1997) presents evidence that exposure to external risk, measured by the interaction between trade openness and the standard deviation of a country's terms of trade, is positively correlated with growth volatility. But Iversen and Cusack (2000) present evidence that, at least for advanced economies, there is no correlation between trade- or capital-market openness and volatility in output, earnings or employment.

12 Note that there is some disagreement in the literature about the contribution of trade liberalization to growth – that is, the dynamic gains to trade. See, for example, Rodriguez and Rodrik (2001).

13 It may be useful to think about the wage effects best describing the consequences of policy change in countries with relatively flexible labor markets. In less flexible labor markets, these effects may be more likely to be observed in employment/unemployment rates.

14 What about the preferences of workers in non-traded industries? Unlike in the HO model, here non-traded workers are insulated from international product-market competition to the extent that domestic non-traded prices, by definition, are not directly affected by trade pressures. But insofar as freer trade raises national income, if income elasticities of demand for non-traded goods are positive then freer trade should raise non-traded prices by raising demand for non-traded goods. So in an RV model workers in non-traded sectors support freer trade, but perhaps less than do comparative-advantage-sector workers because trade policy's effect on non-traded prices works indirectly through non-traded demand. If some factors remain mobile across sectors in the RV model, factor prices are not so clearly linked to product-price changes. Changes in real factor prices for these mobile factors depend on the consumption basket of these mobile factors. In the above discussion we focus only on the specific factors.

15 Note that this trade question was not asked in the 1994 NES survey, so our analyses are limited to 1992 and 1996.

16 As discussed earlier, marginal responses in the United States to questions on trade and immigration policy do appear to be somewhat sensitive to the question frame. For example, does the question mention any reasons why trade may be good or bad? If so, do those reasons include price effects, wage effects, employment effects, or all three? The key results reported in this section that focus on divisions in public opinion have been replicated across a number of different question frames.

17 We recognize that this assumption abstracts from other interesting facts about the distribution of the skills of US immigrants. For example, Borjas *et al.* (1997: 7) show that the skill distribution of US immigration has been somewhat bimodal at both the high-skill and low-skill ends of the distribution.

18 These conclusions about the determinants of individual trade and immigration policy preferences are robust to a wide variety of sensitivity tests. These include, for example, inclusion or exclusion of a number of control variables including sex, age, race, immigration status, party identification, ideology, union membership, measures of ethnic and racial tolerance, retrospective evaluations of economic performance, skill mix of the immigrants in the respondent's region and state unemployment rates. Further, we investigated the impact of possible omitted variables based on the idea of issue linkage – for example, including measures of individual environmental concerns as independent variables in the trade analysis. We also evaluated the possibility that degrees of political awareness might account for the correlation between skill type and opinions, particularly for trade in which one might argue elite messages are predominantly favorable toward freer trade and so more politically aware citizens may be more likely to consume these messages and adopt the mainstream opinion. The main results reported in this section do not depend on the inclusion or exclusion of these regressors. See Scheve and Slaughter (2001a, b, c) for a number of alternative analyses exploring such issues as different measurement strategies for key variables of interest and alternative substantive interpretations of the results, all of which further verify our findings.

19 This measure and all other national level variables unless otherwise noted are from the *World Development Indicators Online* (World Bank 2003).

20 Occupations were coded according to the following rules based on the categories available in the World Values Survey: 1 = agricultural worker; 2 = farmer; 3 = unskilled manual worker; 4 = semi-skilled manual worker; 5 = skilled manual worker; 6 = foreman or supervisor; 7 = non-manual office worker in non-supervisory role; 8 = supervisory office worker; 9 = professional worker; 10 = employer manager of establishment with less than ten employees;

11 = employer manager of establishment with ten or more employees. Since these categories do not necessarily measure differences in skills of equal intervals, it is important to note that the results here are robust to a number of alternative codings of this variable. Further, and perhaps more importantly, the results are robust to employing a measure of skill based on the age that the respondent completed his or her formal education.

21 In alternative specifications, we followed the procedure of regressing the policy measures on *Occupational Skill* and a number of demographic and political control variables. This did not substantively alter the results.

22 Consistent with the literature on trade-policy opinions, the results reported here can be replicated for alternative measures of national factor endowment – for example, GDP per capita, country tertiary enrollment ratio, and country scientists and engineers in research and development per one million persons.

23 This estimate is robust to dropping potentially influential observations. With that said, obviously the comparative evidence presented here is based on small-*n* cross-sectional analyses and thus some caution should be made with respect to all the inferences made based on this evidence.

24 The ISSP data was not featured in the previous section because overall it has fewer country observations and does not include nearly as many developing countries (thus variation in factor endowments is truncated in the ISSP data). Nonetheless, key results from the analyses of the WVS data can be replicated using the ISSP surveys, which have in fact been the primary dataset used in the literature (O'Rourke and Sinnott 2001; Mayda 2002; Beaulieu *et al.* 2002; Mayda and Rodrik 2005).

25 Despite the strong empirical reasons for thinking macroeconomic conditions are an important determinant of trade opinions, we note again that unemployment is not a feature of the standard models of international trade typically employed in the political economy literature. We view the link between unemployment and trade opinions as largely reflecting the differences in the real adjustment costs that workers face when macroeconomic conditions are good and when they are not. See Wallerstein (1987) for a theoretical explanation for the connection between unemployment and the demand for the protection that depends on the existence of collective bargaining.

26 The specific question wording in the ISSP data was "How much do you agree or disagree with the following statements: (R's country) should limit the import of foreign products in order to protect its national economy." The variable *Trade Opinion* was coded so that those respondents giving the "agree" or "agree strongly" responses were coded a 1, while those respondents giving one of the remaining three valid responses were coded a 0.

27 Note that in some studies using the 1995 ISSP data, East and West Germany are treated as separate countries and thus the analyses reported include 24 rather than 23 countries.

28 This finding is also true if potentially influential observations such as Spain and Latvia are omitted from the analysis. It is also robust to including a number of possible control variables such as the natural log of per capita GDP and trade openness. For the ISSP data the natural log of per capita GDP is negatively correlated with protectionist trade opinions while trade openness is not significantly correlated with average trade opinions.

29 Boix (forthcoming) points out that, of course, both openness and social insurance policies are endogenous and it often may be equally feasible to meet the demands of workers through either protection and/or generous social insurance. This point is surely correct and thus an individual's policy opinions about trade and social insurance may be simultaneously determined. We will return to this possibility in the concluding discussion. The argument pursued in this

section requires only that we assume that when individuals form an opinion about trade they take existing government labor-market policies as exogenous. Among other considerations, the historical basis of and persistence of cross-national differences in labor-market policies makes this a tenable assumption.

30 The main results of this section can be replicated for much more aggregated "subsidies and transfers" data from the World Bank, which allow inclusion of 20 of the original 23 observations.

31 A couple of qualifications to Figure 2.4 should be kept in mind. First, there is not evidence in this data that employment protection policies also lessen differences in opinion across workers. Second, the correlation is not evident between the more aggregated measure of spending discussed earlier and the marginal effect of skill type on trade opinions in the WVS data. This may indicate a problem with the argument, simply suggest that the appropriate measure for social insurance spending is that spending targeted for labor-market programs, or reflect the fact that the WVS data is populated mostly by relatively poorer countries for which there is often no skill division in opinion for social insurance spending to attenuate.

32 These numbers are based on using the Golden *et al.* (2002) measures for centralization. Similar or fewer observations would be available using alternative sources for measures of wage bargaining centralization.

33 We thank an anonymous referee for suggesting the issues presented in this paragraph.

34 There is also evidence in the literature that other economic considerations may be important determinants of opinion formation. For example, Scheve and Slaughter (2001a) argue that asset ownership may also be important for trade-policy preferences and provide evidence that home ownership in geographic regions with a manufacturing mix concentrated in comparative-disadvantaged industries is correlated with support for trade protection. Baker (2003, 2005) argues that the consumption gains to trade are critical in understanding support for trade reform in Latin America. Hanson *et al.* (2002) argue that the perceived fiscal impact of immigration may play an important role in opinion formation.

35 One other result emphasized in the O'Rourke and Sinnott study is the gender gap in opinion over trade, with women having more protectionist opinions. This result is evident in most other studies (see, for example, Scheve and Slaughter 2001c). The theoretical basis behind the gender gap has not been developed in the literature. One possibility is simply that labor markets are partially segmented by sex and that women face greater risks in the labor market from trade-policy liberalization.

36 Note that one practical task for future research is simply to gather comparative surveys in which the industry of employment of respondents is recorded in detail. To our knowledge, only Scheve and Slaughter (2001a) employ survey data with this information and thus are able to construct reasonable measures of industry exposure (Mayda and Rodrik's (2005) industry results are derived without actually knowing what industry individuals are employed in).

37 See Busch and Reinhardt (2000), Darden (2002), and Hainmueller and Hiscox (forthcoming) for three very different studies on belief formation about trade policy. Note also the importance of exploring low-information rationality perspectives on opinion formation about international economic policies. It is quite likely that individuals gather information about policy alternatives via work experiences, group affiliations, and the media and construct summary evaluations broadly consistent with their interests and values without actually forming complex causal beliefs about the effects of different alternatives.

## References

Alt, J. E. and Gilligan, M. (1994) "The Political Economy of Trading States: Factor Specificity, Collective Action Problems, and Domestic Political Institutions," *Journal of Political Philosophy*, 2/2: 65–192.

Baker, A. (2003) "Why is Trade Reform so Popular in Latin America?," *World Politics*, 55/April: 423–55.

—— (2005) "Who Wants to Globalize? Consumer Tastes and Labor Markets in a Theory of Trade Policy Preferences," *American Journal of Political Science*, 49/4: 924–38.

Baldwin, R. E. and Cain, G. G. (1997) "Shifts in US Relative Wages: The Role of Trade, Technology, and Factor Endowments," *NBER Working Paper*, No. 5934, February.

Balistreri, E. J. (1997) "The Performance of the Heckscher-Ohlin-Vanek Model in Predicting Endogenous Policy Forces at the Individual Level," *Canadian Journal of Economics*, 30/1: 1–17.

Beaulieu, E. (2002) "Factor or Industry Cleavages in Trade Policy? An Empirical Test of the Stolper-Samuelson Theorem," *Economics and Politics*, 14/2: 99–131.

Beaulieu, E., Benarroch, M. and Gaisford J. (2002) "Intra-Industry Trade Liberalization: Why Skilled Workers Everywhere Resist Protectionism," unpublished typescript, University of Calgary.

Bernard, A. B. and Jensen, J. B. (2002) "The Death of Manufacturing Plants," *NBER Working Paper*, No. 9026.

Bhagwati, J. (1991) "Free Traders and Free Immigrationists: Strangers or Friends?," Russell Sage Foundation Working Paper.

Boix, C. (forthcoming) "Between Protectionism and Compensation: The Political Economy of Trade," in P. Bardhan, S. Bowles and M. Wallerstein (eds) *Globalization and Egalitarian Redistribution*, Princeton: Princeton University Press.

Borjas, G. J. (1999a) *Heaven's Door: Immigration Policy and the American Economy*, Princeton: Princeton University Press.

—— (1999b) "The Economic Analysis of Immigration," in O. C. Ashenfelter and D. Card (eds) *Handbook of Labor Economics*, Amsterdam: North-Holland, 1697–760.

Borjas, G. J., Freeman, R. B. and Katz, L. F. (1996) "Searching for the Effect of Immigration on the Labor Market," *American Economic Review*, 86/2: 247–51.

—— (1997) "How Much Do Immigration and Trade Affect Labor Market Outcomes?," *Brookings Papers on Economic Activity*, 1: 1–90.

Bronfenbrenner, K. (2000) "Uneasy Terrain: The Impact of Capital Mobility on Workers, Wages, and Union Organizing," Working Paper, September.

Busch, M. and Reinhardt, E. (2000) "Geography, International Trade, and Political Mobilization," *American Journal of Political Science*, 44/4: 703–19.

Cameron, D. (1978) "The Expansion of the Public Economy," *American Political Science Review*, 72: 1243–61.

Card, D. (2001) "Immigrant Inflows, Native Outflows, and the Local Labor Market Impacts of Higher Immigration," *Journal of Labor Economics*, 19/1: 22–64.

Cassing, J., McKeown, T. and Ochs, J. (1986) "The Political Economy of the Tariff Cycle," *American Political Science Review*, 80/3: 843–62.

Chicago Council on Foreign Relations (2002a) *Worldviews 2002: American Public Opinion and Foreign Policy*, Chicago: CCFR.

Chicago Council on Foreign Relations (2002b) *Worldviews 2002: European Public Opinion and Foreign Policy*, Chicago: CCFR.

Darden, K. (2002) *Liberalism and Its Rivals*, unpublished typescript, Yale University.

*Economic Report of the President* (1997, 2000) Washington, DC: US Government Printing Office.

Epstein, D. and O'Halloran, S. (1996) "The Partisan Paradox and the US Tariff, 1877–1934," *International Organization*, 50/2: 301–24.

Fabbri, F., Haskel, J. E. and Slaughter, M. J. (2003) "Does Nationality of Ownership Matter for Labor Demands?" *Journal of the European Economics Association* 1/(2/3): 698–707.

Feenstra, R. C. and Hanson, G. H. (1997) "Foreign Direct Investment and Relative Wages: Evidence from Mexico's Maquiladoras," *Journal of International Economics*, 42/May: 371–93.

—— (1999) "The Impact of Outsourcing and High-Technology Capital on Wages," *Quarterly Journal of Economics*, August: 907–40.

Freeman, R. (1995) "Are Your Wages Set in Beijing?" *Journal of Economic Perspectives*, 9/3: 15–32.

Friedberg, R. (2001) "The Impact of Migration on the Israeli Labor Market," *Quarterly Journal of Economics*, 116: 1373–408.

Gabel, M. (1998) *Interests and Integration: Market Liberalization, Public Opinion, and European Union*, Ann Arbor: University of Michigan Press.

Garrett, G. (1998) *Partisan Politics in the Global Economy*, New York: Cambridge University Press.

Golden, M., Lange, P. and Wallerstein, M. (2002) "Union Centralization among Advanced Industrial Societies: An Empirical Study," Dataset available at www.shelley.polisci.ucla.edu/data, accessed 19 September 2002.

Gorg, H. and Strobl, E. (2003) "Footloose Multinationals?," *Manchester School*, 71/1: 1–19.

Gottschalk, P. and Moffitt, R. (1994) "The Growth of Earnings Instability in the US Labor Market," *Brookings Papers on Economic Activity 2*, Washington, DC: Brookings Institution, 217–54.

Hainmueller, J. and Hiscox, M. (forthcoming) "Learning to Love Globalization? Education and Individual Attitudes Toward International Trade," *International Organization*.

Hanson, G. H. and Harrison, A. (1999) "Trade Liberalization and Wage Inequality in Mexico," *Industrial and Labor Relations Review*, 52: 271–88.

Hanson, G. H., Scheve, K., Slaughter, M. J. and Spilimbergo, A. (2002) "Immigration and the US Economy: Labour-Market Impacts, Illegal Entry, and Policy Choices," in T. Boeri, G. H. Hanson and B. McCormick (eds) *Immigration Policy and the Welfare System*, London: Oxford University Press, 169–285.

Hanson, G. H. and Slaughter, M. J. (2002) "Labor-Market Adjustment in Open Economies: Evidence from US States," *Journal of International Economics*, 57/1: 3–29.

Haskel, J. E. and Slaughter, M. J. (2001) "Trade, Technology, and UK Wage Inequality," *The Economic Journal*, 111/January: 163–87.

—— (2003) "Have Falling Tariffs and Transportation Costs Raised US Wage Inequality?," *Review of International Economics*, 11/4: 630–50.

Hays, J., Ehrlich, S. and Peinhardt, C. (forthcoming) "Government Spending and Public Support for Trade in the OECD: An Empirical Test of the Embedded Liberalism Thesis," *International Organization*.

Helpman, E. (1984) "A Simple Theory of Trade with Multinational Corporations," *Journal of Political Economy*, 92: 451–71.

Hiscox, M. (2001) *International Trade and Political Conflict: Commerce, Coalitions, and Mobility*, Princeton: Princeton University Press.

—— (2003) "Through a Glass and Darkly: Framing Effects and Individuals' Attitudes Toward International Trade," unpublished typescript, Harvard University.

Inglehart, R. (2000) *World Values Surveys and European Values Surveys, 1981–1984, 1990–1993, and 1995–1997* [Computer File], ICPSR Version. Ann Arbor: Institute for Social Research [producer], Ann Arbor: ICPSR [distributor] 2000.

International Social Survey Programme (ISSP) (1995) *National Identity*, Archived by Zentralarchiv Für Empirische Sozialforschung, Koeln.

Iversen, T. and Cusack, T. (2000) "The Causes of Welfare State Expansion," *World Politics*, 52/April: 313–49.

Johnson, G. and Slaughter, M. J. (2001) "The Effects of Growing International Trade on the US Labor Market," in R. Solow and A. B. Krueger (eds) *The Roaring Nineties: Can Full Employment Be Sustained?*, Russell Sage Foundation, 260–306.

Katzenstein, P. (1985) *Small States in World Markets: Industrial Policy in Europe*, Ithaca: Cornell University Press.

Lawrence, R. Z. and Slaughter, M. J. (1993) "International Trade and American Wages in the 1980s: Giant Sucking Sound or Small Hiccup?," in M. N. Baily and C. Winston (eds) *Brookings Papers on Economic Activity: Microeconomics*, 2: 161–211.

Leamer, E. E. (1984) *Sources of International Comparative Advantage*, Cambridge: The MIT Press.

—— (1998) "In Search of Stolper-Samuelson Linkages Between International Trade and Lower Wages," in S. M. Collins (ed.) *Imports, Exports, and the American Worker*, Washington, DC: Brookings Institution Press, 141–202.

Mayda, A. M. (2002) "Who Is Against Immigration?: A Cross-Country Investigation of Individual Attitudes toward Immigrants," Harvard University Working Paper.

Mayda, A. M. and Rodrik, R. (2005) "Why Are Some People (and Countries) More Protectionist Than Others?" *European Economic Review*, 49/6: 1393–430.

Mussa, M. (1978) "Dynamic Adjustment in the Heckscher-Ohlin-Samuelson Model," *Journal of Political Economy*, 86/September.

Neary, P. (1978) "Short-Run Capital Specificity and the Pure Theory of International Trade," *The Economic Journal*, 88/September: 448–510.

OECD (1997) "Economic Performance and the Structure of Collective Bargaining," *OECD Employment Outlook*, Paris: OECD.

O'Rourke, K. and Sinnott, R. (2001) "The Determinants of Individual Trade Policy Preferences: International Survey Evidence," in S. M. Collins and D. Rodrik (eds) *Brookings Trade Forum: 2001*, Washington, DC: Brookings Institution Press.

Rama, M. (1994) "Endogenous Trade Policy: A Time-Series Approach," *Economics and Politics*, 6/November: 215–32.

Richardson, J. D. (1995) "Income Inequality and Trade: How to Think, What to Conclude," *Journal of Economic Perspectives*, Summer: 33–55.

Rodriguez, F. and Rodrik, D. (2001) "Trade Policy and Economic Growth: A Skeptic's Guide to the Cross-National Evidence," in B. Bernanke and K. Rogoff (eds) *Macroeconomics Annual 2000*, Cambridge: The MIT Press.

Rodrik, D. (1995) "Political Economy of Trade Policy," in G. Grossman and

K. Rogoff (eds) *Handbook of International Economics*, vol. 3, Amsterdam: Elsevier Science Publishers, 1457–94.

—— (1997) *Has Globalization Gone Too Far?*, Washington, DC: Institute for International Economics.

—— (1998) "Why Do More Open Economies Have Bigger Governments?," *Journal of Political Economy*, 106/5: 997–1032.

Rybczynski, T. M. (1955) "Factor Endowments and Relative Commodity Prices," *Economica*, 22: 336–41.

Sapiro, V., Rosenstone, S. J., Miller, W. E. and the National Election Studies (1998) American National Election Studies, 1948–1997 [CD-ROM]. ICPSR ed. Ann Arbor, MI: Inter-university Consortium for Political and Social Research [producer and distributor].

Scheve, K. F. (2000) "Comparative Context and Public Preferences over Regional Economic Integration," paper presented at the 2000 Annual Meetings of the American Political Science Association.

Scheve, K. F. and Slaughter, M. J. (2001a) "What Determines Individual Trade-Policy Preferences?" *Journal of International Economics*, 54/2: 267–92.

—— (2001b) "Labor-Market Competition and Individual Preferences Over Immigration Policy," *Review of Economics and Statistics*, 83/1: 133–45.

—— (2001c) *Globalization and the Perceptions of American Workers*, Washington, DC: Institute for International Economics.

—— (2004) "Economic Insecurity and the Globalization of Production," *American Journal of Political Science*, 48/4: 662–74.

Schmidt, S. R. (1999) "Long-Run Trends in Workers' Beliefs about Their Own Job Security: Evidence from the General Social Survey," *Journal of Labor Economics*, 17/4: S127–S141.

Slaughter, M. J. (2000) "What Are the Results of Product-Price Studies and What Can We Learn From Their Differences?," in R. C. Feenstra (ed.) *The Impact of International Trade on Wages*, National Bureau of Economic Research Conference Volume, 129–70.

—— (2001) "International Trade and Labor-Demand Elasticities," *Journal of International Economics*, 54/1: 27–56.

Takacs, W. (1981) "Pressures for Protectionism: An Empirical Analysis," *Economic Inquiry*, 19/October: 687–93.

Wallerstein, M. (1987) "Unemployment, Collective Bargaining, and the Demand for Protection," *American Journal of Political Science*, 31: 729–52.

—— (1999) "Wage-Setting Institutions and Pay Inequality in Advanced Industrial Societies," *American Journal of Political Science*, 43: 649–80.

World Bank (2003) *World Development Indicators Online*. Available at: devdata.worldbank.org/dataonline/, accessed March 2003.

# 3 Economic insecurity and the globalization of production

*Kenneth Scheve and Matthew J. Slaughter*[1]

## Introduction

Determining whether international economic integration in advanced economies increases worker insecurity is critical to competing explanations of welfare-state policymaking and the politics of globalization. An influential argument in the welfare-state literature is that increases in economic insecurity from globalization generate demands for more generous social insurance that compensates workers for a riskier environment (e.g. Boix forthcoming; Burgoon 2001; Cameron 1978; Garrett 1998; Hays *et al.* 2002; Rodrik 1997, 1998). The connection between globalization and welfare spending in this argument depends on the causal mechanism that international economic integration increases worker insecurity. Claims that no such link exists undermine this explanation for variation in welfare-state spending.

The link between economic integration and worker insecurity is also an essential element of explanations for patterns of public opposition to policies aimed at further liberalization of international trade, immigration and foreign direct investment (FDI) in advanced economies. Economic insecurity may contribute to the backlash against globalization in at least two ways. First is a direct effect in which individuals that perceive globalization to be contributing to their own economic insecurity are much more likely to develop policy attitudes against economic integration. Second, if globalization limits the capacities of governments to provide social insurance, or is perceived to do so, then individuals may worry further about globalization and this effect is likely to be magnified if labor-market risks are heightened by global integration.

Previous empirical research has focused on whether one particular component of globalization, international trade, generates economic volatility. This research has been inconclusive. Among others, Rodrik (1997, 1998) argues in the affirmative and presents evidence that exposure to external risk from trade, measured by the interaction between trade openness and the standard deviation of a country's terms of trade, is positively correlated with growth volatility. In contrast, Iversen and Cusack

(2000) contend that there is no convincing evidence that international trade increases economic insecurity. They argue that Rodrik's correlation is not sufficient and that it is necessary either that price volatility in international markets be greater than in domestic markets or that trade concentrate rather than diversify economic risks. Iversen and Cusack then present evidence that, at least for advanced economies, there is no correlation between trade openness and volatility in output, earnings, or employment.

In this chapter, we investigate whether international economic integration increases economic insecurity. Our analysis makes a substantial departure from existing research by focusing on a relatively overlooked dimension of globalization: the cross-border flow of FDI within multinational enterprises (MNEs). This focus on FDI rather than trade is rare in the literature, and we argue that this omission matters for both empirical and theoretical reasons.

Empirically, in recent decades, cross-border flows of FDI have grown at much faster rates than have flows of goods and services. UNCTAD (2001) reports that from 1986 through 2000, worldwide cross-border outflows of FDI rose at an annualized rate of 26.2 percent, versus a rate of 15.4 percent for worldwide exports of goods and services. In the second half of the 1990s this difference widened to 37.0 percent versus just 1.9 percent. Moreover, it is the multinationalization of production that a number of scholars have pointed to as the distinguishing feature of the current phase of globalization compared to previous eras (e.g. Bordo *et al.* 1999).

This lack of attention to FDI also matters because, as we will discuss, there are strong theoretical reasons to believe that FDI can substantially influence economic insecurity. The globalization of production by MNEs gives firms greater access to foreign factors of production and thus greater ease of substitution away from workers in any single location. As a result, workers feel more insecure. Stated in terms of the underlying labor economics, the central idea is that FDI by MNEs increases firms' elasticity of demand for labor. More-elastic labor demands, in turn, raise the volatility of wages and employment – and thereby raise worker insecurity.

This theoretical framework motivates our empirical analysis of the relationship between the multinationalization of production and the economic insecurity of workers. We present new evidence, based on analysis of individual-level panel data from Great Britain over 1991–1999, that FDI activity in the industries in which individuals work is positively correlated with individual perceptions of worker insecurity. This correlation holds in analyses accounting for individual-specific effects and a wide variety of control variables. Moreover, FDI exposure has one of the largest substantive effects in accounting for the within-individual variation in insecurity. We regard these individual-level panel results as the first valid evidence consistent with a causal relationship from FDI to worker insecurity.

There are four remaining sections to the chapter. The next section provides a theoretical framework for the economics of FDI and worker insecurity. The third section describes the data to be used in the study and the econometric models to be estimated. The fourth section reports the empirical results, and the final section concludes.

## Theoretical framework for FDI and worker insecurity

### *Defining worker insecurity*

Although there are a number of alternative definitions of economic insecurity, most often it is understood to be an individual's perception of the risk of economic misfortune (Dominitz and Manski 1997). Consequently, researchers have focused on the risk of events such as the loss of health insurance, being a victim of a burglary, losing a job and significant decreases in wages (e.g. Anderson and Pontusson 2001; Mughan and Lacy 2002).

It is likely that most people's perceptions of economic insecurity depend heavily on their purchasing power, which in turn depends on both their asset ownership and their labor-market status – both employment and income earned there from. In reality, the large majority of people rely much more on labor income than capital income for purchasing power. Accordingly, we think labor-market status is the main determinant of perceptions of economic insecurity.

In light of this labor-market focus, we conjecture that the economic misfortunes underlying people's economic insecurity stem mainly from more volatile employment and/or wage interactions with their employers. That is, risk-averse workers are not indifferent between employment options that yield the same amount of expected earnings but with differing degrees of certainty. More certain earnings outcomes – due to more certain wage and/or employment realizations – are preferred to less certain ones, and insecurity rises with this uncertainty.[2]

### *Worker insecurity in labor-market equilibrium: why FDI matters*

Equilibrium in a standard competitive labor market is set by the intersection of labor supply and labor demand. The labor-supply curve is aggregated across individuals, and at each point along it the elasticity of labor supply, $\eta^S$, is defined as the percentage change in the quantity of labor supplied by workers in response to a 1 percent increase in the price of labor. Higher wages typically induce a greater quantity of labor supplied.

The labor-demand curve is aggregated across firms, and at each point along it the elasticity of labor demand, $\eta^D$, is defined as the percentage decline (in absolute value) in the quantity of labor demanded in response to a 1 percent increase in the price of labor. This elasticity consists of two parts. The substitution effect tells, for a given level of output, how much firms substitute away from labor towards other factors of production when wages rise. The scale effect tells how much labor demand falls after a wage increase thanks to the rise in the firms' costs and thus the fall in their output and so demand for labor and all other factors. When wages rise, both the substitution and scale effects reduce the quantity of labor demanded.

In accord with a wide range of empirical evidence, we introduce volatility into the labor market by assuming that the labor-demand schedule is stochastic. To see what forces drive this volatility, note that each firm's labor-demand schedule traces out the *marginal revenue product* of its workers as the wage rate varies. A profit-maximizing firm hires workers until the revenue generated by the last worker hired equals the market wage that firm must pay that last worker.

For each firm, its product prices and technology are two key determinants of marginal revenue products. Aggregated across firms, then, the position of the labor-demand schedule depends crucially on all relevant product prices and production technologies. Define $m\hat{r}p$ as the percentage shift in the labor-demand schedule due to shocks to prices and/or technologies. It is straightforward to then show that the resulting percentage change in wages ($\hat{w}$) and employment ($\hat{e}$) are respectively given by

$$\hat{w} = \left(\frac{\eta^D}{\eta^S + \eta^D}\right) m\hat{r}p \text{ and } \hat{e} = \left(\frac{\eta^D \eta^S}{\eta^S + \eta^D}\right) m\hat{r}p.$$

If $m\hat{r}p$ is a random variable, then we can write

$$Var(\hat{w}) = \left(\frac{\eta^D}{\eta^S + \eta^D}\right)^2 Var(m\hat{r}p) \text{ and } Var(\hat{e}) = \left(\frac{\eta^D \eta^S}{\eta^S + \eta^D}\right)^2 Var(m\hat{r}p).$$

The above expressions demonstrate that greater volatility in labor-market outcomes – and thus greater economic insecurity – can arise either from greater aggregate volatility in prices and technology, $Var(m\hat{r}p)$, or from a higher elasticity of demand for labor, $\eta^D$. The former can be thought of as the volatility of aggregate shocks to labor demand, and the latter can be thought of as the pass-through of those shocks into volatility of wages and employment. In this framework, the link between globalization and labor-market volatility depends on some component of globalization, such as trade or FDI, altering one of these quantities, $Var(m\hat{r}p)$ or $\eta^D$.

We argue that an important channel through which FDI can affect labor-market volatility is by increasing labor-demand elasticities via the substitution effect. Suppose that a firm is vertically integrated with a number of production stages. A multinational firm can move abroad some of these stages (e.g. Helpman 1984). This globalization of production within multinationals gives access to foreign factors of production, either directly through foreign affiliates or indirectly through intermediate inputs. This expands the set of factors firms can substitute towards in response to higher domestic wages beyond just domestic non-labor factors to include foreign factors as well. Thus, greater FDI can raise labor-demand elasticities – and so worker insecurity because of more volatile wage and employment outcomes.

This argument does not exclude other mechanisms through which globalization may increase economic insecurity. For example, openness to international trade may increase the volatility of aggregate shocks to labor demand ($Var(\hat{mrp})$). As discussed in the introduction, this is the link examined in much of the previous research on globalization and economic insecurity, and its empirical importance remains an open question. Another example is that theoretically, international trade in final goods – whether mediated by multinationals or not – could also affect insecurity by making labor demands more elastic through the scale effect. This pro-competitive effect of trade has been well-studied, and FDI can also work on the scale effect (e.g. as foreign firms compete with domestic incumbents).

We have focused on the substitution effect of FDI for several reasons. Most importantly, the substitution effect is direct in that it places domestic workers in competition with foreign labor for employment within the same firm. It is thus likely to have a larger effect on labor demand elasticities.[3] Further, other researchers have emphasized in theory its possible role in generating insecurity (e.g. Rodrik 1997), but no compelling empirical evidence has been produced.

Before turning to an empirical test of the link between FDI and insecurity, we note one other important aspect of MNEs and labor markets. Many studies across a variety of countries have documented that establishments owned by MNEs pay *higher* wages than do domestically owned establishments. This is true, even controlling for a wide range of observable worker and/or plant characteristics such as industry, region and overall size. The magnitudes involved are usually quite big.[4]

This multinational wage premium may reflect several forces. It could be accounted for by higher worker productivity due to superior technology and/or capital; or by higher worker productivity due to unobservable worker qualities; or by greater profits and therefore more rent sharing with workers. Our theory framework suggests another possibility: that MNEs pay more to compensate workers for the greater labor-market volatility associated with MNEs.

Regardless of the cause(s) of the multinational wage premium, its existence is important for considering how the globalization of production affects economic insecurity. All else equal, this premium likely makes multinational employees feel *more* secure. Our focus on elasticities and labor-market volatility highlights MNE influences on different dimensions of the overall worker-firm relationship. These contrasting issues of labor-demand elasticities and wage premia suggest that the net impact of MNEs on worker insecurity is *ex ante* unclear. Whether wage premia fully compensate for increased risks from higher elasticities is an empirical question.

## Data description and empirical specification

### *Data description*

In light of the theory discussion above, the objective of our empirical work is to examine the impact of FDI on economic insecurity. Specifically, we will evaluate how individual self-assessments of economic insecurity correlate with the presence of mobile capital in the form of FDI in the industries in which individuals work. Our data cover Great Britain, which we think is an excellent case to examine both because inward and outward FDI have long figured prominently in the overall economy and because of the high quality of data available.

The individual data are from the *British Household Panel Survey* (BHPS 2001). This survey is a nationally representative sample of more than 5,000 UK households and over 9,000 individuals questioned annually from 1991 to 1999.[5] It records detailed information about each respondent's perceptions of economic insecurity, employment, wages and many other characteristics. The most important pieces of survey information required for our analysis are a measure of economic insecurity, identification of the respondents' industry of employment, and repeated measurement of the same individual over time.

We measure economic insecurity by responses to the following question asked in each of the nine years of the panel.

> I'm going to read out a list of various aspects of jobs, and after each one I'd like you to tell me from this card which number best describes how satisfied or dissatisfied you are with that particular aspect of your own present job – job security.

The ordered responses are on a seven-point scale ranging from "not satisfied at all" to "completely satisfied." Consistent with our interest in the labor-income dimension of economic insecurity, this question measures perceptions of employment risks. We constructed the variable *Insecurity* by coding responses in the reverse order from the original question, with a range from 1 for individuals who give the response "completely satisfied" to a 7 for those individuals giving the response "not satisfied at all." Higher values of *Insecurity* thus indicate less satisfaction with job security.

Our theoretical framework hypothesizes that high FDI activity in industries may generate economic insecurity among workers by increasing labor-demand elasticities. Theory does not offer clear guidance on how to measure this crucial concept of FDI exposure, so to test our key hypothesis we constructed three alternative measures.

First, from the UK Office of National Statistics (ONS) we obtained data on inward and outward FDI investment positions in all two-digit 1992 Standard Industry Classification (SIC92) UK industries from 1991 through

1999.[6] The BHPS records respondent industry of employment by the 1980 Standard Industry Classification (SIC80), so we concorded the FDI data to two-digit SIC80 industries.[7] We then merged the industry-level FDI data with the BHPS survey.

Our first, and main, measure of FDI exposure is a dichotomous industry-level variable: *FDI Presence*. We set *FDI Presence* equal to one if two conditions were met: if the industry had any positive FDI investment, inward or outward, and if the industry's activities do not require producers and consumers to be in the same geographic location. If either of these conditions were not met, we coded *FDI* equal to zero. As with all our FDI measures, *FDI Presence* varies by both industry and year.

Our logic in defining *FDI Presence* with these two conditions runs as follows. The first condition of positive FDI investment is straightforward. Any inward or outward FDI activity satisfies this. The second condition recognizes that FDI activity is less likely to alter labor-demand elasticities if business activities cannot be outsourced across countries because the consumer and producer must be in the same geographic location.

Consider the examples of wholesale trade, retail trade and personal services (e.g. haircuts). The large majority of business activities in these industries require the colocation of producers and consumers: e.g. customers sitting in the barber's chair. The notions of economic insecurity related to FDI that we discussed in the second section focus on the substitutability of business activities across countries. In reality, in many industries, FDI does not have this characteristic; indeed, FDI may arise precisely because foreign customers cannot be served at a distance via international trade. Accordingly, *FDI Presence* identifies not all industries with FDI, but instead only those industries with FDI in which business activities can be outsourced across countries. So for industries such as wholesale trade, retail trade and personal services we coded *FDI Presence* as zero regardless of the level of actual FDI.

It is theoretically ambiguous if, in addition to the *existence* of FDI activity, the *magnitude* also matters. It may be that more FDI activity indicates greater capital mobility, which in turn raises labor-demand elasticities and perceptions of employment risks. Since the dichotomous *FDI Presence* does not distinguish FDI magnitudes once any FDI is present, we also constructed two continuous measures of FDI exposure that account for magnitudes relative to industry size.

The variable *FDI Total Share* equals the sum of inward and outward FDI stocks divided by UK gross value added (again, except for industries that require producers and consumers to colocate, for which the variable was coded zero). The main concern about this measure is that its denominator covers UK activity only, but the numerator covers not just inward FDI into the UK but also outward FDI out of the UK. This mismatch of scope cannot be addressed (in part because the data do not disaggregate host countries for outward FDI), but it likely introduces error in our measurement of the underlying concept of FDI exposure.

Our second continuous measure of FDI exposure addresses this concern by including in the numerator only inward FDI. Thus, *FDI Inward Share* equals inward FDI divided by gross value added (again, except for industries that require producers and consumers to colocate, for which the variable was coded zero). This measure generates the opposite trade-off: no mismatch of scope, but in theory outward FDI can matter for FDI exposure just as inward FDI does. Inward and outward FDI flows tend to be highly correlated, however, which suggests that on balance *FDI Inward Share* might be preferred to *FDI Total Share.*

It is important to recognize the level of aggregation for the FDI regressors. Our use of two-digit industries is dictated by ONS rules on public data dissemination. Theoretically, we could imagine measuring FDI exposure more finely at the level of the respondent's company, rather than at the more aggregated industry level.[8] Our specification implicitly assumes that within each industry, all workers perceive FDI threats equally regardless of whether each works for a firm with some FDI. This assumption seems reasonable. We are simply assuming that important features of the labor demand faced by workers are set in the industry of employment rather than the firm.[9]

Beyond FDI exposure, perceptions of economic insecurity may also be shaped by a number of characteristics of individuals and the industries in which they are employed. Accordingly, for our main analyses we constructed four individual-level and two industry-level variables. The variable *Income* measures annual household income in thousands of UK pounds.[10] *Union* equals one if the individual belongs to a workplace union and zero if not. *Education* is a categorical variable ranging from one to four, with higher values for more educational attainment.[11] The variable *Age* equals the respondent's age in years at the time of the survey. *Manufacturing* is an indicator variable equal to one if the respondent's industry of employment is in the manufacturing sector and equal to zero otherwise. Finally, *Sector Unemployment* measures the share of workers unemployed in each respondent's industry of work.[12]

Each of these six control variables is likely to account for some of the differences among individuals in perceptions of economic insecurity. However, it must be acknowledged that other unmeasured or unobservable differences among individuals may also matter. For example, individuals almost surely vary in their degree of risk aversion. In addition, individuals probably vary in their interpretation of the BHPS question. One individual may think about job security in compensated terms conditional on wages and any perceived compensating wage differential. But another observationally similar individual may think without conditioning in this way.

Unmeasured or unobservable individual heterogeneity is, of course, a problem that faces all survey research. But it seems particularly acute here because our key variable to be explained measures perceptions of risk. So to address this heterogeneity, we use the fact that the BHPS records repeated observations for the same individual over many years. We exploit this panel structure by including an individual-specific effect for each respondent. These individual-specific effects capture any time-constant factors across people that drive variation in perceptions of employment risks.

For each year of our panel, Table 3.1 reports summary statistics of our key variables. The summary statistics and our subsequent analyses are based on the BHPS subsample of private sector, full-time workers who are not self-employed. It is for this group of workers that our theoretical framework most directly applies. *Insecurity* averages just below three in most years, suggesting that the average respondent was fairly satisfied with his or her job security.

*FDI Presence*, our main measure of exposure to the globalization of production, averages slightly over half in most years – i.e. in most years just over half of respondents worked in FDI-exposed industries. Industries with positive values for *FDI Presence* include metal manufacturing, mechanical engineering, and banking and finance. Among these industries in 1991, the sector with the most respondents was mechanical engineering. The industries meeting our two conditions for being FDI exposed vary over time, with sectors such as instrument engineering and business services being added to the list.

### *Econometric models*

By matching each BHPS observation with the relevant industry FDI information, we examine how self-assessments of economic insecurity relate to FDI exposure. We formalize the determinants of economic insecurity as follows:

$$Insecurity_{it} = \alpha_i + \beta \text{FDI}_{it} + \gamma Z_{it} + \epsilon_{it} \quad (1)$$

where the subscript $i$ indexes individuals; the subscript $t$ indexes years; $Insecurity_{it}$ is our measure of economic insecurity; $\text{FDI}_{it}$ is one of our measures of FDI exposure; the vector $Z_{it}$ includes dichotomous indicators for each year and, in many specifications, the control regressors discussed above; $\alpha_i$, $\beta$, and $\gamma$ are parameters to be estimated; and $\varepsilon_{it}$ is an additive error term.

The coefficient estimates of $\beta$ in equation (1) indicate whether and to what extent individual perceptions of economic insecurity are correlated with FDI exposure. Exposure to FDI activity is increasing in each of our three FDI variables, and we expect this to be positively correlated with the dependent variable *Insecurity*. This is the central hypothesis of our empirical analysis. Thus, our null hypothesis is that $\beta = 0$, with the alternative $\beta > 0$.

*Table 3.1* Summary statistics

| *Variable* | *Year* | | | | | | | | |
|---|---|---|---|---|---|---|---|---|---|
| | *1991* | *1992* | *1993* | *1994* | *1995* | *1996* | *1997* | *1998* | *1999* |
| Insecurity | 2.978 | 3.021 | 2.916 | 2.941 | 2.881 | 2.789 | 2.681 | 2.663 | 2.726 |
| | (1.982) | (1.748) | (1.663) | (1.708) | (1.641) | (1.563) | (1.532) | (1.465) | (1.579) |
| FDI presence | 0.424 | 0.424 | 0.612 | 0.548 | 0.567 | 0.604 | 0.592 | 0.577 | 0.565 |
| | (0.494) | (0.494) | (0.487) | (0.498) | (0.496) | (0.489) | (0.492) | (0.494) | (0.496) |
| FDI total share | 0.388 | 0.394 | 0.424 | 0.389 | 0.405 | 0.459 | 0.465 | 0.570 | 0.732 |
| | (0.600) | (0.597) | (0.634) | (0.575) | (0.552) | (0.598) | (0.683) | (0.798) | (1.129) |
| FDI inward share | 0.189 | 0.190 | 0.167 | 0.151 | 0.172 | 0.178 | 0.185 | 0.223 | 0.236 |
| | (0.299) | (0.294) | (0.290) | (0.246) | (0.247) | (0.258) | (0.300) | (0.313) | (0.368) |
| Education | 2.262 | 2.325 | 2.391 | 2.437 | 2.469 | 2.511 | 2.539 | 2.558 | 2.538 |
| | (0.897) | (0.894) | (0.900) | (0.911) | (0.905) | (0.901) | (0.884) | (0.870) | (0.876) |
| Age | 35.471 | 35.696 | 35.597 | 35.646 | 35.650 | 35.550 | 35.499 | 35.809 | 36.122 |
| | (12.029) | (11.747) | (11.616) | (11.619) | (11.564) | (11.527) | (11.725) | (11.885) | (11.698) |
| Income | 23.766 | 25.219 | 25.817 | 26.377 | 27.807 | 29.319 | 29.650 | 30.572 | 30.721 |
| | (13.560) | (14.209) | (13.632) | (14.698) | (15.788) | (16.417) | (17.259) | (20.565) | (22.784) |
| Union | 0.279 | 0.260 | 0.231 | 0.209 | 0.227 | 0.210 | 0.193 | 0.188 | 0.205 |
| | (0.449) | (0.439) | (0.421) | (0.407) | (0.419) | (0.407) | (0.395) | (0.391) | (0.404) |
| Manufacturing | 0.341 | 0.329 | 0.318 | 0.298 | 0.314 | 0.310 | 0.298 | 0.286 | 0.276 |
| | (0.474) | (0.470) | (0.466) | (0.458) | (0.464) | (0.462) | (0.458) | (0.452) | (0.447) |
| Sector unemployment | 0.091 | 0.089 | 0.088 | 0.077 | 0.073 | 0.065 | 0.051 | 0.051 | 0.048 |
| | (0.035) | (0.033) | (0.031) | (0.025) | (0.024) | (0.021) | (0.017) | (0.017) | (0.017) |
| Observations | 2,654 | 2,292 | 2,153 | 2,247 | 2,379 | 2,525 | 2,698 | 3,060 | 4,058 |

Note

The BHPS sample in each year is private-sector, full-time workers who are not self-employed. Each cell reports the variable mean and, in parentheses, its standard deviation.

The panel nature of the BHPS data is indicated in (1) by the $i$ and $t$ indexes. Pooling individuals across years has obvious advantages but generates a number of estimation issues regarding individual heterogeneity. It is likely that observations over time for the same individual will be more similar than observations across different individuals. This might be due to persistence in or unmodeled characteristics of individual perceptions of economic insecurity. This is particularly pertinent to our analysis because, as discussed above, there are good reasons to think that unobserved factors may affect perceptions of economic insecurity. So (1) allows $\alpha$ to vary across individuals to capture unmeasured or unobserved heterogeneity.

Equation (1) can be estimated via random- or fixed-effects estimators. The random-effects estimator generates consistent parameter estimates if the individual effects are uncorrelated with the other explanatory variables. The fixed-effects estimator is also consistent under this assumption, but is less efficient. Under the alternative hypothesis that the individual effects are correlated with other explanatory variables, only the fixed-effects estimator is consistent. We will use both methods to estimate (1) and report diagnostics to evaluate the estimators. We will also use a number of alternative econometric specifications, including a dynamic panel model with a lagged dependent variable.

## Empirical results

### *Baseline specifications and results*

Table 3.2 reports random-effects and fixed-effects results for equation (1) for our main measure of FDI exposure, *FDI Presence*. In the first two sets of estimates reported, the only control variables are the year indicator variables. Across these two sets of results, the main substantive finding is a positive correlation between *FDI Presence* and *Insecurity*. The magnitude of the estimated effect is over twice as large in the random-effects specification. The coefficients for the year variables indicate deviations in mean levels of insecurity in each year from the base year 1991. In both specifications the parameter estimates are negative for every year except 1992 and turn significantly negative after 1995. This indication of lower average levels of insecurity in later years is broadly consistent with the UK macroeconomic performance over the 1990s: initial recession followed by increasingly strong economic growth.

Although the main substantive story is the same across these first two specifications in Table 3.2, it is still necessary to determine our relative confidence in the two estimators. We employed the Hausman specification test: if the random-effects assumption that the individual-specific effects are uncorrelated with the explanatory variables is true, then coefficient estimates from the two models should not be statistically different.

*Table 3.2* Panel analysis of economic insecurity, 1991–1999

| *Regressor* | *Random effects* | | | *Fixed effects* | | | *Fixed effects* | | |
|---|---|---|---|---|---|---|---|---|---|
| | *Coef.* | *S.E.* | *p-value* | *Coef.* | *S.E.* | *p-value* | *Coef.* | *S.E.* | *p-value* |
| FDI presence | 0.238 | 0.024 | 0.000 | 0.103 | 0.032 | 0.001 | 0.101 | 0.037 | 0.006 |
| Education | | | | | | | 0.098 | 0.049 | 0.046 |
| Age | | | | | | | 0.021 | 0.045 | 0.637 |
| Income | | | | | | | −0.002 | 0.001 | 0.052 |
| Union | | | | | | | 0.100 | 0.048 | 0.036 |
| Manufacturing | | | | | | | −0.009 | 0.046 | 0.848 |
| Sector unemployment | | | | | | | 3.032 | 0.603 | 0.000 |
| Year 1992 | 0.068 | 0.038 | 0.071 | 0.099 | 0.039 | 0.012 | 0.090 | 0.059 | 0.124 |
| Year 1993 | −0.093 | 0.039 | 0.016 | −0.027 | 0.041 | 0.508 | −0.048 | 0.098 | 0.622 |
| Year 1994 | −0.070 | 0.038 | 0.070 | −0.014 | 0.041 | 0.737 | −0.019 | 0.141 | 0.895 |
| Year 1995 | −0.090 | 0.039 | 0.021 | −0.020 | 0.042 | 0.635 | −0.044 | 0.185 | 0.813 |
| Year 1996 | −0.194 | 0.038 | 0.000 | −0.126 | 0.042 | 0.002 | −0.144 | 0.228 | 0.527 |
| Year 1997 | −0.284 | 0.038 | 0.000 | −0.207 | 0.041 | 0.000 | −0.203 | 0.273 | 0.457 |
| Year 1998 | −0.291 | 0.037 | 0.000 | −0.200 | 0.041 | 0.000 | −0.217 | 0.318 | 0.496 |
| Year 1999 | −0.241 | 0.036 | 0.000 | −0.171 | 0.042 | 0.000 | −0.206 | 0.362 | 0.569 |
| Constant | 2.831 | 0.031 | 0.000 | 2.856 | 0.032 | 0.000 | 1.693 | 1.427 | 0.235 |
| Observations | | 24,671 | | | 24,671 | | | 24,075 | |
| Individuals | | 7,328 | | | 7,328 | | | 7,163 | |
| T | | $1 \leqslant T \leqslant 9$ | | | $1 \leqslant T \leqslant 9$ | | | $1 \leqslant T \leqslant 9$ | |

The test statistic, distributed $\chi^2$ with degrees of freedom equal to the number of coefficients (here, nine), equals 55.15. This strongly rejects the null hypothesis that the coefficients do not differ statistically and suggests violation of the key random-effects assumption. Consequently, we prefer the fixed-effects estimator.

The third set of estimates of (1) reported in Table 3.2 continues with the fixed-effects estimator but adds to the year indicators six additional control variables: *Education, Age, Income, Union, Manufacturing* and *Sector Unemployment.* The main result is that *FDI Presence* continues to be positively correlated with *Insecurity*. The size and statistical significance of this correlation is virtually unchanged from that in our second specification. Results for the control variables are also of interest. Respondents tend to be more insecure who are more educated, in households with lower income, in unions, or working in sectors with higher unemployment.

The impact of unemployment rates seems straightforward. The result for education may reflect the "aspiration effect" documented in previous studies of job satisfaction: more educated workers tend to "expect more" from all aspects of their jobs, perhaps including job security. The negative correlation between *Insecurity* and *Income* may reflect two influences: individuals may be less concerned about prospective job losses if higher household income offers some insurance, or if they believe their income compensates for those risks. And the union-membership effect may be due to unionized workers having more information about prospective job losses than their non-unionized counterparts. Finally, note that this specification shows no correlation between worker insecurity and either age or working in manufacturing and also that the precision of estimates on all year indicators has fallen below standard significance levels.

To assess the substantive impact of forces shaping worker insecurity, we calculate an "average" effect for each regressor by multiplying each coefficient estimate by each variable's sample variation. We do not, however, want to use the sample variation reported in the summary statistics of Table 3.1. This is because the year-by-year standard deviations in Table 3.1 reflect variation across individuals at each point in time, whereas our fixed-effects estimates in Table 3.2 reflect variation within individuals across time. Consequently, for the estimation subsample in our final specification of Table 3.2, we decomposed the total variation in each regressor of interest into one part reflecting variation within years across individuals and the other part reflecting variation within individuals over time. For each regressor we then multiplied the standard deviation of the latter by the related coefficient estimate to calculate the impact of one-standard-deviation change in each regressor on the reported values for *Insecurity*.

These calculations indicate that a one-standard-deviation increase in *FDI Presence* translates into a 0.027 increase in *Insecurity*. This amount is larger than the increases in *Insecurity* stemming from one-standard-deviation changes in *Union* (0.018), *Education* (0.017), or *Income* (0.016),

*Table 3.3* Panel analysis of economic insecurity with alternative measures of FDI exposure, 1991–1999

| *Regressor* | *Fixed effects* | *Fixed effects* | *Fixed effects* | *Fixed effects* |
|---|---|---|---|---|
| FDI total share | 0.042 | 0.041 | | |
| | (0.020) | (0.020) | | |
| | 0.034 | 0.043 | | |
| FDI inward share | | | 0.159 | 0.153 |
| | | | (0.050) | (0.052) |
| | | | 0.002 | 0.004 |
| Year dummies | Yes | Yes | Yes | Yes |
| Control variables | No | Yes | No | Yes |
| Observations | 24,662 | 24,066 | 24,662 | 24,066 |
| Individuals | 7,325 | 7,160 | 7,325 | 7,160 |
| T | 1≤T≤9 | 1≤T≤9 | 1≤T≤9 | 1≤T≤9 |

Note
Each cell reports the coefficient estimate; in parentheses, its standard error; and its p-value.

and is exceeded only by the *Insecurity* increase correlated with *Sector Unemployment* (0.058). We think that *Sector Unemployment* is driven mainly by business-cycle fluctuations and thus that among our remaining "structural" controls, FDI exposure appears to be the substantively most important determinant of worker perceptions of job insecurity.

What do we conclude from Table 3.2? Holding other factors constant, individuals employed in FDI sectors systematically report less satisfaction with their job security. This is strongly consistent with the hypothesis that FDI exposure generates economic insecurity in workers. To verify this central conclusion, we now turn to a number of robustness checks.

### *Robustness checks*

Our first check was for robustness to alternative measures of FDI exposure. Table 3.3 replicates our fixed-effects specifications of Table 3.2 but replaces *FDI Presence* first with *FDI Total Share* in columns 1 and 2 and then with *FDI Inward Share* in columns 3 and 4. In columns 1 and 3 the $Z_{it}$ vector includes just year indicators; columns 2 and 4 add the six additional controls from Table 3.2. Both estimated coefficients on *FDI Total Share* are approximately 0.04 with a standard error of 0.02. Similarly, both estimated coefficients on *FDI Inward Share* (which, recall, may be the preferred to *FDI Total Share*) are approximately 0.15 with a standard error of 0.05. Thus, we again find a positive and statistically significant correlation between FDI exposure and perceptions of economic insecurity.

Next, we evaluated the sensitivity of our results to alternative approaches to accounting for persistence in panel data. Modeling individual-specific effects is one way of accounting for this correlation. But this approach does not allow us to differentiate between the idea that persistence in observations of insecurity is accounted for by the influence of past experiences of insecurity on present perceptions and the alternative idea that certain individuals just have unobserved characteristics that lead them to have certain types of perceptions (Green and Yoon 2002; Wawro 2002). To make this assessment, it is necessary to add a lag of the dependent variable to the right-hand side of equation (1).

A lagged dependent variable is obviously correlated with the individual-specific effects; consequently, this specification cannot be estimated via random effects. Moreover, the fixed-effects estimator is also biased and inconsistent in the presence of a lagged dependent variable when, as in our data, the number of periods is small. There are a number of alternative estimators for this situation, some of which first-difference the data to deal with individual-specific effects and then use instrumental variables to address the correlation between the error term and lagged dependent variable generated by differencing (see Wawro 2002). We use the Arellano-Bond generalized method-of-moments estimator.

The first three columns of Table 3.4 report results for this estimator, which adds a lag of the dependent variable to our econometric model of economic insecurity. In comparing these results with those earlier, note that the number of individuals and total observations has significantly declined. First differencing, and the use of lagged instruments, results in the loss of the 1991 and 1992 data altogether. It also means that individuals must be retained in the panel for three years to be included in the analysis.

The estimated coefficient on the lagged dependent variable is 0.198 with a standard error of 0.021. This suggests that past shocks to individual perceptions of economic insecurity do affect current perceptions, above and beyond the influence of individual-specific characteristics, though the magnitude of this effect is not large. The estimated $\beta$ is 0.107 with a standard error of 0.051. This estimate divided by one minus the coefficient estimate on the lagged dependent variable yields the *long-run* effect of FDI exposure on economic insecurity. This long-run impact is 0.133, which is approximately the same magnitude as the analogous fixed-effects estimates in Table 3.2, and it is statistically significant at the 0.05 level. We regard this to be a quite rigorous test of our central hypothesis. A significant correlation between exposure to FDI and perceptions of economic insecurity remains conditional on controls for individual heterogeneity, for the persistence of perceptions of economic insecurity, and for year-to-year shocks in insecurity.

To assess the validity of these results, we conducted three diagnostic tests recommended by Arellano and Bond (1991).[13] Consistency of their estimator requires the errors to be serially uncorrelated, in which case first-differenced residuals should display negative first-order serial correlation but not second-order serial correlation. The z-value for the hypothesis

*Table 3.4* Dynamic panel analysis of economic insecurity, 1993–1999

| | *Arellano-Bond* | | | *Arellano-Bond with instruments for FDI* | | | *Arellano-Bond with instruments for FDI* | | |
|---|---|---|---|---|---|---|---|---|---|
| *Regressor* | *Coef.* | *S.E.* | *p-value* | *Coef.* | *S.E.* | *p-value* | *Coef.* | *S.E.* | *p-value* |
| Δ Insecurity$_{(t-1)}$ | 0.198 | 0.021 | 0.000 | 0.231 | 0.016 | 0.000 | 0.231 | 0.016 | 0.000 |
| ΔΔ FDI presence | 0.107 | 0.051 | 0.037 | 0.266 | 0.181 | 0.142 | 0.281 | 0.195 | 0.150 |
| ΔΔ Education | | | | | | | −0.045 | 0.085 | 0.593 |
| ΔΔ Age | | | | | | | −0.039 | 0.059 | 0.509 |
| ΔΔ Income | | | | | | | 0.001 | 0.001 | 0.353 |
| ΔΔ Union | | | | | | | 0.150 | 0.082 | 0.068 |
| ΔΔ Manufacturing | | | | | | | −0.042 | 0.132 | 0.750 |
| ΔΔ Sector unemployment | | | | | | | 0.210 | 1.083 | 0.846 |
| Δ Year 1993 | −0.091 | 0.041 | 0.027 | −0.118 | 0.052 | 0.023 | −0.120 | 0.055 | 0.029 |
| Δ Year 1994 | −0.043 | 0.042 | 0.310 | −0.059 | 0.046 | 0.200 | −0.054 | 0.047 | 0.250 |
| Δ Year 1995 | −0.003 | 0.041 | 0.949 | −0.019 | 0.044 | 0.666 | −0.014 | 0.044 | 0.747 |
| Δ Year 1996 | −0.087 | 0.039 | 0.026 | −0.110 | 0.042 | 0.009 | −0.103 | 0.043 | 0.016 |
| Δ Year 1997 | −0.173 | 0.036 | 0.000 | −0.188 | 0.038 | 0.000 | −0.175 | 0.038 | 0.000 |
| Δ Year 1998 | −0.092 | 0.033 | 0.005 | −0.099 | 0.034 | 0.004 | −0.084 | 0.034 | 0.015 |
| Constant | −0.026 | 0.009 | 0.003 | −0.033 | 0.011 | 0.002 | 0.005 | 0.060 | 0.930 |
| Observations | | 13,397 | | | 13,397 | | | 13,178 | |
| Individuals | | 3,785 | | | 3,785 | | | 3,735 | |
| T | | $1 \leq T \leq 7$ | | | $1 \leq T \leq 7$ | | | $1 \leq T \leq 7$ | |

test under the null hypothesis of no first-order autocorrelation is −20.45, suggesting rejection of this null. The z-value for the hypothesis test under the null hypothesis of no second-order autocorrelation is 1.15, suggesting retention of this null. These two test results are consistent with the assumptions of the Arellano-Bond estimator.

Arellano and Bond (1991) also develop a Sargan test that helps further assess whether the assumptions about serial correlation hold. The null hypothesis of this test is that the model's overidentifying restrictions are valid; rejection of the null suggests the need to respecify the model. The test statistic, distributed $\chi^2$ with 27 degrees of freedom, equals 29.75, indicating that we do not have evidence to reject the null hypothesis that the overidentifying restrictions are valid. Overall, none of the three diagnostic tests raises significant concerns about the basic assumptions required for valid implementation of the Arellano-Bond estimator as in Table 3.4.

A third important robustness issue is the possibility of estimation bias due to endogeneity and/or measurement error. On endogeneity, it might be argued that individual FDI exposure is not strictly exogenous because individuals may choose their industry of employment based (at least partly) on their perceptions of economic insecurity. Less-secure risk-averse workers might choose not to work in FDI-exposed sectors, while risk-loving workers might choose the opposite. On measurement error, it might be argued that all of our FDI regressors are imperfect measures of the underlying economic concept of interest, labor-market riskiness linked to multinationals.

The endogeneity of worker industry choice is certainly a possibility. That said, in our panel a substantial proportion of changes over time in individual FDI exposure arise from changes in industry FDI status, which are clearly exogenous relative to individual perceptions, rather than from changes in individual industry of employment. Moreover, to the extent that people do switch industries endogenously, this should bias the coefficient on FDI exposure down, away from our hypothesized positive effect. These considerations mean that our results reported thus far may *underestimate* the effect of FDI exposure on perceptions of economic insecurity.

Nonetheless, both to relax the strict exogeneity assumption and to address measurement concerns, we used the panel structure of the data by allowing previous errors (i.e. unforecasted realizations of *Insecurity*) to influence future changes in *FDI Presence*. The model estimated is the same dynamic panel as in the first part of Table 3.4, but now *FDI Presence* is instrumented for using its lagged levels and changes in the same way that the Arellano-Bond estimator instruments for lagged *Insecurity*. This approach accounts for potential endogeneity, and it also yields consistent estimates on *FDI Presence* in the case of random measurement error.

The results of this analysis are reported in the balance of Table 3.4 for specifications with and without a full set of control variables. As expected, the coefficient estimate on *FDI Presence* is substantially larger than in the first part of Table 3.4: the implied long-run effect is now 0.35, well over twice as large as before. The standard error is also now larger, but the coefficient estimate is still significant at the 0.15 level. One method for evaluating whether relaxing the strict exogeneity assumption is warranted is to compare the p-value of the Sargan test across specifications. For the three sets of estimates in Table 3.4 the p-values are essentially identical, which yields little information on the value of instrumenting. Based on these results and our related discussion, we conclude that endogeneity and measurement error are not serious problems for the key finding that FDI exposure influences perceptions of economic insecurity.[14]

A fourth important robustness issue we considered was specification choice and potential omitted-variable bias. Tables 3.2 through 3.4 include as controls time-constant person-specific factors as well as a core set of six additional regressors. We verified that our FDI-insecurity correlation of interest maintained for specifications including other possible controls. We investigated a number of other possibilities including industry unionization rates and possible measures of "deindustrialization" (proxied with changes in absolute or relative levels of industry employment or sales). Including these variables did not substantially change our results, nor were these variables significantly correlated with the dependent variable *Insecurity*.

A fifth and final robustness check we mention is sensitivity to estimation sample. Our core results are for a sample of private-sector, full-time, not-self-employed workers: the labor-market participants for which the theoretical framework most directly applies. Our FDI-insecurity correlation of interest was maintained in estimates of key specifications using broader samples.

## Conclusion

A central question in political and academic debates about international economic integration is whether globalization increases worker insecurity. Previous empirical research has focused on whether one particular component of globalization, international trade, generates economic volatility. The findings in this research have been mixed. In this chapter, we argue that FDI by multinational enterprises is an important aspect of globalization generating worker insecurity. FDI gives firms greater access to foreign factors of production, and thus greater ease of substitution away from workers in any particular location. As a result, workers feel more insecure. Stated in terms of the underlying labor economics, the central idea is that FDI by MNEs increases firms' elasticity of demand for labor. More elastic labor demands, in turn, raise the volatility of wages and employment, all of which tends to make workers feel more insecure.

The chapter provides the first empirical test at the individual level of the relationship between the multinationalization of production and the economic insecurity of workers. Our analysis of panel data from the UK over the 1990s finds that FDI activity in the industries in which individuals work is positively correlated with individual perceptions of economic insecurity. This relationship holds even in fixed-effects specifications for which only variation within rather than across respondents is used to estimate the correlation between exposure to FDI and perceptions of insecurity.

We regard these individual-level panel results as the first valid evidence consistent with a causal relationship between FDI and worker insecurity. While the role of trade in increasing worker insecurity remains an open question, our findings establish a clear link between international economic integration – through the mechanism of FDI – and insecurity.

Our use of UK data offers some important advantages. The key idea of MNEs raising worker insecurity via labor-demand elasticities assumes both cross-country FDI mobility and competitive labor markets. With its high degree of FDI inflows and outflows and relatively flexible labor markets, the UK closely matches this theoretical framework. Moreover, publicly available UK data allowed us to create a dataset with key ingredients including individual measures of economic insecurity over many years, industry of employment, and FDI exposure for those industries. In countries with less flexible labor markets, increases in labor-demand elasticities from increases in FDI might not alter the employment risks facing workers. Understanding how national labor-market institutions mediate the link from FDI to worker insecurity seems a fruitful agenda for future research.

Our findings have significant implications for the politics of globalization and for the determinants of welfare-state policymaking. On the politics of globalization, our findings extend existing explanations for public backlash against globalization in advanced economies. This literature suggests that the backlash is not purely a constructed phenomenon and that the labor-market consequences of liberalization affect policy opinions. Individuals whose real and/or relative wages are lowered by liberalization are likely to have more skeptical opinions (Gabel 1998; Mayda and Rodrik 2001; O'Rourke and Sinnott 2001; Scheve and Slaughter 2001a, 2001b, forthcoming). These labor-market arguments, however, largely focus on the relationship between globalization and the level and distribution of earnings.

In contrast, the approach of our article recognizes that risk-averse workers care about the volatility of their earnings, in addition to their level – in particular, volatility from the risk of unemployment. These concerns about volatility are likely to help shape opinions about economic integration (see also Hays *et al.* 2002).

In broadening the focus of labor-market concerns from just earnings levels to earnings volatility, we note that our findings suggest possible ambivalence in policy attitudes towards FDI. On the one hand, multinationals tend to pay higher wages. But as this article has analyzed, on the other hand multinationals also tend to have more elastic labor demands.

Indeed, the higher wages may be a compensating differential for the riskier outcomes. Higher wages should tend to make workers favor policies to attract FDI, but riskier employment should pull in the opposite direction. We regard this tension to be an important issue in any research attempting to explain the politics of foreign-investment policies in advanced economies.

On the welfare state, our research provides compelling individual-level evidence of a link between globalization and perceptions of worker insecurity. It is left for future research to determine whether there is, in turn, a link from increased insecurity to greater demand for social insurance. Nevertheless, our findings are critical to this debate because they provide strong evidence for the premise of the argument connecting globalization to worker demands for social insurance – that is, that international economic integration raises worker insecurity. Moreover, if globalization limits the capacities of governments to provide social insurance, or is perceived to do so, then individuals may worry further about globalization and this effect is likely to be magnified by increased labor-market risks from global integration.

## Notes

1 This chapter was first published in *American Journal of Political Science*, 48/4/:662–74, (October 2004). For financial support we thank the National Science Foundation for award #SES-0213671, the Yale Center for the Study of Globalization, the Carnegie Corporation's Globalization and Self-Determination Project at the Yale Center for International and Area Studies, the Leitner Program in International Political Economy, and the Institution for Social and Policy Studies. For very helpful data assistance we thank Simon Harrington at the UK Office of National Statistics and Ralf Martin. For helpful comments and discussion we thank Chris Anderson, Samuel Bowles, José Cheibub, Rafaela Dancygier, Keith Darden, Esther Duflo, Jonathan Haskel, Michael Hiscox, Hyeok Kwon, Lisa Martin, Fredrik Sjoholm, Mike Tomz, Michael Wallerstein, three anonymous reviewers, the editors and seminar participants at Binghamton University, Cornell University, Duke University, the Santa Fe Institute, the University of Michigan and the University of Nottingham.

2 It is important to note that there is now a large body of evidence that labor-market volatility has been rising in many countries, especially in the 1990s, in terms of greater earnings volatility, declining job tenure and self-reports. Gottschalk and Moffitt (1994) report substantial increases in year-to-year earnings volatility for the United States over the 1970s and 1980s. Looking at the 1990s as well, a symposium issue of the *Journal of Labor Economics* (1999) documented declines in US job stability, especially in the 1990s for large groups of workers such as those with more tenure. Within that symposium issue, Schmidt's (1999) analysis of individual surveys finds that US workers in the 1990s were more pessimistic about losing their jobs than they were during the 1980s – despite the ongoing economic expansion of the 1990s.

3 There are several recent empirical studies documenting that MNEs and FDI do increase labor-demand elasticities through the substitution effect. Slaughter (2001) estimates that demand for US production labor in manufacturing became more elastic from 1960 to the early 1990s and that these increases were

correlated with FDI outflows by US-headquartered MNEs. Fabbri *et al.* (2003) estimate that both UK-multinational plants and foreign-owned plants each had larger increases than did UK domestic plants in the elasticity of demand for production labor in manufacturing over 1973–1992. An important margin on which MNEs may affect elasticities is on the extensive margin of plant shutdowns. MNEs may be more likely than domestic firms to respond to shocks by closing entire plants. For the manufacturing sectors in at least three countries it has now been shown that plants that are part of an MNE are more likely to close than are their purely domestic counterparts: the UK (Fabbri *et al.* 2003); the US (Bernard and Jensen 2002); and Ireland (Gorg and Strobl 2003).

4 Doms and Jensen (1998) document that for US manufacturing plants in 1987, multinational wages exceeded domestically owned wages by a range of 5–15 percent, with larger differentials for production workers rather than non-production workers. Griffith (1999) presents similar evidence for the UK; Globerman *et al.* (1994) for Canada; Aitken *et al.* (1996) for Mexico and Venezuela; and Te Velde and Morrissey (2001) for five African countries.

5 The BHPS is ongoing, but our data are through 1999 only.

6 For his assistance in generating this data, we thank Simon Harrington.

7 The BHPS records industry of employment according to the SIC80 classification scheme in all years but does report this information according to the SIC92 system in two of the years in our sample.

8 Of course, this is only a theoretical possibility. Even if we had firm-level FDI data, it would not be usable because the BHPS does not report the respondent's firm.

9 Our focus on industries as a relevant aggregate for labor-market effects is also consistent with many empirical findings in the labor-economics literature. For example, a common finding in studies of profit-sharing is that wage-bargaining keys off of industry profits above and beyond firm considerations. Of course, over longer time horizons than we consider in this article, workers could be assumed to be facing an economy-wide labor demand curve.

10 Annual household income is a variable calculated by the BHPS to include income from all sources in the 12 months prior to the September of the survey year, as virtually all of the fieldwork for each survey year is done from September to December.

11 For example, category one indicates no qualifications or still in school and no qualifications, while category four includes teaching qualifications, first degree or higher degree.

12 These data were obtained directly from the ONS and are based on its Labour Force Survey.

13 Following Arellano and Bond (1991), we report coefficient estimates based on their one-step estimator with robust standard errors and diagnostics based on their two-step estimator.

14 For measurement error, we also investigated whether small changes in the industry-by-industry coding of the *FDI* variable had any effect on its coefficient estimates. For example, we reestimated all tables when agriculture and mining industries were not included as possible FDI-exposed industries. All changes we investigated had minimal impact on our core results.

## References

Aitken, B., Harrison, A. and Lipsey, R. E. (1996) "Wages and Foreign Ownership: A Comparative Study of Mexico, Venezuela, and the United States," *Journal of International Economics*, 40/3–4: 345–71.

Anderson, C. and Pontusson, J. (2001) "Welfare States and Employment

Insecurity: A Cross-National Analysis of 15 OECD Countries," presented at the annual meetings of the American Political Science Association.

Arellano, M. and Bond, S. (1991) "Some Tests of Specification for Panel Data: Monte Carlo Evidence and an Application to Employment Equations," *Review of Economic Studies*, 58/2: 277–97.

Bernard, A. B. and Jensen, J. B. (2002) "The Death of Manufacturing Plants," *National Bureau of Economic Research Working Paper*, No. 9026.

Boix, C. (forthcoming) "Between Protectionism and Compensation: The Political Economy of Trade," in P. Bardhan, S. Bowles and M. Wallerstein (eds) *Globalization and Egalitarian Redistribution*, Princeton: Princeton University Press.

Bordo, M., Eichengreen, B. and Irwin, D. (1999) "Is Globalization Today Really Different from Globalization a Hundred Years Ago?" in D. Rodrik and S. Collins (eds) *Brookings Trade Forum 1999*, Washington: Brookings Institution Press, 1–50.

Burgoon, B. (2001) "Globalization and Welfare Compensation: Disentangling the Ties that Bind," *International Organization*, 55/3: 509–51.

Cameron, D. (1978) "The Expansion of the Public Economy: A Comparative Analysis," *American Political Science Review*, 72/4: 1243–61.

Dominitz, J. and Manski, C. F. (1997) "Perceptions of Economic Insecurity," *Public Opinion Quarterly*, 61/2: 261–87.

Doms, M. E. and Jensen, J. B. (1998) "Comparing Wages, Skills, and Productivity Between Domestically and Foreign-Owned Manufacturing Establishments in the United States," in R. Baldwin, R. Lipsey and J. Richardson (eds) *Geography and Ownership as Bases for Economic Accounting*, Chicago: University of Chicago Press, 235–55.

Fabbri, F., Haskel, J. E. and Slaughter, M. J. (2003) "Does Nationality of Ownership Matter for Labor Demands?," *Journal of European Economic Association*, 1/2: 698–707.

Gabel, M. (1998) "Economic Integration and Mass Politics: Market Liberalization and Public Attitudes in the European Union," *American Journal of Political Science*, 42/3: 936–53.

Garrett, G. (1998) *Partisan Politics in the Global Economy*. Cambridge: Cambridge University Press.

Globerman, S., Ries, J. and Vertinsky, I. (1994) "The Economic Performance of Foreign Affiliates in Canada," *Canadian Journal of Economics*, 27/1: 143–56.

Gorg, H. and Strobl, E. (2003) "Footloose Multinationals?" *The Manchester School*, 71/1: 1–18.

Gottschalk, P. and Moffitt, R. (1994) "The Growth of Earnings Instability in the U.S. Labor Market," *Brookings Papers on Economic Activity 2*, Washington: Brookings Institution, 217–54.

Green, D. P. and Yoon, D. H. (2002) "Reconciling Individual and Aggregate Evidence Concerning Partisan Stability: Applying Time-Series Models to Panel Survey Data," *Political Analysis*, 10/1: 1–24.

Griffith, R. (1999) "Using the ARD Establishment Level Data to Look at Foreign Ownership and Productivity in the U.K.," *Economic Journal*, 109/June: F416–42.

Hays, J., Ehrlich, S. and Peinhardt, C. (2002) "Globalization, the Size of Government, and Labor Market Institutions: Maintaining Support for Openness among Workers," presented at the annual meeting of the Midwest Political Science Association.

Helpman, E. (1984) "A Simple Theory of International Trade with Multinational Corporations," *Journal of Political Economy*, 92/3: 451–71.

Iversen, T. and Cusack, T. (2000) "The Causes of Welfare State Expansion," *World Politics*, 52/April: 313–49.

*Journal of Labor Economics* (1999) Symposium Issue on "Changes in Job Stability and Job Security," 17/4, Part 2.

Mayda, A. M. and Rodrik, D. (2002) "Why Are Some People (and Countries) More Protectionist Than Others?," *National Bureau of Economic Research Working Paper*, No. 8461.

Mughan, A. and Lacy, D. (2002) "Economic Performance, Job Insecurity, and Electoral Choice," *British Journal of Political Science*, 32/3: 513–33.

O'Rourke, K. and Sinnott, R. (2001) "The Determinants of Individual Trade Policy Preferences: International Survey Evidence," *Brookings Trade Forum: 2001*, Washington: Brookings, 157–206.

Rodrik, D. (1997) *Has Globalization Gone Too Far?*, Washington: Institute for International Economics.

—— (1998) "Why Do More Open Economies Have Bigger Governments?" *Journal of Political Economy*, 106/5: 997–1032.

Scheve, K. F. and Slaughter, M. J. (2001a) "What Determines Individual Trade-Policy Preferences," *Journal of International Economics*, 54/2: 267–92.

—— (2001b) "Labor-Market Competition and Individual Preferences Over Immigration Policy," *Review of Economics and Statistics*, 83/1: 133–45.

—— (forthcoming) "Public Opinion, International Integration, and the Welfare State," in P. Bardhan, S. Bowles and M. Wallerstein (eds) *Globalization and Egalitarian Redistribution*, Princeton: Princeton University Press.

Schmidt, S. R. (1999) "Long-Run Trends in Workers' Beliefs about Their Own Job Security: Evidence from the General Social Survey," *Journal of Labor Economics*, 17/4: S127–S141.

Slaughter, M. J. (2001) "International Trade and Labor-Demand Elasticities," *Journal of International Economics*, 54/1: 27–56.

Te Velde, D. W. and Morrissey, O. (2001) "Foreign Ownership and Wages: Evidence from Five African Countries," CREDIT Discussion Paper.

United Nations Conference on Trade and Development (2001) *World Investment Report: Promoting Linkages*, New York: United Nations.

Wawro, G. (2002) "Estimating Dynamic Panel Data Models in Political Science," *Political Analysis*, 10/1: 25–48.

# Part II

# More threats from the outside

## International economic institutions and national autonomy

# 4 The International Monetary Fund and the global spread of privatization

*Nancy Brune, Geoffrey Garrett and Bruce Kogut*[1]

The sale of state-owned assets – privatization – has been a defining characteristic of the global economy in the last two decades of the twentieth century. More than 8,000 acts of privatization were completed around the world between 1985 and 1999 (Brune 2003).[2] These sales were valued at more than $1.1 trillion (in constant 1985 US dollars). After an initial large spike in 1987 (when almost US$120 billion in state-owned assets were sold in only 77 transactions, mostly by Organization for Economic Cooperation and Development (OECD) countries), privatization swept the globe in the 1990s (see Figure 4.1). From an average of roughly US$50 billion per year (on 500–1,000 transactions) in the early 1990s, revenues from global privatizations grew to US$87 billion on more than 1,700 transactions by 1995, peaking in 1998 at US$171 billion of assets sold in 2,500 transactions. Although almost two-thirds of the privatization activity in terms of revenues took place in high-income countries, the bulk of privatization transactions occurred in low- and middle-income countries (see Table 4.1).

Appendix 4.1 presents country-level data for 1985 to 1999. Privatization revenues exceeded US$100 billion (in 1985 dollars) in Italy, Japan and the United Kingdom, and over US$50 billion in Australia, Brazil and France. Relative to their GDPs, the five largest privatizers were Bolivia, Guyana, Hungary, Panama and Portugal, each of which had sold state-owned assets worth more than 30 percent of their 1985 GDPs by 1999. Privatization revenues exceeded 25 percent of 1985 GDP in another four countries – Australia, Chile, Malaysia and New Zealand. By 1999, total revenues from privatization exceeded 5 percent of 1985 GDP in 60 countries.

What explains the spread of privatization around the world? In most economic theories, privatization increases productivity, efficiency and output. Even though the empirical evidence is somewhat mixed, most economists continue to support privatization. But if it is efficient to sell off state-owned assets, why have we observed dramatic variations among countries in the extent and pace of privatization? Were countries more likely to privatize if they had large state-owned sectors initially, or if they confronted economic crises, or for other reasons?

In this chapter we concentrate on the impact of lending by

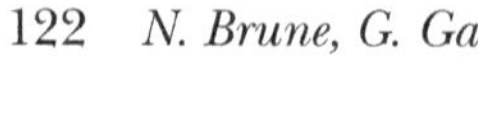

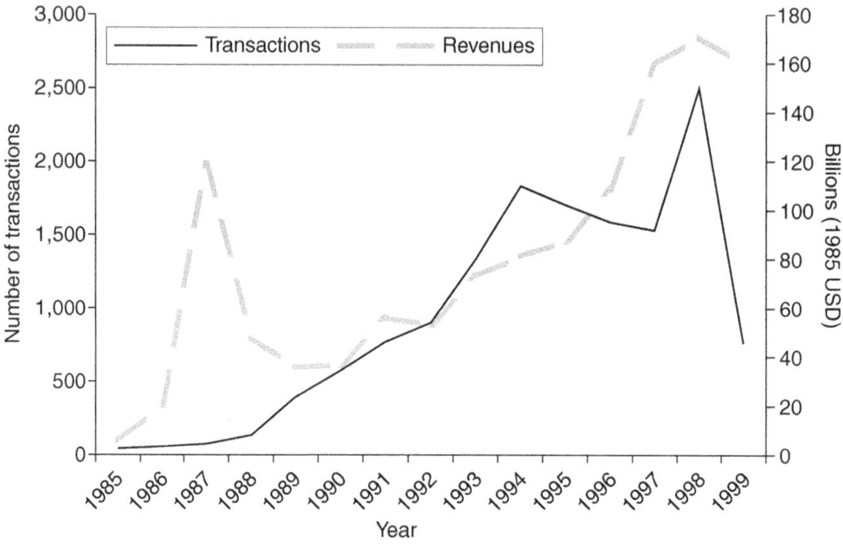

*Figure 4.1* Privatization over time.

international financial institutions, both the IMF and World Bank, on privatization around the world. We demonstrate that countries that borrowed from the IMF subsequently privatized more assets (in terms of market valuations at the time of sale), controlling for the effects of the initial size of the state-owned sector, fiscal imbalances, per capita income, the depth of capital markets, and the quality of government. Indeed, we estimate that for every dollar a country owed the IMF, it subsequently privatized assets worth approximately 50 cents. In contrast, World Bank loans were not significantly associated with increased privatizations revenues, though there was no evidence that countries with loans from the World Bank privatized less.

Two interpretations are consistent with these results. On the one hand, IMF conditionality (which is generally considered to be more constraining than that imposed by the World Bank) could have forced recipient governments to privatize more state-owned assets (in terms of volume). On the other hand, global capital markets could have valued more highly the sale of (a given volume of) state assets in countries that received assistance from the IMF as a result of the increased credibility of commitments to market-promoting policies in these countries. We cannot easily distinguish between the conditionality and credibility interpretations because it is extremely difficult to isolate the volume of privatized assets independently from their valuation. Our results show that IMF conditionality was associated both with higher privatization revenues and with more privatization transactions, but the revenues' effects were stronger and very robust.

*Table 4.1* Privatization by region and per capita income, 1985–1999

| | *Revenues (billions, 1985 US$)* | *Average revenues (% 1985 GDP, unweighted)* | *Transactions* | *Average revenues per transaction (millions, 1985 US$)* |
|---|---|---|---|---|
| *By region* | | | | |
| East Asia and the Pacific | 318.0 | 13.3 | 831 | 382.7 |
| Eastern Europe and Central Asia | 23.3 | 14.0 | 2,453 | 9.5 |
| Latin America and the Caribbean | 197.3 | 13.9 | 1,601 | 123.2 |
| Middle East and North Africa | 19.9 | 6.9 | 419 | 47.5 |
| North America and Western Europe | 522.2 | 8.9 | 871 | 599.5 |
| Southeast Asia | 11.4 | 5.2 | 335 | 34.1 |
| Sub-Saharan Africa | 9.5 | 5.4 | 1,662 | 5.7 |
| *By per capita income** | | | | |
| Low income | 62.0 | 8.4 | 2,782 | 22.3 |
| Middle income | 265.9 | 10.2 | 4,269 | 62.3 |
| High income | 773.7 | 9.9 | 1,121 | 690.2 |
| Total | 1,101.6 | 9.6 | 8,172 | 134.8 |

Source: Brune (2004).

Note
*Based on per capita GDP (atlas method) in 1980.

Thus, we subscribe to the credibility interpretation of our IMF effect over a simpler conditionality interpretation: the imposition of IMF conditions in a country won the approval of global capital markets for its privatization program (in a similar argument to that proposed by Perotti and van Oijen 2001).

## Privatization: efficiency or commitment?

Privatization is an economic policy whose cross-national spread has a familiar logistic S-shape. After the initial wave of sales of state-owned assets in Britain in the early 1980s (and earlier still in Chile), privatization programs began to emerge in other countries: at first in other OECD nations but then in developing and transition economies as well.[3]

Why did privatization spread in this fashion? There is some prima facie evidence that countries with larger state-owned sectors were also in economic difficulty in the early 1980s, particularly with respect to fiscal imbalances. It is plausible that they privatized in response to these problems. But the connection between economic distress and privatization presupposes that countries were confident that privatization would help their economies.

The evidence on this critical point, however, is mixed – particularly from studies completed before the mid-1990s. Research on early privatizations in the United Kingdom suggested that firm and sector performance improved only when privatization was coupled with the creation of truly competitive markets (Vickers and Yarrow 1988). Some cross-national studies subsequently found that privatization improved performance at the firm level (Galal *et al.* 1994; Galal and Shirley 1994; Megginson *et al.* 1994; Megginson and Netter 2001; Ramamurti 1996, 1997), but other studies disputed this conclusion (Bevan *et al.* 2001; Black *et al.* 2000). In an important recent article, Dewenter and Malatesta (2001) found that firms that were subsequently privatized performed better in the three years before they were sold off (as governments prepared them for sale) but that the performance of these firms once privatized was no better than that of other firms. But even if one were to accept Megginson and Netter's (2001) conclusion that privatization, on balance, has been good for firms and economies, it would still be important to note that the empirical evidence was not available to the governments that chose to privatize in the late 1980s and early 1990s. The lateness of empirical support for the benefits of privatization coupled with its relative weakness should caution against a rapid endorsement of a simple efficiency explanation for the spread of privatization in the past couple of decades.

In this chapter, we explore another potential causal path that does not require the assumption that privatization directly improves firm or sector performance. Governments in countries with economic problems, as well as high levels of state ownership, face a credibility problem. Even good firms will not attract sufficient funding because of political uncertainty.

Perotti and van Oijen (2001) argue that privatization provides the appropriate commitment technology to attract investors in the case of distressed economies. They present evidence that national credit ratings subsequently improved in countries that privatized significant state-owned assets.

If this line of argument is correct, privatization could still be beneficial to economies by attracting investment, even if it does not improve the efficiency of either privatized firms or the product markets in which they compete. There is, however, a chicken and egg problem in this privatization-credibility dynamic. Governments without strong credit ratings, particularly in emerging economies, are likely to be forced to privatize initially at discounted prices to attract investors, given the time needed for investors to gain confidence that governments are indeed credibly committed to pro-market reforms.

It is at this point that the international financial institutions (IFIs) may play a pivotal role. Both the IMF and the World Bank provide loans (and in the latter case, some grants as well) to developing countries, but they stipulate conditions for disbursement.[4] Since governments in developing countries often need IFI financing to stabilize their economies or fund their development programs, conditionality may generate credible commitments to the IFIs' agendas – at least to the extent that the IMF and the World Bank themselves are internationally credible market reformers. In turn, this credibility could increase future investors' confidence in buying shares in firms privatized in countries that owe money to the IMF or the World Bank.

IMF conditionality is generally considered to be much more binding than is the World Bank's. The Fund plays a strong role in monitoring and enforcing compliance, and failure to meet any specified condition often means that the next tranche of loans is not released. In contrast, World Bank performance criteria for loans are often not stated as quantitative targets, and punishment for failure to perform is rare (Polak 1994). It should also be noted that the Fund and World Bank do not stipulate cross-conditionality, whereby failure to meet a condition of one institution's loan constitutes suspension of the other institution's loans to that country.

Since 1997, the IMF has made information on its conditionality requirements publicly available. Recent agreements (letters of intent) confirm what was previously conjecture – namely, that for more than a decade, the IMF has included privatization as a standard condition of its structural adjustment lending (Davis *et al.* 2000). Insiders often attribute the birth of the idea of privatization conditionality to a speech by Secretary of State James Baker at the Seoul meetings of the IMF and World Bank in 1985 (Polak 1994). The idea quickly gained other adherents inside the Washington-based international policy community beltway so much so that John Williamson (1993) included privatization among the policies in the Washington Consensus between the US Treasury and the IFIs in the late 1980s and early 1990s.[5]

It is not clear whether the IFIs' efforts to condition financing on privatization and other reforms has improved macroeconomic performance. Przeworski and Vreeland (Przeworski and Vreeland 2000; Vreeland 2003) recently found that participation in IMF loan programs actually reduced national economic growth, even after selection bias among slow-growth countries was taken into account. Using a similar methodology, Abouharb (2001) argued that World Bank loans have had no discernible impact on growth rates in recipient countries.

As we have suggested, the case for privatization need not rest upon direct efficiency gains. The value of an acquisition or share purchase is influenced by expectations about the future, with respect both to economic performance (at the firm, sector and national levels) and to government policy (regulation, taxes, nationalization etc.). Participation in IFI programs may signal that a country is credibly committed to economic reforms from which asset holders will benefit. If a country privatizes when it is subject to an IFI program, investors may be more likely to buy shares in state assets that are sold and to pay a higher price for them, expecting that government policy will be more market friendly.

Recent studies have explored the effect of IFI lending on capital flows. Bird and Rowlands (1997) find limited support for the argument that IMF lending has a catalytic effect on capital flows in general. Mody and Saravia (2003), however, claim that the IMF does have a catalytic effect but only when country conditions (debt and reserve ratios) are such that the IMF has a credible influence on policies. In this chapter, we extend the inquiry by exploring whether there is a more focused effect of IMF (and World Bank) lending on privatization.

## The data

### *Data sources*

The privatization data used in this chapter are derived from the Global Privatization Database (GPD) (Brune 2004). Almost half of the privatization transactions in GPD were originally reported in the World Bank Privatization Database (WBPD) (2000) on developing countries.[6] Three other published sources were used to compile GPD: the World Bank Private Participation in Infrastructure Database (PPID) (2000) for developing countries; the World Bank African Privatization Database (WBAPD) (2002); and the Thomson Financial IFR Platinum Privatization International Database (PID) (1999) focusing on high and upper middle-income countries. GPD also includes almost 6,000 transactions derived from a variety of other sources, including government documents, international organizations, academic journals, newspapers, industry and consulting reports, and other previously published volumes on privatization.[7]

We analyze annual observations on privatizations from 1985 to 1999 in

96 countries for which all relevant data are available (see Appendix 4.1). Of these (both developing and developed) economies, 91 privatized assets during the analysis period.[8] We also include another five countries that did not privatize but for which all the other data are available (Bahamas, Botswana, Cyprus, Suriname and Syria). Our analysis draws on a much larger sample of countries than those used in other cross-national studies of privatization, such as Bortolotti *et al.* (1998, 2001) and Megginson *et al.* (1994).

The generic version of our estimated equations regressed privatization revenues (as a percentage of GDP) on the following variables: (the log of) per capita income; the size of the state-owned sector in 1980; the national budgetary balance; an index of the quality of government institutions; the presence of a functioning stock market; our variables measuring IFI obligations; and region and time dummies. We also use privatization transactions as a dependent variable in an effort to distinguish the market's valuation of a privatized asset (i.e. revenues derived from privatization) from the amount of assets privatized (transactions). But since the transactions measure counts equally – for example, the wholesale selling off of a national telecoms monopoly with the bit-by-bit sale (in tranches) of a small company – we concentrate on privatization revenues.

The initial extent of government ownership of the economy placed an upper limit on the amount of privatization a country could subsequently have undertaken. Hence we expect a positive coefficient on this parameter. Theoretically, the most desirable measure of the size of the state-owned sector is the share of GDP derived from state-owned enterprises. But these data are available for only a relatively small set of countries beginning in the late 1980s, and it is not clear precisely how these estimates were calculated. Instead, we rely on a simpler ordinal indicator (0–10) of the size of the state-owned sector from *Economic Freedom of the World*, which contains information on a large sample of developing and developed countries going back to the mid-1970s (Gwartney *et al.* 1996).[9]

It is commonly assumed that governments tend to privatize when they need to generate revenues to balance the public fiscal balance sheet. To test this argument, we include the central government's budget balance as a portion of GDP. Since positive scores denote fiscal surpluses, we expect the budget balance coefficients to be negative in the privatization regressions.

GDP per capita was included to control for the effects of a country's level of development on privatization revenues. Positive coefficients would imply that higher per capita incomes promoted privatization, perhaps because more developed countries were better equipped to undertake privatization. Negative parameter estimates would suggest that less developed countries had a greater need to privatize.

We explore arguments about development with some more fine-grained measures as well. It has been argued that countries with developed market-promoting institutions are more likely to privatize. To measure the overall quality of governance in a country, we use an index derived from a set of International Country Risk Guide indicators first employed by Knack and Keefer (1995): the sum of scores for corruption; bureaucratic quality; and the rule of law (all measured on a 0–10 scale, with higher scores reflecting better governance). We would expect estimated parameters for the government quality index to be positive.

Our analyses also control for whether a country had a functioning stock market (a 0–1 dummy variable). It is likely that privatized assets would be valued more highly in countries with well-functioning domestic capital markets that reduce information asymmetries and emphasize corporate governance (Holmström and Tirole 1993; Levine 1997). Controlling for these governance and market effects, we expect the residual impact of per capita income on privatization to be negative – because poorer countries have a greater need to privatize.

The central hypothesis we wish to test, however, is that countries that enter into binding relationships with international financial institutions (for whatever reason) subsequently privatize more state-owned assets. We use the outstanding level of financial obligations (relative to national GDP) to measure the strength of a country's relationships with the IFIs and hence the potential magnitude of the market credibility boost.

The IMF variable comprises repurchase obligations to the IMF for all uses of IMF resources (excluding those resulting from drawings on the reserve tranche), including credit tranches, enlarged access resources, all special facilities (the buffer stock, compensatory financing, extended fund and oil facilities), trust fund loans, and operations under the structural adjustment and enhanced structural adjustment facilities. The World Bank variable comprises all International Bank for Reconstruction and Development (IBRD) loans (at market rates) and International Development Association credits (at concessional rates).

We have hypothesized that the impact of the IFIs on privatization is increasing with the size of a country's obligations to them – especially for the IMF. Hence the coefficients on both IFI variables would be positive if the effect of conditionality has been to increase the sale of state-owned assets and market valuations of these sales.

### *Descriptive statistics*

Table 4.2 presents aggregate data on the financial impact of the IMF and World Bank on the developing (low- and middle-income, based on 1980 GDP per capita incomes) countries in this study between 1980 and 1999. High-income countries are not eligible for World Bank assistance, and none of the high-income countries in this study owed the IMF money in the 1980s and 1990s.

The top panel of Table 4.2 demonstrates the large role played by the

*Table 4.2* Developing countries and the IFIs, 1980–1999

| | *Outstanding IMF obligations (% of GDP each year)* | *Outstanding World Bank obligations (% of GDP each year)* |
|---|---|---|
| Low-income countries | 5.1 | 16.5 |
| Middle-income countries | 1.5 | 3.5 |
| All developing countries | 3.1 | 9.2 |
| *Top 10* | | |
| Zambia | 29.1 | 28.4 |
| Guyana | 26.1 | 30.6 |
| Jamaica | 12.7 | 13.5 |
| Gambia, The | 11.0 | 28.7 |
| Ghana | 9.7 | 22.4 |
| Uganda | 8.5 | 20.5 |
| Malawi | 7.5 | 50.4 |
| Congo, Dem. Rep. | 7.1 | 12.8 |
| Senegal | 7.0 | 17.0 |
| Togo | 6.2 | 27.3 |
| *Bottom 10* | | |
| Botswana | 0.0 | 5.3 |
| Syrian Arab Republic | 0.0 | 2.9 |
| Oman | 0.0 | 0.4 |
| Iran, Islamic Rep. | 0.0 | 0.3 |
| Malta | 0.0 | 0.0 |
| Bahamas, The | 0.0 | 0.0 |
| Greece | 0.0 | 0.0 |
| Ireland | 0.0 | 0.0 |
| Singapore | 0.0 | 0.0 |
| Suriname | 0.0 | 0.0 |
| IMF-World Bank correlation for all developing countries | | 0.58 |

Note
We present aggregate data on the financial impact of the IMF and World Bank on the developing (low- and middle-income) countries in this study over the period 1980–1999.

IFIs in the developing world. Over the 1980s and 1990s, low-income countries had outstanding obligations to the IMF and the World Bank that each year averaged 5.1 percent and 16.1 percent of GDP, respectively. The numbers were smaller for middle-income countries, but combined annual IMF and World Bank obligations constituted about one-eighth of GDP. In the developing world as a whole, outstanding loans from the World Bank were about three times as large in dollar terms as those from the IMF. However, since IMF conditionality was more constraining than the World Bank variant, it is possible that the impact on privatization of IMF obligations was greater than that of World Bank loans.

The middle panel of the table represents the ten countries with the largest outstanding obligations to the IMF in the last two decades. Zambia and Guyana each had outstanding IMF debt that averaged annually more than one-quarter of their GDP, whereas the amounts ranged between 6 percent and 13 percent per year for the other eight most heavily indebted countries. At the same time, countries with large IMF obligations invariably borrowed considerable sums from the World Bank as well. In the cases of Guyana and Zambia, IFI obligations constituted almost 60 percent of GDP each year during the 1980s and 1990s. Outstanding World Bank credit annually constituted fully one-half of Malawi's GDP in the same period. The other top ten IMF debtors owed the World Bank between 13 percent and 29 percent of their GDPs. Not surprisingly, eight of the countries in this top ten list were in sub-Saharan Africa.

The bottom panel lists the ten developing countries that were least dependent on the IFIs in the 1980s and 1990s. With the exception of residual unpaid debts from IMF programs in the 1970s in Botswana, Iran, Oman and Syria, these countries owed the IFIs no money in the 1980s and 1990s. Some of the countries on this list were not surprising. After all, by the end of the 1980s Greece, Ireland and Singapore were all high-income countries. The other seven nations were already classified as middle-income countries by 1980 and hence were less likely to receive IFI assistance than their low-income colleagues. In contrast to the biggest IMF and World Bank debtors, the bottom ten countries were dispersed across several continents.

In aggregate, there was a strong positive correlation ($r = 0.58$) between outstanding obligations to the two IFIs among all the developing countries in our dataset. Countries that owed the IMF more money were likely also to have larger lines of credit at the World Bank. This correlation, however, was far from perfect. Given the differences in the types of conditionality agreements written by the IMF and World Bank, it is important to analyze their effects on privatization separately.

### *Comparative cases*

Before moving to the multivariate statistics, it is useful to consider a paired comparison of the experiences of two countries to illustrate the plausibility of the broader relationship we propose between privatization and IFI lending. Ghana and Nigeria are low-income, non-democratic countries in West Africa with functioning stock markets. However, whereas Ghana was heavily dependent on IMF (and World Bank) lending – particularly in the late 1980s and early 1990s – Nigeria was much less so. Ghana was a successful and large privatizer in the latter 1990s; Nigeria was not (see Table 4.3).

In 1993, Ghana passed a privatization law and established the Divestiture Implementation Committee to oversee the sale of its state-owned assets. The country subsequently privatized food-manufacturing enterprises (related to cocoa, one of its primary exports), breweries, state-owned banks, and a minority stake in its state-owned telecommunications operator, Ghana Telecom. The lion's share of its privatization revenues

*Table 4.3* Ghana and Nigeria

| | *Average IMF obligations (1990–1999) as % of GDP* | *Privatization revenues (1990–1999) as % of 1985 GDP* | *Size of state-owned sector (1980)*[a] | *Deficit*[b] | *GDP per capita*[c] |
|---|---|---|---|---|---|
| Ghana | 9.3 | 21.6 | 10 | −1.5 | 379 |
| Partial list of major privatized enterprises: food manufacturing enterprises (cocoa), breweries (Achimota Brewery), Ashanti Goldfields Company, banking (Ghana Commercial Bank), telecommunications (Ghana Telecom – 30%). | | | | | |
| Nigeria | 0.0 | 4.2 | 10 | −5.1 | 257 |
| Partial list of major privatized enterprises: tourism (hotels), Nigerian National Petroleum Corporation, banking (First Bank of Nigeria, United Bank), cement (Ashaka, Benue), food manufacturing and production. | | | | | |

Notes

Both countries are low-income and nondemocratic and have functioning stock markets.

a Code for size of state-owned sector: 2 low, 4 low-medium, 6 medium, 8 medium-high, 10 high.

b Budget balance as share of GDP (1990–1999 average).

c GDP per capita (constant 1995 US$) (1990–1999 average).

resulted from the sale of the Ashanti Goldfields company (in the mining sector). The total revenues received from privatization during the 1990s were valued at 21.6 percent of Ghana's 1985 GDP. In 1990, Ghana's outstanding IMF obligations totaled 12.7 percent of GDP. By 1999, Ghana had reduced those obligations to 4.0 percent as a share of GDP, reflecting at least in part the successes of its privatization program.

Nigeria, Ghana's neighbor to the east, had much less success with its privatization program. Under the direction of the National Council on Privatization (NCP), the sale of state-owned assets got off to a quick start in Nigeria in the early 1990s. By 1993, it had divested a number of enterprises in the financial (banking and insurance), agriculture, food-manufacturing, tourism and transport (railroads) sectors, as well as a share of the Nigerian National Petroleum Company. But because of lack of investor interest, Nigeria's privatization program abruptly stalled. The national government has been unable to sell off several firms it considers "crown jewels." For example, the sale of the state-owned telecommunications operator, NITEL, has been repeatedly postponed. In 1999, the government attempted to reinvigorate its failing privatization program by creating the Bureau of Public Enterprises to oversee the NCP. But this new initiative has yet to kick-start the sale of the large set of assets that remain in the hands of the Nigerian state. During the 1990s as a whole, Nigeria privatized assets worth 4.2 percent of its 1985 GDP, but almost all of these were sold before 1993.

Nigeria was among the sub-Saharan African countries least reliant on the IFIs in the 1990s. The country had no outstanding obligations to the IMF during the decade, and World Bank assistance was less than a third as large (relative to GDP) as in neighboring Ghana. Interestingly, Nigeria stopped participating in all IMF programs in 1994 – the same year that its privatization program came grinding to a halt – because of disagreements about the terms of policy conditionality attached to IMF loans.[10] It was not that Nigeria did not need external financing. By 1991 Nigeria owed an estimated US$34 billion to members of the Paris Club and foreign commercial banks. According to the Nigerian Federal Ministry of Finance, the total external debt outstanding at the end of 1999 was US$28 billion. Of the total outstanding debt, the Paris Club constituted the highest source, with a share of 73.2 percent in 1999.[11]

This Ghana–Nigeria comparison is consistent with our argument that there may be an indirect benefit of accepting IFI loans, and the conditions attached to them, in terms of generating investor confidence in national privatization programs. Ghana seems a real success story with respect to privatization, with the IMF playing a leading role in economic policy formulation during the 1990s. Nigeria was much more independent from the IFIs, and the IMF in particular, precisely because it was unwilling to accept the policy conditions attached to IMF loans. But after a promising start, its privatization program collapsed because of a lack of investor interest, which we surmise was because of a lack of confidence that the Nigerian government, acting independently, would pursue the kinds of market reforms required to make its privatized firms good investments. We now demonstrate that this lesson of the Ghana–Nigeria comparison holds for the rest of the developing world as well.

## Results

This section reports our statistical analyses of the determinants of privatization, focusing on the effects of outstanding obligations to international financial institutions. We begin with an aggregated cross-sectional analysis of privatization between 1985 and 1999, regressed on variables for the first half of the 1980s. We then estimate panel regressions to examine year-to-year relationships. Finally, we check the robustness of our results by analyzing privatization dynamics and selection bias in privatization outcomes. In each set of analyses, there was a consistent and strong relationship between IMF lending and privatization – privatization was greater in countries with larger outstanding obligations to the IMF.

### *1985–1999 cross-section*

Table 4.4 reports the cross-sectional results for equations that regressed privatization proceeds between 1985 and 1999 (as a proportion of 1985 GDP) on a series of variables measured from 1980 to 1984 (to mitigate potential problems with reverse causality). In our baseline model presented in column 4.1, countries with larger state-owned sectors and larger budget deficits in the early 1980s privatized more of their economies. The parameter estimate for GDP per capita was positive and close to statistical significance, implying that more developed countries privatized more. Privatization revenues were greater in the countries of East Asia and the Pacific than in the excluded reference regions of North America and Western Europe.

Most importantly, the variable measuring outstanding obligations to the IMF was positive, substantively large, and statistically significant, whereas the estimated parameter for World Bank debt was negative and insignificant. For every dollar of outstanding debt to the IMF in 1980–1984, a recipient country privatized assets worth almost 50 cents over the next 15 years.

The remainder of our empirical analysis tests the robustness of this IMF-privatization association. We exclude all high-income countries to ascertain whether the IMF effect was influenced by the inclusion of 26 countries with no outstanding obligations to the IFIs in the early 1980s. Column 4.2 shows that this was not the case, though the IMF coefficient was somewhat smaller on the sample of developing countries only. In column 4.3, we reestimate the baseline equation using Tobit because our privatization data are left-censored at zero. The IMF coefficient was larger using the Tobit estimator than was the case in the Ordinary Least Squares (OLS) equation, whereas the other estimated parameters were similar to those reported in column 4.2.

*Table 4.4* Total privatizations, 1985–1999

| | 4.1 | 4.2 | 4.3 | 4.4 | 4.5 |
|---|---|---|---|---|---|
| | *Baseline* | *Developing countries only* | *Tobit* | *Excluding outliers* | *Transactions as dependent variable* |
| GDP per capita (log) | 1.631<br>(1.299) | 1.591<br>(1.561) | 1.514<br>(1.258) | 1.20<br>(1.19) | −0.390**<br>(0.159) |
| Size of the state-owned sector in 1980 | 1.124**<br>(0.499) | 0.94<br>(0.669) | 1.070**<br>(0.485) | 0.598<br>(0.379) | 0.152**<br>(0.061) |
| Budget balance (% of GDP) | −0.299**<br>(0.134) | −0.397**<br>(0.192) | −0.292*<br>(0.147) | −0.308**<br>(0.137) | −0.012<br>(0.023) |
| Functioning stock market | 1.381<br>(2.059) | 1.681<br>(2.466) | 2.199<br>(2.096) | 2.54<br>(1.83) | 1.236***<br>(0.276) |
| Government quality | −0.048<br>(0.285) | 0.09<br>(0.400) | 0.001<br>(0.301) | −0.029<br>(0.265) | 0.052<br>(0.040) |
| World Bank outstanding obligations (% of GDP) | −0.07<br>(0.394) | −0.034<br>(0.421) | −0.018<br>(0.368) | −0.266<br>(0.253) | −0.026<br>(0.050) |
| IMF outstanding obligations (% of GDP) | 0.493**<br>(0.234) | 0.434*<br>(0.262) | 0.532*<br>(0.299) | 0.601***<br>(0.187) | 0.068*<br>(0.041) |
| East Asia and the Pacific | 6.720*<br>(3.696) | −0.929<br>(6.685) | 6.886**<br>(3.297) | 7.88**<br>(3.62) | 0.088<br>(0.430) |
| Eastern Europe and Central Asia | 4.779<br>(8.315) | 0.111<br>(9.428) | 5.864<br>(5.734) | 0.868<br>(3.92) | 3.060***<br>(0.751) |
| Latin America and the Caribbean | 4.164<br>(3.620) | −0.989<br>(6.067) | 4.395<br>(3.185) | 5.11<br>(3.36) | 0.104<br>(0.419) |
| Middle East and North Africa | −3.61<br>(3.981) | −10.801*<br>(6.268) | −3.195<br>(3.758) | −0.635<br>(3.33) | −0.820*<br>(0.497) |
| South Asia | −4.203<br>(4.361) | −9.244<br>(6.709) | −4.043<br>(5.567) | −1.71<br>(3.82) | −0.76<br>(0.703) |
| Sub-Saharan Africa | −3.255<br>(4.305) | −8.38<br>(6.483) | −3.304<br>(4.130) | 0.042<br>(3.63) | −0.218<br>(0.551) |
| Constant | −14.497<br>(10.957) | −9.074<br>(14.428) | −14.793<br>(11.308) | −10.3<br>(10.1) | 4.705***<br>(1.471) |
| Observations | 96 | 70 | 96 | 93 | 96 |
| R-squared | 0.33 | 0.38 | 0.0558 | 0.37 | 0.0687 |
| log likelihood | | | −316.45 | | −477.34 |
| chibar2(01) = | | | | | 3,978.85 |
| Prob. > = chibar2 | | | | | 0.000 |

Note

We report the cross-sectional results for equations that regressed privatization proceeds in 1985–1999 (as a % of 1985 GDP) on a series of variables measured in 1980–1984. Standard errors in parentheses. ***indicates $p < 0.01$; **indicates $p < 0.05$; *indicates $p < 0.10$.

See Appendix 4.2 for a description of data and sources.

In column 4.4, we exclude the largest outliers from the baseline regression that arguably were unduly influential on the results reported. We calculate DFITs statistics of influence, or the scaled difference between predicted values for the *i*th case when the regression is estimated with and without the *i*th observation, for each observation and then drop the three countries (Bolivia, Hungary and Portugal) from our sample that were excessively influential on conventional interpretations of DFITs (DFITS > 2* $\sqrt{}$(k/n)) (Bollen and Jackman 1985). Not surprisingly, the overall fit of our regression equation increases substantially when we remove these outliers. More importantly, the IMF coefficient also increased indicating that for every dollar of outstanding debt to the IMF in 1980–1984, a country privatized assets worth almost 60 cents on the dollar over the next period.

Finally, in column 4.5 we change the dependent variable from the value of privatized assets (relative to GDP) to the number of privatization transactions, using a negative-binomial estimator to take into account the left-hand censoring of the transactions variable at zero. Whereas the total revenues measure combines both the volume of assets privatized and the market's valuation of them, the transactions variable is only a volume measure. The number of privatizations measured by transactions varied enormously. In the sample of countries we use, the mean number of transactions completed over the period was 68 with a standard deviation of 152. Countries like Luxembourg and Papua New Guinea privatized only one enterprise, whereas Romania sold 1,180.

With the transaction variable as the dependent variable, the IMF effect was marginally positive – for every percentage point of GDP owed to the IMF in 1980–1984, a country subsequently engaged in 0.07 privatization transactions. While we cannot wholly reject the argument that IMF loans caused countries to privatize more assets – a direct effect of conditionality – it is clear that this effect was magnified many times in terms of the markets' valuations of privatized assets. We estimate that a dollar owed to the IMF in the early 1980s resulted in the privatization of assets worth between 40 and 60 cents more. This suggests a very powerful credibility effect associated with IMF lending.

There are, however, limitations to the inferences that can be drawn from Table 4.4. In particular, we should be cautious about drawing causal connections between a country's relationship with the IMF in the early 1980s and its privatization program through the end of the 1990s. We now reconsider this relationship using annual data.

### *Panel analysis*

The first column of Table 4.5 replicates column 4.1 but uses rectangular annual panel data for 95 countries over 1985–1999.[12] In this equation, all the regressors (except initial size of the state-owned sector) were lagged one year and we include (but did not report in the table) dummy

*Table 4.5* Annual privatizations, 1985–1999

| | *5.1* | *5.2* | *5.3* |
|---|---|---|---|
| | *Baseline* | *Before and after 1990* | *Additional variables* |
| GDP per capita (log) | 0.072 | 0.063 | 0.135 |
| | (0.082) | (0.084) | (0.115) |
| Size of the state-owned sector in 1980 | 0.053* | 0.048 | 0.041 |
| | (0.030) | (0.030) | (0.031) |
| Budget balance (% of GDP) | −0.006 | −0.008 | −0.009 |
| | (0.009) | (0.009) | (0.009) |
| Functioning stock market | 0.275** | 0.263** | 0.230* |
| | (0.126) | (0.127) | (0.138) |
| Government quality | 0.014 | 0.011 | 0.015 |
| | (0.022) | (0.022) | (0.025) |
| World Bank outstanding obligations (% of GDP) | 0.011 | 0.011 | 0.014 |
| | (0.007) | (0.009) | (0.010) |
| World Bank *X* 1990s | | −0.009 | −0.009 |
| | | (0.008) | (0.008) |
| IMF outstanding obligations (% of GDP) | 0.007 | −0.024* | −0.024* |
| | (0.012) | (0.013) | (0.013) |
| IMF *X* 1990s | | 0.067*** | 0.068*** |
| | | (0.022) | (0.021) |
| Democracy | | | −0.132 |
| | | | (0.163) |
| Trade (% of GDP) | | | −0.001 |
| | | | (0.001) |
| FDI inflows (% of GDP) | | | 0.001 |
| | | | (0.037) |
| British legal heritage | | | 0.316** |
| | | | (0.130) |
| French legal heritage | | | 0.314** |
| | | | (0.140) |
| Socialist legal heritage | | | 0.654* |
| | | | (0.359) |
| Constant | −1.237* | −1.045 | −1.736* |
| | (0.747) | (0.754) | (1.007) |
| Observations | 1,236 | 1,230 | 1,170 |
| Number of countries | 95 | 94 | 91 |
| R-squared | 0.0609 | 0.0714 | 0.0770 |
| Joint Hypothesis Test (IMF and IMF *X* 1990) | | $F(1, 1208) = 10.04$ | |
| | | Prob. > F = 0.0016 | |

Note

The first column of Table 4.5 replicates column 4.1 in Table 4.4 but uses *annual* panel data for 95 countries in 1985–1999. All regressors were lagged one year. In column 5.2, we interacted our IFI variables with a dummy variable for the 1990s. In column 5.3, we assessed the sensitivity of our IMF result to the effects of other mediating variables common in work on international development. Standard errors in parentheses. ***indicates $p<0.01$; **indicates $p<0.05$; *indicates $p<0.10$.

variables for each year as well as for each region. Not surprisingly the coefficients in Table 4.5.1 are much smaller than those in Table 4.4.1 because they measured annual effects rather than those aggregated over 15 years. The positive effect of the presence of a functioning stock market on privatization revenues was more pronounced in the time series, whereas the effects of budget deficits and larger initial state-owned sector were weaker. As was the case in our cross-section analysis, the parameter estimate for outstanding financial obligations to the World Bank was again insignificant (though stronger than in the cross-section).

The most important coefficient in Table 4.5.1 was the positive – but insignificant – impact of last year's outstanding IMF credit on this year's privatization revenues. The positive and significant finding from Table 4.4 combined with the insignificant effect in this equation suggests that the IMF-privatization revenues relationship may have changed over time. Indeed, we would expect the relationship to have grown increasingly strong over time, because the IMF's commitment to privatization, and to conditioning loans on the execution of national privatization programs, increased significantly during the 1990s. We tested this hypothesis in column 5.2 by interacting our IFI variables with a dummy variable for the 1990s.

As expected, column 5.2 shows that whereas outstanding IMF obligations had a small negative impact on privatization revenues in the next year, this estimate was reversed in direction and doubled in size for the 1990s; the yearly impact during the 1990s is estimated to be 0.043 (i.e. $-0.024+0.067=+0.043$). That is, for every dollar a country owed the IMF in the previous year during the 1990s, it privatized assets worth four cents more in the current year. Over the whole decade, this effect would have been 40 cents – quite similar to the aggregate effect estimated in the cross-section regression in Table 4.4. In contrast with this over-time change in the IMF-privatization relationship, outstanding obligations to the World Bank did not have a significant positive effect on privatization revenues in the 1980s, and this effect lessened to near zero in the 1990s. These results are quite consistent with general views about differences in the lending practices and policy views of the two institutions.[13]

In column 5.3 we assess the sensitivity of our IMF result to the effects of other mediating variables common in work on international development. We consider the effects of democracy, international economic openness (measured by levels of trade and foreign direct investment) and differences in legal systems (legal heritage) on privatization revenues. Though some of these variables were significant (notably, differences in legal heritage), the IMF coefficient for the 1990s was unaffected by their inclusion. In sum, Table 4.5 reinforces our central finding from Table 4.4, with the modification that the positive effect of IMF obligations on privatization revenues was a 1990s phenomenon.

### *Additional robustness checks: selection and dynamics*

We conduct two final robustness checks for our central IMF-privatization result. First, we correct for selection bias in the extent of national privatization programs, using the procedure advocated by Heckman. Second, we take into account the fact that countries' privatization programs tended to last for several years (i.e. creating dynamic connections between last year's and this year's privatization revenues). The results of these analyses are reported in Table 4.6.

The selection-corrected estimates are presented in column 6.1. The model specification is full maximum likelihood, which permitted using the inverse Mills ratio to calculate the probability density over the cumulative density function. This ratio was then used in the estimating equation, along with the other regressors. We use three variables to estimate the selection equation: a country's budget balance, domestic fixed investment, and foreign exchange reserves (all lagged one year). The results of the likelihood test indicate that the selection model and the estimating model were very highly correlated and that the bias (downward) significant. But once these selection effects are taken into account, it is still the case that the more money a country owed the IMF in a given year, the more privatization revenues were generated in the following year.

Column 6.2 includes a country's lagged privatization revenues as a regressor to take into account the fact that national privatization programs typically last several years. We would expect that once a country began privatizing it would continue to do so and hence that the lagged dependent variable would have a positive and significant impact on this year's privatization revenues. Column 6.2 demonstrates that this dynamic was strongly evident in our privatization data. Nonetheless, even when we control for past privatization, a country's outstanding obligations to the IMF were still positively associated with its subsequent privatization revenues. Given that we controlled for the propensity for privatization programs to persist over time, this annual incremental IMF effect is striking.

In summary, Table 4.6 confirms that IMF lending had a positive impact on privatization revenues. This positive impact persisted even after correcting for the propensity of countries already committed to market reform to also participate in IMF programs and after taking into account that once a country began to privatize state-owned assets, it was likely to continue privatizing for several years.

## Conclusion

We analyze the relationships between the IFIs and privatization in three steps. First, we use cross-section regressions from 1985 to 1999 to ascertain whether outstanding IFI obligations affected the scale of a country's overall privatization programs. The central result of this analysis was that

*Table 4.6* Selection effects and dynamics

| | *6.1* | *6.2* |
|---|---|---|
| | *Selection* | *Dynamics* |
| Privatization (% of GDP), lagged | | 0.223*** |
| | | (0.066) |
| GDP per capita (log) | 0.090* | 0.065 |
| | (0.052) | (0.041) |
| Size of the state-owned sector in 1980 | 0.056*** | 0.041*** |
| | (0.019) | (0.016) |
| Budget balance (% of GDP) | −0.003 | −0.004 |
| | (0.005) | (0.004) |
| Functioning stock market | 0.178** | 0.150** |
| | (0.090) | (0.075) |
| Government quality | 0.002 | 0.001 |
| | (0.015) | (0.012) |
| World Bank outstanding obligations (% of GDP) | 0.007 | 0.004 |
| | (0.005) | (0.004) |
| IMF outstanding obligations (% of GDP) | 0.017** | 0.012** |
| | (0.007) | (0.005) |
| Constant | −1.44*** | −1.06*** |
| | (0.415) | (0.323) |
| *Selection equation* | | |
| Budget balance (% of GDP) | 0.031*** | 0.031*** |
| | (0.006) | (0.006) |
| Domestic investment (% of GDP) | 0.019** | 0.019** |
| | (0.008) | (0.008) |
| Foreign exchange reserves (% of GDP) | −0.019*** | −0.019*** |
| | (0.002) | (0.002) |
| Constant | 3.36*** | 3.36*** |
| | (0.372) | (0.374) |
| athrho | −0.050 | −0.046 |
| | (0.034) | (0.030) |
| lnsigma | 0.051 | 0.028 |
| | (0.116) | (0.125) |
| Lambda (Mills ratio) | −0.052 | −0.047 |
| | (0.036) | (0.031) |
| Observations | 1,265 | 1,265 |
| Number of countries | 96 | 96 |
| log likelihood | −1,864.15 | −1,835.11 |
| Wald chi2 | 193.17 | 393.57 |
| Prob. > chi2 | 0.0000 | 0.0000 |
| Wald test of independent equations chi2(1) = | 2.14 | 2.35 |
| Prob. > chi2 | 0.1438 | 0.1256 |

Note

We conducted two final robustness checks on our central IMF-privatization result. In column 6.1, we used the Heckman model to correct for selection effects. In column 6.2, we included a country's lagged privatization revenues as a regressor to take into account the fact that privatization programs typically last several years. Standard errors in parentheses. ***indicates $p<0.01$; **indicates $p<0.05$; *indicates $p<0.10$.

the more countries owed the IMF before 1985, the greater were their subsequent revenues raised from the sale of state-owned assets. Second, we analyze panel data to see whether this aggregated effect was evident in year-to-year data: did how much a country owed the IMF last year increase its privatization revenues this year? Our analysis answered this question affirmatively but with an important qualification. The impact of IMF lending on privatization revenues was a 1990s phenomenon – when IMF conditionality with respect to privatization hardened. Third, we control for significant selection effects and for over-time persistence in national privatization programs. Doing so did not weaken our central IMF-privatization result.

What do these results mean? They have little to say about the efficiency of privatization, per se. But they do point to a critical role played by the IMF in altering market perceptions of country risk. It has long been a theoretical defense of IMF bailouts that they are required not only to provide short-term liquidity but also to stave off disastrous self-fulfilling fears in the market place. Consistent with this line of argument and with recent studies questioning the direct impact of the IMF on economic growth, our results suggest that the primary value of the IMF may be financial market enhancement rather than the provision of capital.

Recent evidence has failed to find a strong catalytic role for IMF programs with respect to overall capital flows into developing countries. Our results indicate, however, that IMF programs have attracted capital for the specific purpose of purchasing formerly state-owned assets. In the longer run, of course, this program success could have important implications for broader processes of economic development through attracting more capital investments at more favorable discount rates. Even if the efficiency-enhancing effects of privatization do not seem as powerful in practice as they are in theory, and even if IMF lending does not have direct effects on economic growth, privatization is more attractive to investors in cases where the privatizing government owes the IMF money and is subject to the policy conditionality.

This conclusion points to an important development tool available to countries and the Fund. Of course, the implication should not be that privatization is recommended to all countries at all times. If enhancing credibility is a primary contribution of the IMF, it is important to consider other policy measures that might deliver this outcome more efficiently and at less cost in social and economic terms. Critics of international financial organizations have long noted that the IMF is an economic institution influencing the political economy of investment. Our findings confirm that financial markets perceive the IMF as playing an important role in enhancing the credibility of governments in raising foreign capital and in increasing the revenues from the massive privatization of the past two decades. The increased revenues represent a large, important capital flow to poor countries that should not be underestimated.

## Appendix 4.1

*Appendix 4.1* Country-level privatizations, 1985–1999

| | *Revenues (billions, 1985 US$)* | *Average revenues (% of 1985 GDP, unweighted)* | *Transactions* | *Size of the state-owned sector in 1980*[a] |
|---|---|---|---|---|
| *East Asia and the Pacific* | | | | |
| Australia | 68.91 | 25.2 | 118 | medium-low |
| China | 22.22 | 8.1 | 281 | high |
| Indonesia | 6.26 | 6.4 | 50 | medium-high |
| Japan | 164.39 | 4.3 | 12 | low |
| Korea, Rep. | 15.37 | 7.2 | 30 | medium-low |
| Malaysia | 11.45 | 28.2 | 91 | medium |
| New Zealand | 13.63 | 27.0 | 66 | medium |
| Papua New Guinea | 0.24 | 8.2 | 1 | medium |
| Philippines | 5.32 | 10.1 | 118 | medium-low |
| Singapore | 4.80 | 13.3 | 25 | medium-low |
| Thailand | 5.44 | 8.0 | 39 | medium |
| *Eastern Europe and Central Asia* | | | | |
| Hungary | 15.52 | 31.6 | 1,037 | high |
| Romania | 2.32 | 5.6 | 1,180 | high |
| Turkey | 5.49 | 4.9 | 236 | medium-high |
| *Latin America and the Caribbean* | | | | |
| Argentina | 42.68 | 22.1 | 230 | medium |
| Bolivia | 1.84 | 37.6 | 98 | medium-high |
| Brazil | 73.12 | 13.4 | 215 | medium-high |
| Chile | 7.87 | 25.3 | 89 | medium |
| Colombia | 9.09 | 15.3 | 65 | medium-high |
| Costa Rica | 0.06 | 0.8 | 8 | medium |
| Dominican Republic | 0.43 | 5.1 | 6 | medium |
| Ecuador | 0.13 | 1.0 | 16 | medium-high |
| El Salvador | 1.14 | 18.0 | 23 | medium-low |
| Guatemala | 1.32 | 12.8 | 8 | low |
| Guyana | 0.18 | 36.5 | 32 | high |
| Haiti | 0.02 | 0.8 | 3 | medium-low |
| Honduras | 0.11 | 3.8 | 41 | medium-low |
| Jamaica | 0.70 | 20.7 | 47 | medium-high |
| Mexico | 40.36 | 16.5 | 317 | medium-high |
| Nicaragua | 0.14 | 6.6 | 78 | high |
| Panama | 1.92 | 30.7 | 21 | medium |
| Paraguay | 0.02 | 0.4 | 5 | low |
| Peru | 8.80 | 19.5 | 196 | medium |
| Trinidad and Tobago | 0.46 | 8.2 | 22 | medium-high |
| Uruguay | 0.02 | 0.2 | 12 | medium |
| Venezuela, RB | 6.88 | 12.0 | 69 | medium-high |
| *Middle East and North Africa* | | | | |
| Bahrain | 0.30 | 8.1 | 4 | medium |

*Appendix 4.1* continued

| | *Revenues (billions, 1985 US$)* | *Average revenues (% of 1985 GDP, unweighted)* | *Transactions* | *Size of the state-owned sector in 1980*[a] |
|---|---|---|---|---|
| Egypt, Arab Rep. | 5.31 | 12.8 | 165 | medium-high |
| Iran, Islamic Rep. | 0.02 | 0.0 | 3 | medium-high |
| Israel | 7.26 | 14.0 | 50 | medium-high |
| Jordan | 0.06 | 1.2 | 6 | high |
| Kuwait | 2.19 | 12.4 | 21 | medium-high |
| Morocco | 3.91 | 15.4 | 84 | medium-high |
| Oman | 0.06 | 0.8 | 8 | medium-high |
| Tunisia | 0.58 | 4.5 | 76 | high |
| United Arab Emirates | 0.19 | 0.6 | 2 | medium-low |
| *North America and Western Europe* | | | | |
| Austria | 11.05 | 6.0 | 51 | medium-high |
| Belgium | 8.68 | 3.9 | 13 | medium-low |
| Canada | 23.90 | 5.2 | 77 | low |
| Denmark | 9.33 | 6.1 | 13 | medium-low |
| Finland | 10.74 | 9.4 | 46 | medium-low |
| France | 89.28 | 7.1 | 58 | medium |
| Greece | 9.86 | 10.0 | 46 | medium-high |
| Iceland | 0.33 | 5.7 | 27 | low |
| Ireland | 5.97 | 14.2 | 17 | medium-low |
| Italy | 102.20 | 11.4 | 89 | medium |
| Luxembourg | 1.07 | 10.4 | 1 | medium-low |
| Malta | 0.28 | 15.0 | 2 | medium |
| Netherlands | 17.22 | 5.4 | 52 | low |
| Norway | 2.65 | 2.3 | 14 | medium |
| Portugal | 24.65 | 32.7 | 92 | medium-high |
| Spain | 49.67 | 11.3 | 90 | medium |
| Sweden | 12.86 | 6.2 | 21 | medium |
| Switzerland | 4.60 | 1.7 | 3 | low |
| United Kingdom | 130.09 | 14.7 | 139 | medium |
| United States | 7.75 | 0.1 | 20 | low |
| *Southeast Asia* | | | | |
| Bangladesh | 0.06 | 0.3 | 32 | medium-high |
| India | 8.29 | 4.1 | 96 | high |
| Pakistan | 2.22 | 6.1 | 109 | high |
| Sri Lanka | 0.84 | 10.2 | 98 | medium-high |
| *Sub-Saharan Africa* | | | | |
| Burkina Faso | 0.02 | 0.9 | 35 | medium-high |
| Cameroon | 0.09 | 0.9 | 31 | medium |
| Congo, Dem. Rep. | 0.00 | 0.0 | 23 | high |
| Congo, Rep. | 0.04 | 1.6 | 67 | high |
| Cote d'Ivoire | 0.68 | 7.8 | 96 | high |
| Ethiopia | 0.35 | 8.9 | 162 | medium-high |
| Gabon | 0.03 | 0.8 | 8 | medium-high |
| Gambia, The | 0.01 | 4.1 | 32 | medium-high |

*Appendix 4.1* continued

| | *Revenues (billions, 1985 US$)* | *Average revenues (% of 1985 GDP, unweighted)* | *Transactions* | *Size of the state-owned sector in 1980*[a] |
|---|---|---|---|---|
| Ghana | 0.90 | 21.6 | 227 | high |
| Guinea-Bissau | 0.01 | 2.8 | 21 | medium-high |
| Kenya | 0.23 | 3.7 | 190 | high |
| Malawi | 0.06 | 5.5 | 73 | high |
| Mali | 0.07 | 3.2 | 68 | medium |
| Niger[b] | 0.00 | 0.3 | 29 | medium |
| Nigeria | 0.85 | 4.4 | 95 | high |
| Senegal | 0.23 | 6.3 | 54 | medium |
| South Africa | 4.53 | 3.4 | 33 | medium-high |
| Togo | 0.06 | 5.4 | 55 | high |
| Uganda | 0.17 | 5.4 | 101 | medium-high |
| Zambia | 0.38 | 11.2 | 253 | high |
| Zimbabwe | 0.78 | 14.6 | 9 | medium-high |

Source: Brune (2004).

Notes
a Gwartney *et al.* (1996).
b Not included in panel analyses because of data limitations.

## Appendix 4.2

*Appendix 4.2* Description of the variables

| *Variable* | *Definition* | *Source* |
|---|---|---|
| Privatization | Lagged value of privatization revenues as percent of GDP | Brune (2004). Global Privatization Database |
| SOE80 | Size of state-owned sector in 1980; (0–10 score, with 10 = extensive state ownership) | Gwartney, Lawson and Black (1996); supplemented using imputation analysis and other sources. |
| GDP PC (log) | Gross domestic product per capita (constant US$), logged | World Bank Development Indicators 2002 CD-ROM |
| Budget balance | Overall budget balance as share of GDP | IMF IFS 2002 CD-ROM and World Development Indicators 2002 CD-ROM |
| IMF | IMF financing as a share (%) of GDP | World Bank Development Indicators 2002 CD-ROM |
| World Bank | EBRD and IBRD loans as a share (%) of GDP* | World Bank Development Indicators 2002 CD-ROM |
| Stock market | Dummy variable = 1 if country has stock market | Authors |
| Trade | Exports plus imports as share of GDP | World Bank Development Indicators 2002 CD-ROM |
| FDI inflows | Foreign direct investment, net inflows as share of GDP | World Bank Development Indicators 2002 CD-ROM |

*Appendix 4.2* continued

| *Variable* | *Definition* | *Source* |
|---|---|---|
| Democracy | Dummy = 1 if country has democratic regime | Przeworski, Alvarez and others, (2001) |
| Quality of government | Sum of corruption, rule of law, and bureaucratic quality scores (0–18, with 18 = high quality of government) | La Porta and others (1999); Easterly and Yu (1999) |
| British legal heritage | Dummy = 1 if country has British (common law) legal heritage | La Porta and others (1999); Easterly and Yu (1999) |
| French legal heritage | Dummy = 1 if country has French (civil law) legal heritage | La Porta and others (1999); Easterly and Yu (1999) |
| Socialist heritage | Dummy = 1 if country has socialist legal heritage | La Porta and others (1999); Easterly and Yu 1999) |

Note
European Bank for Reconstruction and Development (EBRD); International Bank for Reconstruction and Development (IBRD).

## Notes

1 The research for this paper was supported by the Reginald H. Jones Center of the Wharton School and a grant from the Carnegie Corporation of New York to Yale University. The authors thank Edward Leamer, Enrico Perotti, James Vreeland, and the anonymous reviewers for their helpful comments.
2 These numbers do not include, nor do we analyze, the disposition of assets by mass/voucher privatization in the former socialist countries. Our analysis of privatization transactions counts separately different tranches of a firm's assets where it was not completely sold in one transaction.
3 Bangladesh, Germany, Mali and South Africa also privatized tiny shares of their state-owned assets in the early 1980s.
4 Though the Bretton Woods-era charters of the two organizations differ significantly, they have evolved into institutions with overlapping jurisdictions regarding structural adjustment lending.
5 Williamson originally formulated the term Washington Agenda, or the Washington Consensus, in a background paper "What Washington Means by Policy Reform" for a conference held by the Institute for International Economics in November 1989, which was published as the opening chapter in the conference volume *The Progress of Policy Reform in Latin America* (1990).
6 For all World Bank privatization information, see www.privatizationlink.org.
7 In the compilation of GPD, data that overlapped but were discordant were reconciled based on the following rank order of data quality (in descending order): PPID, WBPD, WBAPD and PID. Data and information gathered from the search of additional primary and secondary materials helped supplement and correct missing information on individual privatization transactions.
8 The regional distributions among these countries were as follows: East Asia and the Pacific – 11 countries; Eastern Europe and Central Asia – 3; Latin America and the Caribbean – 22; Middle East and North Africa – 10; North America and Western Europe – 20; South Asia – 4; sub-Saharan Africa – 21.
9 In countries with a score of 10, more than 30 percent of the economy was

derived from economic activity of the state-owned sector; in countries that scored a 0, less than 1 percent of economic output was derived from state-owned enterprises.

10 As late as 2001, Nigeria had failed to reach agreed policy targets with the IMF.

11 Source: Central Bank of Nigeria: www.cenbank.org/extern_debt/htm.

12 Niger had to be excluded from the panel data analysis because of missing data on some independent variables in the late 1980s and early 1990s.

13 Because panel estimates are biased with fixed effects and lags, we also used the Arellano-Bond specification of generalized method of moments (GMM). With a single lag on the privatization variable, the IMF effect remained significant at the 0.01 percent level (coefficient of 0.075); the World Bank variable was not significant.

## References

Abouharb, R. (2001) "World Bank Structural Adjustment Loans and Their Impact on Economic Growth" unpublished paper, State University of New York Binghamton.

Bevan, A., Estrin, S., Kuznetsov, B., Schaffer, M., Angelucci, M., Fennema, J. and Mangiarotti, G. (2001) "The Determinants of Privatized Enterprise Performance in Russia," *William Davidson Institute Working Paper Series*, No. 452.

Bird, G. and Rowlands, D. (1997) "The Catalytic Effect of Lending by the International Financial Institutions," *The World Economy*, 20: 967–91.

—— (2004) "Do IMF Programmes Have a Catalytic Effect on Other International Capital Flows?" *Oxford Development Studies*.

Black, B., Kraakman, R. and Tarassova, A. (2000) "Russian Privatization and Corporate Governance: What Went Wrong?," *Stanford Law Review*, 52: 1731–808.

Bollen, K. A. and Jackman, R. W. (1985) "Regression Diagnostics: An Expository Treatment of Outliers and Influential Cases," *Sociological Methods and Research*, 13/4: 510–42.

Bortolotti, B., Fantini, M. and Siniscalco, D. (1998) "Privatizations and Institutions: A Cross-Country Analysis," unpublished paper, Milan: FEEM.

—— (2001) "Privatization: Politics, Institutions, and Financial Markets," *Emerging Market Review*, 2: 109–36.

Brune, N. (2004) "Privatization Around the World," Ph.D. dissertation, Yale University.

Davis, J., Ossowski, R., Richardson, T. and Barnett, S. (2000) *Fiscal and Macroeconomic Impact of Privatization*, Occasional Paper No. 194, Washington, DC: International Monetary Fund.

Dewenter, K. and Malatesta, P. H. (2001) "State-Owned and Privately Owned Firms: An Empirical Analysis of Profitability, Leverage, and Labor Intensity," *American Economic Review*, 91/1: 320–34.

Easterly, W. and Yu, H. (1999) *Global Development Network Growth Database*, Washington: World Bank.

Galal, A., Jones, L., Tandon, P. and Vogelsang, O. (1994) *Welfare Consequences of Selling Public Enterprises: An Empirical Analysis*, New York: Oxford University Press.

Galal, A. and Shirley, M. (1994) *Does Privatization Deliver? Highlights from a World Bank Conference*, Washington: World Bank.

Gwartney, J., Lawson, R. and Block, W. (1996) *Economic Freedom of the World: 1975–1995*, Toronto: Fraser Institute.

Holmström, B. and Tirole, J. (1993) "Market Liquidity and Performance Monitoring," *Journal of Political Economy*, 101/4: 678–709.

Knack, S. and Keefer, P. (1995) "Institutions and Economic Performance: Cross-Country Tests Using Alternative Institutional Measures," *Economics and Politics*, 7/3: 207–27.

La Porta, R., Lopez-de-Silanes, F., Shleifer, A. and Vishny, R. (1999) "The Quality of Government," *Journal of Law, Economics, and Organization*, 15/1: 222–79.

Levine, R. (1997) "Financial Development and Economic Growth: Views and Agenda," *Journal of Economic Literature*, 35: 688–726.

Megginson, W., Nash, R. and van Randenborgh, M. (1994) "The Financial and Operating Performance of Newly Privatized Firms: An International Empirical Analysis," *Journal of Finance*, 49: 403–52.

Megginson, W. and Netter, J. (2001) "From State to Market: A Survey of Empirical Studies on Privatization," *Journal of Economic Literature*, 39: 321–89.

Mody, A. and Saravia, D. (2003) "Catalyzing Capital Flows: Do IMF Programs Work as Commitment Devices?" *IMF Working Paper* 03/100.

Perotti, E. and van Oijen, P. (2001) "Privatization, Political Risk, and Stock Market Development in Emerging Economies," *Journal of International Money and Finance*, 20/1: 43–69.

Polak, J. (1994) "The World Bank and the IMF: A Changing Relationship," in D. Kapur, J. P. Lewis and R. Webb (eds) *The World Bank. Its First Half Century. Volume 2: Perspectives*, Washington: Brookings Institution Press.

Przeworski, A., Alvarez, M. E., Cheibub, J. A. and Limongi, F. (2000) *Democracy and Development: Political Institutions and Well-Being in the World, 1950–1990*, Cambridge: Cambridge University Press.

Przeworski, A. and Vreeland, J. (2000) "The Effect of IMF Programs on Economic Growth," *Journal of Development Economics*, 62/August: 385–421.

Ramamurti, R. (1996) *Privatizing Monopolies: Lessons from the Telecommunications and Transport Sectors in Latin America*, Baltimore: Johns Hopkins University Press.

—— (1997) "Testing the Limits of Privatization: Argentine Railroads," *World Development*, 25/December: 1973–93.

Vickers, J. and Yarrow, G. (1988) *Privatization: An Economic Analysis*, Cambridge, Massachusetts: MIT Press.

Vreeland, J. R. (2003) *The IMF and Economic Development*, New York: Cambridge University Press.

Williamson, J. (1993) "Democracy and the 'Washington Consensus'," *World Development*, 21/August: 1329–36.

# 5 The MDBs and the nation-state

*Gustav Ranis*

## Introduction

The relationship between the Multilateral Development Banks (MDBs), led by the World Bank (WB), and the borrowing nation-states remains the subject of considerable controversy. Critics on the left complain that the MDBs, using their conditionality clout, have involved themselves in a neo-imperialist fashion in the most sensitive domestic policy arenas and threaten countries' self-determination efforts, while critics on the right point to what they see as a lack of overall development success as an indication that development should really be left to private markets. But both sets of critics can agree – and here they are joined by the Bank itself – that the adjustment assistance era of the 1980s and 1990s has not proved highly productive.

In this chapter I hope to first briefly trace the evolution of the MDBs changing modus operandi over the past 60 years, then focus on what I perceive to be the present situation and conclude with an assessment of where the relationship should be heading if countries' self-determination is to be consistent with MDBs fulfilling their charter obligations.

## The first 60 years

During the 1950s and 1960s bilateral aid, especially by the US, was dominant. With the help of "long-run assistance strategy" papers, the US tried to assert considerable influence on host country policies, with program loans of substantial magnitude playing an important leverage role. From the initial focus on balance of payments support in the Marshall Plan days focused on Europe, US assistance to developing countries started with projects and then shifted to program lending. The growing realization that the collection of even inherently sound projects does not necessarily add up to a good country program meant an increasing emphasis on exercising influence on recipient country policies. In this context both quantitative as well as qualitative targets were set. For example, in the course of aid programs to Pakistan, Taiwan and Korea, AID found it useful to distinguish between rewarding past performance and inducing future performance change. In negotiations with Pakistan the US offered to provide substantial additional commodity assistance as part of an agreed program of import liberalization and the freeing up of domestic agricultural commodity markets. A similar pattern was in evidence in the case of Taiwan when substantial aid ballooning between 1959 and 1963 was accompanied by the adoption of the famous 19 points of reform. In the case of South Korea, $1 million was allocated for each of five specific reform steps. The elements of such programs were stated in official documents following comprehensive dialogue, but supported by the then overwhelming view that donors possessed superior wisdom, along with the required resources.

Accordingly, there was relatively little hesitation about getting deeply involved in the internal affairs of recipient countries. Donors recognized that they could maximize their influence by program assistance when the country is viewed as the project, or by sectoral assistance when the sector is the project; in both cases, the advantage was the relationship between a fast flow of resources and exercising maximum leverage on country policies. After all, the volume of program lending is usually based on an analysis of the overall balance of payments or budget requirements which almost begs to be broadened into a general review of the overall economic situation and the total budget of the recipient, complete with joint quarterly reviews of the economic situation and of progress on particular problems relating to the tranched disbursement of aid. The systematic use of influence in these sensitive areas, of course, requires detailed knowledge, or at least the assertion of such knowledge, in order to determine what are the most important components of any conditionality list. It was recognized even in the 1950s and 1960s that the donor/recipient relationship is an inherently delicate one since there is always the risk of the donor being viewed as a neo-colonial entity interfering in the internal affairs of the recipient. However, it should be emphasized that during these early postwar decades there was still a honeymoon in place, with probably exaggerated expectations on both sides as to what the partnership would yield in the way of development.

In contrast to the dominant bilateral donors, the MDBs, even though presumably less suspect of political motives and neo-imperialist ambitions, chose to maintain their concentration on project assistance during this period. However, by the 1970s the WB, with the coming of McNamara into the presidency of the WB, began to shift to a concern with poverty alleviation, accompanied by an increasing resort to non-project lending. As the WB and the other MDBs, if lagging somewhat behind, moved towards non-project lending, under the label of structural adjustment, the risk of trespassing on internal decision makers in recipient countries, of course, increased. But it is also fair to say that there was an initial abundance of hubris on the part of donors in terms of their assumed superior wisdom as to what needed to be done and as to how recipients could be made to recognize this, with the help of conditionality and fast-disbursing loans. While recipients were supposed to understand that the executive branch in the US, for example, could propose but that Congress would dispose, there was continuously inadequate recognition given to the fact that recipients had similar problems, i.e. their ability to comply with agreed-on commitments was subject to veto players, i.e. presumed losers from reforms who could torpedo a sincere desire by the executive branch of government to comply with the package.

All of this, of course, relates very much to the question of how well or how poorly the Bank was able to affect the quality of country performance during the 1970s, 1980s and 1990s as a consequence of its provision of dollars and advice, coupled with conditionality. The MDBs' catalytic effect, much ballyhooed, has to be assessed in terms of the extent to which the policies reached make sense, the extent to which the behavior of recipient countries was, in fact, affected and, last but not least, the extent to which the aid itself actually eased adjustment pains, bought off vested interests, alleviated inflationary pressures, etc.

There seems to be general agreement, even within the WB and the other MDBs, that traditional conditionality embodied in the structural adjustment packages of that era have generally not been very successful. The Bank's own major evaluation reports in the 1990s admitted to many failures of adjustment lending because of the frequent absence of a true domestic constituency for reform. There are, I believe, some other reasons for the relative lack of success of the structural adjustment packages embodying the so-called Washington Consensus during these three decades. For one, the World Bank, in particular, was unduly centralized, had very few full-fledged resident missions abroad, with most of the decision-making locus for both commitments and advice located in Washington, supplemented by relatively brief visiting missions, with changing membership. In fact, the recent Volcker Commission found that the typical World Bank staff member spent less than 10 percent of his/her time on recipient country contacts. Given their typically brief in-country presence, such missions usually gathered information on the run, while raising friction by insisting on meeting with high-level officials on a more or less automatic basis. Consequently intrusiveness was not always accompanied by the requisite in-depth understanding, especially with respect to the institutional and political economy dimensions of the recipient government's reform tasks. In brief, while the World Bank continued to preach decentralization to its customers in the context of its emphasis on improved governance, it did not really practice it consistently.

However, when all is said and done, undoubtedly the most telling criticism of past MDB policy-based lending is that both donor and recipient are in too much of a hurry; they all too frequently rush to judgment, putting together packages that can be signed off on so that money can be disbursed quickly. In that sense, both WB and recipient personnel are similarly motivated. The former see their rewards and promotions in terms of the volume of commitments made and agreements signed; the latter anticipate the relief expected from the quick flow of funds. All the consistent rhetoric about the importance of package quality to the contrary, neither side is therefore really inclined to take the time and the potential flak to carefully assess more precisely what the needs are, what should be done in a broader socio-political and institutional context and how to ensure that the package was more than just superficially "owned" by the recipient.

There has, of course, been a continuous evolution of what is meant by reform quality, given the changing topics focused on for priority attention, especially at the World Bank. But the question remains: how does this evolving search for the "key" levers of successful development ultimately affect the lending decisions. It is this "disbursement dilemma," i.e. the desire to lend being overwhelmingly strong and the list of conditions unduly long, as well as insufficiently differentiated to reflect specific local institutional, political, and even economic realities, which lies at the heart of the matter. All too frequently a laundry list of conditions, sometimes additive or even conflicting as between the WB, the regional banks, the IMF, and frequently bilateral donors, was put together without a clear idea of what was really important and what a country can reasonably be expected to accomplish over any given period of time. The ideal sequencing of reform components, by no means a trivial issue, also took a back seat. As a consequence, it should not be surprising that, over time, the level of friction and disappointment rose exponentionally – especially when it became increasingly obvious that ultimately the need to lend would overcome the need to ensure that the laundry list of conditions had indeed been met.

At the risk of some exaggeration, what often takes place is a rather time-consuming and expensive ritual dance. Most structural adjustment lending releases don't get cancelled; they may be delayed, and few countries have ever had prolonged breakdowns in their relations with the MDBs as a consequence of non-compliance. And all this in spite of the fact, reported by Tony Killick, that in the early 1990s only a quarter of the WB's structural adjustment loans moved forward according to their intended schedule. Once lender and borrower both know that the commitment to a fast-disbursing loan has been made, it is clearly difficult to maintain a credible threat of cutting off that loan in case of non-compliance. Even non-compliance is a highly ambiguous concept since it always comes down to a judgment call. Aware of the fact that the donor is likely to insist on compliance early in the game and anxious to disburse later on, both parties have an incentive to fashion and then implement superficial agreements. Paradoxically, moreover, while additional resources are supposed to ease the pain of adjustment they often have the very opposite effect, i.e. they take the pressure off and permit the recipient to avoid making often painful adjustments. The MDB achieves the desired commitment of resources and the recipient has the pressure for change relieved by the flow of resources. Both parties can claim that reform and loan disbursement targets have been met, more or less, and, in the absence of any externally verifiable measures of the effectiveness of the program, can declare it a success and go on to the next year's negotiations. But all this is not without a high cost in terms of increasing mixtures of fatigue, cynicism and friction, plus at least the appearance of excessive interference in the internal affairs of the nation-state, without, in return, having the benefit of actually achieving progress on reforms – indeed possibly retarding it as a consequence of taking the pressure off, i.e. via an extension of the "Dutch Disease" problem.

One of the complications in tracing the relations between the MDBs impacting on the nation-state from above is that such pressure is sometimes utilized by the recipient as a convenient lightning rod to blame for unpopular policies or to permit the reform wing of any government to convince its more recalcitrant conservative wing that changes are necessary. Such hoary arguments, however, don't have a long half-life in this repeated game context. It is always easy and convenient for the borrower to blame the lender both for excessive intervention in domestic affairs and, subsequently, for the failure of the program.

We should also remember that the falling credibility of structural adjustment lending packages was due to the fact that donor motives have become increasingly suspect over time, including the exercise of G7 political pressures exerted through the MDBs and the influence of private investor pressures leading to the differential treatment among recipient countries. In fact, it is sometimes argued that the situation is not the WB as the principal and the recipient as the agent, but G7 private interests as the principal and the MDBs as the agent impacting on recipient countries.

Clearly contributing to the increased lack of credibility has been the aforementioned large number of conditions, sometimes resulting from cross-conditionality between the MDBs and the IMF and bilateral donors which have made it easy to determine that a sufficient number of conditions have been complied with if there is a critical desire to do so, or, in the case of smaller or less "important" countries, to insist on a judgment of non-compliance. All this, of course, frustrates recipients, given the implied intrusiveness, combined with a lack of realism, plus the fact that most countries aren't able to actually perform on more than three or four reform items at any one time. Indeed, while the average number of conditions has now been reduced from about 60 in the 1980s to 30 in 2000, it is still unduly large in terms of the realistic implementation capabilities of most countries. This very much contributes to the notion of both parties going through ritual dances which are time-consuming and friction-laden, especially expensive in terms of the attention of scarce high-level manpower in the recipient nation-states.

I believe that the Rubicon on this issue was crossed at the WB early on, i.e. during the presidency of Robert McNamara, when annual and global country lending targets were established, even though – unlike the case of congressionally funded bilateral agencies – there existed no external mandate for the MDBs to do so. As usual, the regional banks soon followed suit, and while there has been a continuous evolution of what is meant by quality, reflecting the continuous search for "silver bullets," the quantity of lending has consistently won out as an indicator of success, for reasons already referred to. Indeed, this point is no longer hotly denied by the MDBs, especially in the Wolfensohn era. However, what to do about it remains an outstanding issue which I intend to return to later on.

In this connection, it is useful to acknowledge the existence of two circulatory systems in operation within all the MDBs to differing degrees, but especially in the WB. One system focuses on the President's office, the research departments, and is focused on the ever-changing realm of ideas, with changing subjects for emphasis, moving, say, from basic needs to poverty, to human development and institutional reforms over time. This system continuously changes and enhances the quality of the policy papers, of country analyses, of the annual World Development Reports. The second system resides in the realm of the operating departments where what matters is commitments on project and structural adjustment lending. The fact is generally recognized that the longer term chances for individual personal recognition and promotion still largely relate to commitments made. Of course, lip service continues to be paid and additional relevant qualitative performance indices tend to be produced by the operating branches of the MDBs, but this is not what determines lending decisions, very much in the tradition of *ex post* cost/benefit analysis on projects. The existence of these two circulatory systems, with relatively little capillary action between them, means that the MDBs continue to suffer from a case of schizophrenia, in spite of admittedly valiant efforts by the Wolfensohn administration to alleviate the problem. It also means that recipients are in a position to exploit that very lack of capillary action. The difficulty of the problem is demonstrated by the fact that management recognizes the need to change the culture of the Bank but, according to Mr Wolfensohn himself, has not found a way to tackle the issue successfully.

## The current situation

Even as the WB is complaining about its lack of capital and as its importance has continued to decline in relation to private capital flows, money continues to chase programs and projects. Of course, the need to shift to country "ownership" is being appealed to more and more frequently by all parties, and in that sense the pressure on the self-determination of the nation-state should have been relieved. But, in fact, the MDBs, directly or indirectly, still take the initiative in most instances, convince the borrowing country of what it should ask for, what it must do in the way of policy change, and what conditionality terms it must accept. In fact, it is no exaggeration to state that both the MDBs and the borrowers, having gone through this particular annual procedure many times, recognize fully that while loans may be linked to conditionality *ex ante*, *ex post* the need to lend still overcomes the need to ensure that the conditions have really been met. Few countries, certainly not politically important or large ones, experience prolonged breakdowns in their relations with the MDBs. Relations between the MDBs and the recipients have deteriorated to the point where structural adjustment lending has now been basically abandoned and new devices, including PRSPs (poverty reduction strategy papers), are being promoted.

One persistent difficulty still attending MDB programs, including the PRSP lending of today, is a certain amount of persistent and unwarranted insularity and self-assurance, especially on the part of the WB which has typically paid relatively little attention to the output of the academic community, bilateral organizations, the UN agencies and even the regional MDBs. While there is much cross-referencing and footnoting in most of the WB's output, relatively less consideration is given to work outside the institution, especially in terms of the attention paid to research and applied policy work in the developing countries themselves, in many of which there has been a substantial development of human capital over the past decades. The concentration of a large number of highly qualified professionals within one institution, all anxious to show their ability to superiors, and less anxious to refer to the work of others, adds up to a high cost of this insularity. There is insufficient encouragement of dissent or controversy. Especially non-Anglo-Saxon academic and policymaking communities in which subtle or not so subtle modifications to current paradigms are currently being advanced are ignored, dismissed or, at best, taken lightly. For example, it took a major effort by Japan not long ago to get the WB to re-examine its rather orthodox views on the role government played in East Asia's historical development successes. Such relative lack of flexibility and openness to alternative assessments of situations and inadequacies constrains the breadth of policy actions that recipients are able to explore when designing reform programs acceptable to the MDBs.

It should be noted that the WB's dominance, bordering on arrogance, continues to extend to its attitude towards the regional MDBs who have been more or less following, rather slavishly, the WB's leadership. They are generally treated as poor cousins who might be invited, along with bilateral donors, to support WB-orchestrated packages, but are otherwise expected not to get in the way. Even though the regional MDBs presumably have more local knowledge and are, by nature, more decentralized, there has been no discernible effort to evolve towards a sensible division of labor. In dealing with other lenders, the WB typically prefers to privately criticize their admittedly inferior professional capacities and then proceed to ignore them. If a new conceptual issue arises, whether in academia or in one of the UN agencies, the World Bank has a tendency to "take over" the issue and hire additional in-house staff to pursue the matter. The alternative of staying out of a given dimension of development, while helping to build up the capabilities of others, is generally viewed as generally too thankless and time-consuming and not consistent with the overriding view that the WB is the main instrument capable of both thought and action affecting what goes on in recipient countries.

Finally, we should remember that private capital is increasingly dwarfing public flows to the recipient nation-states. Quite aside from what the MDBs can do in supporting domestic private sector activities directly, given the charter restrictions relevant to all but the European Development Bank, the most important function remains one of signaling, i.e. providing housekeeping seals of approval to other contributors. Private investors continue to depend heavily on both published and unpublished country analysis work provided by the MDBs, especially the World Bank. We should also keep in mind that, while the World Bank differentiates clearly between IDA (soft loan), World Bank (harder loan) and Blend (a mix of the two) countries, the question of the extent of the complementarity rather than displacement between public and private flows and various types of graduation has received inadequate attention. Much of Africa, selected parts of Central and South America and parts of South Asia will continue to require IDA type financing for some time to come. As for the rest, MDB lending, in terms of both project and program flows, will probably be directed more towards facilitating domestic as well as complementary foreign private flows, with the objective of the earliest possible graduation from public flows.

Given the poor report card that structural adjustment lending has received, both inside and outside the MDBs, we are now witnessing a two-pronged, differentiated approach in donor activity. On the one hand, with respect to the heavily indebted poor countries, the HIPCs, forward-looking PRSPs are now insisted on before MDB relief is given. The PRSPs are supposed to be more participatory than the structural adjustment loans of the past, but in practice the ownership dimension remains rather token. While not necessarily representative, it is worth noting that, at a Kampala meeting in May 2001, 39 organizations and regional networks in 15 African countries agreed that PRSPs were simply window dressing and really resembled the Structural Adjustment Loans of yester-year under different clothing. We do know that the IMF has issued a large-sized detailed manual on how to prepare the PRSPs, which would seem to indicate that the HIPC initiative offers only limited and still highly conditional resources, most of which, incidentally, might also turn out to be not really additional.

The other current innovation is the Millennium Challenge Account, proposed by the US, which will reward countries which have already done well, clearly favoring the speediest rather than the neediest. Here again the question of conditionality remains relevant, with the US executive branch proposing an increase in total aid flows. As a consequence, a substantial middle-income group of countries is likely to be left out, i.e. countries which are not in the debt relief category nor doing so well as to be able to receive funds from the Millennium Challenge Account. Admittedly it is a bit early to tell how this new bilateral window will operate, nor are we suggesting that the HIPC initiative should be abolished, only that at the moment we still seem to be faced with the same defects in MDB activity previously referred to, plus having to deal with the illusion that we have now discovered a key solution of how to combat pervasive poverty. Indeed, we may instead have found a way to reward countries which behave "appropriately," not only in terms of developmental progress, but also in terms of meeting certain political criteria. This could, in fact, bode ill for increased intrusion into sensitive internal affairs, political as well as economic, of the recipient nation-state.

By around 2000 the realization grew, in other words, that what was needed was a shift of emphasis, with the MDBs focusing more on becoming knowledge banks rather than purveyors of capital, with the PRSP for the poor and a multi-lateralized MDA for middle-income countries, on offer. The question still arises then whether self-determination in countries still requiring support from the MDBs can be made consistent with an effective contribution by the latter, a subject to which we will now turn.

## Is self-determination consistent with an effective contribution by the MDBs?

The fact that past performance by the MDBs, using fast disbursing loans cum conditionality packages as a chosen instrument, has been far from optimal, should not lead one to the conclusion that the instrument itself is faulty. On the contrary, when deployed appropriately, such loans may still represent a very good, if not the best way, of promoting development objectives in the Third World. In any case, I am convinced that yielding to the temptation to return to the safe ground of a "projects only" approach, complete with dams and other large infrastructural projects, would be an equally large mistake. The components of any individual country reform program supported by non-project lending, if properly negotiated and truly owned by the recipient nation-state, remains, I believe, the best device to assist reform in developing countries.

The first step in that direction must be a recognition by the MDBs that a sine qua non of success is full joint conceptualization and an agreement which is not only economically but politically feasible as to what needs to be done in the way of reform and what additional resources may be required to help the country get there. In its absence, no amount of conditionality is likely to work. This, I think, requires the abandonment of the sometimes explicit, often implicit, annual MDB country lending targets. While I recognize that it is pretty unrealistic from the political relationship point of view to expect the MDBs to completely abandon some sort of low-level annual country loan targets, the point here is that major ballooning in lending, associated with the aforementioned type of agreement on policy change, would probably be negotiated only occasionally on a when-and-if basis. This requires greater passivity on the parts of MDBs and much more initiative on the part of the borrowing nation-state, a non-trivial change in the past behavior of both parties. It would be necessary for new windows to be opened permitting the MDBs to behave more like the banks they are supposed to be, in a position to sit back, encouraging would-be borrowers to approach whenever they are ready with plans for substantial reform initiatives. Such so-called "new windows" would give the MDBs an opportunity to initiate a fresh approach emphasizing substantial country selectivity while safeguarding country self-determination. This selectivity could differ from the current Millennium Challenge Account set-up which unfortunately still proposes 16 criteria for purposes of assessment and is heavily biased towards already good performers, presumably mostly middle-income countries. Moreover, the anticipated success, country by country, could be expected to lead to increased resources and a greater willingness of donor countries to support the MDBs and the development process generally over time. Nation-states which are not yet fully capable of taking such an initiative could, of course, request technical assistance to help them put together their proposal but the help should come from third parties. Self-destructing quasi-independent teams would be able to draw on the substantial expertise and experience of the MDBs but there should be no link between the advice and the possible subsequent lending activities.

If the "business as usual" annual country lending could be kept to a minimum, the annual ritual dance that I have described above could be replaced by serious bargaining and ultimate agreement on what needs to be done, once countries decide to approach the international community. A credible process would thus require the fullest possible commitment by the borrowing country and a willingness by the MDBs to respond when proposals are made, though they, of course cannot be expected to sign on the dotted line. Both parties must always keep in mind that the reform package has to be accepted both economically and politically. Moreover, it must be supported over a period long enough so that the borrower's twin risks can be taken into account. We would not expect conditionality to be abandoned but it would have to be converted into "self-conditionality," with the MDBs acting neither paternalistically nor in an interventionist fashion, but ready to discontinue providing resources in the case of noncompliance with an agreed self-conditionality list. Future reform packages would be reasonably restrictive in the number of conditions contained since there clearly exists an inverse relationship between the number of conditions and their credibility. The recipient country would have to put itself on notice that in order to ensure the continued flow of resources this reduced number of home-grown conditionality rules would have to be adhered to, with the financial flows needed not only to buy off vested interest groups and ease the pain of adjustment, but also to provide the required reassurance to presumptive winning stakeholders. This procedure would at the same time acknowledge the growing professional competence of LDC policy makers, as well as the need to inject much-needed credibility into a process which has become fatigued and unproductive.

This also means that there might be some fallow years, possibly even decades, when only low level "business as usual" country programs are being pursued in particular borrowing countries. It also means that, with respect to the big packages, the MDBs must occasionally refuse to respond and be willing to stop lending when self-conditionality provisions have been materially violated. In other words, the new window involving major reform packages and the ballooning of resource flows would presumably be relevant to only a handful of countries at any given time.

The safeguarding of self-determination by recipients would also be furthered if the MDBs agreed on and implemented a more effective division of labor within the family. Given the World Bank's admittedly superior analytical capability, it would probably make sense to have it focus more on macro analysis and let the various regional development banks focus more on microeconomic, sectoral and institutional matters likely to be very country-specific and requiring extra doses of local knowledge. Such detailed country-specific analysis is clearly necessary when there is recognition that institutional differences may, in fact, be among the key issues preventing countries from putting together a viable reform program. It is, moreover, quite in keeping with the notion of the MDBs – not just the WB – as knowledge banks to have them focus on institutional interventions to help markets function better. The regional banks' location should place them in a better position to respond to relevant reform proposals in a realistic fashion. WB and regional bank efforts should, in other words, be viewed increasingly as complementary efforts instead of as WB subcontracts under which regional banks are asked to accept WB intellectual leadership and supplement WB resource flows. While self-determination might seem to be threatened by anything approaching a monolithic stance by the international lending community, such enhanced interplay between the World Bank, the regional banks and bilateral donors, in the context of recipient initiative, can be expected to improve overall efficiency. This is not to suggest any rigid blueprint for an improved division of labor on a country basis, but that a less dismissive and paternalistic attitude by the WB is warranted. If the posture becomes one of encouragement, of sharing information, of assisting the build-up of human capital in the regional banks and the UN agencies, instead of reinforcing inferiority complexes by the sheer weight of its lending and intellectual capital, a more realistic and productive division of labor could, in fact, result.

A major obstacle to the proposed new window and its suggested operations is, of course, the aforementioned deeply entrenched culture within the World Bank. As long as the signals governing personnel evaluations and promotions continue to favor lending commitments, rather than longer term and harder to assess qualitative results on the ground, safeguarding self-determination objectives in the recipient countries will be difficult to accomplish. Nevertheless, the current re-examination of globalization as an unalloyed benefit or curse should help concentrate the mind. There is a real risk that the deficiencies of the earlier structural adjustment era as well as, I submit, the current PRSP initiative will continue increasingly to drive a wedge between amended Washington Consensus adherents and those who reject the benefits of open markets, import liberalization and price flexibility.

Abandoning religion on the part of the MDBs is part of the challenge; for example, there already has been a change in how capital market liberalization is viewed, differentiating between FDI, which is favored, and short-term portfolio capital, which is shunned. The same is true for a more catholic attitude towards what constitutes optimal exchange rate policy. Evidence of greater sensitivity to differences in country conditions, deferring much more to third party expertise and, most of all, a willingness to be patient and passive would all be of great help. Whether or not the reward system within the MDBs can be made consistent with the emphasis on long-term quality as opposed to short-term quantity is still not clear and represents a critical challenge for the MDB management.

An additional device to ensure that donor activity from above, by MDBs and the IMF, can be made consistent with national self-determination is to take a leaf from the Marshall Plan experience, i.e. by installing peer reviews by countries in a given region passing judgment on whether the few self-conditionality items set by each of the members have, in fact, been met. The selectivity proposed here may indeed be the best way to protect recipient countries' sovereignty while also ensuring that MDB dollars are effectively deployed. Neither current friction-laden ritual dances nor selectivity by front-loading where conditions have already been met, come close to addressing the basic issue. As an important actor among the poorest countries and an increasingly minor actor as countries move up the ladder, the MDBs would be well advised to put themselves in a position where they can respond to country proposals instead of pressing their ideas on them. It is a relatively tall order, acquiring a substantial shift in the direction and culture of the MDBs but would be extremely helpful not only in safeguarding self-determination for the recipients but also in permitting the MDBs to regain real relevance in spite of their shrinking quantitative importance relative to private flows.

# 6 The political impact of WTO membership in urban China

*Mary C. Cooper and Pierre F. Landry*

Globalization – and particularly the role of the World Trade Organization (WTO)[1] in this process – has inspired controversy in both academic and popular circles among new member states of the global trading regime. Yet, studies of public opinion toward globalization are primarily conducted in democratic systems (Koehler 2001; Scheve and Slaughter 2001; Greven 2003; Hanson *et al.* 2005), even though most of the 34 countries that have joined the WTO since 1994 are either authoritarian regimes or very young democracies (see Appendix 6.1). Few detailed empirical studies of the dynamics of public opinion with respect to globalization have been conducted in non-democratic societies.

China's membership in the WTO has come at the price of tougher admission standards than most other developing countries. Although WTO accession is likely to benefit the economy as a whole, the costs of adaptation to this new regime are not evenly distributed across sectors and regions (Bhalla 1998; Wei 2000; Clark and Mountjoy 2001; Jussila *et al.* 2001). Integration into the global economy will certainly involve painful adjustment costs for some segments of the population, particularly farmers, internal migrants, and employees of historically protected state-owned enterprises (Lardy 2002; Bhalla and Qiu 2004; Zhai *et al.* 2004). Nevertheless, public debate about the WTO focuses mainly on the advantages China will gain through membership (Wang *et al.* 2004).

The Chinese state has attempted to impose a view of WTO membership that not only limits political resistance from "losers" of globalization, but also undercuts the legitimacy of any potential resistance. The Chinese Communist Party (CCP) has portrayed China's internationalization as a positive outcome that will bring considerable economic benefits to the population while strengthening China's international standing. At the same time, the Chinese party state is risk averse, insisting that the future of reforms hinges on the ability of the CCP to maintain social stability. Yet, in the light of the considerable pressures on the Chinese labor market (Zeng 2005), China's compliance with its WTO commitments entails a level of political risk. Obviously, these risks are reduced if only a minority of citizens becomes net losers post-WTO accession, but regardless of the distribution of economic costs and benefits, the Chinese state can mitigate the risks of social instability by activating nationalist sentiments about China's proper international role. State-controlled media can play a crucial role by presenting the benefits of membership in non-economic terms, thus raising support for the WTO even among groups that are expected to do poorly under the new rules of the game. In this chapter, we rely on public opinion surveys from very different economic regions in order to examine the attitudes of ordinary Chinese citizens toward the WTO. These unusual data put us in a better position not only to gauge the overall level of support for WTO membership in China, but also allow us to explore the reasons that motivate likely net-losers to maintain their support for China's globalization drive.

## Public opinion and globalization

### *Comparative findings*

In the existing literature, the main framework for predicting an individual's preferences on the globalization debate is based on economic self-interest. Cleavages may be sectoral, class-based, or gender-based. A focus on sectoral differences argues that workers in exporting industries benefit from globalization, while employees of import-competing industries are harmed by globalization. On the other hand, class-based analyses argue that the benefits and opportunities (not to mention the costs) of globalization are differentially distributed among income groups. Organized labor – whether workers are in an import-competing sector or not – is commonly counted as an opponent of globalization (French 2002; Kunkel 2002). Gender may form a third source of differentiation in preferences. Many authors describe globalization as a process of feminization of labor. Gills (2002) argues that women's social movements have been a source of resistance to globalization because it increases the vulnerability of female labor to exploitation.

Clearly, economic interest alone does not determine preferences with respect to globalization. A variety of ideational considerations may also influence popular perceptions of globalization. Opposition to globalization may derive from "concerns about loss of sovereignty, security, identity and culture" (Kunkel 2002: 248). In Australia, for example, "fear of trade deals undermining health, education and media regulation is shared on both the right and the left" (Kunkel 2002: 249). On the positive side, globalization can be part of a foreign policy strategy of building closer links with key allies. In Taiwan, membership in international organizations is not only a source of economic benefit, but also can be part of a strategy to break the island's diplomatic isolation and provide formal channels for communication with foreign governments (Cho 2002). Polls reveal that many Taiwanese believe that membership in the WTO will promote cross-strait peace and security (Kuo 2000). Membership in international institutions can also be a source of national prestige, as in the case of Italy's membership in the European Union (Tossutti 2002).

Individual preferences may also be shaped by one's location in the global economy. A small state such as Singapore is extremely dependent on continued access to, and healthy development of, international economic institutions, which constrains both policy options and popular views of globalization (Dent 2002). Larger economies, in contrast, have a more plausible alternative to economic globalization. Furthermore, regions within a larger economy are not necessarily uniformly situated with respect to globalization. Within a given national economy, large coastal cities with relatively wealthy and cosmopolitan populations and skilled human capital will be more favorable toward globalization than regions with less skilled labor. For example, it is easy to predict that residents of Manhattan will have more to gain and less to lose from globalization than residents of West Virginia.

Within any type of political regime, elites are able to exercise "opinion leadership." Nevertheless, authoritarian states are likely to be more successful than democratic states in limiting the parameters within which "acceptable" debates on globalization may occur. For example, Singapore's policymaking structure limits the independence of organized civil society interests. The Singapore Environment Council and the National Trade Union Congress, which might be expected to give voice to anti-globalization concerns, instead take a stand in favor of free trade, and are "essentially state constructs, formed as the main official representative organizations in their respective fields of labour and environment" (Dent 2002: 160). These three sources of preferences are summarized in Figure 6.1.

| | *Likely to favor globalization* | *Likely to oppose globalization* |
|---|---|---|
| *Economic self-interest* | • Export industries<br>• Capital<br>• Greater education | • Import-competing industries<br>• Labor<br>• Women<br>• Less education |
| *Ideology* | • Belief that economic integration enhances national security (e.g. Taiwan) | • Concern with sovereignty, culture, identity<br>• Concern with environment<br>• Belief that economic integration threatens national security |
| *State-level variables* | • Small economy<br>• Authoritarianism (States favoring globalization may have the capacity to limit the dissemination of alternate views) | |

*Figure 6.1* Preferences on globalization.

The obvious question is under what circumstances ideological and state-level variables can override individual self-interest. In the United States, economic self-interest is a strong predictor of opinions on globalization. A Pew Research Center Survey conducted in 2000 found that Americans with greater education, higher family incomes, and in younger age groups were more likely to see free trade and WTO membership as good for the United States. After controlling for demographic variables, neither union membership nor political party affiliation has a significant effect on opinions toward globalization (Pew 2000).

Other studies fail to find a strong relationship between economic position and opinion on globalization, and instead highlight the role of ideological beliefs. For example, a survey conducted among local bureaucrats in Shanghai in 1997 and 1998 found that levels of support for WTO membership were nearly uniform across gender, age brackets, current positions, Communist party affiliation and income. Those who favored cultural and other contact with the West were more likely to be strongly in favor of WTO membership. Nevertheless, respondents held distinct opinions on specific aspects of globalization, as those who favored WTO membership did not necessarily favor increased foreign direct investment (FDI) (Koehn 2002). Although the implications of joining the European Union are substantially different than those of joining an institution such as the WTO, public opinion on this issue has some similarities with the WTO debate. Opinions on the EU are shaped by competing considerations including economic benefit and national sovereignty. Despite the fact that the tangible benefits of economic globalization have been concentrated mainly in northern Italy, Tossutti (2002) found that demographic variables (such as sex, age, income and location) were not significant predictors of whether respondents believe that EU membership benefits Italy. A study by White *et al.* (2002) draws on surveys in Belarus, Moldova, Russia and Ukraine, finding that attitudes toward the EU were generally positive, and more committed democrats tended to be more enthusiastic about the EU.

## *China and the WTO*

Based on existing theoretical propositions about opinions on globalization, and on the empirical findings of existing work, what can we expect in the Chinese case? First, China's regions have experienced highly uneven growth rates during the reform era (Hu and Wang 1999). As a result, as shown in Table 6.1, GDP per capita is substantially higher in Eastern China than in other regions (see Appendix for additional details).

### *Local economic performance*

All else being equal, different perceptions of the impact of WTO are likely to be based on recent local economic performance. Coastal regions have

*Table 6.1* Regional variation in wealth

| | *GDP per Capita (RMB)* |
|---|---|
| East | 10,465 |
| Northeast | 8,600 |
| Central | 5,661 |
| West | 5,401 |

Source: SSB: *Zhongguo Chengshi Tongji Nianjian 2000*. These data match the time when the survey was conducted.

seen rapid growth, large-scale foreign investment, growing integration with the global economy, and overall prosperity. Northeastern China, in contrast, remains dominated by state-owned industry. It has seen very little foreign investment, and has little reason to believe that its industry will successfully adapt to increased competition in the global market. Western China is in a more ambivalent position. Long neglected under the pro-coastal development strategy, the official "Go West" policy is building expectations that despite western China's few natural advantages when it comes to integration with the global economy, the prospect of substantial state-driven investment will improve the region's prospects under the WTO.

### *Human capital*

A second potential source of difference in opinion with respect to the WTO arises from endowments of human capital. As is the case in other countries, Chinese citizens who are old, poor or uneducated are likely to fare worse in the global economy than their younger, wealthier or better-educated counterparts. The process of globalization in China has already created a shift from guaranteed lifetime employment to massive layoffs and the phenomenon of migrant laborers (Chan 2001; Solinger 2001). Therefore, we expect that ordinary workers will be more insecure about their job security under WTO than cadres or managers.

The debate about globalization in the PRC has not for the most part been as divisive as in other countries, in no small part because the authorities have required the official media to embrace globalization. This is not to say that the globalization critique or the risks inherent to the rapid opening of protected sectors to international competition, particularly debt-burdened and inefficient state-owned enterprises (SOEs), are unknown to ordinary citizens. In fact, high level officials frequently used pending membership in WTO to accelerate reforms of the state sector and justify the policy of laying off workers from state firms that will no longer enjoy easy access to state subsidies and easy loans from state banks under the rules of accession.

The comparison between SOE workers (particularly those with little human capital) with wealthy urban consumers crystallizes the contrast between potential winners and losers of China's globalization. Wealthy consumers will gain from reduced tariff and non-tariff barriers such that had up to now greatly restricted access to prized consumer products such as automobiles. At the other end of the spectrum, increased competition and the implementation of the principle of "national treatment" for all firms are very likely to further damage many state firms that had developed under the planned economy. In northeast China, layoffs in SOEs have already affected millions of workers who sometimes take to the streets to demand payment of back-wages. Figure 6.2 outlines these expectations about Chinese public opinion on WTO accession.

### *Nationalism*

A third important factor influencing Chinese public opinion about the WTO is nationalism. China's leadership was committed to achieving membership in the WTO, framing the debate in terms of Chinese national pride. The dynamics of "face nationalism" (Gries 2004, 2005) did in fact loom very large during the long negotiations for membership. Beyond expected economic gains for many segments of Chinese society, party leaders and the Chinese media stressed that in order for China to play its role as a powerful and important country in the world, it must be part of global organizations. The question of WTO was further charged, because it was entwined with the Taiwan issue. China insisted on joining the WTO first, and only then "allow" Taiwan to join as a separate customs unit.

| | *Likely to favor globalization* | *Likely to oppose globalization* |
|---|---|---|
| *Economic self-interest* | | |
| By region | • Coastal/East<br>• West (hopeful) | • North |
| By sector | | • State sector |
| By human capital | • Younger<br>• High income<br>• Greater education | • Older<br>• Low income<br>• Less education<br>• Low-skill workers |
| *Ideology* | • Belief that economic integration strengthens China's international standing | |
| *State-level variables* | • Authoritarianism (The Chinese state favors globalization, has capacity to limit dissemination of alternate views) | |

*Figure 6.2* Expectations of Chinese preferences on globalization.

Accordingly, Chinese media dutifully focused on the advantages of WTO membership, and China's entry was hailed as a great moment of national pride. Though the message delivered is uniform across regions and social groups, the question remains whether this message is uniformly accepted by an increasingly diverse and differentiated public.

From ordinary citizens' viewpoint, the debate about China's membership in the WTO revolves around two distinct dimensions. National pride, artfully reinforced by the media, reinforces support for membership. Furthermore, those who anticipate personal benefits from market liberalization should also support it (Figure 6.3).

The theoretical and empirical challenge focuses on the indeterminate cases. Does self-interest among likely beneficiaries suffice to generate support for the organization? The bottom right cell presents the greatest political challenge: do citizens who are likely to suffer as a result of membership but exhibit a high level of pride that China has finally joined WTO actually support the organization? If they do, we would conclude that the CCP has made a safe political bet to join because it can rely on a reserve of "selfless globalists" to push its globalization drive. On the other hand, if nationalistic arguments fail to persuade individuals who are clearly at risk, the odds of serious political instability under economic liberalization are much higher, especially if these groups are large and geographically concentrated.

The rest of the chapter is structured as follows. The next section explains how we estimate the differences in expected individual benefits under WTO. It provides an overview of the four cities that were selected as sample sites, and explains the variables used in our analysis and their operationalization. The following section discusses the selection-bias issues associated with conducting surveys in authoritarian countries. Next, we explain the statistical model used in our analysis, and discuss our results. We find that the Chinese state has been quite successful in shaping public perception of WTO accession as a positive step that will strengthen China's international standing. Our results indicate that nationalism

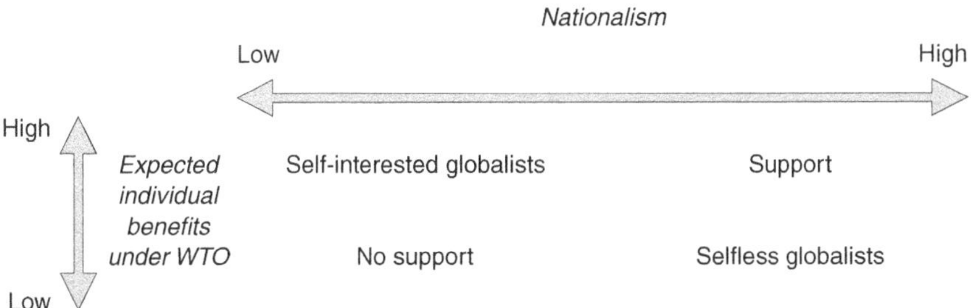


*Figure 6.3* Hypothetical effect of self-interest and nationalism on individual support for globalization.

outweighs individual benefit considerations when explaining public support for the WTO in China.

## Accounting for individual expected gains and losses under WTO

We did not attempt to measure individual subjective assessments of future gains from WTO. We rely instead on objective measures of our respondents' prospects based on their city of residence, employment status and income levels.

### *Overview of four cities*

We examine the political implications of the Chinese leadership's embrace of globalization based on mass survey data of four Chinese cities in the summer of 2002. Our sample was designed to survey residents, aged 15–70, of cities that expect large economic benefits from WTO membership, cities that expect significant economic harm from membership and cities facing more uncertainty about their prospects under WTO. As a condition of conducting these surveys, we agreed to avoid identifying the specific cities used in this study. The cities will be labeled *northeast, eastern, north OCC (Open Coastal City) and west.*

An obvious way to assess a city's prospects under WTO membership is to examine its level of integration with the global economy prior to WTO accession. Regional development in China has been highly uneven since the open-door policy began in 1979. In general, eastern China has attracted much greater levels of foreign direct investment (FDI) than other areas. Foreign investment not only provides an influx of capital to coastal regions, but also creates transfers of technology, managerial expertise and connections with foreign markets. Therefore, coastal cities generate the bulk of China's exports. Table 6.2 illustrates the differences in integration with the global economy among the four cities used in this

*Table 6.2* Openness of sampled cities

| | *Foreign trade/GDP (%)* | *FDI/GDP (%)* |
|---|---|---|
| Northeast | 20 | 4 |
| Eastern | 112 | 6 |
| North OCC | 113 | 8 |
| West | 10 | 1 |
| All Chinese cities | – | 5 |

Sources: *Zhongguo Chengshi Tongji Nianjian 2000*, Municipal Statistical Yearbooks.

Note
Numbers are purposefully rounded to preserve the anonymity of the research sites.

*Table 6.3* Demographics of sampled cities

| | *GDP/capita (RMB)* | *Per capita annual disposable income* | | *College students/capita (%)* | *Local education expenditures per capita (RMB)* | *Official unemployment (%)* |
|---|---|---|---|---|---|---|
| | | *Urban* | *Rural* | | | |
| Northeast | 10,000 | 5,500 | 2,400 | 1.4 | 90 | 1 |
| Eastern | >15,000 | 11,700 | 5,600 | 1.4 | 570 | 2 |
| North OCC | >14,000 | 8,000 | 3,600 | 0.5 | 70 | 1 |
| West | 12,000 | 7,600 | 2,900 | 1.1 | 40 | 5 |
| All cities | 8,000 | 6,300 | 2,200 | 0.4 | 50 | 3 |

Sources: *Zhongguo Chengshi Tongji Nianjian 2000*, Municipal Statistical Yearbooks.

Note
Numbers are purposefully rounded to preserve the anonymity of the research sites.

study. The table makes clear that globalization is already well under way in eastern China. In the two coastal cities surveyed here, trade openness[2] already exceeds 100 percent of GDP. Similarly, FDI inflows as a percentage of GDP in the two coastal cities are above the national average for all Chinese cities.

Demographic factors such as the wealth and education levels of each city's population are also relevant for anticipating its ability to compete in the global economy. Both coastal cities are much wealthier than the national average, but this wealth does not neatly translate into a better-educated population. Despite being the poorest city in the sample, the northeast site has a similar number of college students on a per capita basis to the eastern site, and has greater local education expenditures per capita than either the west or the northern OCC. Another interesting point highlighted by the table above is that although there are large differences among these cities, on the GDP and income measures they are all above the national average. If it is true that residents of poorer cities are more fearful of the costs associated with WTO accession, the true level of anxiety in large parts of China may be even higher than estimated by this study.[3]

### *Individual-level variables*

Our survey included a number of variables that are useful in assessing individuals' likely prospects after WTO accession. These individual-level variables capture different aspects of vulnerability to globalization. For example, age and education level provide measures of an individual's ability to adapt to a changing economic environment. Respondents were asked their highest level of study. A variable called "tertiary education" is coded 0 if the highest level of study achieved was elementary school, middle school or high school, and is coded 1 if the highest level of study achieved was technical college, university, MA, or Ph.D. Income per capita is another variable that captures the relative benefits (through lower prices on consumer goods) and risks (through potential job insecurity) an individual may anticipate.[4]

Even given a certain age, education or income level, some groups are expected to face better prospects under WTO. Given the Chinese political system, Chinese Communist Party (CCP) members are likely to face less objective economic risk than non-members. First, since top enterprise management is comprised of party members, it is reasonable to expect that if layoffs are necessary managers will attempt to protect the jobs of party members at lower levels. Second, even if a party member does become unemployed, membership in the CCP is a relatively scarce and valuable resource that will facilitate finding new employment or starting an independent business.[5] Two other variables that identify groups facing relatively favorable prospects under WTO are "cadre power" (measured by rank) and "elite status," measured by the number of employees under the direct supervision of the respondent.

Other groups may be particularly fearful of the adjustment costs associated with WTO membership. As discussed above, some of the globalization literature argues that pressure to achieve export competitiveness has particularly negative effects on women's wages. It is certainly true that a significant proportion of China's export-oriented manufacturing firms rely heavily on young, unmarried female laborers. Therefore, we also test whether gender is associated with differences in the level of support for globalization.

Several variables specifically address the question of job insecurity. One variable measures the effect of employment in a state-owned enterprise, as opposed to employment in party-government units, science or education units, or collective, private, individual or foreign enterprises. Due to their already precarious financial state, many SOEs will be unable to survive expanded competition with foreign firms. Therefore, all else being equal, respondents employed in SOEs face a higher level of job insecurity. A second variable captures the effect of job position. Within any type of work unit, employees at the lowest ranks are likely to be the most vulnerable to globalization. The variable "worker" identifies respondents who identified themselves as "worker," "ordinary employee," or "low level technician." A third variable identified respondents who are unemployed. Finally, two variables measure respondents' perception of the level of unemployment. One survey question asked if the respondent knew friends or family members laid off within the previous year. A second question asked if unemployment in the respondent's city was a serious problem compared to the situation in the rest of the country. It seems plausible that even if the respondent's own job appears to be secure, those who perceive unemployment as a more serious problem are likely to be more concerned about the costs of adjustment to WTO.

### *Non-response as a non-random assignment problem*

We recognize that conducting opinion research in authoritarian regimes increases the risk that respondents may choose to provide "safe" or "politically correct" answers when the questions posed relate to well-publicized and important state policies. Respondents may choose not to participate at all (survey non-response) or, having accepted to participate, decide to skip specific questions (item non-response) (Zhu 1996).

We do not have sufficient information about the respondents who were randomly selected but opted not to participate in the study to analyze the problem of survey non-response explicitly. However, we know a great deal about those who for any reason chose not to provide a substantive answer to the question: "*Do you think that the WTO is beneficial to, does not have much impact on, or is detrimental to China?*"

Consider the pathway to a substantive answer: respondents were first asked whether they had heard of the WTO or not. We do not believe that the question is politically sensitive. Answering "No" or "I don't know" simply denotes a lack of awareness about international organizations and/or issues. It may well depend upon a person's educational level, job status or knowledge of the national affairs. We explicitly treat the filter question "*Have you ever heard of the WTO*" as a non-random assignment problem because the sub-population that is aware of the organization is highly unlikely to constitute a random subset of respondents. If the reasons why respondents have never heard of the WTO are systematically related to the question of interest, the coefficients in an ordinary probit model of support for the WTO will be biased (Chow *et al.* 1979; Heckman *et al.* 1985; Heckman 1988a, 1988b; Klein and Wellek 1989; Choi 1992; Farley *et al.* 2002; Geddes 2003).

In contrast, the follow up question (if one has heard of the WTO) *is* politically sensitive. Openly expressing views that the organization is detrimental to China certainly challenges official policy that membership – secured in 2001 after ten years of arduous negotiations – is one of the major achievements of the Jiang-Zhu administration. Beyond the few brave souls who explicitly challenged this received wisdom, we also take the view that the analysis must discriminate between individuals who, having heard of the WTO, explicitly affirmed that it benefits China and those who, given the option, chose to answer that the WTO's impact on China is "neutral" or did not answer the question at all (DK/NA). As a result, we coded our dependent variable "support for the WTO" 1 if respondents explicitly affirmed the position that it is beneficial to China. All other answers are coded 0, because they denote either open opposition of government policy, ambivalence (or the refuge for a neutral

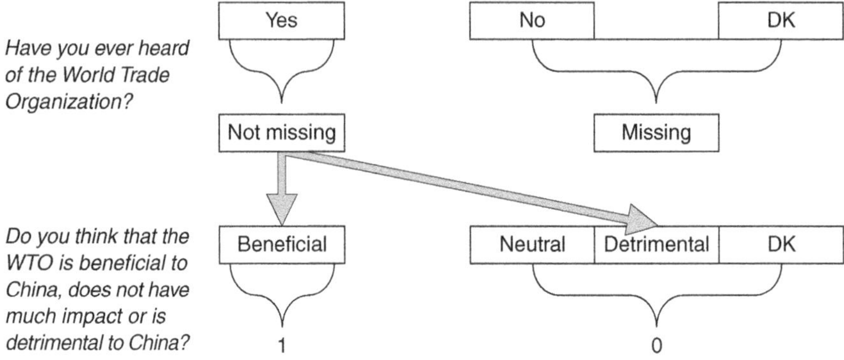


*Figure 6.4* Coding rule for "support for the WTO".

answer among those who may be reluctant to state their opposition) or the politically safe refusal to provide any answer at all. Simply put, our dependent variable captures explicitly stated support for China's membership in the WTO (Figure 6.4).

### *Causes of selection bias*

#### *Age and location*

In practice, awareness of the WTO varies geographically and seems strongly correlated with age. In the two open coastal cites in north and east China, the age gap between those who are aware of the organization is considerable (9.3 and 12.1 years, respectively). This is probably the product of the openness of the local economies. Through physical presence of the foreign direct investors, media discussions of the implications of membership for their city and the overall relevance of the global economic trends to citizen's lives, awareness of the WTO is much more widespread on the coast than in regions that have not been widely exposed to China's open door policy (the northeast and the west).

#### *Gender*

Awareness is also correlated with gender, and the extent of the gender gap is geographically systematic. In the northeastern and western samples, the absolute number of women unaware of the WTO is not only large (23.4 percent and 17.6 percent of the total sample respectively), but it is also twice as large as the number of men (9.4 percent and 8.6 percent). In open coastal cities, the gender gap narrows considerably, and is not even statistically significant in the eastern city.

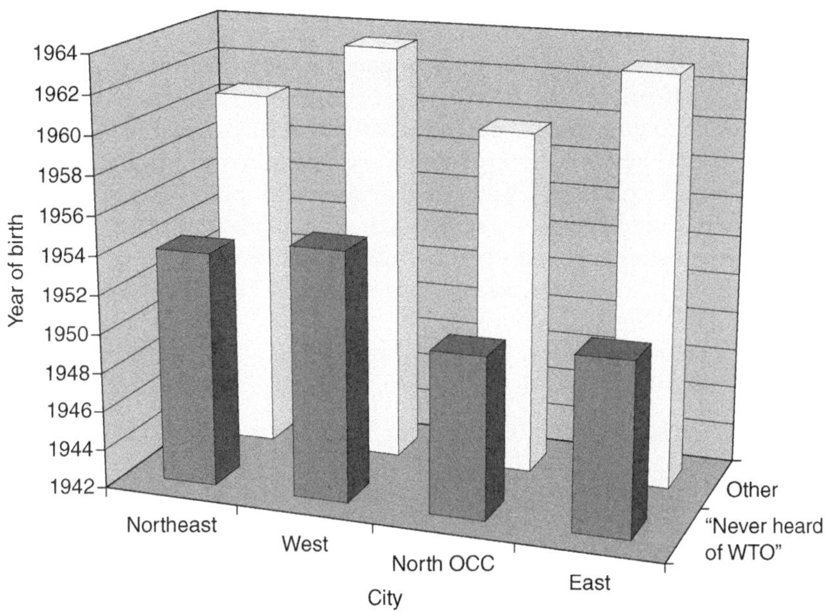


*Figure 6.5* Impact of age on respondents' awareness of the WTO, by city.

*Table 6.4* Gender and awareness of the WTO

| | *Male* | *Female* | *Total* |
|---|---|---|---|
| *Northeast* | | | |
| No answer | 47 | 117 | 164 |
| Answer | 448 | 388 | 836 |
| Total | 495 | 505 | 1,000 |
| | $\chi^2_{(1)} = 34.0877$ Pr = 0.000 | | |
| *West* | | | |
| No answer | 43 | 88 | 131 |
| Answer | 457 | 412 | 869 |
| Total | 500 | 500 | 1,000 |
| | $\chi^2_{(1)} = 17.7883$ Pr = 0.000 | | |
| *North OCC* | | | |
| No answer | 13 | 46 | 59 |
| Answer | 478 | 463 | 941 |
| Total | 491 | 509 | 1,000 |
| | $\chi^2_{(1)} = 18.3787$ Pr = 0.000 | | |
| *East* | | | |
| No answer | 17 | 29 | 46 |
| Answer | 452 | 502 | 954 |
| Total | 469 | 531 | 1,000 |
| | $\chi^2_{(1)} = 1.9143$ Pr = 0.166 | | |

*Awareness of national affairs*

Following Zaller (1992), we also account for the public's knowledge of political affairs by asking a number of specific factual questions that vary in level of difficulty.[6] Each respondent received a score that sums the number of correct answers, ranging from 0 to a theoretical maximum of nine. Clearly, a person's propensity to hold a substantive opinion about the WTO is related to her level of engagement with political issues. Figure 6.6 plots the distribution of our dependent variable against the political awareness score for the northeastern sample. Political awareness is a mere 1.7 among those who have never heard of the WTO, against 3.5 for non-supporters and 4.5 for supporters. The results hold across samples: political awareness is very low when cases are "missing" in the selection-bias sense and tends to be higher among WTO supporters than others (Table 6.5).

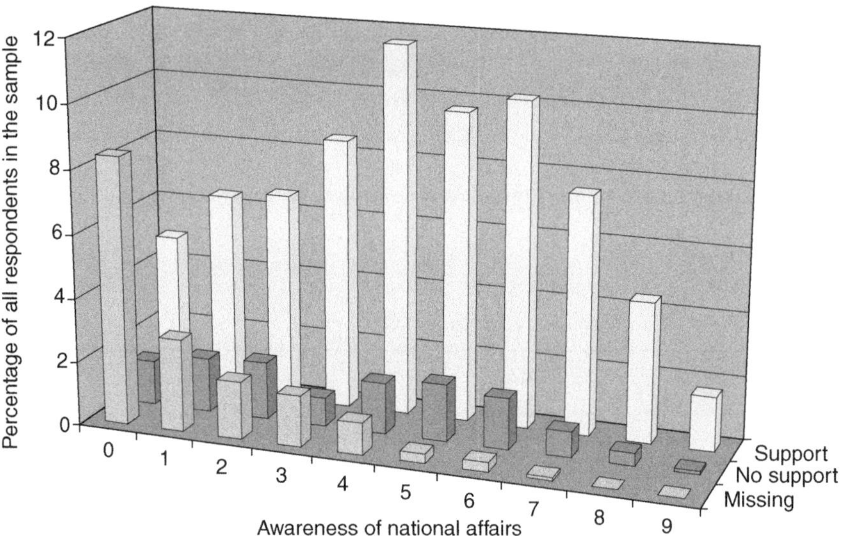


$\chi^2_{(18)}=271.15$ Pr=0.000
Kendall's $\tau_{-b}=-0.25$ ASE=0.03

*Figure 6.6* Political awareness and support for the WTO.

*Table 6.5* Average political awareness score (0–9 scale), by city and category of the dependent variable

| | *Missing* | *No support* | *Support* |
|---|---|---|---|
| Northeast | 1.7 | 3.5 | 4.5 |
| West | 1.5 | 3.2 | 4.6 |
| North OCC | 1.1 | 3.5 | 4.6 |
| East | 1.8 | 4.4 | 4.9 |

*Education*

The vast majority of the respondents who have never heard of the WTO is concentrated among those who have not completed a high school education. This result may seem rather obvious, but this important selection affect must be accounted for in the analysis because the subset of respondents who expressed an opinion about the WTO is clearly more educated than ordinary citizens. Figure 6.7 displays the results for the northeastern sample, but the point holds across all cities: the lack of awareness of the WTO is concentrated among individuals who have little education while support for the WTO increases with schooling. Furthermore, average educational levels for all categories of the dependent variable increase with the city's degree of openness (Table 6.6).

*Table 6.6* Average schooling, by city and category of the dependent variable

| | *Missing* | *No support* | *Support* |
|---|---|---|---|
| Northeast | 6.0 | 8.7 | 10.1 |
| West | 6.4 | 9.4 | 10.6 |
| North OCC | 6.5 | 9.8 | 10.7 |
| East | 7.6 | 10.5 | 11.4 |

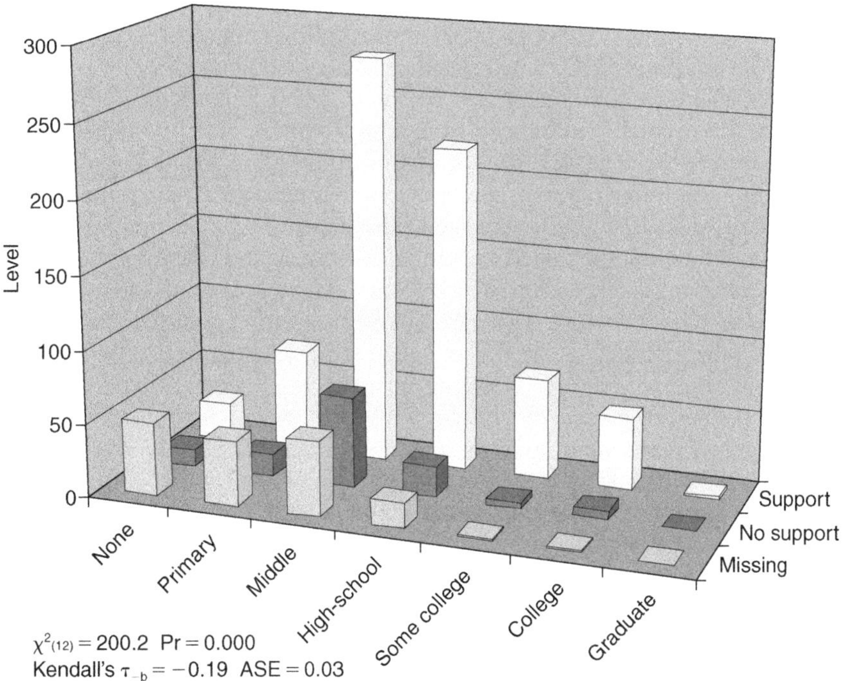


*Figure 6.7* Level of education and support for the WTO.

## Modeling support for the WTO

Since our dependent variable is binary and we explicitly account for sample selection, we estimate a maximum likelihood bivariate probit model. The dependent variable "support for the WTO" is only observed if a respondent has ever heard of the WTO. The selection equation models the probability of observing the dependent variable based on a respondent's gender, age, level of education and degree of political awareness. The outcome equation predicts whether a respondent who is aware of the WTO agrees that it is beneficial to China or not. Since our respondents were selected within neighborhood committees, all robust standard errors are computed assuming clustering by neighborhood committee.[7]

### *Findings*

Although the selection equations are powerful predictors of awareness of the WTO in the northeastern, western and northern samples, awareness is not – in turn – systematically correlated with the respondent's substantive support of the WTO. However, there is very strong evidence of selection bias in the eastern sample.

Two variables stand out as both substantively important and statistically significant predictors of support for the WTO. Nationalism clearly outweighs the importance of other factors in the explaining popular support for the WTO, but economic factors (namely estimated income) also contribute to higher levels of support for membership. Figure 6.8 illustrates how nationalism and self-interest interact, based on the eastern China sample.[8] The fitted values assume a male worker with college education born in 1942 with a political awareness score of 4.5 (the sample mean). Nationalism has the biggest discriminating impact among lower income earners. At a per capita annual income of RMB 10,000, the expected probability of support among respondents who do not agree that WTO enhances China's international standing is only 90 percent, as opposed to nearly 98 percent among respondents who do agree with this statement. The gap narrows around the sample mean, and disappears completely in the higher income brackets. In fact "self-interested globalism" seems to be the defining characteristic of the urban economic elite who stand to gain from cheaper high-end consumer products (such as automobiles) that remain unaffordable for average and low income earners, but are becoming affordable to a rising proportion of wealthier urbanites.

The regime's policy of portraying WTO as a foreign policy accomplishment makes even more sense considering the much reduced levels of support in cities that are unlikely to benefit very much (western sample) or even suffer (northeast) under WTO. Notice that in the northwest, where layoffs in SOEs are widespread, workers are substantially (and significantly so, at the 0.01 level) less likely to support the WTO. In fact, without the nationalist card, the odds of supporting the WTO are barely

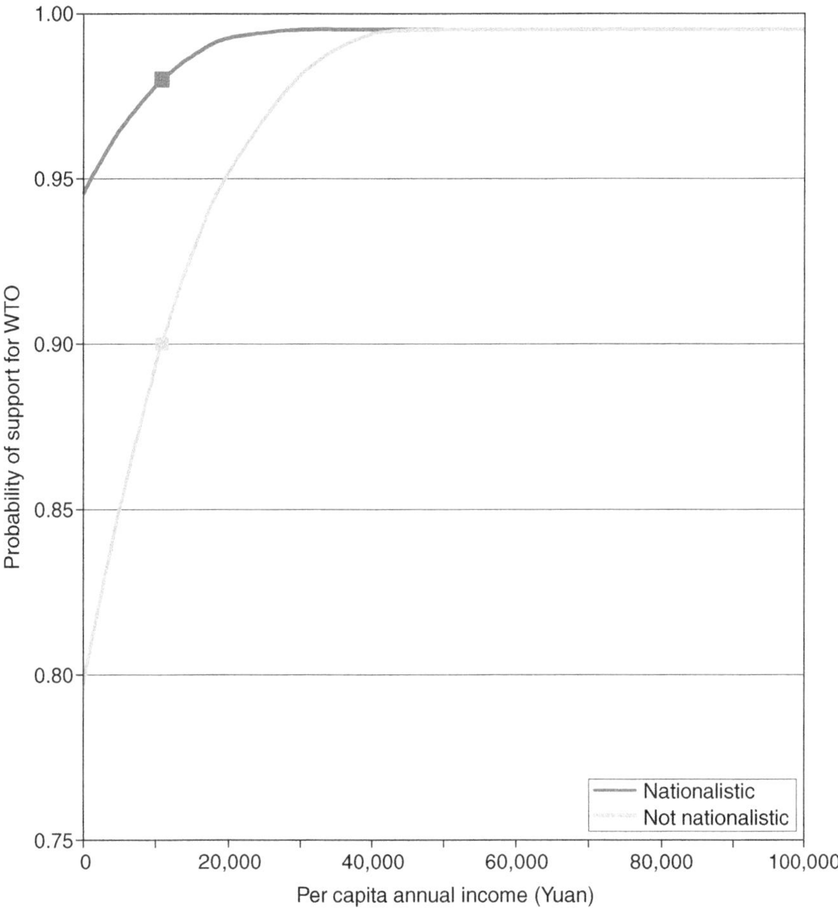


*Figure 6.8* Fitted impact of income and nationalism on the probability of support for the WTO (eastern sample).

above 30 percent. The fitted odds almost double if the same respondent is assumed to be nationalistic (Figure 6.9).

The models also support the hypothesis that – *ceteris paribus* – current levels of economic openness – along with employment opportunities – have a positive impact on the level of support for the WTO. Workers in the northeast are probably rational to be skeptical of the WTO because the local economies are so dependent on the state sector that finding alternative employment is unlikely if they are laid off. In contrast, in the eastern sample, only workers who fear being laid off express lower levels of support, while even ordinary workers who believe that layoffs are an issue but do not personally feel that their own job is at risk support the WTO.

In conclusion, our analysis shows that the Chinese case does not fit

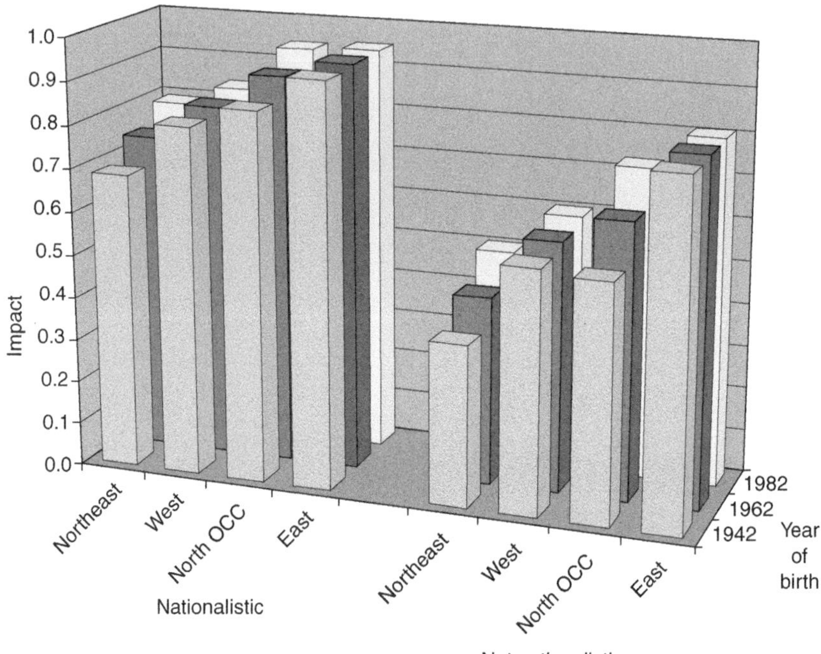


*Figure 6.9* Fitted impact of nationalism and age on the probability of support for the WTO, by city.

neatly with the standard assumptions in the globalization literature. The conventional wisdom holds that the main framework for predicting an individual's preferences on the globalization debate is based on economic self-interest. In China, however, instead of a cleavage of public opinion pitting expected winners against expected losers, we find a very different kind of public. Contrary to the expectations based on economic self-interest, we do not find strong opposition to the WTO among SOE employees, among the working class as a whole, or among women. Throughout the Chinese public, it appears that ideational considerations – most particularly, the consideration of national power and dignity – exert a strong influence on popular perceptions of globalization.

It remains to be seen whether these high levels of support can be sustained in the longer run. We analyze data collected on the eve of China's entry in the WTO, a period when the benefits of accession were front-loaded, while the more difficult adjustments are scheduled to occur during the transitory phase of five years, in most instances. The public's optimism is also to some extent the product of China's impressive macroeconomic performance since 1978. Fortunately for the leaders in Beijing, the PRC has yet to experience a severe economic downturn that would test the extent to which economic nationalism alone can legitimize China's globalization drive.

*Table 6.7* Probit estimation with sample selection of support for the WTO

| | *Northeastern city* | | *Western city* | | *North coastal city* | | *Eastern city* | |
|---|---|---|---|---|---|---|---|---|
| Number of observations | 826 | | 566 | | 59 | | 636 | |
| Censored obs. | 162 | | 131 | | 751 | | 46 | |
| Uncensored obs. | 664 | | 435 | | 102 | | 590 | |
| LLK | −515 | | | | −371 | | −303 | |
| Wald chi2(15) | 66.38 | | 84.53 | | 102 | | 73 | |
| Prob > chi2 | 0.000 | | 0.000 | | 0.000 | | 0.000 | |
| *Support for WTO* | *Coef.* | *RSE* | *Coef.* | *RSE* | *Coef.* | *RSE* | *Coef.* | *RSE* |
| Nationalism | 0.806 | 0.140*** | 0.729 | 0.230*** | 0.950 | 0.159*** | 0.770 | 0.166*** |
| Estimated income/cap | 0.097 | 0.000*** | 0.041 | 0.000** | 0.021 | 0.000 | 0.042 | 0.000*** |
| Female (1 = fem; 0 = male) | 0.101 | 0.134 | 0.170 | 0.201 | 0.183 | 0.151 | −0.238 | 0.148 |
| Year of birth | 0.008 | 0.007 | 0.002 | 0.007 | 0.012 | 0.006** | 0.000 | 0.007 |
| Tertiary education | −0.377 | 0.285 | 0.569 | 0.287 | −0.025 | 0.196 | −0.117 | 0.209 |
| CCP member | 0.196 | 0.245 | 0.888 | 0.337*** | 0.065 | 0.253 | −0.293 | 0.259 |
| Cadre power | −0.091 | 0.139 | 0.126 | 0.341 | −0.136 | 0.139 | −0.063 | 0.256 |
| Elite | 0.190 | 0.332 | −0.101 | 0.906 | 0.488 | 0.456 | 0.167 | 0.532 |
| Political awareness | −0.053 | 0.051 | −0.027 | 0.056 | 0.078 | 0.036** | −0.049 | 0.031 |
| Employed in SOE | 0.390 | 0.170** | 0.204 | 0.203 | −0.013 | 0.102 | −0.224 | 0.148 |
| Worker | −0.550 | 0.156*** | 0.241 | 0.216 | −0.292 | 0.350 | 0.269 | 0.342 |
| Worker × Fear layoff | 0.152 | 0.149 | −0.099 | 0.218 | 0.201 | 0.214 | −0.478 | 0.216** |
| Believe layoff is a problem | 0.030 | 0.153 | 0.242 | 0.274 | −0.372 | 0.177** | 0.386 | 0.210* |
| Know someone laid off | −0.098 | 0.167 | 0.275 | 0.232 | −0.152 | 0.217 | 0.142 | 0.184 |
| Unemployed | 0.168 | 0.185 | −0.320 | 0.206 | −0.196 | 0.202 | 0.243 | 0.196 |
| Constant | −14.793 | 14.062 | −4.035 | 14.569 | −22.679 | 11.283** | 1.249 | 12.984 |
| *Selection equation* | | | | | | | | |
| Female (1 = fem; 0 = male) | −0.235 | 0.134* | −0.278 | 0.110*** | −0.132 | 0.157 | 0.395 | 0.149*** |
| Year of birth | 0.012 | 0.004*** | 0.006 | 0.005 | 0.014 | 0.006** | 0.017 | 0.006*** |
| Level of education [0–6 scale] | 0.275 | 0.066*** | 0.341 | 0.074*** | 0.239 | 0.112** | 0.220 | 0.089*** |
| Political awareness | 0.311 | 0.025*** | 0.199 | 0.033*** | 0.358 | 0.054*** | 0.296 | 0.050*** |
| Constant | −24.401 | 7.853*** | −13.083 | 9.287 | −27.250 | 11.719** | −33.576 | 12.189*** |
| *Wald test of independence of equations* | | | | | | | | |
| $\rho$ | −0.332 | 0.446 | −0.266 | 0.528 | −0.155 | 0.262 | −0.999 | 0.003*** |
| $\rho = 0$: $\chi^2_{(1)}$ | | 0.470 | | 0.230 | | 0.340 | | 4.100 |
| Prob > $\chi^2$ | | 0.490 | | 0.630 | | 0.560 | | 0.040 |

Note
Standard errors are heteroskedastic-consistent, assuming clustering by neighborhood committee.

## Appendix 6.1

*Appendix 6.1* WTO accession, 1994 – 16 February 2005

| | |
|---|---|
| *1994* | Angola |
| | Djibouti |
| | Grenada |
| | Guinea |
| | Guinea-Bissau |
| | Honduras |
| | Liechtenstein |
| | Papua New Guinea |
| | Paraguay |
| | Qatar |
| | Slovenia |
| | Solomon Islands |
| | St. Kitts and Nevis |
| | United Arab Emirates |
| *1995* | Bulgaria |
| | Ecuador |
| *1996* | Mongolia |
| | Panama |
| *1998* | Kyrgyz Republic |
| *1999* | Estonia |
| | Latvia |
| *2000* | Albania |
| | Croatia |
| | Georgia |
| | Jordan |
| | Oman |
| *2001* | China |
| | Lithuania |
| | Moldova |
| *2002* | Taiwan |
| *2003* | Armenia |
| | Macedonia |
| *2004* | Cambodia |
| | Nepal |

Source: WTO web site: www.wto.org/english/thewto_e/whatis_e/tif_e/org6_e.htm.

## Appendix 6.2

*Appendix 6.2* GDP by province, 1999

| | *Population (10,000 persons)* | *GDP (RMB 100 million)* | *GDP/Capita (RMB)* |
|---|---|---|---|
| *Eastern region* | | | |
| Beijing | 1,250 | 2,174 | |
| Tianjin | 910 | 1,450 | |
| Hebei | 6,602 | 4,899 | |
| Shanghai | 1,313 | 4,035 | |
| Jiangsu | 7,009 | 7,637 | |
| Zhejiang | 4,220 | 5,874 | |
| Fujian | 2,962 | 3,679 | |
| Shandong | 7,724 | 7,187 | |
| Henan | 7,553 | 4,010 | |
| Guangdong | 7,299 | 9,504 | |
| Guangxi | 2,766 | 1,423 | |
| Hainan | 101 | 144 | |
| Total | 49,709 | 52,018 | 10,465 |
| *Northern region* | | | |
| Neimenggu | 1,205 | 693 | |
| Liaoning | 4,103 | 4,215 | |
| Jilin | 2,398 | 1,712 | |
| Heilongjiang | 3,070 | 2,648 | |
| Total | 10,776 | 9,267 | 8,600 |
| *Central region* | | | |
| Shanxi | 1,354 | 945 | |
| Anhui | 5,641 | 2,590 | |
| Jiangxi | 2,179 | 1,124 | |
| Hubei | 4,957 | 3,471 | |
| Hunan | 6,261 | 3,415 | |
| Total | 20,392 | 11,544 | 5,661 |
| *Western region* | | | |
| Chongqing | 3,072 | 1,480 | |
| Sichuan | 6,477 | 3,257 | |
| Guizhou | 1,280 | 538 | |
| Yunnan | 1,208 | 1,086 | |
| Shaanxi | 2,991 | 1,475 | |
| Gansu | 851 | 469 | |
| Qinghai | 134 | 73 | |
| Ningxia | 351 | 210 | |
| Xinjiang | 186 | 351 | |
| Tibet | | | |
| Total | 16,550 | 8,939 | 5,401 |
| National average | | | 8,393 |

## Notes

1 Prior to 1995, the General Agreement on Tariffs and Trade (GATT) was the organization regulating global trade. On 1 January 1995 the WTO replaced GATT.
2 Trade openness is measured as (Imports + Exports)/GDP.
3 Nevertheless, as discussed in more detail below, awareness of the WTO tends to vary geographically. Poorer inland cities are likely to have lower levels of awareness of the WTO, which is likely to mitigate overall levels of WTO-related anxiety in these cities.
4 Income per capita is measured as (Annual Household Income/Number of Persons Depending on that Income). In cases where the respondent did not provide a figure for annual household income, we estimated annual household income as (Previous Month Household Income × 12).
5 Of course, it is difficult to disentangle the economic and political effects of the CCP membership variable. A party member may express support for China's WTO membership because he expects to benefit (or at least does not anticipate significant economic risk) from WTO accession. In this case, a favorable response indicates a "self-interested globalist" orientation. On the other hand, a party member may feel constrained to express support for the government's policy positions, whether or not he expects any personal benefit, indicating a more "selfless globalist" orientation.
6 Specifically, the respondent was asked to identify the current vice-president of the PRC (Hu Jintao at the time), the current governor of their home province, the Party secretary of their city, the highest organ of the state empowered to pass legislation (National People's Congress), the Prime Minister of Japan, one of China's eight recognized "democratic parties," the US vice-president, the head of the Hong-Kong SAR (Tung Chee-hua) and the Secretary General of the United Nations.
7 We need not account for stratification and probability weights. Each urban sample is drawn from a single stratum, and the probability of selecting a respondent is equalized by design. Thirty neighborhood committees were randomly selected in each city (40 in the eastern city). Within each neighborhood, respondents were directly selected from lists of residents supplied at the local level. We thus directly obtained an equal probability sample of adults (age 15–70) – not households – without the need to randomly draw a single adult from a number of eligible respondents across of varying size. Probability weights are thus unnecessary.
8 In probit models with sample selection where $y_1 = X\beta + \varepsilon_1$ (outcome equation), $y_{1,select} = (Z\gamma + \varepsilon_2 > 0)$ represents the selection equation that determines the observability of $y_1$, and $\rho = corr(\varepsilon_1, \varepsilon_2)$, the probability that $y_1 = 1$ conditional upon $y_2 = 1$ is equal to $\Phi(X\beta, Z\gamma, \rho)$, where $\Phi$ is the bivariate normal distribution function.

## References


Bhalla, A. S. (1998) *Globalization, Growth and Marginalization,* New York: St. Martin's Press.

Bhalla, A. S. and Qiu, S. (2004) *The Employment Impact of China's WTO Accession,* London: RoutledgeCurzon.

Chan, A. (2001) *China's Workers Under Assault: The Exploitation of Labor in a Globalizing Economy,* Armonk: M.E. Sharpe.

Cho, H. (2002) *Taiwan's Application to GATT/WTO: Significance of Multilateralism for an Unrecognized State,* Westport: Praeger.

Choi, K. (1992) *Identification and Estimation of Nonparametric and Semiparametric Sample Selection Models*. Microform.

Chow, W., Mitchell, B. M. and Los Angeles Dept. of Water and Power (1979) *Sample Selection in the Los Angeles Electricity Rate Study*, Santa Monica: Rand.

Clark, C. and Montjoy, R. S. (2001) *Globalization's Impact on State-Local Economic Development Policy*, Huntington: Nova Science Publishers.

Dent, C. M. (2002) "Reconciling Multiple Economic Multilateralisms: The Case of Singapore," *Contemporary Southeast Asia*, 24/1: 146–65.

Farley, D., Wynn, B. O. and Rand Corporation (2002) *Exploration of Selection Bias Issues for the DoD Federal Employees Health Benefits Program Demonstration*, Santa Monica: Rand.

French, J. D. (2002) "From the Suites to the Streets: The Unexpected Re-emergence of the 'Labor Question,' 1994–1999," *Labor History*, 43/3: 285–304.

Geddes, B. (2003) *Paradigms and Sand Castles: Theory Building and Research Design in Comparative Politics (Analytical Perspectives on Politics)*, Ann Arbor: University of Michigan Press.

Gills, D. S. (2002) "Globalization of Production and Women in Asia," *Annals of the American Academy of Political and Social Science*, 581/May: 106–20.

Greven, T. (2003) *Clash of Globalizations? The Politics of International Labor Rights in the United States*, Frankfurt and New York: Peter Lang.

Gries, P. H. (2004) "Popular Nationalism and State Legitimation in China," in P. H. Gries and S. Rosen (eds) *State and Society in 21st Century China: Crisis, Contention, and Legitimation*, London: Routledge, 180–94.

—— (2005) "Nationalism and Chinese Foreign Policy," in Y. Deng and F. Wang (eds) *China Rising: Power and Motivation in Chinese Foreign Policy*, New York: Rowman & Littlefield, 103–20.

Hanson, G. H., Scheve, K. F., Slaughter, M. J. and National Bureau of Economic Research (2005) *Public Finance and Individual Preferences over Globalization Strategies*, Cambridge: National Bureau of Economic Research.

Heckman, J. J. (1988) *The Microeconomic Evaluation of Social Programs and Economic Institutions; The Value of Longitudinal Data for Solving the Problem of Selection Bias in Evaluating the Impact of Treatments on Outcomes, Chung-Hua Series of Lectures by Invited Eminent Economists; No. 14.* Nankang, Taipei, Taiwan, Republic of China: Institute of Economics Academia Sinica.

Heckman, J. J., Singer, B. and Social Science Research Council (US) (1985) *Longitudinal Analysis of Labor Market Data*, Cambridge: Cambridge University Press.

Hu, A. and Wang, S. (1999) *The Political Economy of Uneven Development: The Case of China*, Armonk: M.E. Sharpe.

Jussila, H., Marjoral, R. and Delgado-Cravidao, F. (2001) *Globalization and Marginality in Geographical Space: Political, Economic and Social Issues of Development in the New Millennium, Dynamics of Marginal and Critical Regions*, Burlington: Ashgate.

Klein, R. and Wellek, R. (1989) *Sample Selection, Aging, and Reactivity of Coal*, New York: J. Wiley.

Koehler, G. and California State Library California Research Bureau (2001) *The Public's View of Foreign Trade: Pragmatic Internationalism*, Sacramento: California State Library California Research Bureau.

Koehn, P. H. (2002) "The Shanghai Outlook on the WTO: Local Bureaucrats and Accession-Related Reforms," *Pacific Affairs*, 75/3: 399–417.

Kokubun, Y. and Wang, J. (2004) *The Rise of China and a Changing East Asian Order*, Tokyo and Washington, DC: Japan Center for International Exchange.

Kunkel, J. (2002) "Australian Trade Policy in an Age of Globalisation," *Australian Journal of International Affairs*, 56/2: 237–51.

Kuo, D. (2000) "Taiwan Poll: Social Elite Sees WTO Entry Crucial to Cross-Strait Peace Process," Taiwanese Central News Agency (November 9). (Obtained from BBC Monitoring, Record Number 0E82CEB5F489C1F5).

Lardy, N. (2002) *Integrating China into the Global Economy*, Washington, DC: Brookings Institution Press.

Pew Research Center for the People and the Press (2000) "Post-Seattle Support for WTO," (March 2). Online. Available at: people-press.org (accessed 15 July 2005).

Scheve, K. F. and Slaughter, M. J. (2001) *Globalization and the Perceptions of American Workers*, Washington, DC: Institute for International Economics.

Solinger, D. J. (2001) "Globalization and the Paradox of Participation: The Chinese Case," *Global Governance*, 7/2: 173–96.

SSB (State Statistical Bureau of China) *Zhongguo Chengshi Tongji Nianjian* [Statistical Yearbook of Chinese Cities], various years, Beijing: China Statistics Publishing.

Tossutti, L. S. (2002) "Between Globalism and Localism, Italian Style," *West European Politics*, 25/3: 51–76.

Wei, Y. D. (2000) *Regional Development in China: Globalization, the State and Regions*, London: Routledge.

White, S., McAllister, I. and Light, M. (2002) "Enlargement and the New Outsiders," *Journal of Common Market Studies*, 40/1: 135–53.

World Trade Organization (2003) Online. Available HTTP: http://www.wto.org (accessed 15 July 2005).

Zaller, J. (1992) *The Nature and Origins of Mass Opinion*, New York: Cambridge University Press.

Zeng, D. Z. and the World Bank (2005) *China's Employment Challenges and Strategies after the WTO Accession*, Washington, DC: World Bank.

Zhai, F., Hertel, T. W. and the World Bank (2004) *Labor Market Distortions, Rural-Urban Inequality, and the Opening of China's Economy*, Washington, DC: World Bank.

Zhu, J. (1996) "'*I don't know*' in Public Opinion Surveys in China: Individual and Contextual Causes of Item Non-response," *Journal of Contemporary China*, 5/12: 223–45.

# 7 Temptation versus coercion

## Trade agreements and the nation-state

*Philip I. Levy*

### Introduction

Multilateral trade agreements used to be considered dull. Negotiators would settle upon non-linear formulae for tariff reductions and then haggle over exclusions and phase-in periods. Only trade aficionados and industries with a pecuniary interest would pay any attention. Negotiators still haggle in the same way, but now they do it behind a security cordon as multitudinous protesters rail against the injustices they claim are being perpetrated in the negotiating hall. In 2002, trade negotiations were so controversial that the US Congress was only able to grant negotiating authority to the executive branch by the slimmest of margins.

To a large extent, these alleged injustices stem from perceived threats to sovereignty, whatever that may be. There is a sense that a supranational organization is challenging nations' rights to set environmental policy, support farmers, or determine whether food is safe. Since all of those decisions are the normal domain of elected national or subnational legislatures, the idea that they are being settled by unelected international bureaucrats seems to be *prima facie* evidence that the process of globalization has undermined the sovereign rights of the nation-state.

While there is a superficial appeal to this reasoning, it does not stand up to close analysis. At one level, the allegations fail because they are based on misunderstandings of the legal status of trade agreements and dispute settlement. The allegations do, however, raise some serious and challenging questions about what the term "sovereignty" means and whether it is possible to draw a bright line between international transactions that preserve sovereign rights and those that diminish sovereign powers.

This chapter reviews some of the literature's existing definitions of sovereignty and argues for a definition that hinges on coercion. If a country is physically prevented from exercising the normal functions of government within its borders or from engaging in voluntary commercial transactions with others, one can reasonably say that the country's sovereignty has been infringed. Even this conservative definition allows for ambiguous scenarios. However, those scenarios are not of the sort that arise in international trade negotiations or in the enforcement of the agreements that emerge. International trade agreements do not pose a threat to the sovereign rights of nations, properly understood.

In the next section we review some of the arguments about sovereignty that have flourished recently and present the case for a coercion standard. We then consider the nature of international trade agreements and their legal standing in relation to sovereign nations. The next section contemplates whether the sovereignty argument is affected by the geographic scope of the trade agreement – regional or global.

## What is sovereignty?

### *Political, economic and legal approaches*

Krasner (2001) reviews thinking on sovereignty and its evolution over recent centuries. He argues that sovereignty does not have a single, well-accepted definition. It can mean control of movement across borders, control of domestic behavior, exclusion of external sources of authority, or the mutual recognition of "juridically independent territorial entities."

There is an interesting distinction to be drawn between *de jure* and *de facto* control. There may be universal acknowledgement that France has the right to set rules governing the length of the work week, but this does not mean that the French central government necessarily has *de facto* control. Its control could be undermined by domestic changes, such as advances in communication facilitating the functioning of a black market in labor, or by international changes, such as increased competition through trade increasing the costliness of regulation. If one were to adopt a definition based on *de facto* control, two immediate difficulties present themselves. First, there have been few, if any, historical instances in which even strong and independent governments have enjoyed complete control over their citizens. In assessing the novelty of globalization's challenges to sovereignty, Krasner provides examples of past challenges to government authority. He writes: "It is not that globalization has had no impact on state control, but rather that controlling transborder movements, not to speak of developments within a state's boundaries, has always been a challenge" (236).

If no one is truly sovereign, the concept is not particularly useful for assessing the impact of trade agreements. The second problem is related: if we adopt a definition of sovereignty such that it is a continuous rather than a binary variable, assessing the effect of trade agreements will be substantially more difficult. One would have to try to distinguish fluctuations in measured sovereignty due to the trading regime from those due to other factors. Thus, the discussion would be better served by a more robust and binary definition of sovereignty that focused more on *de jure* control.

Bagwell and Staiger (2004) inadvertently demonstrate the perils of an excessively narrow definition of sovereignty. They focus on two of Krasner's four types of sovereignty: the maintenance of internal control (interdependence sovereignty) and the absence from foreign interference (Westphalian sovereignty). They refine Krasner's definitions to fit their economic model. Interdependence sovereignty exists in a choice problem when a government's payoff from a choice problem is unaffected by the choices of other governments. A government has Westphalian sovereignty in a choice problem if all other governments are indifferent to the outcome of its choice problem. Unsurprisingly, with the further narrowing of these definitions, Bagwell and Staiger (2004: 11) argue that governments frequently lose sovereignty in trade agreements: "If the level of a policy instrument is directly negotiated between or among governments, it seems reasonable to conclude that national sovereignty over that policy instrument has been lost, at least as long as the agreement is in force."

Not only does this have the direct implication that all cooperative agreements diminish sovereignty, but it also treats sovereignty not as an attribute of a state but rather as the attribute of a state in the context of a particular choice problem. In a footnote, they allow for, but ultimately dismiss, a definition of sovereignty that says a country maintains sovereignty so long as a national government has the right to withdraw from an agreement.

While the Bagwell and Staiger definition is precise and works well within the two-goods model that they analyze, it does little to capture the more general sense that countries have either retained or abandoned their rights to independent action as they have pursued international trade agreements.

### *Where is the GATT army?*

A popular but unhelpful conception of sovereignty is that of Friedman (2000). This is the idea of a "golden straitjacket." Ostensibly, countries enjoy the nominal freedom to engage in or disengage from international commerce. The costs of disengagement are so high, however, that *de facto* the countries are compelled to adopt a homogenous set of policies that reduces domestic politics to quibbles over trivialities. Friedman's analysis is a bit more subtle than his metaphor:

> I am not saying that you have to put on the straitjacket . . . If you want to resist (the changes of globalization), that is your business. And it should be your business. But if you think that you can resist these changes without paying an increasingly steep price, without building an increasingly high wall and without falling behind increasingly fast, then you are deluding yourself.
>
> (Friedman 2000: 109)

The problem with the straitjacket metaphor is that it implies compulsion. Though Friedman writes of countries choosing whether or not to don a straitjacket, it is apparel that usually connotes a complete lack of choice. It is the outfit of an individual who has been committed to an institution and whose freedom has been forcibly curtailed.

Rather than the lurid image of a golden straitjacket, Friedman might have called it the "dilemma of the good job" (though he would certainly have sold fewer books). Consider a young college graduate hoping to succeed as an actor. Our aspiring thespian faces the choice each morning of heading off to an audition where he has a slim chance of landing a low-paying role. What if he decides he would rather sleep in on a given morning? The expected cost to sleeping in is just the meager wage weighted by the odds of landing the part. He can rest easy.

Suppose, though, that a friend calls and offers our young graduate a job with a six-figure salary and demanding hours. What has happened to the cost of sleeping in? It has risen dramatically. An absence would likely threaten not only the day's wages, but also the job itself, possibly years of lucrative work. He is likely to set his alarm.

The young man's changed circumstances parallel the story Friedman tells at the national level. The costs of misbehaving in international commerce can be dauntingly high. The virtue of drawing the analogy to an individual is that we can distinguish between incentives and true compulsion. Compulsory labor – slavery or indentured servitude – is abhorrent to civilized nations and is generally banned. That is the true analogue to the golden straitjacket. The young man of our story may say to himself, "I really have to get in to work," but he faces a choice in the way a slave does not. We see free individuals renounce materialism and decide to live simpler, more austere lives. We see hermits renounce modernity and isolate themselves in a world of bare subsistence. Though the vast majority of people would prefer the six-figure job, the existence of a choice is fundamentally important to the argument that individuals have benefited from modern changes. It allows us to invoke revealed preference – we know individuals prefer a modern lifestyle to rustic subsistence because both are available and they choose modernity. We cannot say the same of slaves, even if they were to be well-treated and housed in sumptuous quarters.

At the national level, the observation that few countries choose to withdraw from international commerce and capital markets does not diminish the fact that countries have the choice. Decreased trade barriers and a well-functioning international financial system do raise the cost of autarky, as Friedman argues, but this is irrelevant for the analysis of sovereignty.

What would constitute an infringement of sovereignty? What is the counterpart to slavery? The use or threat of force is the clearest analogue. In the Cold War, the Soviet Union's occupation of Central and Eastern European nations denied them sovereignty over economic and political choices. Were nations faced with the choice of granting economic concessions or facing attack, the threatened nations could legitimately claim infringed sovereignty.

Military attack marks out an extreme. What about an embargo? This allows the target nation to preserve its territorial integrity and to operate as it likes within its borders. But it is being physically prevented from engaging in commerce with willing partners. We can count this, too, as an infringement of sovereignty, though a careful argument along these lines would require a more sophisticated parsing of extra-territorial rights. This is the equivalent of preventing our aspiring graduate from reaching his lucrative workplace by placing him under house arrest.

We can continue along the spectrum of influence by considering economic sanctions.[1] Suppose country A tells country B to adopt a particular policy or face the end of trade between the two. Depending on trade flows, this could prove as painful to country B as the embargo considered in the previous example. However, consistent with the argument in that example, country A should have the sovereign right to trade (or not trade) with whatever partner is willing to engage. The parallel to our individual might be a workplace requirement that the young man wear a tie. He may not like ties, but the employer can choose to employ only well-dressed workers. The individual is left with the real choice between dressing up and quitting. Country B has a real choice between adopting the policy or rearranging its trade flows. In both cases, the end of the relationship may be painful, but in both cases adoption of the policy is not compelled. Hence, this seems to be on the other side of the dividing line between actions that do and do not infringe sovereignty.

As a final example, consider a positive incentive. Country A could offer country B aid if it adopted a specified policy (conditionality). This seems intuitively less offensive to sovereignty than the case of sanctions above, but it is qualitatively similar. In each case, country B will be worse off if it rejects A's policy. The difference is that in the incentive scenario country B is guaranteed its status quo level of welfare whether or not it adopts the policy. Whatever additional appeal this guarantee might have is immaterial, since it will not affect the conclusion that a positive offer would not be an infringement of sovereignty.

These examples do not present a clear demarcation of where sovereignty ends and infringement begins, but they do illustrate that a definition of sovereignty that is based on freedom from compulsion would not be trivial (we observe infringements). The last two examples, in which sovereignty remained intact, can be loosely linked to common scenarios in international trade enforcement and negotiation. These linkages are drawn in the next section. We conclude here by noting that there was no army fielded under the banner of either the General Agreement on Tariffs and Trade (GATT) nor the World Trade Organization (WTO). As noted by Lash and Griswold (2000: 3):

> In reality, the WTO wields no power of enforcement. It has no authority or power to levy fines, change tariff rates, or modify domestic laws in any way to bring about compliance. *The WTO has no power to make any member do anything the member doesn't want to do* (emphasis in original).

## Do trade agreements impinge upon sovereignty?

### *Trade agreements and national law*

The previous section considered particular actions that might be applied to get a target country to adopt a policy. This is something quite different from the popular concern about a supranational body imposing its will. The fault lies with popular misconceptions about the functioning of international trade agreements. We will focus on the interaction of World Trade Organization agreements with US law, though the principles are similar worldwide.

The US Constitution grants Congress the power to regulate international trade. For a variety of reasons, most Congresses in the postwar period have chosen to partially delegate the negotiating power to the executive branch. Most recently, this delegation has been known as "fast track authority" and then "trade promotion authority." Given the assignment of powers in the Constitution, however, Congress is limited in its ability to delegate. The President and his representatives can negotiate a trade agreement under the WTO but it must ultimately be voted upon by Congress. The important aspect of the delegation is Congress' self-imposed ban on amendments. This prevents an agreement from being unwound piece by piece. Under US law, a trade agreement takes effect not when agreement is reached at a ministerial conference but when Congress passes implementing legislation.

The remarkable aspect of the process is how limited the role is for WTO officials. The Director General and the chairmen of negotiating committees have the power to persuade participants and to suggest potential compromises, but they have no powers to impose an outcome on the membership. The WTO, like the GATT before it, operates on the basis of consensus.[2] There is not even super-majority voting, much less autocratic powers for the WTO secretariat. Countries are affected by each other's policies and therefore have preferences over those policies. The WTO provides a forum in which countries can seek mutually beneficial policy packages. Trade theory offers one illustration of how large countries might each seek to apply a tariff, but there will be mutual gains from reciprocal liberalization. The range of issues under consideration in WTO negotiations has expanded considerably beyond tariffs, as discussed below. Nonetheless, the principle remains that if and only if an agreement offers mutual benefits, it will be adopted by all member countries. The WTO as an organization serves to help its members seek such an agreement.

This discrepancy between public perceptions of the WTO's role as an enforcer and its actual role as a facilitator is mirrored in a split in the academic literature over how to analyze the negotiation process. There are two distinct branches of game theory that have been applied. The more realistic is the non-cooperative bargaining approach used by Bagwell and Staiger (1990) and others. In this approach, trade agreements are upheld in an infinitely repeated game. At each stage, the participating countries decide whether or not to pursue an agreed-upon policy. If the country chooses not to follow the agreed-upon policy, it will take whatever actions it deems will maximize its immediate self-interest. If the partner country observes such a defection, it will cease to follow the agreed-upon policy in all future periods.[3] This has the virtue of resembling the dispute settlement mechanism in the GATT and WTO (discussed below). It does not have any role for an enforcer or facilitator at all; the agreement that is supportable through such a scheme is known as self-enforcing.

The alternative approach draws upon the machinery of cooperative game theory, which is frequently used to describe bargaining (see, e.g. Busch and Horstmann 2001 in a more general context). This approach can more easily accommodate such institutional features as an organization to oversee bargaining. It also makes important issues such as the scope of negotiations significantly more tractable. Unfortunately, the basic premise of the cooperative approach is that whatever accord is reached between the parties is externally enforceable. Thus, all the realism of the process is abandoned in its description of how an international trade agreement functions.

Returning to the question of a trade agreement's impact on sovereign rights, once a package is agreed, a country faces a choice akin to the positive incentive scenario in the previous section. By assumption, it gains from the overall policy package (if not, it simply rejects it). Almost certainly, however, the package will offer benefits on net; the gains will outweigh the costs, as perceived by the relevant decision-making body in a country. The gains offer a positive incentive to adopt the policies that are perceived as costly. The country retains the option of the status quo and retains the sovereign right to make no change.[4]

### *Dispute settlement mechanisms*

Once a WTO agreement is adopted by all member countries, the membership faces the question of how it will be enforced. Suppose country A had agreed to remove its tariff on good X in exchange for country B's removal of a tariff on good Y. What happens if country B fails to remove its tariff on good Y? The most obvious punishment would be for country A to cancel its plans to drop its tariff on good X. This would not seem to leave any role for a dispute settlement mechanism.

Here economic modeling is too transparent for its own good. In the example above, it should be obvious whether or not country B has retained a tariff on the import of good Y – the duty must either be paid or not at customs. In practice, commitments are made over more complex issues and it is harder to discern whether or not a member has reneged on those commitments. Disputes have hinged on whether a country's health regulations have a suitable scientific basis, whether a complicated tax system served to subsidize exports, and whether agricultural programs distort production or trade.

In each of these cases, the WTO dispute settlement system offered an opinion. One innovation of the Uruguay Round that created the WTO was the introduction of an appellate mechanism to review the initial panel decisions in disputes. The WTO approach to dispute settlement also makes the adoption of these findings the default (the GATT rules made it easy to block a finding).

It is perhaps unfortunate that the dispute settlement mechanism of the WTO bears a superficial resemblance to the US judicial system. When newspapers announce that the WTO has ruled against a popular measure, it sounds like reports that a US court has thrown out a law as unconstitutional. There are crucial differences. When the US Supreme Court finds a law unconstitutional, the executive and judicial branches of government treat that decision as law. When the Supreme Court ruled that schools must be integrated, federal marshals were dispatched to enforce the ruling.

When a WTO panel rules against the US, the basis for the ruling must be that the US has acted in a way inconsistent with its earlier obligations (as opposed to inconsistent with some general principles). When the WTO adopts such a finding, it does not become law. It serves as a call for the US to change its law or practices. That may require action by the executive or the legislative branch. Those branches retain the right to act as they please. The effect of the WTO ruling is not to compel action, but rather to authorize the complaining country to reciprocally withdraw a concession. The virtue of such authorization is to limit the possibility of an escalating trade war in which each country perceives a campaign of illegitimate actions. If the US – or any other WTO member – fails to comply with a ruling, the outcome is essentially that of the simple tariff case: a mutually beneficial deal is set aside.

Once reciprocal withdrawal of concessions is authorized, we have a scenario similar to that described in the sanctions example above. Country A wants country B to adopt a policy (removal of the transgression) and is threatening B with a sanction should it fail to do so. Country B will be better off if it complies, but it retains the right to choose the unwinding of the deal instead. We have seen countries make this choice on important issues in recent years. By the previous reasoning, the dispute settlement mechanism does not threaten national sovereignty.

### *The changing content of trade agreements*

One reason that questions have emerged about the encroachment of international trade agreements on sovereign territory is the expanded scope of those agreements. In the early rounds of GATT negotiations, the principal subject of negotiation was border barriers – tariffs and quotas. More recent negotiations have dealt with issues such as sanitary and phytosanitary regulation, government procurement and intellectual property protection. Decisions over whether to address issues such as labor, environmental and investment policy have been among the most divisive at the WTO.

At one level, the expanded scope of trade negotiations is easily understandable. International trade is the difference between domestic consumption and domestic production. While border barriers can be an obvious hindrance to international commerce, it is no less of a hindrance if a government declares that imported food is unhealthy or that all government computers must run on domestically produced software. The impact of such actions on trade and on exporters is indistinguishable from that of an equivalent tariff or quota. Yet government procurement and health regulation are traditionally domestic concerns, and that makes international restrictions appear all the more intrusive.

Even if the topics are traditionally domestic ones, if there are international effects they may be candidates for inclusion in international negotiations. The essential point is that countries retain the sovereign right to walk away from an agreement either in the process of its negotiation or subsequently.

One particularly contentious dispute in the 1990s concerned Europe's restrictions on imports of bio-engineered food.[5] The stated purpose of the European restrictions was to defend public health, clearly a central right of a sovereign state. The difficulty is how one distinguishes between legitimate health concerns and an unjustifiable stance that conveniently serves to protect domestic agricultural interests. There are a number of standards one could adopt: ban food if it has not been completely proven safe; or ban food only if there is sound scientific evidence that it poses a risk. Or, of course, one could choose to keep this area of regulation entirely free from any international encumbrances.

The difficulty for the European Union was that it chose, in the Uruguay Round negotiations, to agree to a standard that required scientific evidence that a product might be harmful. Presumably, its willingness to adopt such a standard allowed it to elicit concessions that it deemed valuable from the US and others. When it later decided to restrict the import of products that had not been shown to pose a health risk, a WTO dispute settlement panel found that it had violated its obligations under the Uruguay Round agreements. As described above, the European Union was allowed to retain its restrictions, but exporters were allowed to withdraw an equivalent value of concessions.

One might ask whether there is a natural boundary between issues that should be considered in international trade negotiations and those that should be exclusively the concern of unfettered domestic politics. This has been one of the most controversial questions before the members of the WTO. One cause of the failed WTO Ministerial meeting in Cancun, Mexico in 2003 was a sharp disagreement over the inclusion of new issues in the negotiating mandate for the Doha Development Agenda.

We restrict our consideration here to those measures that can have an extra-territorial economic impact.[6] In the abstract, we can consider a hypothetical candidate issue, Z, and ask whether its inclusion in negotiations makes countries better off than they would be if it were excluded. For demandeur countries that would like to see policies on Z changed, they are at least weakly better off from Z's inclusion; if Z is included there is at least the possibility the demandeurs' concerns will be addressed. What about the demandee countries? At first blush, it might seem that they can only lose. Presumably, they already have the Z policies that maximize their well-being. If there were no other issues for which these countries are demandeurs, this would be the end of the analysis. However, if there is at least one other issue V on which the Z-demandees are demandeurs, there is the possibility that a $(V', Z')$ combination could be put forward in an agreement that would make the Z-demandee better off than under the status quo, which we can denote as $(V_o, Z_o)$.

The key to the argument for inclusion of Z was also the key to the revealed preference argument above: the Z-demandee country can be no worse off for the inclusion of Z so long as countries retain their sovereign rights to reject an agreement, as they do in international trade negotiations. If the country accepts an agreement $(V', Z')$ it must be because it at least weakly prefers that agreement to $(V_o, Z_o)$. The advantage of including additional issues is that the additional dimensionality of agreements allows for more possible agreements under which all nations gain. This increased scope for agreement has grown in importance as the membership of the WTO has soared to nearly 150 countries.

To argue that an agreement should be kept off the negotiating agenda is either to argue that there is no possibility that any policy other than $Z_o$ will be agreed and that there will be some negotiating cost associated with its inclusion, or to argue that the negotiating dynamic is sufficiently different from this simple rational choice model that the inclusion of an issue in negotiations can negatively alter the outcome of the negotiations. This statement seems to be beyond the analytical capabilities of current non-cooperative game theory, but would be an interesting topic for further investigation.

## Regional versus multilateral agreements

To this point, the discussion has focused on the multilateral trade negotiations that have occurred under the auspices of the GATT and the WTO.

Concurrently, most of the membership of the WTO has been negotiating bilateral or plurilateral agreements with other nations. The US commonly negotiates agreements of differing degrees of complexity and commitment, from Trade and Investment Framework Agreements (TIFAs) and Bilateral Investment Treaties (BITs) to the more visible free trade agreements such as the North American Free Trade Agreement (NAFTA). Among opponents of globalization in the US, the most visible free trade agreements have engendered at least as much hostility as WTO agreements.

To a large extent, a US regional trade agreement[7] is similar in structure and enforcement to WTO agreements. In lieu of the WTO dispute settlement mechanism, there will be a dispute settlement mechanism specific to that agreement or a set of agreements. There is significant overlap in the issues covered: market access, services, intellectual property rights, and more. Countries still must individually decide that the agreement is in their best interest and they retain the right to abandon the agreement.

We briefly consider two ways in which regional agreements differ from multilateral agreements. First, in the majority of US regional agreements, the US is paired with one or several significantly smaller and less economically developed partner countries. Second, regional agreements have dealt more extensively with controversial issues such as labor, environmental and investment policies.

The disparity in size between the US and many of its regional trade agreement partners might or might not tilt the outcome of negotiations in favor of the US, relative to the outcome one might achieve in the WTO. At the WTO negotiations, smaller developing nations at least theoretically have the option of allying themselves with a large number of similarly situated countries. However, there are also more developed nations. Further, the intricacies of WTO negotiations have meant that agreements take much longer to reach. The narrower coverage of WTO agreements may mean that they are less useful for developing nations in signaling their commitment to pro-investor policies. All of these points address whether regional or multilateral agreements better serve the interests of developing nations. While this is an interesting question, it is separate from whether the agreements infringe upon the sovereignty of those nations. The fundamental lack of coercion remains. A regional trade agreement with the US may be more tempting for a developing nation than a WTO agreement, but this is a quantitative not a qualitative difference.

The other question concerns the scope of regional agreements. Although the inclusion of labor and environmental agreements could be criticized as unnecessary in a trade agreement, or even as an intrusion into traditionally sovereign matters that are not the legitimate concerns of a trading partner, they are still undertaken voluntarily and may be abandoned at will (albeit along with other benefits of the agreement). One feature of US regional trade agreements that has been held up as a particular threat to sovereignty is the policy on arbitration of investment disputes. Such policies, as with NAFTA, discussed in Chapter 11, try to protect member countries' investors against malicious actions by host countries. The expropriation of a factory would be a clear violation. The challenge, as with health regulation, is distinguishing between legitimate and illegitimate measures. What if a country adopts a regulation that only affects foreign investors and has the effect of rendering the foreign investment worthless? Few investors are happy to entrust adjudication of such a question entirely to the courts of the host country. Hence, agreements have created international bodies to hear such disputes. This has caused concern because of the appearance that an international judicial body is sitting in judgment on domestic regulatory matters.

The distinction that was made previously between Supreme Court rulings and the findings of dispute settlement panels applies here as well. While international arbitration raises complicated international legal questions, so long as decisions require voluntary adoption by a member country government, there is no coercion, countries are free to walk away from an agreement, and one can argue that sovereignty remains intact.

## Conclusion

The question of whether international trade agreements impinge on the sovereignty of the nation-state is absolutely central to the protests against globalization of recent years. While the concept of sovereignty has been analyzed for years, many of the definitions that have emerged from this analysis fail to capture popular notions of a threat to a nation's right to independent action. To be precise, they fail to limit themselves to this meaning.

It is not immediately obvious that popular conceptions are right and carefully-developed analyses with long pedigrees are wrong. The purpose of the analysis, though, is to assess the validity of popular discontent with international trade diplomacy. To that end, one wants a definition that accurately reflects the charges being leveled.

If one perceives international trade negotiations as allowing, but not requiring, a country to reach mutually beneficial agreements with trading partners that will be followed so long as it is in a country's self-interest, it is difficult to stir a crowd to rabid opposition. If one accepts the premise that countries have choices, the main argument that can be used for opposition to international accords is the much less appealing one that protests on the international stage allow groups that have failed to advance their views in the domestic political process to have a second chance at achieving their goals. If, however, one portrays the WTO as an organization that imposes its supranational will from afar, it is much easier to stir righteous nationalist indignation.

A detailed examination of the negotiation process under the WTO, regional trade agreements, and the subsequent functioning of the dispute settlement mechanisms shows that there is no point at which external force is applied. The only plausible way one could argue for an infringement of sovereignty is with an expansive conception of sovereignty that equates any offering of incentives with erosion of sovereign rights. A definition that broad only renders an otherwise useful concept useless.

This chapter has not offered a precise definition of sovereignty. We have opted instead to move towards such a definition by the process of elimination. A useful objective for future work would be to make this definition more precise and to show that it provides a useful demarcation between instances in which countries exercise free choice and instances in which countries face coercion.

## Notes

1 This would meet Drezner's (2003) definition of economic coercion: "The threat or act by a sender government or governments to disrupt economic exchange with the target state, unless the target acquiesces to an articulated demand." We reserve the term "coercion" for forcible interventions.

2 Steinberg (2002) considers the extent to which the consensus rule really reflects equality among WTO members. He concludes that "the GATT/WTO consensus decision-making process is organized hypocrisy in the procedural context." That reflects differing degrees of influence rather than the presence of forcible coercion.

3 In fact, this describes a "trigger-strategy" approach. There are other ingenious schemes for wringing additional cooperation out of such a setting, but the difference is quantitative rather than qualitative.

4 The statement that a country retains the option of the status quo requires qualification. There are arguments that the world trading system is like a bicycle – it must keep moving forward or it will fall over. At worst, such an argument would remove the status quo as an option but would not alter the conclusions on sovereignty.

5 See Hanrahan (1998) for a discussion.

6 One can have interesting philosophical discussions about whether one country has legitimate interests in events that occur exclusively within a nation's boundaries. In fact, such discussions are central to the idea of Westphalian/Vattelian sovereignty (Krasner 2001), in which countries abjure from intervention in others' internal affairs. Examples of recent issues on which countries have attempted to involve themselves include human rights and the extinction of non-migratory species.

7 We adopt the phrase "regional trade agreement" that is in common use at the WTO, despite the fact that a number of US agreements are with individual far-flung partners (e.g. separate agreements with Australia, Singapore and Chile).

## References

Bagwell, K. and Staiger, R. W. (1990) "A Theory of Managed Trade," *American Economic Review*, 80/4: 779–95.

—— (2004) "National Sovereignty in an Interdependent World," *NBER Working Paper*, No. 10249.

Busch, L. and Horstmann, I. J. (2001) "The Game of Negotiations: Ordering Issues and Implementing Agreements," unpublished paper, University of Western Ontario.

Drezner, D. W. (2003) "The Hidden Hand of Economic Coercion," *International Organization*, 57/Summer: 643–59.

Friedman, T. (2000) *The Lexus and the Olive Tree*, New York: Anchor Books.

Hanrahan, C. E. (1998) "US-European Agricultural Trade: Food Safety and Biotechnology Issues," Congressional Research Service, 98–861 ENR. Online. Available at: www.ncseonline.org/NLE/CRSreports/agriculture/ag-51.cfm.

Krasner, S. D. (2001) "Abiding Sovereignty," *International Political Science Review*, 22/3: 229–51.

Lash III, W. H. and Griswold, D. T. (2000) "WTO Report Card II: An Exercise or Surrender of U.S. Sovereignty?" *Cato Institute Trade Briefing Paper*, No. 9.

Steinberg, R. H. (2002) "In the Shadow of Law or Power? Consensus-Based Bargaining and Outcomes in the GATT/WTO," *International Organization*, 56/2: 339–74.

# Part III

# Threats from the inside

## Globalization, autonomy movements and political organization

# 8 Globalization, decentralization and secession

## A review of the literature and some conjectures

*Nicholas Sambanis*

### Introduction

Since 1945, more than 300 groups have organized to demand a greater degree of self-determination.[1] Some of these movements simply demand greater financial or cultural independence from the center (e.g. the right to retain more of their locally raised tax revenues to finance local expenditures and satisfy region-specific preferences over public goods consumption), while others want to secede and establish a new state. In all cases, the presence of these movements suggests a persistent demand for self-determination across more than half the countries of the world.

Self-determination – the freedom of a people living in a well-defined area to govern themselves – is the expression of nationalism. I use the term here as a synonym for sovereignty. Sovereignty can be defined both at the level of the country and the level of the region or any politically significant administrative jurisdiction smaller than an internationally recognized state.[2] Sovereignty is a public good: if a nation or state is sovereign, then all its members enjoy the privileges associated with sovereignty (e.g. citizenship; protection under the law). And sovereignty can only be achieved through collective action and the expression of public will.

Where preferences between a region and the rest of the country are different, the meaning of sovereignty will differ across geographical units of the country. There may be competition among various regions for greater sovereignty, which implies that greater independence and policy autonomy for one region may result in less autonomy and resources for other regions. Groups and/or regions may strive to increase their sovereignty by demanding more autonomy over fiscal policy, or greater independence in designing cultural policies, or by seeking to secede from the state. Demand for sovereignty is defined here as an organized effort to increase political power and representation relative to the center of political authority or, alternatively, to attain greater administrative and legislative independence from the center and greater control over the territory in which a group demanding sovereignty lives. Demand for sovereignty is different from an outcome of greater self-determination. Such an outcome (e.g. an outcome of territorial partition) depends not only on the demand for secession, but also on the "supply" side of the equation – i.e. on the government's reaction and the international community's norms regarding self-determination.

Political and economic decentralization and secession have been the focus of many academic and policy debates, particularly since the collapse of the Soviet Union led to the creation of several new states. The norm of state sovereignty, embedded in the UN Charter, has prevented the articulation and implementation of self-determination demands by regions or minority groups for the largest part of the post-1945 period (Zacher 2001). This norm, however, is being revisited, following the collapse of the USSR and the dissolution of Yugoslavia. As more groups demand greater economic and political autonomy, governments and international organizations are increasingly considering the merits of a policy of decentralization to reduce the risk of violent conflict aimed at secession.

In this chapter, I review some contributions to the literature on decentralization and secessionism and consider the link between the two as well as the relationship between globalization, decentralization and secessionism. The literature on decentralization offers a good handle with which to analyze the likely effects of globalization on secessionism.[3]

This chapter is organized as follows: in the next section, I provide a literature review on the causes and likely effects of political and economic decentralization – the objective of self-determination movements. I also discuss the complementarities between economic and political decentralization. Following this, I review the literature on secession and suggest some likely causes of the demand for self-determination. I focus on some of the conditions under which increased decentralization is likely to lead to secessionism. Next, I turn to globalization and explain how globalization is likely to affect the demand for sovereignty. I do so by revisiting some of the theoretical arguments and empirical results reported in the previous two sections and thinking through the likely relationship between globalization and each of the key variables that have been shown to influence the demand for sovereignty. A key mechanism through which globalization might influence the prevalence of secessionism and political violence around the world is by reducing the level of decentralization. This is likely to create excess demand for sovereignty in some regions, though only under a specified set of conditions. Throughout the chapter, I refer to several illustrative examples to make my arguments more concrete, but data limitations prevent me from presenting a systematic empirical test. The chapter is therefore not designed to present and test a theory of the relationship between globalization and secessionism. Rather, it offers some conjectures that can be further developed and tested in other studies.

## When is decentralization more likely?

Political and economic decentralization are strategies aimed at reducing the potential of conflict arising out of regional inequities and minority groups' claims to greater self-determination. I discuss the effects of decentralization on patterns of civil conflict, but I first review some of the literature that helps us understand the conditions under which countries are likely to become politically decentralized.

There are several determinants of when and where we are likely to see decentralization policies, but no study to date has established a set of necessary and sufficient conditions for decentralization. The following determinants are frequently discussed in studies of decentralization: the number of major ethnic groups; the degree of territorial concentration of those groups; the existence of ethnic networks and communities across the border of the state; the country's dependence on natural resources and the degree to which those resources are concentrated in the region's territory; and the country's per capita income relative to that in other regions. Persistent self-determination movements are also more likely to get attention: both the Catalans of Spain and the Quebequois of Canada have had long-standing demands for greater autonomy and were able to secure constitutionally-provided autonomy concessions from the state.

In democratic countries that are already well-integrated in the international system, we are less likely to observe a trend towards more decentralization, as this may lead to increased risk of secession and, consequently, to suboptimal scale of provision of public goods for the state.[4] To avoid this, democratic states will offer inducements to minorities so that they remain committed to the state. These inducements could range from land reform in the periphery to income redistribution at the center. Decentralization is also likely to be used as a concession to minorities who may be forced to pursue secession as a means towards self-administration on cultural and economic matters (several examples in India as with the Nagas and Tripuras).

Even in countries that have experienced civil war, decentralization can be a good way to organize politics between the central government and an ethnic minority. There are several examples of government-negotiated and internationally arbitrated decentralization in civil war settlements: the Dayton accords in Bosnia; the autonomy agreements reached to end the war in Mindanao in the Philippines; the federal political structure created in Ethiopia after the fall of the Mengistu regime; and the solution pushed by NATO countries in Kosovo to prevent the partition of the province from Yugoslavia while restoring a level of regional autonomy that would protect the rights of the Kosovar Albanian majority.

Political decentralization – understood as the delegation of powers and authority for autonomous decision-making to subnational units – is aimed at a more efficient and equitable solution to problems associated with the provision of public goods. The best-known efficiency argument on the local provision of public services is Tiebout (1956), who explains local efficiency as the result of competition between subnational governments to attract investment, firms or residents. If economies of scale are not too large, decentralization can lead to more efficient allocation of resources by targeting public goods provision to the preferences of particular local communities (Oates 1972). Decentralization can also act as a way to insert checks and balances in federal institutions (Weingast 1995) and can facilitate policy innovation (Kollman *et al.* 1996) and government efficiency in the implementation of economic reforms (Treisman 2000). Meaningful political decentralization is characterized by the presence of lower/subnational levels of government with constitutionally determined or residual rights of control of several important issue areas (Riker 1964).

The benefits of decentralization will depend on the optimal scale of production of particular public goods (Alesina and Spolaore 1997; Lake and Rothschild 2001). We would therefore not expect to observe decentralization where the assumptions underlying efficiency models of decentralization do not apply. Specifically, decentralization will most likely not be effective if there is imperfect factor mobility across regions; if there are high transaction costs to mobility (e.g. ethnic networks in the professions); or if we have semi-permanent heterogeneity in local preferences due to the region's political geography as when we have ethnically mixed and immobile populations.[5] In countries with such characteristics, we would expect central governments to have less interest in decentralization. Decentralization is more likely to be observed in countries that started out as federations or were the result of merging distinct ethnic and religious groups into a unified state. It is less likely to be observed in countries that started out with a highly centralized political system or in cases where large inflows of migrant populations become territorially concentrated, changing the regional demographics of a country, and demand peripheral autonomy and more resources from the center. But this need not mean that there will not be latent demand for decentralization in the country's periphery even where the central government believes that decentralization is unlikely to quell the demand for more sovereignty. Where the actual and demanded level of decentralization/self-determination differ, we are likely to observe separatist conflict, including violence (Sambanis and Milanovic 2004).

### *The relationship between economic and political decentralization*

Economic and political decentralization are conflict prevention or conflict resolution strategies. Secessionist demands and possibly even violence might be caused by actual or perceived regional inequalities in public goods provision. Economic and/or political decentralization might be one way to reduce the risk of secessionist conflict. Demand for more decentralization should be observed in those regions where there are significant preference differences from the center.

One could distinguish between economic decentralization (income and asset redistribution; regional fiscal decentralization) and political redistribution (democratic reform; political decentralization; federalism). But the two forms should be positively correlated. In this section, I present simple tests of the bivariate relationship between economic and political decentralization.

I have identified a list of countries that could be characterized as federal or semi-federal using information provided in large databases of political institutions. A total of 48 countries can be classified as politically decentralized for the most recent year for which data has been available. Drawing on raw data from the Polity III project (Jaggers and Gurr 1996), I coded three binary variables denoting the level of centralization of the political system (federal, semi-federal and centralized) for all sovereign countries from 1960–1995 (the last year for which annual coding on centralization measures was available).[6]

Coding economic decentralization for such a large set of countries is much more difficult. Decentralization is typically measured in terms of the size of regional (i.e. subnational) expenditures as a share of total government spending (Fisman and Gatti 2000). Fisman and Gatti have compiled such a measure of expenditures of state and local governments over total spending by all levels of government, including central government, using the International Monetary Fund's *Government Finance Statistics* (GFS) for the period 1980–1995. Their variable, *decentralization*, is defined as "the share of local and state government expenditure over total government expenditure." I use this readily available measure to compute partial correlations between the level of economic decentralization and political decentralization.[7]

For the last coded year in my data (1994), I cross-tabulated *federal* and a variable denoting economically decentralized countries (*dec2*=*1 when decentralization*>0.3)[8] and this yields a positive and significant relationship between political and economic decentralization (Pearson $\chi^2(1) = 6.88$). A much less significant relationship emerges between countries with only partially decentralized political systems (*semi-federal*) and *dec2* (Pearson $\chi^2(1) = 3.63$). A highly significant and negative relationship emerges between politically centralized and economically decentralized countries. These results are intuitive and suggest that political and economic decentralization go hand-in-hand and they may even be complementary. Thus, while most of the discussion in the rest of the chapter focuses on economic (fiscal) decentralization, the arguments should also apply to other (political) measures.

*Decentralization* is also positively correlated with the level of democracy.[9] I created a binary variable (*dec*) code 1 if *decentralization* was equal to or greater than its mean (0.2) and 0 otherwise and conducted an equality of means tests of *pol* and its components to see if any significant differences emerged across countries that could be classified as decentralized and countries that could be classified as centralized. Note that only aggregate scores for *decentralization* are available, so I repeated the test for several years during the period which corresponds to the measurement of *decentralization* (1980–1995). The test assuming equal variances across the two samples suggests that, for the period from 1985–1992, the decentralized group of countries is systematically more democratic than the group of non-decentralized countries. That difference becomes more pronounced if we classify countries into centralized or decentralized according to a higher threshold of *decentralization* (e.g. if we code *dec2* = 1 if *decentralization* > = 0.3). This classification separates countries more equally than the former (40 centralized v. 89 decentralized if the cutoff point is 0.3). A Spearman test of independence of the net level of democracy (*pol*) and the level of economic decentralization (*decentr*) is resoundingly rejected both for specific years and for the entire sample.[10] These very simple tests establish, in a bivariate framework, that there is a systematic relationship between the level of economic decentralization and the openness of political institutions.

Turning now to separatism and separatist violence, I cannot fully explore the impact of decentralization on the risk of secession or civil war, as the data used to compile *decentralization* are available only for 17 countries that have experienced civil war and there is reason to suspect that missing data are systematically related to the occurrence of a civil war.[11] Also, in almost all of the cases of civil war countries for which economic decentralization data are available, *decentralization* is measured for years that correspond to the post-civil war period. Thus, our discussion will have to be limited to bivariate correlations between decentralization and other variables of interest and will also be limited to the period for which decentralization data are available.

## *Decentralization's effects on political conflict and violence*

### *What are the likely effects of decentralization on separatism and political violence?*

Political decentralization is a reactive or reflective political system, regardless of whether it is pursued before or after civil war.[12] It is a reflective system because it takes cultural or political divisions as given and works around them by providing a system of quasi-independence, reducing the level and depth of interaction between the periphery and the center. After civil war, decentralization often reflects and/or justifies the war's military outcomes, as warring factions can gain greater autonomy as a result of their struggle. The fact that decentralization is the outcome of civil war implies that this policy is ridden with significant moral hazard problems.

The international community, in its efforts to stop the violence, may inadvertently be rewarding the most violent and uncooperative groups at the expense of the rest of society. Not only can this create bad precedent for other potentially secessionist groups, but it can increase resentment at the center and mobilize other groups to demand greater centralization. But the opposite may also be true: denying the right to self-determination to groups that have significant grievances against the center may lead to prolonged conflict.

The scholarly literature on the effects of political decentralization on large-scale political violence is inconclusive. The greatest focus has been on the stability of decentralization agreements within the context of civil war settlements, but even that literature is limited.[13] Decentralization, or more generally federalism, may actually exacerbate the time consistency problems associated with civil war settlements or even with less violent political conflict. According to Lake and Rothschild (2001: 4), there are limited conditions for successful political decentralization after civil war:

> Only where multiple groups cohabit the same national space, none can achieve control over the state, each is led by moderates willing to accept the desires of others for cultural, linguistic, and religious autonomy, and democracy is robust is decentralization likely to prove a stable and effective long term solution.

In addition, Zartman's (1995) well-established insight that a "hurting stalemate" is needed to induce parties to negotiate on dividing the state implies that wars will continue unabated until such a stalemate is reached if groups think that this is the only way to achieve self-determination. In most cases of civil war settlement, the parties will have to disarm and rebel troops will be demobilized. This increases the rebels' anxiety about the government's credibility, its commitment to the peace, and the likelihood of future reneging on the war settlement. Where these risks are high, parties may be reluctant to agree to federal frameworks unless they can protect their basic liberties under such frameworks.

While commonsensical arguments can be put forth both in favor and against the use of decentralization agreements to induce political stability, we do not yet have substantial cross-national evidence to support any argument empirically. In one important study of India, Wilkinson (2004) analyzed the determinants of ethnic violence (riots) at the state (subnational) level over a span of several decades and one of his interests was to see if consociationalism limited violence. Wilkinson conducted a micro-level study, collecting data on the ethnic composition of the police force and considered if that was relevant for preventing violent riots. He focused on Muslim-Hindu riots and on Muslim (minority) representation in police forces and found that states with the highest degree of under-representation of Muslims in police forces often had as bad a record of human rights and rioting as states with relatively low under-representation of Muslims. Thus, he argued that there was a low and non-significant statistical relationship between indicators of ethnic proportionality and the lack of violence in India during the period from 1975–1999. He attributed this finding to the fact that basic statistics on representation mask the real or effective level of representation and freedom for minorities, which is often determined by the operation of institutions and the actions of elites and not by constitutional rules. Also, the salience of identity may be different across Indian states and the type of institutions that have been created may be endogenous to identity salience. Thus, in some states it may be enough to have relatively small minority representation in police forces to keep the peace. Wilkinson's critique of consociational solutions to the risk of ethnic violence notwithstanding, no cross-national study to date has shown that minority representation in government and in local policing has a negative effect (increasing ethnic violence). There is sufficient case-study evidence (e.g. from Bosnia and Cyprus, among others) to suggest that such representation is a necessary element in every post-civil war negotiated settlement to increase confidence in effective monitoring of violations of the peace. But in the end, Wilkinson's study shows that the link between consociationalism and risk of violence is too complex and we lack the data necessary to analyze that relationship properly at the cross-national level.

From a theoretical perspective, one could argue that another condition for the success of federal or semi-federal postwar institutions is that parties must define their utility in terms of their absolute gains from the agreement. If they are instead interested in relative gains (i.e. in what their rivals are getting in return), then the space for a feasible agreement narrows and conflict is likely.[14] An example of the prevalence of concern with relative gains in a peace process was the negotiation over resettlement of the town of Varosha, in Cyprus. After the end of the Cypriot civil/international war, UN-sponsored talks focused on the return of the Greek residents of Varosha in exchange for economic concessions to the Turkish-Cypriot side, which included opening up the border at Varosha to allow tourists and businessmen to enter the Turkish-occupied part from Varosha. The resettlement plan would have returned 40,000 Greek refugees to their homes without upsetting the military balance and the economic concessions would have increased Turkish-Cypriot GDP by more than 20 percent.[15] These negotiations, however, failed because each party was more concerned with what the other party was getting out of the deal than with the direct benefits of the agreement to itself.[16]

Given the potential instability of decentralization agreements, might centralization be a better alternative? Scholars have in fact observed a trend towards greater centralization after civil war, with the consolidation of power occurring during the peace process (Lake and Rothschild 2001). Perhaps this trend is what we should expect, if decentralization would afford regional parties the means and space necessary to re-organize their rebellion.[17]

However, centralization also involves risks of renewed violence if groups are systematically excluded from governance (Atlas and Licklider 1999). Yet, only in a small number of cases did we see semi-federal institutions established after civil war (Lake and Rothchild 2001). And in some of these cases (e.g. Nigeria), these institutions were the continuation of prewar political institutions, so there does not seem to be overwhelming evidence of a correlation between war-related hostility and the need to establish separate administration of subnational regions. In cases such as South Africa, where the system adopted in 1993 gave provincial legislatures the authority to legislate on several issue areas (e.g. health, housing, transport), there was a steady trend towards more centralization. Such cases may suggest that reflective systems may not need to last long after civil wars end and that they may have to be gradually transformed into proactive, inclusive systems. Yet the question still remains why such systems will offer credible guarantees of inclusion to minority groups.

Lake and Rothschild (2001) argue that most countries that have adopted federal institutions in their early years as independent states have eventually moved towards more centralization. Examples they give are Argentina, Nigeria, Pakistan and Venezuela. But there are also examples of states that remained decentralized, such as Australia, Canada, the US, Austria, Belgium and Brazil. Malaysia is an example of a country that successfully moved from semi-federalism to full federalism. Similarly, Comoros, Swaziland, South Africa, Tanzania, Trinidad and Tobago all moved from centralized systems to a more decentralized federal structure in the 1990s (according to the Polity III database).

Decentralization must offer some degree of support against discriminatory government policies as it denies the government its monopoly power over the provision of public goods, such as education or policing in the region. When this autonomy extends to the means of defense and regions become able to defend themselves against the government, decentralization can either be a stable outcome within a unitary state (since the minority groups will be satisfied that their key concerns and fears are addressed), or it can be seen as a stepping stone towards secession.

Thus, in post-civil war situations where there is a clear pattern of hostility between the central government and peripheral groups, we are likely to see decentralization agreements only when we have the pre-conditions for a credible government commitment towards peace (i.e. sufficient military power for the regions to enforce the agreement or some external guarantor of peace) *and* where the region's capacity for and likely benefits from secession are low (e.g. when the regional armies' capacities have been damaged by war; or where the group size is small and the region's economy is too specialized and too small to be viable without support from the center). In other words, secession must be costly for the regions and denial of some autonomy must not be viable or costless for the government. Under these conditions, some violent secessionist campaigns that have been "settled" through the force of arms can result in relatively stable decentralization. Examples are the autonomy agreements with the Chittagong Hill Tribes in Bangladesh and the Nagas in northeast India. In those cases, increased regional autonomy does not carry extreme risk of escalating demands for autonomy and more violence because past attempts at secession were violently and effectively suppressed by the government. If there is no doubt about the government's resolve or its capacity to suppress secession, granting some regional autonomy can be an effective way to reducing tension and achieving the efficiency gains typically associated with decentralization.

In the next section, I take up the question of the demands for self-determination and outline the conditions under which secessionist movements are likely to grow including in regions with some positive prior level of decentralization. In the absence of these conditions, decentralization may be a stable and effective policy. The link to globalization will be considered in the final section of the chapter.

## Causes of secessionist movements

A growing literature on secession has identified several conditions that help determine which groups are unlikely to be satisfied with lesser degrees of autonomy and are likely to demand secession. If the government offers insufficient decentralization, groups demanding greater sovereignty might attempt to secede. The pursuit of secession seems more likely if all or most of the following conditions occur:

- the distribution of costs and benefits of political integration is unequal among regions or groups;[18]
- groups have a distinct cultural identity,[19] they are territorially concentrated,[20] and there is significant group-level grievance, possibly driven by economic inequality, political discrimination, or a threat of cultural annihilation;[21]
- regional modes of production and economic specialization coincide with ethnic cleavages and reinforce patterns of economic inequality among ethnic groups;[22]
- the center encroaches on previously acquired rights of independence and replaces indirect with direct rule;[23]
- the economic benefits of membership to the state are not significant for the aggrieved group;[24]
- cleavages are not cross-cutting[25] and the conflict is concentrated between the government and specific ethnic minorities;[26]
- locational interdependence among people sharing a polity does not militate against separation;[27]

- federal or other regional political institutions are controlled by elites who gain by mobilizing public opinion against the central government;[28]
- the political benefits of membership for the group's elites are smaller than their expected political gains within the context of a new state;
- there are no security benefits to remaining in the state (in terms of having access to a larger military to protect against external threat) and there may, instead, exist internal security dangers.

Secession may reduce economies of scale in the provision of public goods like health and education, but this is a tradeoff that groups may be willing to take, if secession implies that the group will have greater access to these goods (even if their production is costlier). Moreover, secession will be more likely if regional elites have greater access to private goods as a result of secession.

These criteria define the conditions favoring the development of secessionist movement, but they do not necessarily explain secession or partition as an outcome. To explain secession as an outcome we must consider not only what motivates the demand for secession but also what defines its supply. We must explain the government's response to secessionist movements. Government acquiescence to secessionist demands is unlikely as long as international norms are against secession (witness the reluctance of the international community to agree to the secession of Kosovo, even after the Serbian-NATO war). There have only been a few cases of a "velvet divorce," where secession was the outcome of negotiation between the parties. Examples include the partition of Czechoslovakia in 1993, Norway's secession from Sweden in 1905 and Iceland's secession from Denmark. Peaceful secession could only happen when the seceding group is relatively "backward" in relation to the dominant group (Horowitz 1985) and secession does not involve severe economic costs to the dominant group in the predecessor country. In addition, the groups must be territorially concentrated without significant residual minorities that may, in turn, wish to secede; the backward group must not possess a disproportionate share of resource endowment of the country and separation must not create massive "tax" for the predecessor state; the two entities must have clearly delineated borders and a previous history of independent, distinct culture.

The government is also less likely to acquiesce to demands for more autonomy if the country does not have many ethnic groups (Toft 2001, 2003). In such countries, one group's secession will not incite secessionist claims by other groups, whereas in multi-ethnic countries the government cannot afford to acquiesce to one group's secessionist demands. The likely response in such a case will be to make some concessions in the form of greater decentralization, but violently suppress any persistent secessionist movement. A good example of this is India's conflict with the Nagas, a culturally distinct group, due to their adoption of Christianity and rejection of the caste system, who live in the northeast region of India near Burma. The Nagas developed a non-violent movement for more autonomy since the era of British colonial rule and their movement turned violent in the 1950s. Under the Hydari agreement signed during India's independence, Nagaland would have a government with significant administrative and legislative authority, but Nehru and the Indian Congress did not ratify the agreement, fearing that granting independence to Nagaland would lead to similar demands elsewhere in India and, eventually, to the dissolution of the Indian state. The Indian government's strategy, therefore, has been to grant a substantial measure of self-administration, but to violently repress any persistent movement towards secession. The credibility of that strategy has been confirmed by the government's policies and military presence in the area (Yonuo 1974).

The difficulty in observing all these conditions implies that we are much more likely to observe violent opposition to secession by central governments (for similar reasons that we are unlikely to observe more decentralization).

Some of the literature on ethnic conflict suggests that the presence of cross-cutting cleavages is likely to prevent the coordination of concerted opposition to central authority (Horowitz 1985; Collier 2000), which implies that decentralization arrangements in countries with significant cross-cutting cleavages should be more stable. These cleavages can make it harder to coordinate political opposition to specific policies and demand secession on the grounds of a distinct identity that cannot be preserved or nurtured in the context of a decentralized, yet unitary state. However, there are exceptions to this "rule" as evidenced by the multicultural composition of rebel groups in southern Sudan. The Southern-Sudanese secessionist movement consists of several distinct groups (several western Nilote and eastern Nilote groups as well as central Sudanic groups). This case is instructive in demonstrating the unifying effects of extreme cultural repression, as Khartoum's insistence on the imposition of Islamic law has unified all non-Moslem groups despite the cultural and political differences of those groups. However, these differences may also account for the lack of success of the southern rebellion, as the unity of a new state of Southern Sudan is questionable.

Similar to the problems associated with the demands and supply of decentralization, secessionist conflict and violence is frequently due to the time-inconsistent nature of government agreements to respect minority rights.[29] The time inconsistency is magnified when there is a change in the balance of capabilities between rebels and government (due, for example, to external intervention); and the central government's commitment to increased regional autonomy is not credible or time consistent. The problem is that almost all decentralization or power-sharing agreements are time-inconsistent. We can point to the second civil war in the Sudan and the Biafran war as examples of the consequences of time-inconsistent federalism. The Sudanese government agreed to respect the southern Sudanese's cultural and religious rights after a first bout of civil war that ended in a peace agreement in 1972. However, the Khartoum government reneged on its promise and attempted to enforce Islamic law in 1983. This renewed violent opposition in the South, leading to a new bout of war. The Biafran civil war in Nigeria resulted after massacres of Ibo tribesmen in 1966 and rising repression from the capital revealed the federal government's reneging on its prior agreements with regional governments after the coup of January 1966 (Tamuno 1970; Nixon 1972; Heraclides 1991).

The above discussion feeds into a model of the demand for self-determination developed by Sambanis and Milanovic (2004). The model integrates several of the arguments surveyed up to this point and adds new hypotheses to develop further the theory of the demand for sovereignty. I briefly summarize the model and, in the next section, link it to how globalization might influence the demand for self-determination partly through its negative effects on levels of economic decentralization.

Sambanis and Milanovic (2004) argue that secessionist movements will develop where they seem *ex ante* profitable for the minority group seeking secession.[30] They focus on region-specific demand-side variables and argue that, while a normal good, sovereignty is not the most precious good, so that its tradeoffs with other goods (such as income) must be considered. Their model posits that a region's demand for sovereignty will be greater as the region's share of total GDP (income) of the country increases; as regional ethnic, religious or racial differentiation from the rest of the country increases; as the regional endowment in terms of natural resources increases; as the historical basis for regional distinctiveness is greater; as inequality between regions (differences in regions' mean incomes) is greater; and it should be lower as regional inter-personal inequality increases.

The model revolves around the argument that there is a tradeoff between sovereignty and income. While more of each good is better, there are costs associated with sovereignty and those costs should be weighed against its benefits.[31] As in other studies (e.g. Alesina and Spolaore 1997), Sambanis and Milanovic (2004) assume that there are increasing returns to scale in the production of sovereignty.[32] This means that in the production of "sovereign" goods (such as defense, or the sustainability of an advanced economy), the cost of producing the good declines with group size. If this were not the case, each and every individual would want to enjoy sovereignty.

Let us also briefly consider the other variables in the model and outline the key hypotheses with reference to each variable. Income inequality – as measured by a region's share in the country's total income – should be important because in countries with unequal income distribution, poorer regions will threaten to secede unless they receive transfers from the center. This is particularly true in the case of federal unions, which is the set of countries for which the Sambanis-Milanovic theory has been developed. Fiscal transfers to the center make membership in the federal union less appealing to the net transfer providers (the richer countries). Thus, the larger the income differential, the greater should be the demand for more sovereignty by rich regions. The same should be true for more populous regions, for reasons mentioned earlier (group size is a factor, given the increasing returns to scale in the production of sovereignty).

At the same time, greater interpersonal inequality within each region should reduce the region's demand for sovereignty. Such inequality should hamper efforts to organize a political movement or insurgency demanding more sovereignty, as the expectation should be that any gains from greater independence will be more unequally divided among the people living in that region. Thus, the economic incentives for secession or greater autonomy for the average person should be lower.

Greater territorial concentration of natural resources in the region should increase the demand for self-determination. This follows straightforwardly from rational choice theory, as the benefits of independence should be greater, the greater the wealth of the separatist region.[33] The greater the importance of natural resources in total national *and* regional GDP, the greater will be the demand for sovereignty by the region. Aceh in Indonesia and Scotland in the UK are two of several examples that illustrate this hypothesis.[34] In resource-rich regions in resource-dependent countries, the region will be a net transfer provider and because the central role of resources in the region's economy would imply that in order for the region to attain the per capita level of income that it deems appropriate given its importance to the national economy, it would have to keep a disproportionate amount of revenues from resource exports. Such an arrangement might not be viable for the center hence it will not be credible.[35] The degree of concentration of natural resources in the region is very important. If resources straddle administrative boundaries, secessionist demands will be lower and predatory groups might resort to other strategies to control the resources (such strategies might include organized crime or an attempt to control the central government so as to extract rents from resources in other regions).

The greater the ethnic or cultural differences of the region vis-à-vis the rest of the country, the greater should be the demand for self-determination. This hypothesis follows directly from a large literature on nationalism (see, in particular, Hechter 2001). It is also a hypothesis consistent with political economy models of decentralization, some of which I reviewed earlier. According to Tiebout's (1956) decentralization model, differences across local preferences will determine the level of decentralization in a given territory, as jurisdictions will come to represent the preferences of the people living in it. What determines the diversity of preferences across jurisdictions is more difficult to establish.[36] Economists have used location models to represent the heterogeneity of preferences among voters over the provision of public goods. In an influential model, Alesina and Spolaore (1997) modeled heterogeneity of preferences as a function of physical distance between groups.[37] Sambanis and Milanovic do not model the complex process through which preferences are formed, but rather draw on the literature on nationalism and ethnicity to argue that one of the main determinants of separatist preferences is regional differentiation from the rest of the country in terms of ethnicity and religion. This may be because people who are culturally similar have similar preferences over public goods consumption. Organizing demands for sovereignty will be easier if there are no difficulties of forming coalitions among potential members of a seceding group (Buchanan and Faith 1987). Thus, cultural differentiation will influence transaction costs (they will rise with the degree of ethno-cultural difference) and, to the extent that trust is a function of ethno-cultural difference, the strength of political coalitions should decrease as ethno-cultural differences increase. An assumption implicit in this is that ethnic fractionalization essentially reduces the degree of solidarity of the group (Hechter 1999, 2001). Ethnic solidarity may derive from the greater ease of social communication among members of the group (Deutsch 1966), to the sense of belonging that ethnic or national identity cultivates (Weber 1978), or a mixture of "willed adherence" and external factors pushing individuals to join a national or ethnic group (Gellner 1983: Chapter 5).

Within a given territory, greater group size should increase the demand for sovereignty.[38] But not all ethnic groups will seek self-determination. A critical conditioning variable is the territorial concentration of ethnic groups. The main difference between an ethnic group and a nation is that nations are concentrated in a region that they perceive as their homeland. But we are not interested in regional concentration or homogeneity per se, but rather in how *different* each region is from the rest of the country in terms of its ethnic/religious composition. For example, in a country such as Japan, where both the regions and the entire country are very homogeneous and a single group is dominant in all regions, we would expect the regions' demand for sovereignty to be weak. Similarly, if a region is ethnically heterogeneous, but so is the rest of the country (e.g. the US), then the difference between the regional and country-wide level of ethnic fragmentation of the population would be small and we would expect the demand for sovereignty to also be small. Demand for sovereignty would be greatest when a region is homogeneous *and* very different from the rest of the country. *Prima facie* support of this hypothesis is the fact that countries that were faced by centrifugal movements have often tried to reduce their intensity by gerrymandering the administrative borders to "dilute" the homogeneity of the restive regions. This was the case, for example, in the pre-World War II Yugoslavia, where regional borders were intentionally created to cut across ethnic lines. The same was true for Nigeria, after the Biafran war, and Francoist Spain.[39]

Finally, cultural-historical factors may also influence a region's sense of distinctiveness and may support nationalist ideology. Thus, we might expect the demand for sovereignty to be greater in regions that had experienced a period of independent statehood before being conquered by another region that ultimately dominated the identity of the central government of a new country (e.g. Catalonia in Spain). It may also be the case that prior conflict and violence would similarly feed into a greater demand for sovereignty by calcifying ethnic cleavages and increasing levels of suspicion and hostility between the regions and the center.

I can now turn to a discussion of the effects of globalization on the demand for sovereignty using the Sambanis and Milanovic (2004) model to frame the discussion.

## How does globalization fit into theories of separatism?

Globalization has many uses and definitions, both economic and non-economic. Non-economic interpretations of globalization can include the proliferation of peace-building and humanitarian operations as they intrude upon areas that have been traditionally perceived as being the purview of state; or globalization can refer to increases in immigration, the widespread ratification of human rights instruments and the growing use of international law to settle disputes between states, or the convergence of political systems with the spread of democracy. There are several economic interpretations of globalization, including increased capital mobility, trade and foreign direct investment, convergence in technical standards, freer labor mobility. All of these interpretations of globalization have in common that they restrict domestic sovereignty.

Perhaps "globalization" should be understood as referring to all those areas combined. It would be difficult to consider the combined effect of such an "extreme" view of globalization, but my hunch is that "extreme" globalization would make self-determination and nationalist ideologies politically irrelevant or unnecessary and would certainly decrease the risk of separatist movements. However, studies of globalization typically take a more narrow view and refer to incomplete globalization – i.e. they focus only on the greater exposure of national economies to the world market through a greater dependence on international trade. To engage with those studies, I also take this narrow view of globalization in this chapter. I argue that narrow globalization can indeed have an impact on self-determination movements. But this is only because we are talking about incomplete globalization – i.e. about a set of policy choices that increase domestic economic risk to specific groups and regions within countries while preserving the pre-existing state system, thereby limiting the risk-management instruments available to affected groups/regions. In this section, I make this point clearer by considering, in the context of the theories of separatism and decentralization reviewed in previous sections, the effect of increased trade exposure on the demand for self-determination. I argue that globalization understood as increased trade as a percentage of GDP can both fuel and quell self-determination movements under different conditions and I outline some of those conditions that are likely to lead to more demand for sovereignty.

I consider globalization's effects on each of the key variables in the Sambanis-Milanovic model of separatism reviewed earlier: the share of the region in total GDP (income) of the country; the regional ethnic, religious, or racial differentiation from the rest of the country; the regional endowment in terms of natural resources; regional interpersonal inequality; the historical basis for regional distinctiveness and autonomy; and inequality between regions (differences in regions' mean incomes).

### Globalization and level of income

Globalization implies increased access to larger world markets. One clear implication of this fact is that globalization can make regional economies sustainable while reducing their reliance on the central government, so it should increase the demand for self-determination for a group of a given size. The more public services can be procured from the private sector, the lower the reliance of rich regions on the state. National defense is the last (and most important) obstacle to complete independence, but it will be less of a problem for rich *and* populous regions, which will be better able to provide their defense. According to the Alesina and Spolaore model I touched on earlier, globalization should increase the demand for separatism because it makes it easier for small markets to survive and cover the costs of public goods.[40]

Small and backward regions will be less likely to demand sovereignty unless they are large/populous. Typically, backward groups are not "pulled" by secessionist ideology if a system of redistribution affords them a higher standard of living within the federation than in an independent state.[41] An example that illustrates this point is the Central Asian Republics, which spearheaded the effort to prevent the dissolution of the USSR (Bartkus 1999). These Republics were net beneficiaries of the USSR's fiscal federalism, as they were allowed to retain 100 percent of their income tax collections (Roeder 1991). This is an example of a successful policy of economic redistribution, which facilitated political stability and was unlikely to develop into secessionism precisely because of the absence of some of the key pre-conditions for the demand of greater self-determination (size of the economy being the first one). However, at the other end of the spectrum are the Baltic states, which were the more advanced groups and net creditors in the Soviet Federation, and were allowed to retain less than 75 percent of their income taxes. These groups were among the first to seek secession from the USSR. Increased access to European markets helped fan secessionism in those regions, as did the fact that they are culturally very different from the rest of the federation and they had a history of conflict with Russia.

### *Globalization and natural resource endowment*

Regions whose economies are heavily dependent on trade in natural resources (minerals, precious stones, agricultural commodities) will be those most affected by globalization as those regions are particularly vulnerable to terms of trade shocks (see Humphreys 2002; Ross 2002). A good example is the case of the Chiappas rebellion in Mexico. Mexico's joining of the North American Free Trade Association (NAFTA) increased demands for greater autonomy in the poorer indigenous areas and economic grievances due to the implications of NAFTA fueled the Chiappas rebellion (Wing 2004). The EZLN's (El Ejército Zapatista de Liberación Nacional) uprising started the day that NAFTA went into effect. Programs that the Salinas government implemented to help labor adjust to changes made necessary by the NAFTA accords were not sufficient to make up for the huge income losses in the Chiapas region due to NAFTA's effects on the corn trade (US corn was more competitively priced, so this led to reductions in corn sales from the region and earning from corn made up the major source of income in the region) (Weinberg 2000; Wing 2004). Chiapas was much less developed than other regions of Mexico and was unable to benefit from the government's modernization programs.

Indonesia offers another case of violent separatist conflict that is related to the export trade of natural resources. Indonesia is highly dependent on exports of primary commodities. Greater globalization implies that regions where those commodities are concentrated – regions such as Aceh – will have an added incentive to rebel, but also that the central government will be less likely to allow them to secede, given those regions' importance for the national economy. In the mid-1970s, when the rebellion in Aceh started, Indonesia's resource export-to-GDP ratio was 19.4 percent (Ross 2005). Aceh grew exceptionally fast during the 1970s and 1980s, faster than the rest of Indonesia with a real per capita income growth of 7–8 percent during those two decades. Its economy was heavily dependent on oil and natural gas exports: while in 1976, oil and gas accounted for less than 17 percent of Aceh's GDP, by 1989, this ratio had risen to 69.5 percent (Ross 2005). The fact that control of oil and gas riches is at the core of the separatist insurgency in Aceh is made clear by the government's enactment of decentralization laws in 1999 that enabled the regional government to retain much of the revenue from natural resource exports.[42]

Beyond terms of trade risk, there is also a demand to benefit directly from control of valuable natural resources once the possibility of trading them in the world market becomes real. The case of Aceh just reviewed provides some evidence of that, as does the case of the Biafran rebellion in Nigeria. A long history of ethno-regional conflict has marked Nigeria's politics. In the mid-1960s, that conflict escalated to a civil war when the region of Biafra attempted to secede. At least part of the explanation for the location and timing of the secession can be found in the discovery of large oil reserves that Biafran leadership wanted to control without sharing the profits with the Nigerian government (Zinn 2005).

Elsewhere in Africa, we see ample evidence of secessionist rebellions that were motivated by a desire to control natural resources. In the Democratic Republic of Congo (DRC), two rebellions have taken place in resource-rich Katanga region, which wanted to secede from the rest of the country to take full advantage of its resource wealth. The DRC is heavily dependent on mineral extraction and trade. Katanga produces 70 percent of the country's copper production, and is the sole producer of cobalt. According to Ndikumana and Emizet (2005: 3), at independence, "Katanga accounted for 75 percent of the Congo's mineral output, about 50 percent of total national resources, and roughly 20 percent of the government's total budgetary expenditures." Another rebellion took place in the 1960s in Kasai, the so-called "diamond state." Katanga and Kasai in the 1960s were the main producers of diamonds in the Congo, and the Congo was the single largest producer of industrial diamonds in the world.[43] Control of the profits from the diamond trade was a key motivation for those wars.

Several African rebellions have been financed through profits from clandestine trade in natural resources (Berdal and Malone 2000; Collier and Hoeffler 2004). The more such trade opportunities become available, the greater the ease to finance rebellions against the state. The desire to profit from international trade without government controls or taxes was part of what motivated or at least sustained the war in Chechnya (Zürcher *et al.* 2005). In this case, "trade" was mostly illicit, but the pattern was consistent with the argument made earlier regarding the link between globalization and conflict: the desire for greater independence from government control in taking advantage of the opportunities for trade with the global economy motivated Chechens who wanted to escape the control of the Russian state. Though no study has argued that there was a causal connection between greater globalization and the onset of the Chechen war, the ability for Chechens to engage in trade through Georgia helped finance the rebellion.

### *Globalization and ethnic or cultural difference*

Does globalization have any effect on the degree of cultural difference between regions and the rest of the country? Under some conditions, such pre-existing differences become more salient. First, globalization can create new, supranational identities, as in the case of bureaucrats in international organizations. Such elites might perhaps counteract the growth or influence of more narrowly defined national identities. If so, then we should expect globalization to reduce the demand for self-determination and see a movement for ever closer integration, supported by an ideology of supranationalism. But this sort of influence would have more to do with one of the other views of globalization I outlined above and is not necessarily a result of growing trade. (It is perhaps more reasonable to expect that a European identity might emerge as a result of the deepening integration of European countries than a globalist identity as a result of growing trade among all countries.)

A second view with a more plausible link is that increased trade-related risk can harden ethnic identities and intensify ethnic conflict in societies with overlapping ethnic and professional cleavages, if trade-related risk is differentially distributed across those cleavages. There is a lot of evidence that conflict is more intense where professional and ethnic cleavages overlap (Horowitz 1985). If a region with a territorially concentrated minority and a highly specialized economy is hit by an adverse economic shock, it is likely that this will intensify conflict between that ethnic group and the state.

Closely related to this discussion of ethnic difference is the fact that, despite growing globalization, there is imperfect labor mobility. Thus, labor cannot easily move to take advantage of new trade opportunities or to avoid the risks of adverse economic shocks within regions. This imperfect labor mobility does not only apply for relations between states, but it might also apply to several large multiethnic states where linguistic, religious or caste barriers make it hard for people to migrate in search of better employment opportunities.

In the standard political-economy treatment of decentralization, ethnic differences are a key source of preference heterogeneity across regions and this is what motivates decentralization (e.g. Alesina and Spolaore 1997). Decentralization is an efficient way to allocate resources among heterogeneous regions if there are no barriers to movement of people across regions, and people are free to move to the region most closely reflecting their preferences (see Tiebout 1956; Oates 1972; Buchanan and Faith 1987).

In reality however, because we are discussing incomplete globalization, there are significant barriers to factor mobility. How will this influence the question of national identity? If ethnic groups find it hard to move to richer regions or countries, then their increased vulnerability to economic shocks should increase their demand of either more self-determination, or more transfers and social insurance provided by the center.

### *Globalization and income inequality*

Perhaps the most important and clear mechanism linking globalization and theories of separatism is through the effects of globalization on income inequality. If globalization increases disparities among mean levels of regional incomes, it should increase the demand for self-determination, other things held equal (this follows from the Sambanis-Milanovic theory reviewed earlier). Here, separatism should be demanded by the richer regions since greater inequality would imply the need for greater inter-governmental transfers from richer regions to poorer regions.

Separatism due to growing inequality in the distribution of trade-related risk can be mitigated by another source of transfers, directly from large conglomerates or supranational organizations to regional or central governments of member states. Fiscal transfers to weaker regions of the conglomerate can reduce the burden on the central government, which in turn will reduce the tax burden on the rich regions, removing the added incentive for separatism. But such conglomerates (e.g. the European Union) must raise revenues from their member states, so the net effect of supranational relief for regional inequality on local demands for self-determination is unclear, particularly when the decision to join conglomerates is not shared equally by all regions of the member state. In Catalonia, for example, the demand for self-determination has increased since Spain joined the European Union, as the perception has been that Catalans have traded one set of transfers and rules for another set, both limiting their independence.

What is important in this discussion is the idea that there can be institutional solutions to the management of globalization-related risk. Government policy is an important intervening variable in the relationship between globalization and the demand for self-determination. It is within the government's purview to regulate the regional distribution of both risks and benefits associated with globalization.

This discussion leads us to consider two important arguments in the literature. First, we must consider the need for social insurance schemes to moderate the risks associated with globalization. Second, and related to the first, we must consider the net effect of globalization on the size of government, since larger governments are better able to provide such social insurance schemes. These arguments and empirical evidence showing a positive correlation between exposure to world trade and the size of government can be found in Rodrik (1998a, b, c) and Cameron (1978).

### *Social insurance against globalization*

Globalization can influence the risk of separatist violence through its effects on economic growth. This follows from, among other sources, the quantitative literature on civil war, which has shown a significant negative correlation between growth and large-scale political violence (e.g. Collier and Hoeffler 2004). Rodrik (1998a, b), in a study that tried to explain why economic growth slowed down in several countries in the 1980s whereas in the 1960s and 1970s growth increases were widespread, argued that the main culprit is bad macroeconomic policy. Rodrik (1998a: 149) argued that, in many countries, bad macroeconomic policies are adopted because the country is unable to cope with the social and political fallout of economic shocks and this acts as a constraint on the governments' policy choices. Deep social cleavages and weak conflict management institutions are at the heart of the problem, exacerbating the effects of negative economic shocks and triggering distributive conflicts. This argument is described in a simple formula (Rodrik 1998b: 2), which explains changes in economic growth as the product of external shocks (a negative number in the formula) and the ratio between "latent social conflict" and the society's "institutions of conflict management." This formula is clearly relevant to the question of interest here – the effects of globalization on separatist conflict. It suggests that, while globalization can increase the potential for negative changes in economic growth, thereby increasing social conflict and even separatist war, it is not globalization per se that has this effect, but rather it is how globalization-related risks are managed by the state. Societies with good conflict management institutions or low levels of social conflict should be less vulnerable to external shocks.

This plausible argument suggests that globalization in countries with significant separatist conflict or large-scale regional inequality can indeed increase the risk of conflict escalation through the channel of declining economic growth. In countries with significant cultural rifts and regional inequality, where there is latent demand for self-determination (cf. Sambanis and Milanovic 2004) in one or more regions and where the government cannot credibly commit to resolving those demands peacefully by providing social insurance or economic resources and transfers to the regions, globalization can increase the risk of violent separatist conflict.

In Indonesia, for example, Ross (2005) has pointed to a link between the growth declines associated with the East Asian economic crisis and the escalation of the separatist conflict in Aceh. The Indonesian government had a poor record of providing social insurance to the province (it had a better record of repression of separatist sentiment), so as growth declined, the prospect of trading Aceh's rich natural resources independently from the central government seemed more appealing to many Acehnese. Ross also argues, however, that this was not a sufficient factor to explain mass-level support for the insurgency. Also crucial was the fact that for more than a decade, the Acehnese had suffered at the hands of the Indonesian military. The precedent of East Timor's achievement of independence was also crucial in mobilizing mass support in favor of Acehnese independence in 1999.

***The link between globalization and centralization***

So far we have seen that globalization increases the need for some sort of social insurance or safety net. Social insurance schemes can be most effectively provided by central governments with a fiscally strong position. Thus, we have to consider the likely effects of globalization on the level of fiscal (de)centralization and then look more closely at the relationship between decentralization and separatist conflict.

A common perception is that globalization increases the level of fiscal decentralization. But Garrett and Rodden (2003) have argued that the opposite is true and that globalization leads to more centralization. They have focused on fiscal centralization, which they measure, as Fisman and Gatti do, as the sum of state and local expenditures as a percentage of total public sector expenditures. Their measure of globalization is the standard trade/GDP ratio used to measure the domestic market's integration to the world market for goods and services.[44] Garrett and Rodden argue that globalization increases the risk of asymmetric shocks, so given the uncertainty about the timing of the shocks and uncertainty about which regions are most likely to be affected, regions will want insurance against these risks and a fiscally strong centralized government will be better able to provide that insurance (in the forms of inter-regional transfers). Thus, the need for macroeconomic stabilization will be greater in a globalized economy and fiscal centralization is better suited to provide that stabilization.

The first to observe a trend of expansion in the role of government in advanced industrial economies as a result of growing exposure to international trade was Cameron (1978). Since the end of World War II, governments have provided more social services, but they are also producers of goods and services and their role in economic policy through the use of fiscal and monetary instruments increased in that period. Cameron explained that trend as a result of growing exposure of national economies to world markets. The "size" of governments is measured by the level of revenues and expenditures of the government as a percent of the country's GDP. Exposure to free trade limits countries' capacity to respond to economic shocks. Drawing on the experience of 18 advanced economies, Cameron (1978: 1253) finds that "a high degree of trade dependence is conducive to a relatively large expansion of the public economy." Cameron also found that party politics influence the scope of the public economy (with leftist governments resulting in increases of public revenues as a percent of GDP relative to other countries where the Left was not a big part of the government). What explains this relationship between openness and government size is governments' need to counter the risks associated with external dependence. In the set of countries that Cameron looked at, openness has led to high industrial concentration and high levels of unionization. This fact, combined with the frequent participation of Leftist parties in government, widened the scope of collective bargaining between governments and labor unions, which in turned led to increases in government spending for income supplements, and the expansion of the public economy (Cameron 1978: 1256).[45] This increase in the scope of public economy is also correlated with increased centralization (Cameron 1978: 1253).

Rodrik also found a positive association between trade exposure and size of the government. His explanation was similar to those given above: "societies seem to demand (and receive) an expanded government role as the price for accepting larger doses of external risk" (Rodrik 1998c: 998).[46] If this argument is correct, the implication for the relationship between globalization and separatist conflict and violence is that the relationship should be negative, assuming that the government does indeed provide a social safety net and that this safety net is sufficient to offset the positive effects of globalization on conflict that I discussed earlier.

### *The consequences of globalization-related fiscal centralization*

Something not considered by any of these explanations of centralization as a result of globalization-related demand for social insurance is how or why there is credibility in any national insurance scheme. In Cameron's explanation, there is a defensible argument in the power of labor unions, which could draw support from Leftist political parties. But Rodrik (1998c) notes that labor unions have played a much more limited role in the less developed countries. So, why would social insurance schemes be credible in those countries? This question is particularly important given that separatist war is more likely in less developed countries, and that consociational or other political systems that are designed to protect minority rights before or after civil war are sometimes not credible and there has been a trend towards more centralization over time (cf. Lake and Rothchild 2001). Moreover, fiscal centralization must have repercussions on other forms of regional autonomy, since loss of fiscal autonomy should imply loss of autonomy over the design or implementation of cultural programs and other regional expenditures that are tailored to meet regional preferences for public goods consumption.

Theories of nationalist conflict (see, e.g. Hechter 2001) have identified a causal connection between the imposition of direct rule in regions that were previously mostly self-governed and the rise of nationalist conflict in those regions. Recent empirical evidence (Sambanis and Zinn 2005) supports those theories. Thus, if greater fiscal centralization resulting from globalization also implies greater centralization in political governance, then we should expect growing opposition by ethnic groups in previously autonomous regions. Garrett and Rodden (2003) have argued that fiscal centralization need not imply other forms of centralization and that it is compatible with cultural and political autonomy. But loss of autonomy over raising and spending regional tax revenues should also imply loss of ability to design and implement region-specific policies or programs that cater to the region's cultural distinctiveness.[47] If this is correct, then increased fiscal centralization should increase the demand for autonomy.

These politically and culturally-driven demands for greater autonomy should, however, be offset by the benefit of a centrally-provided safety net to regulate economic risks associated with globalization. This is consistent with the tradeoff between income and sovereignty in Sambanis-Milanovic's theory.

The key question is whether a larger government always implies larger safety nets for groups and regions affected adversely from globalization? While the studies reviewed previously have given some empirical evidence to support that relationship, there are important data limitations to them in that they do not include many of the countries with active ethnic conflict and violence. If conflict over self-determination is already ongoing; if the country is heavily dependent on natural resource trade *and* if those resources are concentrated in one or a few regions; if regions contain significant ethnic concentrations and asset-specific regional economies (those economies would be more vulnerable to terms of trade shocks); if there is a history of conflict or violence between the state and the regions; and if there is significant regional inequality in the distribution of income and services across regions, then the government's pledges to increase its investment in social and economic safety nets to protect the region from the risks associated with globalization will not be credible. In other words, if most of the pre-conditions for high demand for self-determination exist, and if there is an external adverse economic shock to the region as a result of globalization, then I would expect globalization to further intensify separatist conflict between the government and the regions.

Thus, to summarize, countries with greater exposure to the world economy need not, on average, develop new separatist conflicts with their regions or minority groups if no conflict existed previously. In those countries, decentralization could help ease tensions if it satisfies local preferences for the consumption of public goods, but if centralization results from globalization, the added cushion against external shocks that this centralization will afford may offset some of the benefits of more sovereignty for the regions. But, in those regions where there were positive levels of conflict previously, even if governments try to provide social insurance against globalization-related risks, separatist conflict is likely to increase since the government's promises and programs are unlikely to be effective or credible. Patterns of prior group-level and region-level discrimination can be used as proxies for the government's commitment to providing such a safety net. Thus, where we observe a positive prior level of conflict due precisely to such discrimination, globalization is likely to exacerbate separatist conflict.

## Conclusion

International trade may increase global welfare, but it is well-known that it creates winners and losers in different sectors of the economy. It follows that globalization can lead to economic gains, but also losses, and that these can be unevenly distributed across countries and regions. The broad welfare gains associated with trade and globalization should decrease the global incidence of war.[48] Several channels connecting trade to global peace have been identified in the literature, especially in the literature focusing on the "democratic peace." There is less of a consensus on the effects of trade on the incidence of intra-state violence and there is no systematic study of the effects of globalization on separatist conflict that does not rise to the level of war.

Given the data limitations that make such a study difficult to conduct, this chapter has provided some conjectures on the relationship between globalization and separatist conflict and violence. I have reviewed some important contributions to the literature on civil war and secession and outlined some perspectives on the relationship between decentralization and secession. The focus on decentralization is justified by the empirical association between globalization and growing centralization.

According to most theories of secessionism, self-determination is typically demanded when the economic benefits of membership to the predecessor state are low relative to the economic and political gains of independence. More democratic states might be better able to resolve conflicts, increasing the benefits of continued membership (i.e. no secession). It is therefore important that globalization has been occurring alongside a trend towards greater democratization (in fact, democratization might be considered as a form of political globalization). Well-established democracies are unlikely to have civil war because they reduce grievance and facilitate non-violent forms of conflict resolution (Hegre *et al.* 2001), but transitions to democracy can create the conditions for conflict and insurgency (Elbadawi and Sambanis 2002). Moreover, incomplete democratization processes that create regimes that are neither democratic enough to reduce grievance, nor autocratic enough to suppress protest, are prone to civil war (Hegre *et al.* 2001).

This chapter argued that there is a link between decentralization and democracy, but I also reviewed studies that showed increasing centralization as a result of globalization. There may, therefore, be a tension between the two parallel processes of globalization and democratization with respect to their effects on the level of decentralization. Systems that are already democratic may be able to provide a credible commitment to decentralization, as groups are allowed to articulate their demands and pursue them in ordinary politics (Wantchekon and Simon 1998). Or, in deep democracies, peripheral groups may feel sufficiently represented at the center so as not to seek secession or decentralization. However, democracy also allows minority groups to organize politically in their pursuit of self-determination; and the process towards centralization in incomplete democracies may allow aggrieved groups to organize and protest the decline in the level of their autonomy. In response to such protest, majority groups may in turn demand greater centralization. These conflicting demands may make it hard for some countries to manage the risks of globalization by centralizing while also providing sufficiently democratic solutions to the demands of regionally concentrated minority groups. Any significant political change (as the change towards more centralization) can upset the balance and activate secessionist sentiment among populations with latent fears of being victimized at the hands of a majority.[49] I have argued that this sort of conflict is more likely to occur as an indirect result of globalization in countries with already active conflicts over self-determination.

The effects of globalization on the risk of separatist conflict and violence depend largely on how globalization interacts with the other determinants of separatism, especially with pre-existing levels of inequality and ethno-cultural difference across regions. This chapter has argued that globalization will have generally positive effects if it increases levels of income and leads governments to provide social insurance programs to cushion any external shocks to vulnerable populations. But in some regions with prior levels of conflict, globalization is likely to exacerbate those conflicts.

Finally, it is worth remembering that this chapter has taken a narrow view of globalization, as does most of the literature. But globalization is a process that includes much more than increases in the level of trade. We can think of several political, cultural and organizational forms of globalization. Many of these forms co-evolve. Increases in global trade have occurred alongside an expansion of the process of democratization around the world. Foreign investment has risen with trade. Migration flows are also growing and countries are becoming much more closely integrated legally and institutionally in several parts of the world (e.g. in the European Union). World institutions (e.g. the United Nations, the World Trade Organization, International Monetary Fund) have been more active in managing world crises and regulating relationships among states. All of these developments can be expected to have both direct and indirect effects on the demand for self-determination within states. Thus, the perspective that I have given here on the relationship between globalization and the demand for self-determination is a distinctly partial equilibrium one. For a solid understanding of the effects of globalization on separatist conflict, one would have to consider the effects of a broadly defined process of globalization and analyze the total effect from all these parallel processes of global integration.

## Notes

1 See Sambanis and Zinn (2005). Most of these (around 70 percent) were non-violent movements and the others either started out violent or turned violent in the process of demanding more autonomy.
2 There are different and complementary understandings of sovereignty. I define sovereignty simply as policy autonomy within the territory of an internationally recognized state. This definition is close to the definitions of "domestic sovereignty" and "Westphalian sovereignty" in Stephen Krasner's work. For a discussion of the main forms of sovereignty, including how each might be violated by several modalities, see Krasner (1999: Chapter 1).
3 In this chapter, I only consider some of the effects of globalization, not what causes globalization. For such an analysis, see Garrett (2000) among others.
4 This can be inferred from the model developed by Alesina and Spolaore (1997).
5 See Lake and Rothschild (2001) for a relevant and insightful discussion.
6 In of 4,345 country-years, the mean and standard deviation of federal, semi-federal and centralized, are, respectively: 0.122 and (0.327); 0.066 and (0.25); and 0.811 and (0.391).
7 These are only illustrative. There are too many missing countries in the Fisman and Gatti (2000) list, so this could bias the correlations.
8 The mean level of *decentralization* is 0.2. This binary variable identifies all countries above the mean.
9 I used data from the Polity98 project, which codes democracy (*dem*) and autocracy (*auto*) level for all countries on a 0–10 scale, with ten being the highest score for each category. Common practice in the literature is to sum these two indices into an aggregate index of polity (*pol*).
10 Garrett and Rodden (2003) also find that democracy is positively associated with greater decentralization (they present regression results based on a measure of fiscal decentralization regressed on the level of democracy).
11 These countries are less likely than others to report accurate statistics to the IMF's Government Financial Statistics database, which Fisman and Gatti (2000) use to compile their measure of economic decentralization.
12 On the distinction between reactive, reflective, and proactive systems in the context of an evaluation of the state of democratic theory, see Shapiro (2001).
13 See Lake and Rothschild (2001) for an important addition to the literature.
14 Hirschleifer (1995) shows how peace negotiation is impossible in the case of antithetical preferences, making continued conflict a rational outcome.
15 The World Bank and the IMF jointly conducted studies of the expected economic benefits of these proposals and they found that the benefits were significant for both communities, though more so for the TCs, whose GDP would have increased by an estimated 20 percent. Sambanis (1999) cites sources from international financial institutions estimating that the re-opening of the airport alone could have brought an annual income of US$ 43–90 million to the TC community.
16 The parties might also have been uncertain about the future implications of agreement on this issue and how it would impact their future bargaining position. That concern could also explain non-agreement. However, in this case, there were credible external guarantees on the enforcement of the provisions of the agreement and neither party had articulated a clear concern over specific ways in which agreement over Varosha would impact its future bargaining position.
17 This would be consistent with arguments that the collapse of the USSR and Yugoslavia was primarily due to the system of ethno-federalism in those countries, which emphasized and even created regional and cultural differences

across groups while allowing them to organize opposition to the state and demand more autonomy. For such an argument, see Bunce (1999).

18 See Bolton *et al.* (1996). Norway's secession from Sweden in 1905 was at least partly the result of Norway's dissatisfaction with the consular and other services that Sweden was providing to Norwegian sailors (Bartkus 1999: 22). By contrast, the formation of a unified Czechoslovakia in 1918 was only possible due to the Czechs' agreement to establish governmental and educational institutions in Slovakia to safeguard the Slovaks' interests and identity (Bartkus 1999).
19 Bartkus (1999); Hechter (2001: 24–5) and Calhoun (1991).
20 See Toft (1996, 2001, 2003). Smith (1992: 5), like most theorists of nationalists, emphasizes the importance of territorial concentration in identity formation. Class and gender, he argues, are not enduring collective identities partly because they are likely to be territorially dispersed.
21 Gurr (2000); Horowitz (1985) and Rudolph and Thompson (1985).
22 See Brustein (1988) and Meadwell (1991).
23 Hechter (2001, Chapter 3).
24 Bartkus (1999). Note the vocal opposition to secessionism in Quebec by the business community, which appreciates the economic benefits of remaining in the Canadian federation.
25 See Horowitz (1985).
26 The Karens of Burma saw their cultural traditions and identity threatened in the Burman-dominated state (Rotberg 1998). The Karens mutinied at the time of independence and have been continually fighting an insurgency against the government since 1948. In 1979, when eight other groups joined the Karen National Union (KNU) to form the National Democratic Front (NDF), the NDF renounced secession as the ultimate goal of secession. This may have signaled a shift in the Karens' belief in the viability of an independent Karen state (Bartkus 1999), though this argument is contrary to Bartkus (1999: 53), who presents interview evidence from several cases to suggest that the economic viability of the new state does not influence elites' calculations of whether or not to pursue secession. A more plausible explanation was that secession was no longer a feasible or credible strategy given the new multi-ethnic coalition against the government. Each of those ethnic groups would have been threatened by the secessionist demands of the other(s).
27 See Buchanan and Faith (1987). This could mean that the political benefits of continued membership in the predecessor state for group elites are smaller than the expected political gains from secession; or that there are no security benefits to remaining in the state; or that secession will not create new internal or external security threats that make the new state not viable.
28 See Meadwell (1991) and Roeder (1991) for an application to the USSR; and Bunce (1999).
29 This argument is made forcefully by Walter (1997, 2004) and draws on Fearon's (1995) rational choice theory of war.
30 A different perspective is argued by Horowitz (1985: 425), who argues that "most secessionist movements are begun by groups stigmatized as backward."
31 The view of sovereignty as a non-essential good is a component of Hechter's (2001) rational choice theory of nationalism and Milanovic's (1999) theory of state decision-making to join multinational conglomerates.
32 This is because there are "natural" limits to sovereignty, one of which is group size (i.e. it does not make sense to be a sovereign nation of 1). Hechter (2001: 40–1) also considers the question of "which scale of nested control structures is most conducive to the maintenance of social order at the lowest overall cost"? One of his key variables is group size (in multicultural societies).
33 See Collier and Hoeffler (2004). A corollary of this argument is the hypothesis

that greater economic dependence on the center (for the provision of public goods) will reduce the incentives for secession.

34 Conversely, the greater the importance of regionally concentrated resources to *national* GDP, the lower the probability that the center will be accommodating towards demands for greater regional sovereignty or that accommodating policies will be considered credible and time-consistent. Demands for sovereignty are likely to be resisted by force in such cases, particularly in less developed, non-democratic regimes.

35 Ross (2005) develops the case of Aceh in Indonesia as an example.

36 By analogy, we can consider the effects of racial segregation on service provision in US cities. The determinants of racial segregation itself are harder to analyze.

37 Alesina's use of physical distance to model the distance in preferences is odd and rather at variance with reality. Civil wars are usually fought among geographically proximate groups, but in Alesina's model these would be people with similar preferences.

38 Consistent with this hypothesis, there is some empirical evidence in the literature on civil war that war prevalence is greater in polarized or ethnically dominated societies as compared to highly fractionalized societies. See Elbadawi and Sambanis (2002) and Reynal-Querol (2002).

39 In our model, if such tinkering with borders is successful, it should dampen the demand for sovereignty.

40 There is a related argument that globalization makes regional autonomy movements more credible, so they are better able to extract resources from the center. This would increase the "strategic" use of separatist ideology even by groups that do not really want to secede, simply so that they can extract resources from the center. This is a plausible argument, but there is no clear empirical evidence of it on a large set of countries. Van Houten (2003) does not find any evidence of this in his sample of European regions.

41 This is in contrast to Horowitz's (1985) theory that backward groups in backward states will be those that demand secession.

42 According to Ross (2005: 20), decentralization laws no. 22 and 25 of 1999 gave regional and local governments the right to retain 15 percent of the net public income from oil, 30 percent from natural gas, and 80 percent from timber.

43 See Ndikumana and Emizet (2005). The Congo's output was around one-third of total world output (Kaplan 1978: 224). However, this is not to say that all the rebellions in the DRC were due to resource predation. For example, the Kwilu rebellion that took place around the same time as the Katanga and Kasai rebellions in the Congo was unrelated to resource-predation, since that region is not resource-rich (Ndikumana and Emizet 2005).

44 They also use a second measure, capital market openness, but I focus on the trade measure here, since that it is the main measure used in the literature.

45 Rodrik (1998c) writes that in developing countries, the role of labor organizations should not be as large as in the countries in Cameron's sample.

46 The increase in the size of government in Rodrik's paper is measured primarily through increase in government consumption, though he also considers the size of social security and welfare. An assumption underlying the above argument is that increases in government consumption stabilize incomes. This assumption seems to be supported by Rodrik's model and data. This is important because the credibility of the social insurance policy would be low if increases in government consumption increased income volatility (as some other authors had argued), given that more programs with greater coverage would be required and the government would have been less able to provide those programs.

47 Sambanis and Milanovic (2004). See also the correlations between economic and political decentralization in the second section of this chapter.

48 There is a large literature on the relationship between trade and violent conflict. Most of it focuses on inter-state conflict. See, for example, Russett and Oneal (2001); Gowa (1994); Mansfield (1994) and Hegre (2000).

49 Woodward (1999) analyzes the Yugoslav wars of secession as a consequence of external shock (debt crisis and collapse of the communist system) that re-activated old nationalist ideologies among unemployed youth and political elites.

## References


Alesina, A. and Spolaore, E. (1997) "On the Number and Size of Nations," *Quarterly Journal of Economics*, 112: 1027–56.

Atlas, P. M. and Licklider, R. (1999) "Conflict Among Former Allies after Civil War Settlement: Sudan, Zimbabwe, Chad, and Lebanon," *Journal of Peace Research*, 36/1: 35–54.

Bartkus, V. O. (1999) *The Dynamic of Secession*, Cambridge: Cambridge University Press.

Berdal, M. and Malone, D. M. (2000) *Greed and Grievance: Economic Agendas in Civil Wars*, Boulder: Lynne Rienner.

Bolton, P., Roland, G. and Spolaore, E. (1996) "Economic Theories of the Break-Up and Integration of Nations," *European Economic Review*, 40: 697–705.

Brustein, W. R. (1988) *The Social Origins of Political Regionalism: France, 1849–1981*, Berkeley: University of California Press.

Buchanan, J. M. and Faith R. L. (1987) "Secession and the Limits of Taxation: Toward a Theory of Internal Exit," *American Economic Review*, 77: 1023–31.

Bunce, V. (1999) *Subversive Institutions: The Design and the Destruction of Socialism and the State*, Cambridge: Cambridge University Press.

Calhoun, C. (1991) "The Problem of Identity in Collective Action," in J. Huber (ed.) *Macro-Micro Linkages in Sociology*, Newbury Park: Sage: 51–75.

Cameron, D. (1978) "The Expansion of the Public Economy: A Comparative Analysis," *American Political Science Review*, 72/4: 1243–61.

Collier, P. (2000) "Ethnicity, Politics and Economic Performance," *Economics and Politics*, 12/3: 225–46.

Collier, P. and Hoeffler, A. (2004) "Greed and Grievance in Civil War," *Oxford Economic Papers*, 56: 563–95.

Deutsch, K. (1966) *Nationalism and Social Communication*, second edition, Cambridge: MIT Press.

Elbadawi, I. and Sambanis, N. (2002) "How Much War Will We See? Explaining the Prevalence of Civil War," *Journal of Conflict Resolution*, 46/3: 307–34.

Fearon, J. D. (1995) "Rationalist Explanations for War," *International Organization*, 49/3: 379–414.

Fisman, R. and Gatti, R. (2000) "Decentralization and Corruption: Evidence Across Countries," *Journal of Public Economics*, 83/3: 325–46.

Garrett, G. (2000) "The Causes of Globalization," *Comparative Political Studies*, 33: 941–91.

Garrett, G. and Rodden, J. (2003) "Globalization and Fiscal Decentralization," in M. Kahler and D. Lake (eds) *Governance in a Global Economy: Political Authority in Transition*, Princeton: Princeton University Press.

Gellner, E. (1983) *Nations and Nationalism*, Ithaca: Cornell University Press.

Gowa, J. (1994) *Allies, Adversaries, and International Trade,* Princeton: Princeton University Press.

Gurr, T. R. (2000) *Peoples Versus States: Minorities at Risk in the New Century,* Washington, DC: United States Institute of Peace.

Hechter, M. (1999) *Internal Colonialism: The Celtic Fringe in British National Development,* New Brunswick: Transaction Publishers.

—— (2001) *Containing Nationalism,* Oxford: Oxford University Press.

Hegre, H. (2000) "Development and the Liberal Peace: What Does it Take to Be a Trading State?," *Journal of Peace Research,* 37/1: 5–30.

Hegre, H., Ellingsen, T., Gates, S. and Gleditsch, N. P. (2001) "Toward a Democratic Civil Peace? Democracy, Political Change, and Civil War, 1816–1992," *American Political Science Review,* 95/1: 33–48.

Heraclides, A. (1991) *The Self-Determination of Minorities in International Politics,* London: Frank Cass.

Hirschleifer, J. (1995) "Theorizing about Conflict," in K. Hartley and T. Sandler (eds) *Handbook of Defense Economics,* volume 1, Amsterdam: Elsevier, 165–92.

Horowitz, D. L. (1985) *Ethnic Groups in Conflict,* Berkeley: University of California Press.

Humphreys, M. (2002) "Economics and Violent Conflict," Framework Paper, Harvard CPI Portal on Economics and Conflict. Online. Available at: www.preventconflict.org/.

International Monetary Fund (various years) *Government Finance Statistics* (GFS), Washington, DC: IMF.

Jaggers, K. and Gurr, T. R. (1996) POLITY III: Regime Change and Political Authority, 1800–1994. [computer file] (Study #6695). 2nd ICPSR version. Boulder: Keith Jaggers/College Park: Ted Robert Gurr [producers], 1995. Ann Arbor: Inter-University Consortium for Political and Social Research [distributor].

Kaplan, I. (ed.) (1978) *Zaïre: A Country Study,* Washington, DC: The American University.

Kollman, K., Miller, J. and Page, S. (1996) "On States as Policy Laboratories," unpublished typescript, University of Michigan.

Krasner, S. D. (1999) *Sovereignty: Organized Hypocrisy,* Princeton: Princeton University Press.

Laitin, D. (2001) "Secessionist Rebellion in the Former Soviet Union," *Comparative Political Studies,* 34 (8): 839–61.

Lake, D. A. and Rothchild, D. (2001) "Political Decentralization and Civil War Settlements," unpublished typescript, UCSD and UC Davis.

Mansfield, E. (1994) *Power, Trade, and War,* Princeton: Princeton University Press.

Meadwell, H. (1991) "A Rational Choice Approach to Political Regionalism," *Comparative Politics,* 23/4: 401–21.

Milanovic, B. (1999) "Nations, Conglomerates and Empires: Trade-Off Between Income and Sovereignty," in D. Salvatore, M. Svetlicic and J. P. Damijan (eds) *Small Countries in a Global Economy,* London: Palgrave, 25–69.

Ndikumana, L. and Emizet, K. (2005) "The Economics of Civil War: The Case of the Democratic Republic of Congo," in P. Collier and N. Sambanis (eds) *Understanding Civil War: Evidence and Analysis (Volume 1),* Washington, DC: World Bank Publications.

Nixon, C. R. (1972) "Self-Determination: The Nigeria/Biafra Case," *World Politics,* (July): 473–97.

Oates, W. E. (1972) *Fiscal Federalism*, New York: Harcourt Brace Jovanovich.

Reynal-Querol, M. (2002) "Ethnicity, Political Systems and Civil Wars," *Journal of Conflict Resolution*, 46/1: 29–54.

Riker, W. H. (1964) *Federalism: Origin, Operation, Significance*, Boston: Little, Brown.

Rodrik, D. (1998a) "Globalization, Social Conflict, and Economic Growth," *World Economy*, 21/2: 143–58.

—— (1998b) "Where Did All the Growth Go? External Shocks, Social Conflict, and Growth Collapses," *NBER Working Paper Series*, Paper No. 6350.

—— (1998c) "Why do More Open Economies Have Bigger Governments?," *Journal of Political Economy*, 106/5: 997–1032.

Roeder, P. G. (1991) "Soviet Federalism and Ethnic Mobilization," *World Politics*, 43/January: 196–232.

Ross, M. (2002) "Oil, Drugs, and Diamonds: How Do Natural Resources Vary in their Impact on Civil War?," unpublished typescript, UCLA.

Ross, M. L. (2005) "Resources and Rebellion in Aceh, Indonesia," in P. Collier and N. Sambanis (eds) *Understanding Civil War: Evidence and Analysis (Volume 2)*, Washington, DC: World Bank Publications.

Rotberg, Robert I. (ed.) (1998) *Burma: Prospects for a Democratic Future*, Washington, DC: Brookings.

Rudolph, J. and Thompson, R. (1985) "Ethnoterritorial Movements and the Policy Process: Accommodating Nationalist Demands in the Developed World," *Comparative Politics*, 17/April: 291–311.

Russett, B. M. and Oneal, J. (2001) *Triangulating Peace*, New York: Norton.

Sambanis, N. (1999) "United Nations Peacekeeping in Theory and in Cyprus," unpublished Ph.D. dissertation, Princeton University.

Sambanis, N. and Zinn, A. (2005) "From Protest to Violence: An Analysis of Conflict Escalation with an Application to Self-Determination," unpublished typescript, Yale University.

Sambanis, N. and Milanovic, B. (2004) "Explaining the Demand for Sovereignty," unpublished typescript, Yale University and the World Bank.

Shapiro, I. (2001) "The State of Democratic Theory," in I. Katznelson and H. Milner (eds) *Political Science: The State of the Discipline*, New York: W.W. Norton & Co. and Washington, DC: American Political Science Association, 235–65.

Smith, A. (1992) *Ethnicity and Nationalism*, Leiden, New York: E. J. Brill.

Tamuno, T. N. (1970) "Separatist Agitation in Nigeria Since 1914," *Journal of Modern African Studies*, 8/4: 565–77.

Tiebout, C. M. (1956) "A Pure Theory of Local Expenditures," *Journal of Political Economy*, 64: 416–24.

Toft, M. (1996) "The Geography of Ethnic Conflict: Do Settlement Patterns Matter?," paper presented at the Annual Meeting of the Midwest Political Science Association, Chicago, April.

—— (2001) "A Theory of Territory, Indivisibility, and Ethnic War," unpublished typescript, Harvard University.

—— (2003) *The Geography of Conflict*, Princeton: Princeton University Press.

Treisman, D. (1997) "Russia's 'Ethnic Revival:' The Separatist Activism of Regional Leaders in a Postcommunist Order," *World Politics*, 49/2: 212–49.

—— (1998) "Fiscal Redistribution in a Fragile Federation: Moscow and the Regions in 1994," *British Journal of Political Science*, 28/1: 185–200.

—— (2000) "Decentralization and the Quality of Government," unpublished typescript, UCLA.

Van Houten, P. (2003) "Globalization and Demands for Regional Autonomy in Europe," in M. Kahler and D. Lake (eds) *Governance in a Global Economy: Political Authority in Transition*, Princeton: Princeton University Press.

Walter, B. F. (1997) "The Critical Barrier to Civil War Settlement," *International Organization*, 51/3: 335–65.

—— (2004) "The Strategic Logic of Secession," unpublished typescript, UCSD.

Wantchekon, L. and Simon, M. (1998) "Democracy as an Enforcement Mechanism for Elite Power-Sharing Contracts," unpublished typescript, Yale University.

Weber, M. ([1922] 1978) *Economy and Society*, G. Roth and C. Wittich (eds), Berkeley: University of California Press.

Weinberg, B. (2000) *Homage to Chiapas: The New Indigenous Struggles in Mexico*, New York: Verso Books.

Weingast, B. R. (1995) "The Economic Role of Political Institutions: Market-Preserving federalism and Economic Development," *Journal of Law, Economics, and Organization*, 11: 1–31.

Wilkinson, S. I. (2004) *Votes and Violence: Electoral Competition and Ethnic Riots in India*, Cambridge: Cambridge University Press.

Wing, E. (2004) "Grievance and Group Dynamics in Chiappas: A Look at the Formation and Significance of the Zapatista Movement," unpublished typescript, Yale University.

Woodward, S. (1999) *Balkan Tragedy*, Washington, DC: Brookings.

Yonuo, A. (1974) *The Rising Nagas: A Historical and Political Study*, New Dehli: Vivek Publishing.

Zacher, M. W. (2001) "The Territorial Integrity Norm: International Boundaries and the Use of Force," *International Organization*, 55/2: 215–50.

Zartman, W. I. (1995) "Putting Things Back Together," in W. I. Zartman (ed.) *Collapsed States: The Disintegration and Restoration of Legitimate Authority*, Boulder: Lynne Rienner: 267–73.

Zinn, A. (2005) "Theory versus Reality: Civil War Onset and Avoidance in Nigeria Since 1960," in P. Collier and N. Sambanis (eds) *Understanding Civil War: Evidence and Analysis (Volume 1)*, Washington, DC: World Bank Publications.

Zürcher, C., Baev, P. and Koehler, J. (2005) "Civil Wars in the Caucasus," in P. Collier and N. Sambanis (eds) *Understanding Civil War: Evidence and Analysis (Volume 2)*, Washington, DC: World Bank Publications.

# 9 Economic integration and political separatism

## Parallel trends or causally linked processes?

*Annalisa Zinn*

### Introduction

Since 1960, the worldwide volume of trade – a key indicator of economic globalization – has been increasing. In 1960 trade was 24 percent of world gross domestic product (GDP). By 1980 trade accounted for 39 percent of world GDP and in 1999 trade's share of global GDP was 45 percent (World Development Indicators). At the same time there has been an increasing number of ethnic or regional "self-determination movements" seeking greater political autonomy for their respective group. In 1960, 61 groups demanded greater autonomy and the number of active self-determination movements increased to 90 in 1970, 136 in 1980, 219 in 1990 and 261 in 1999 (Sambanis and Zinn 2005).

Observation of these simultaneous processes, particularly in the case of Europe, has led to the popular claim that economic globalization, especially in the form of increasing trade liberalization, and self-determination movements are casually linked in that globalization increases the frequency and intensity of the demand for self-determination (Alesina and Spolaore 1997; Coates 1998; Dragadze 1996; Enriquez 1999; Jones and Keating 1995; Marks and McAdam 1996; Marks *et al.* 1996; Newhouse 1997; Sorens 2004; Talbott 2000). And there are indeed multiple examples that seem to substantiate this claim. Close to home, as the North American Free Trade Agreement (NAFTA) went into effect on the first of January 1994, a rebellion led by the indigenous Zapatista National Liberation Army (EZLN) broke out in the Mexican state of Chiapas. One of the rebels' key demands was greater autonomy for the indigenous communities in the state[1] and a key motivation for the rebellion was the fear that corn imports from the United States would destroy the region's agricultural economy.[2]

Across the Atlantic, as Finland and Sweden prepared in the late 1980s to join the European Union (EU), new separatist organizations arose, in Åland and Scania respectively, to demand EU membership as separate political entities.[3] Older European self-determination movements – such as Plaid Cymru (The Party of Wales) in the United Kingdom, Mouvement

Normand (Normandy Movement) in France, and Libertà Emilia e Rumagna (Emilia and Romagna Freedom), Liga Veneta (Venetian League) and Partito d'Azione Siciliano (Sicilian Action Party) in Italy – also seek greater autonomy for their historic region in the context of a "Europe of the Regions."[4]

At the same time, however, many self-determination movements seem to be concerned with issues that are very different, and possibly also very removed, from how their region is faring in the global economy, or could fare in the global economy if the region were an independent country. For example, a motivation for autonomy shared by many separatist groups – such as Abkhazians in Georgia, Sikkimese in India and the Republic of Texas Movement – has been the claim that their region's historical incorporation into their "host state" was illegal or against their wishes.[5] Other groups – such as the Kachin Independence Army (KIA) in Myanmar, the Moro National Liberation Front (MNLF) in the Philippines, the Sudanese People's Liberation Army (SPLA) and multiple Sikh and Kashmiri separatist movements in India – have cited religious discrimination or domination as a key grievance fueling their quest for independence.[6]

These examples raise the possibility that economic integration may not be a contributing factor to political separatism, as popular wisdom currently suggests, but rather that economic integration and political separatism are merely parallel trends. In this chapter I investigate these possibilities.

With the help of a multivariate statistical analysis of 116 countries from 1980–1999, I find a surprising relationship between economic integration and political separatism: countries with open economies appear *less likely* to be places where ethnic, religious or regional groups form political organizations to demand self-determination, compared to countries with more closed economies. This finding challenges the popular view that globalization amplifies the intensity of subnational threats to state sovereignty and suggests that the increasing level of trade between countries is actually curbing parallel increases in the number of active self-determination movements.

The chapter proceeds as follows. I begin by outlining several hypotheses about how globalization may affect the demand for political reorganization and cite a few examples that illustrate these hypotheses. I then consider alternative explanations for why self-determination movements form and seek greater autonomy. To test both sets of hypotheses, I conduct a multivariate statistical analysis on what determines the number of active self-determination movements in a given country-year.

## Globalization as a cause of political separatism

Political separatism is a term that describes the demands and actions of self-determination movements: organizations consisting of individuals that share a common ethnic, religious, or regional identity and which seek to enhance the power of their identity group by attaining greater administrative and legislative autonomy or even independence (Sambanis and Zinn 2005). As their name implies, self-determination movements ground their actions for greater autonomy in the language of "self-determination": a group-defined claim to the right of self-government within the boundaries of a given territory. For these subnational minority groups, self-government could consist of the authority to raise taxes and spend tax revenues locally; the capacity to maintain a local defense or police force; autonomy over cultural practices; and/or the power to define the territorial boundaries of the region within which the group exercises its right to self-determination (Sambanis and Zinn 2005).

As previously mentioned, in light of the parallel increases in inter-country trade and the number of active self-determination movements over the past 50 years, a common notion is that globalization, specifically in the form of trade liberalization, increases the frequency and intensity of movements for regional autonomy. That is, it stimulates the formation of new movements and fuels existing movements, perhaps by increasing voter support for these movements (Sorens 2004), inducing changes in their strategies, or encouraging them to be more active in their pursuit of greater autonomy.

There are several explanations for the proposed causal relationship between globalization and the demand for greater autonomy. First, opportunistic political actors, especially when they represent interests threatened by globalization, are likely to mobilize popular demands for greater autonomy as a response to globalization (Dragadze 1996). The Lega Nord (Northern League), a separatist political party advocating greater autonomy and sometimes even secession for Italy's northern regions, seems to fit this story well. Survey data reveals that in recent years most Lega Nord supporters have been workers and artisans who tend to overestimate the actual impact of global dynamics on their region. Their electoral support for the Lega Nord therefore suggests that they view the strengthening of local and regional institutions as the best defense against global forces (Beirich and Woods 2000).

Also consistent with Dragadze's hypothesis, the Lega Nord has varied its positions on European economic integration on the basis of whether integration appeared to be a threat or an opportunity for the northern regions. When in the mid-1990s the central government was cutting spending and raising taxes in order to bring Italy's public deficits down to 3 percent of GDP – a requirement for membership in the Economic and Monetary Union (EMU) and subsequent adoption of the euro – the Lega Nord advocated that the northern regions should "secede and join EMU," given that the export-oriented northern regions would both benefit from the euro and easily qualify for EMU membership (*The Economist*, 5 October 1996: 47). However, on 22 January 2004 Umberto Bossi, head of the Lega Nord, slammed the euro as "the hold-up of the century," with claims that since the euro's introduction, "prices doubled and people are now having trouble making ends meet" (Europe Intelligence Wire).

Another explanation for the proposed causal connection between increasing globalization and increasing activity by self-determination movements is that globalization produces new regional and supranational institutions, especially in the case of the European Union, which in turn often become additional targets for political actors interested in mobilizing demands for autonomy (Coates 1998; Marks and McAdam 1996; Marks *et al.* 1996). For example, since the late 1980s over 50 European subnational governments – many of which are led by separatist political parties – have set up offices in Brussels. Although they have no legal or formal place in the EU, these offices provide the European Commission and Parliament with a regional viewpoint on legislation and lobby for greater voice in EU decision-making. They have also succeeded in establishing a consultative Committee of the Regions composed of local and regional representatives across the EU (Marks and McAdam 1996).

A third explanation for the concomitant increases in trade and in the number of active self-determination movements is that economic integration makes political disintegration more feasible and thus encourages both the formation and persistence of self-determination movements (cf. Jones and Keating 1995). In their model of the size of countries, Alesina and Spolaore (1997) show that the equilibrium number of countries is increasing in the amount of economic integration because economic integration minimizes the trade-off between the benefits of large jurisdictions and the costs of heterogeneity associated with large and diverse populations.

More specifically, a benefit of large countries is that they have large internal markets that enable them to take advantage of economies of scale, which in turn increase the efficiency and contingent international competitiveness of the national economy. However, taking advantage of the economies of scale in large countries may come at a political cost. A larger population is more likely to be heterogeneous, which means that in larger countries public choices are less likely to be close to the preferences of the average individual, compared to public choices in smaller, relatively homogeneous countries. But in the case of regional trading blocks in which small countries can freely trade with each other, the economic benefits of a large internal market and the political benefits of a more homogeneous citizenry can be reconciled, suggesting that "regional separatism should be associated with increasing economic integration" (Alesina and Spolaore 1997: 1041).

Finally, as Nicholas Sambanis also argues in his contribution to this volume, globalization may create economic reasons for autonomy, particularly in places where there exists *ex ante* economic disintegration between regions. Assuming that economic integration does indeed exacerbate interregional inequality within countries, relatively rich regions may seek autonomy on the allegation that the central government is exploiting the economic resources of the richer region, e.g. by increased tax rates whose revenue is used to fund transfers to and development projects in the poorer regions.

## Other possible causes of self-determination movements

Given the methodological requirement to consider alternative explanations, any investigation of the cross-national links between globalization and self-determination movements must be part of a larger exploration of the reasons why self-determination movements form in some countries at certain points in time and sometimes persist in demanding greater autonomy. While no comprehensive theory of the causes of self-determination currently exists, the literature does suggest several factors that may render a country more likely to house self-determination movements. First and foremost, there must be at least one, non-dominant group with a separate cultural identity (Bartkus 1999; Dragadze 1996; Hechter 2001). Second, it must be possible for such groups to form an active organization and thus overcome the ubiquitous collective action problem (Sambanis and Zinn 2005).

While these two criteria are mandated simply by the definition of a self-determination movement, they are clearly not the whole story behind the formation of self-determination movements because ethnic groups may – and in fact do – mobilize to press for issues *other* than greater autonomy, such as civil rights, participation in government, better working conditions, use of language and freedom of religion (Davenport 2003). So the literature on political separatism specifies a number of other factors that ought to encourage ethnic groups, which have the possibility of political mobilization, to demand self-determination. These factors include the territorial concentration of a minority group's population (Toft 2003); the historical or current loss of autonomy (Hechter 2001); group-specific discrimination (Gurr 2000), especially economic discrimination as political discrimination may render a group less likely to seek greater autonomy (Marshall and Gurr 2003); regionally-concentrated natural resources (Collier *et al.* 2003); existing self-determination movements among transborder ethnic kin (Marshall and Gurr 2003); and inter-group economic inequality (Horowitz 1985). Such horizontal inequality may result either from regional or group-specific differentials in the benefits of political integration (Bolton *et al.* 1996; Bartkus 1999) or from regional modes of production that coincide with ethnic cleavages (Brustein 1988; Meadwell 1991).

In countries where self-determination movements are more likely to form, a separate set of factors may increase the number of active self-determination movements in any given country-year. These factors include a high degree of ethnic heterogeneity within the country, which increases the number of potential separatist groups; a democratic system of government, which may provide more opportunities for seeking self-determination (e.g. electoral politics and a non-repressive environment for non-violent protest movements) and thus encourage the persistence of active self-determination movements; and an open economy, which may signal the viability of secession and thus also encourage self-determination movements to keep on laboring for independence.

## Empirical analysis

### *Variable measurements*

To gain insight into the determinants of the demand for greater subnational autonomy, I estimate a multivariate events count model of the number of active self-determination movements in a given country-year. The dependent variable in this model, *Self-determination movements*, comes from the Sambanis and Zinn (2005) dataset of self-determination movements and it indicates the number of active self-determination movements in the given country-year. As such, *Self-determination movements* measures not only the frequency of demands for greater autonomy, but also their intensity from the perspective of the relevant central government, given that each self-determination movement within a country represents a distinct ethnic or regional group that is seeking greater autonomy, or even independence, for a distinct territory of the country.

With the exception of democracy, which I measure with Cheibub and Gandhi's (2004) dichotomous coding of regime-type, and ethnic heterogeneity, which I measure with Fearon and Laitin's (2003) ethnolinguistic fractionalization index, to quantify the previously discussed potential determinants of self-determination movements, it is necessary to have data on the demographic characteristics of and state policies towards ethnic groups. Such data can be obtained from the Minorities at Risk (MAR) Project, which monitors and analyzes the status and conflicts of politically active communal groups in all countries with a current population of at least 500,000.[7] While MAR's variables are coded by ethnic group, they can be transformed into country-level variables, such as those needed in the present analysis, given that my indicator of economic globalization – *Trade* (as percent of GDP) from the World Development Indicators – is only available at the country-level.[8]

Specifically, I proxy territorially-concentrated ethnic groups with *Group concentration*, a tripartite variable indicating whether a given country's most concentrated politically-active communal group comprises:

1 less than 50 percent;
2 50–75 percent;
3 75–100 percent of the population of its regional base.

This variable is drawn from MAR's "Regional base – proportion of group members, 1990" (GC6B) indicator, which defines "regional base" as a spatially contiguous region within a country, larger than an urban area, in which 25 percent or more of the minority resides, and the minority constitutes the predominant proportion of the population (Davenport 2003: 19). For a few MAR groups the GC6B indicator could not be coded, so in these cases I measure *Group concentration* using MAR's older and more generic GROUPCON variable, which, for present purposes, is more or less compatible with the GC6B indicator.[9]

My indicator for historical or current loss of autonomy by cultural minorities is a binary variable, *Lost autonomy*, which indicates whether or not one or more cultural minorities in a given country were historically autonomous (i.e. MAR's AUTON variable = 1). As indicators of group-specific discrimination, I code two five-part variables based on MAR's political and economic discrimination indices: *Political discrimination*, which for every country-year takes on the highest level of political discrimination experienced by a communal group living in the given country, and *Economic discrimination*, which, for every country-year, takes on the highest level of economic discrimination experienced by a communal group living in the given country.

Following the MAR indices, there are four positive levels of discrimination:

1 Historical neglect or restrictions leading to substantial under-representation in political participation and/or significant poverty and under-representation in desirable occupations, but public policies are designed to improve the group's political and/or economic status;
2 historical neglect or restrictions etc. (like discrimination level one), but no evidence of remedial policies;
3 substantial under-representation and poverty due to prevailing social practice by dominant groups and formal public policies toward the group are neutral or, if positive, inadequate to offset discriminatory policies;
4 public policies substantially restrict the group's political participation and/or economic opportunities by comparison with other groups (Davenport 2003: 36–7, 39).

Valuable natural resources are many, including oil, mineral deposits and agricultural products, and I have not found any quantitative measure of the intra-country regional concentration of one or more natural resources. Using thematic (economic activity, land use, natural resource and energy) country maps from the Perry-Castañeda Library Map Collection and mineral maps from the US Geological Survey's Minerals Yearbook, I have constructed a rough, first-cut measure of the regional concentration of oil and mineral resources within a given country as these are the natural resources that have been tied to secession (Collier *et al.* 2003: 60–1). Specifically, I have divided each map into quadrants (i.e. a country's northeastern, northwestern, southeastern and southwestern regions) by drawing two perpendicular lines from the country's approximate central point and I have then calculated the relative percentage of distinct mineral and oil deposits sites (i.e. distinct mineral or other symbols on the maps) falling into each quadrant. Based on this information, I have coded *Resource concentration* as a four-part variable indicating whether a given country (0) either has no noteworthy mineral and oil resources or its resources are spread fairly evenly across the country; or whether its most resource-rich quarter contains:

1 26–50 percent;
2 51–75 percent;
3 76–100 percent of the mineral and oil deposit points in the given country.

Once again, it must be emphasized that this is a rough measure of natural resource concentration as for more detailed information, e.g. on the size of each mineral or oil deposit site in each administrative or ethnically-salient region of a given country, it would be necessary to construct a more fine-grained measure.

To test for transborder contagion effects, i.e. the formation of a self-determination movement in response to the promptings of ethnic kin in a bordering country who have already demanded greater autonomy, I have constructed a binary variable called *Separatist kin*, which indicates whether or not in the previous country-year there was an active self-determination movement among transborder ethnic kin (data from Sambanis and Zinn 2005).

Lastly, I measure inter-group economic inequality with a modified version of MAR's economic differentials index. This index, a seven-point scale ranging from −2 (the group is advantaged) to +4 (extreme inter-group differentials, i.e. high inequality), measures inter-group comparisons on six economic dimensions: income; land/property; higher education; presence in commerce; presence in professions; and presence in official positions. Since both advantaged and disadvantaged groups may be predisposed to demand greater autonomy (Horowitz 1985) and the scale points do not measure the intensity of economic inequality in the way that an ordinal scale would require,[10] I recode the MAR economic differentials index into a binary variable, *Inter-group economic inequality*. This variable is coded 1 for every country-year in which a communal group living in the given country experienced economic differentials of some kind (i.e. a non-zero score on the MAR index).

### *Model specification*

The data sample of 116 countries contains 3,921 non-missing country-year observations and 2,028 years of activity by self-determination movements, which signifies meaningful variation in the dependent variable. The countries included in this sample are those where, according to the MAR Project, there are politically mobilized minority groups who suffer or benefit from differential treatment vis-à-vis other groups in the country and for which trade data are available. By the first criterion, each country in the sample should be equally likely, on the basis of the following two necessary conditions for the formation of self-determination movements, to be a place where self-determination movements form: the existence of at least one minority cultural identity within the country; and possibilities for ethnic mobilization. This base-level equal likelihood among all sample cases is essential to the analysis because, without it, the possibility of spurious correlation between the dependent variable and the explanatory variables would be heightened.

It is also very important to note that of the 284 minority groups surveyed by the MAR project, and thus included in the present analysis, less than half have sought greater autonomy at some point since 1945 (Sambanis and Zinn 2005). This means that the MAR-based independent variables (*Group concentration*, *Lost autonomy*, *Political discrimination*, *Economic discrimination* and *Inter-group economic inequality*) do not automatically determine the frequency of self-determination movements. Rather, the MAR-based variables measure social characteristics that could apply to any ethnic group, regardless of their political agenda.

In order to determine the appropriate event-count model for this data, it is necessary to inspect the dependent variable's raw data for evidence of over-dispersion, the condition where the variance in the data is larger than its mean, and to consider whether distinct events are statistically independent of one another. Such inspection is necessary because in some even-count models, namely the Poisson regression model, the mean and unconditional variance are constrained to be equal and distinct events are presumed to be independent.

*Self-determination movements* contains 3,921 observations, ranging from 0 to 45. Its mean is 1.39 and its unconditional variance (standard deviation) is 2.88, which is evidence of over-dispersion. Tabulation of *Self-determination movements* reveals that 48 percent of the counts are zeros, which suggests that over-dispersion is likely due to "zero-inflation" – an excess proportion of zeros in the count data. A zero-inflation Poisson model could therefore still be appropriate, but not in the present analysis where there is not only intra-country dependence between distinct events, but also the possibility that a self-determination movement in one country stimulates co-ethnics in a neighboring country to form a self-determination movement.

So I model the data using zero-inflated negative binomial regression, which allows for "excess zeros" under the assumption that the population is characterized by two regimes, one where members have zero counts (e.g. country-years without active self-determination movements) and one where members have zero or positive counts (e.g. country-years with one or more active self-determination movements). The likelihood of being in either regime is estimated using a logit specification, while the counts in the second regime are estimated using a negative binomial specification.

The explanatory variables in the zero-inflation model – *Economic discrimination, Group concentration, Inter-group economic inequality, Lost autonomy, Political discrimination, Resource concentration, Separatist kin* and *Trade* – are potential determinants of the absence of active self-determination movements in a given country-year. The explanatory variables in the negative binomial model – *Democracy, Ethnic heterogeneity* and *Trade* are potential determinants of the number of active self-determination movements in a given country-year. All explanatory variables have annual frequency from 1980–1999 (the only years which MAR data on political and economic discrimination are available) and since *Economic discrimination, Lost autonomy* and *Political discrimination* may capture government repression of an active self-determination movement, these variables are lagged one year.

### *Results*

Table 9.1 presents the results of the statistically significant zero-inflation negative binomial model. The logit portion of the model indicates that there are eight factors affecting the likelihood that there will be no active self-determination movements in a given country-year. These factors are *Group concentration, Lost autonomy, Resource concentration* and *Separatist kin*, which are negatively correlated with the absence of self-determination movements (i.e. they encourage the formation of self-determination movements) and *Trade, Economic discrimination, Political discrimination* and *Inter-group economic inequality*, which increase the likelihood that no self-determination movements will form in a given country-year. So it seems that economic globalization renders a country less likely to be a place where self-determination movements form, which, although contrary to popular wisdom, is consistent with Van Houten's (2003) finding that European integration has not induced a general rise in demands for greater regional autonomy in EU countries.

Furthermore, it seems that the key grievance motivating self-determination movements is the current or historical loss of autonomy; that the demand for self-determination is likely to spillover to transborder ethnic kin; and that factors increasing the feasibility of secession – high territorial concentration of one or more ethnic groups and a high degree of regional natural resource concentration – are key determinants of whether or not self-determination movements form in a country with

*Table 9.1* Determinants of the number of active self-determination movements, 1980–1999

| | *Logit Zero-Inflation Model (no self-determination movements)* |
|---|---|
| Economic discrimination (lagged one year) | 2.625*** (0.623) |
| Group concentration | −2.031*** (0.420) |
| Inter-group economic inequality | 1.546* (0.643) |
| Lost autonomy (lagged one year) | −29.900*** (2.360) |
| Political discrimination (lagged one year) | 1.974*** (0.383) |
| Resource concentration | −1.576** (0.488) |
| Separatist kin | −28.075*** (1.457) |
| Trade | 0.098*** (0.022) |
| Constant | −15.632*** (3.489) |
| | *Negative Binomial Model (number of self-determination movements)* |
| Democracy | 0.551*** (0.072) |
| Ethnic heterogeneity | 0.442** (0.137) |
| Trade | −0.012*** (0.001) |
| Constant | 0.826*** (0.111) |
| Wald chi-square | 95.88*** |
| Log pseudolikelihood | −2,492.495 |
| Total observations | 1,616 |

Notes
Robust standard errors are in parentheses. Estimations performed using Stata. *$p<0.05$; **$p<0.01$; ***$p<0.001$.

politically-active ethnic, regional or religious groups. By contrast, factors that may decrease the opportunity for political mobilization (i.e. political discrimination) or possibly impoverish a group and thus render independence less economically viable (i.e. economic discrimination and inter-group economic inequality) seem to discourage the formation of self-determination movements. While this latter finding is inconsistent with Horowitz (1985) and Gurr (2000), it supports the common argument that political opportunities and constraints create the most important incentives for initiating new phases of collective action (Tarrow 1998: 7; cf. Fearon and Laitin 2003).

The negative binomial portion of the model indicates that more self-determination movements tend to be active in countries with relatively closed economies, democratic government, and a high degree ethnic heterogeneity. With the exception of the negative effect of economic openness on the formation and number of active self-determination movements, all of the findings presented in Table 9.1 are consistent with at least some works in the literature on political separatism and collective action. This suggests that the statistical model is also theoretically valid, which lends additional credence to the surprising finding that the demand for self-determination tends to be less frequent and intense in more globalized countries, all other things being equal.[11]

But why is there this negative relationship between economic integration and political separatism? A likely possibility is that, as in the case of globalization's effect on internal violent conflict (Hegre *et al.* 2003), the factor doing the work is not economic openness per se, but one of its covariates. This possibility will be the subject of further investigation. In the meantime, the key finding seems to be that recent increases in economic integration and political separatism are parallel processes and that without the increasing level of trade between countries, the number of active self-determination movements worldwide most likely would be higher.

## Conclusion

Chapter after chapter, the recurring theme of this volume is that some of the common notions about globalization and state sovereignty are fallacies, others are only partially valid, while still others are applicable only in a specific, circumscribed context. This chapter on the links between economic integration and political separatism expands on this theme by presenting evidence, contrary to popular wisdom, to suggest that economic globalization decreases, rather than increases, the frequency and intensity of the demand for self-determination. The next line of inquiry will be to investigate further the reasons for this unexpected relationship between economic integration and political separatism.

## Notes

1 MAR, "Assessment for Mayans in Mexico," http://www.cidcm.umd.edu/inscr/mar/assessment.asp?groupId=7002 (1 February 2005).
2 "Chiapas Uprising and Trade," http://www.american.edu/TED/chiapas.htm (1 February 2005).
3 See Minahan (1996: 13–15) and KnowEurope's Directory of European Union Political Parties. Finland and Sweden joined the EU in 1995.
4 See KnowEurope's Directory of European Union Political Parties.
5 See MAR Group Assessments; Minahan (1996: 518–20); Hewitt and Cheetham (2000: 247).
6 Degenhardt (1988: 156–9); Balencie and de La Grange (1996: 18–37, 167–202, 281–307, 470–84).
7 For more information see the MAR website: www.cidcm.umd.edu/inscr/mar/.
8 In the statistical analysis that follows, I tried measuring economic globalization with FDI (net inflows as percent of GDP), but the results were unreliable. I therefore do not report them.
9 Specifically, the GROUPCON variables consists of four categories:

   0 widely dispersed;
   1 primarily urban or minority in one region;
   2 majority in one region, others dispersed;
   3 concentrated in one region.

The latter three categories, though less specific, are comparable to GC6B's three categories. If there did not appear to be a match between the two indicators, I coded *Regional concentration* on the basis of MAR's qualitative group summaries.

10 Rather, the scale points measure on how many dimensions the given group faces inequality. This is not a measure of the degree (i.e. intensity) of inequality because a group facing profound inequality in one dimension is arguably more disadvantaged than a group facing superficial inequality on several dimensions. Since MAR does not provide data on the degree of inequality, for the present purposes it is best to proxy inter-group economic inequality as a binary variable.

11 This result is corroborated by a logit regression covering more countries and years (165 countries, 1960–1999) with *Trade* as the independent variable and *Self-determination activity* as the dependent variable (coefficient = −0.014; significant at the 0.1 percent level).

## References


Alesina, A. and Spolaore, E. (1997) "On the Number and Size of Nations," *Quarterly Journal of Economics*, 112: 1027–56.

Balancie, J. and de La Grange, A. (1996) *Mondes Rebelles: Acteurs, Conflits et Violences Politiques*, vol. 2: Asie, Maghreb, Proche et Moyen-Orient et Europe, Paris: Editions Michalon.

Bartkus, V. O. (1999) *The Dynamic of Secession*, Cambridge: Cambridge University Press.

Beirich, H. and Woods, D. (2000) "Globalization, Workers and the Northern League," *West European Politics*, 23/1: 130–43.

Bolton, P., Roland, G. and Spolaore, E. (1996) "Economic Theories of the Break-Up and Integration of Nations," *European Economic Review*, 40: 697–705.

Brustein, W. R. (1988) *The Social Origins of Political Regionalism: France, 1849–1981*, Berkeley: University of California Press.

Cheibub, J. A. and Gandhi, J. (2004) "Classifying Political Regimes: A Six-fold Classification of Democracies and Dictatorships." Presented at the 2004 Annual APSA Meeting. Dataset available at: http://pantheon.yale.edu/~jac236/DATASETS.htm (accessed February 2005).

Coates, C. (1998) "Spanish Regionalism and the European Community: A Comparative Analysis of Four Spanish Regions," *Parliamentary Affairs*, 51/2: 259–71.

Collier, P., Elliott, V. L., Hegre, H., Hoeffler, A., Reynal-Querol, M. and Sambanis, N. (2003) *Breaking the Conflict Trap: Civil War and Development Policy*, Washington, DC: The World Bank.

Davenport, C. (2003) *Minorities at Risk Dataset Users Manual 030703*. Online. Available at: www.cidcm.umd.edu/inscr/mar/data.asp#quantitative (accessed December 2004).

Degenhardt, H. W. (ed.) (1988) *Revolutionary and Dissident Movements*, London: Longman Publishers.

Dragadze, T. (1996) "Self-Determination and the Politics of Exclusion," *Ethnic and Racial Studies*, 19/2: 341–51.

Enriquez, J. (1999) "Too Many Flags?," *Foreign Policy*, 116: 30–49.

Europe Intelligence Wire (2004) "Northern League's Bossi says Euro was 'Hold-up of the Century.'" 22 January.

Fearon, J. D. and Laitin, D. D. (2003) "Ethnicity, Insurgency, and Civil War," *American Political Science Review*, 97/1: 75–90.

Gurr, T. R. (2000) *Peoples Versus States: Minorities at Risk in the New Century*, Washington, DC: United States Institute of Peace Press.

Hechter, M. (2001) *Containing Nationalism*, Oxford: Oxford University Press.

Hegre, H., Gleditsch, N. P. and Gissinger, R. (2003) "Globalization and Internal Conflict," in G. Schneider, K. Barbieri and N. P. Gleditsch (eds) *Globalization and Conflict*, Boulder: Rowman & Littlefield, 251–75.

Hewitt, C. and Cheetham, T. (2000) *Encyclopedia of Modern Separatist Movements*, Santa Barbara, CA: ABC–CLIO.

Horowitz, Donald L. (1985) *Ethnic Groups in Conflict*, Berkeley: University of California Press.

Jones, B. and Keating, M. (eds) (1995) *The European Union and the Regions*, Oxford: Oxford University Press.

KnowEurope, *Directory of European Union Political Parties*. Online. Available at: www.knoweurope.net/html/toc/b_deupp.htm (accessed December 2004).

Marks, G. and McAdam, D. (1996) "Social Movements and the Changing Structure of Political Opportunity in the European Union," *Western European Politics*, 19/2: 249–78.

Marks, G., Nielson, F. and Leonard, R. (1996) "Competencies, Cracks, and Conflicts: Regional Mobilization in the European Union," *Comparative Political Studies*, 29/2: 164–92.

Marshall, M. G. and Gurr, T. R. (2003) *Peace and Conflict 2003*, College Park: Center for International Development and Conflict Management, University of Maryland.

Meadwell, H. (1991) "A Rational Choice Approach to Political Regionalism," *Comparative Politics*, 23/4: 401–21.

Minahan, J. (1996) *Nations Without States: A Historical Dictionary of Contemporary National Movements*, London: Greenwood Press.

Newhouse, J. (1997) "Europe's Rising Regionalism," *Foreign Affairs*, 76/1: 18–36.

Perry-Castañeda Library Map Collection. Online. Available at: www.lib.utexas.edu/maps/ (June 2005).

Sambanis, N. and Zinn, A. (2005) "From Protest to Violence: An Analysis of Conflict Escalation with an Application to Self-Determination Movements," unpublished manuscript, Yale University.

Sorens, J. (2004) "Globalization, Secessionism, and Autonomy," *Electoral Studies*, 23: 727–52.

Talbott, S. (2000) "Self-Determination in an Interdependent World," *Foreign Policy*, 118: 152–63.

Tarrow, S. (1998) *Power in Movements: Social Movements and Contentious Politics*, second edition, Cambridge: Cambridge University Press.

Toft, M. D. (2003) *The Geography of Ethnic Violence*, Princeton: Princeton University Press.

US Geological Survey (2004) *Minerals Yearbook*, volume 3. Online. Available at: minerals.usgs.gov/minerals/pubs/country/ (June 2005).

Van Houten, P. (2003) "Globalization and Demands for Regional Autonomy in Europe," in M. Kahler and D. Lake (eds) *Governance in a Global Economy: Political Authority in Transition*, Princeton: Princeton University Press.

World Bank (2004) *World Development Indicators*. Online. Available at: devdata.worldbank.org/dataonline/ (December 2004).

# 10 Globalization and ethnonationalist movements

## Evidence from Spain and India

*Meredith L. Weiss*

Ethnonationalism as a political force long predates the contemporary era of economic integration and transborder flows of people, ideas, and resources, but may be significantly tempered by the latter. Moreover, the persistent political salience of ethnic and religious affinities, often regardless of the economic implications of self-determination, buttresses Westphalian principles. The progress of contemporary ethnonationalist movements thus serves to interrogate the implications of globalization. This chapter compares and contrasts four ethnonationalist movements, two in Spain and two in India, to examine when and why ethnonationalist sentiments still carry weight, the significance of domestic and international support and sanctions to these movements, and what such movements reveal about the relative potency and dynamics of nation-states and global forces.

The four cases examined here are Basque, Catalan, Punjabi and Kashmiri nationalist movements. While these four cases are far from collectively exhaustive of possible scenarios, they effectively highlight several significant findings. First, other considerations notwithstanding, ethnic, regional and religious sentiments remain powerful motivators for political behavior. Second, while the international context matters, how states respond to ethnonationalist movements remains more salient. Third, movements supported significantly by a diasporic population or that invoke transnational identities may benefit more from globalization than others. Fourth, the global forces involved may shift over time, with implications for ethnonationalist movements' prospects and strategies.

### Situating ethnonationalism

I premise my analysis upon a straightforward definition of "ethnonationalism." Such a sentiment invokes identities generally deemed primordial rather than civic (Geertz 1995), even if significantly constructed or at least consciously amplified (Calhoun 1993). These identities are ethnic, religious or regional, as indicated by shared language, rituals, sense of communal past and future, physiognomy and the like. Ethnonationalists identify also with a particular territory: the nation-state (cf. Barrington 1997). If prevailing political boundaries do not align with nationalist aspirations, conflict may result – unless, for instance, the state in question succeeds in rallying a broader and stronger sense of belonging within the existing borders. Given that current territorial boundaries are not perfectly in line with national identifications – and can never be, given that individuals have multiple identities and their attachment to various of these may shift over time – members of nations may be found within or across states, creating the possibility of either irredentist or secessionist movements. The cases considered here are, or have the potential to be, primarily secessionist; they are of communities marked by a substate identity, and which would have to secede from the larger political unit to satisfy their nationalist aspirations fully.

At the same time, at least some portion of the relevant community in these cases is currently located outside the primary state in question. Hence, the transborder dimensions of these conflicts are immediately apparent. Some of these aspects are long-standing, such as the role of national diasporic communities. Others are relatively new, and relate more clearly to the contemporary phase of globalization, such as the significance of supranational institutions or need of states to consider seriously the needs of international investors in charting strategies. Regardless, it is how states decide to handle ethnonationalist movements active within their boundaries that is of critical importance, even if on a more general level, states enjoy relatively less autonomy than previously – and even if those nations, were they to secede and form independent nation-states, would also enjoy relatively limited autonomy in the global system. At stake in these contests, now as always, is not so much power in a macro sense, as juridical domination by institutions and individuals not defined as part of one's own appropriately-construed nation-state.

## Overview of the cases

These four cases – Basque, Catalan, Punjabi and Kashmiri nationalist movements – highlight varying trajectories of nationalist conscientization and agitation, differing state and international responses, and different outcomes. The similarly ethnonationalist basis for these movements, however, begs comparative examination. I begin with an overview of each of the movements, then will tease out conclusions in the next section.

### *Basque nationalism*

The Basque Country lies in the northern corner of the Iberian peninsula. The origins of the Basques – the only remaining pre-Aryan race in Europe with a language, Euskadi, unrelated to any other – are unknown. Even after Spain unified politically in the early eighteenth century, the Basque

Country retained a separate constitutional identity and legal and financial administration, enumerated in a set of laws or rights called *fueros* (Payne 1971: 15, 32). The geographic isolation of the region over the years fostered a degree of xenophobia and insistence on Basque historical, ethnic, and linguistic distinctiveness, even though the link between the region and Spain has been largely taken for granted for centuries (Ben-Ami 1991: 493; Guibernau 2000: 56; Payne 1971: 32, 43; Shabad and Gunther 1982: 443, 474 n2).

In the 1890s, a Basque nationalist movement, known initially as Vizcayanism and led by Sabino de Arana y Goiri, took shape to defend Basque traditions and ethnicity against contamination by the Spanish amid industrialization, urbanization and attendant immigration into the region. Opposition to Spain was initially limited, however. The process and timing of development in the Basque Country had led to a dual economy, and class differences undercut nationalist aspirations. A small capitalist class produced capital goods (especially iron and steel), and was dependent upon ties with Spain for protectionist measures and a market. Alongside that class was a larger mass still embedded in a traditional economy (agriculturalists, artisans etc.) and bitter at the capitalists' power. Early Basque nationalism and cultural-linguistic revival emphasized tradition and the past, and were strongly influenced by Catholic clergy and ideologically conservative. The movement appealed most strongly to those displaced or marginalized by processes of modernization, but also to segments of the traditional social elite and bourgeoisie. Given variations in Basque economic and social modernization, however, commitments to nationalism (and socialism) varied (Ben-Ami 1991: 494; Díez Medrano 1995; Douglass and Zulaika 1990: 243; Payne 1971: 35–8).

The first Basque nationalist organization, Centro Vasco, was established in 1893. It later became the Basque Nationalist Party (Partido Nacionalista Vasco, PNV), which has dominated Basque nationalism ever since. The Centro Vasco called for an independent republican confederation of seven internally-autonomous Basque provinces on either side of the Pyrenees (four in Spain and three in France); rejection of Spanish immigration and influence; restoration of the traditional fueros; and subordination of the state to the Catholic church. The movement first entered electoral politics in 1898, but accomplished little. Basque political elites got on well with the regime; Basque language and culture held limited resonance among the general population; and many Basques were more attracted to other prevailing ideologies (Payne 1971: 35–8). During the dictatorship of Primo de Rivera (1923–1930), the movement was outlawed and forced underground, then resurfaced and gained strength (as did other regional nationalist movements and militant trade unionism) with the establishment of the Republic in the 1930s (Douglass and Zulaika 1990: 243; Payne 1971: 38–9, 42–5). The subsequent Spanish Civil War (1936–1937) saw Basques divided between supporters of Franco's Spanish

Nationalists and Basque nationalists.[1] An October 1936 Basque autonomy statute created an autonomous Government of Euskadi, led by the PNV, but only briefly. In 1937, Mussolini's Italy offered to assist in forging an independent Basque country under Italian protection, but negotiations failed. Basque nationalism was effectively routed and so, with the ascendance of Franco, the PNV established a government in exile in Paris (Douglass and Zulaika 1990: 243–4; Payne 1971: 45–9).

Although the Basque economy flourished compared with most of the rest of the country, regional language and culture fared less well under Franco, who sought national integration through linguistic and cultural homogenization, involving sporadic but severe repression especially of Catalan and Basque language and culture (Shabad and Gunther 1982: 443). Moreover, rapid industrialization and an influx of Castilian-speakers into the Basque Country in the 1950s fostered Basques' sense of being colonized by Spain and forced to assimilate into its culture (Guibernau 2000: 58–9). Throughout the Franco years, Basque nationalist organizations persisted at home and abroad, often comparatively "shrill and fanatical" (Payne 1971: 50). Basque nationalists campaigned internationally against Madrid: collaborating with the Allies in World War II, arguing the Basque case before the UN, and establishing networks among expatriate Basques. However, in the early 1950s, hoping to set up military bases in Spain, the US put a halt to international pressure on Spain. Overall, Payne argues that by 1975, the extended political dictatorship "had the counterproductive effect of reawakening intense nationalist feeling in the most distinctive regions, and indeed of sparking a more intense nationalist identity in the Basque provinces" (Payne 1991: 487).

Most notably, in 1959, the revolutionary terrorist group Euskadi ta Azkatasuna (ETA, Basque Land and Liberty), formed out of a student study group as an alternative to the more conservative PNV and less Basque-specific Spanish Socialist and Communist parties. While the ETA's calls for national liberation were in line with previous Basque ideology, the group broke with tradition by proposing the exclusion of the Catholic church from politics and substituting the idea of *ethnos* – shown through commitment to Basque language and culture – for biological race as the basis of Basque identity. The ETA has sought an independent, socialist (Marxist-Leninist), Basque state. Its demands include amnesty for all Basque political prisoners, legalization of even separatist political parties, expulsion of Spanish police agencies from the Basque Country, measures to benefit the working class (although many young ETA supporters are themselves middle-class), and recognition of the right to self-determination for the Basque people. One faction of the ETA has formed the party Euskadiko Eskerra (Basque Country Left) to work within the system (despite ETA-organized electoral boycotts); another faction is represented by the more radical Herri Batasuna (Popular Unity) (Douglass and Zulaika 1990: 248–52; Woodworth 2001: 2, 7).

In the early 1960s, calling for rebellion against Spanish "colonization," the ETA launched a campaign of guerilla insurrection to boost awareness and mobilization. Since then, the group has engaged in bombings, assassinations, bank robberies, kidnappings, intimidation, graffiti and collecting a "revolutionary tax" from Basque businesses. Comprised of atomized cells of primarily young, male, part-time activists; supported internationally by other national liberation movements; able to capitalize at least initially on European (especially French) opposition to Franco; and careful in their selection of targets to force a national state of alert, the ETA has resisted state penetration or suppression. Its existence has lent teeth even to more moderate Basques' demands for concessions, but has also ratcheted up tensions (Douglass and Zulaika 1990: 238, 244–7, 252; Woodworth 2001: 1, 5). Nearly 800 people have been killed since 1968 in ETA-related violence, and "the more democratic Spain became, the more hard-liners within the group accelerated its killing rate," despite rising popular resentment (Woodworth 2001: 1, 5–6).

The backdrop to this radicalization was Franco's death in 1975, Spain's subsequent democratization, and the granting of substantial regional autonomy with the December 1978 constitution.[2] Spain is now one of Europe's most decentralized states, although not constitutionally federal. Vizcaya, Guipuzcoa and Alava are now known as the Autonomous Community of the Basque Country. To some extent, the central government diminished the claims to full nationhood of the Basque Country as well as Catalonia by establishing 15 additional autonomous communities as well (some historically and culturally distinct and others created by fiat). However, while ever-increasing powers have been devolved to all these regions, only the Basque Country and the Basque province of Navarre collect taxes and pay the central government for services it provides rather than relying on handouts from the center. Moreover, in a nod to the significance of language to nationalist claims, the Basque and Catalan autonomy statutes grant Euskera and Catalán co-official status with Castilian and ensure the right of residents to learn and use them (Shabad and Gunther 1982: 462). Bargaining among regional and national parties has resulted in differing levels of autonomy for the "historic nationalities" (Catalans, Basques and Galicians) versus other regions and decentralization for the whole country. While nearly all the powers listed in the Statutes of Autonomy had been transferred by 1987, devolution to the regions of fiscal resources and authority continued through the 1990s (Colomer 1998; *The Economist* 2000a; Edwards 1999; Guibernau 2000).

Nationalist concerns have dominated the Basque political agenda since Franco's death and the first regional elections in 1980 (Ross 1996: 488–9) – won by the PNV, who have governed since. However, Basques are divided among supporters of Spanish parties and the 1978 constitution; Basque nationalists willing to work within existing democratic structures, even if they do not support the constitution; and Basque separatists aligned with the ETA (Colomer 1998). Guibernau posits, "the system which permits regional nationalisms to play an active part in all-Spanish politics seems to have reduced pro-independence nationalist movements to the status of minority parties in Catalonia and the Basque Country" (Guibernau 1997: 30). Conversely, Woodworth argues that, especially given the weakness and difficulty of Euskera as a language, many Basques believe "anything less than full independence . . . would spell the end of their cultural, linguistic, and national identity within a very short time" (Woodworth 2001: 8).

Spain has pursued multiple strategies to quell ETA violence, with only limited success. In addition to tightening laws on terrorism, the Spanish Interior Ministry launched a "dirty war" against the ETA in the 1980s, incurring persistent allegations of human rights abuses in the process. Links established through judicial investigations by the late 1990s among the socialist government, the security forces, and death squads have exacted a cost on Spanish democracy, forced a cleanup of the anti-terrorist high command, and corroborated for impressionable young Basques the oppressive tendencies of the Spanish state. Crackdowns have generally had the counterproductive effect of spurring antagonism toward the regime and support for the ETA rather than discouraging radical militancy. With continuing indiscriminate repression in response to ETA attacks, "The radicals' thesis that 'nothing has changed here since Franco' became self-fulfilling to those who were already disposed to believe it" (Woodworth 2001: 5–6). In 1998, after a campaign in the 1990s to "socialize the suffering" (broadening their targets so all would share the Basques' pain), the ETA initiated a truce modeled on Northern Ireland's.[3] Self-determination for the Basque Country (including the three French Basque provinces and Navarre) would be pursued non-violently by a united front of both radicals and moderates. Talks broke down after 14 months and the ETA returned to violence (Douglass and Zulaika 1990: 247; Mees 2001: 799; Woodworth 2001: 1–2, 5–10). The ETA's campaign has heightened fear and social polarization, plus dampened tourism and economic development, despite state-led efforts at infrastructure development and economic diversification. The Basque Country remains comparatively prosperous, but political vandalism and the extortion of revolutionary taxes cost it tens of millions of dollars each year (*The Economist* 2000b: 12; Woodworth 2001: 1).

Taking another tack, in July 1998, the main nationalist parties in the Basque Country, Catalonia and Galicia signed the joint Declaració de Barcelona, calling for Spain to be redefined as a multilingual, multicultural and multinational state. While the 1978 Spanish constitution asserts that Spain contains "nationalities and regions," it still deems Spain a single nation and intends eventual parity among historical and newly-created autonomous communities. Acceptance of the Declaration would thus require revision of Spain's constitutional framework. The main Spanish parties opposed the Declaration, but regional institutions have fostered and strengthened regional identities, and not just in the historical regions. Regardless, it is not clear that meeting the demands of the Declaration would prove sufficient; the historical regions – certainly the Basques – might still press for full independence (Guibernau 2000: 62–6).

The high costs of violence and vandalism, coupled with the granting of increased autonomy to the region over time, the rise of a grassroots Basque peace movement since the late 1980s, and the possibility of cooperation among a broader array of nationalist forces make a settlement to the conflict seem possible (Mees 2001: 811–14). Still, what distinguishes the Basque conflict from others is its intractability and continuing violence despite significant concessions since 1978. Key priorities now include negotiating an end to ETA violence and reaching a compromise on Basque autonomy (since Spain is unlikely to concede independence to the region). Given the primordial character of Basque nationalism, embodied in regular allusions to Basque race and blood, Basque nationalist demands for independence may prove non-negotiable – even moderate nationalists in the PNV have come to demand independence (Guibernau 2000: 58–9). A referendum seems inevitable, but would pose a dangerous example for Catalonia and other regions. Decisions on the extent of devolution or the possibility of secession reverberate, impacting upon the nature and performance of Spanish democracy and quasi-federalism, as well as upon demands from even newly-created regions and the tenacity of claims to self-determination by others in Spain.

### *Catalan nationalism*

Catalonia is a province with a population of around six million in northeastern Spain, bordered to the north by France and Andorra, and to the south and east by the Mediterranean Sea. Initially independent and constitutionally advanced, Catalonia was integrated into Spain in the early eighteenth century, retaining few special rights. The push for regional autonomy in Catalonia dates back at least to the mid-nineteenth century, although secession did not become a significant goal until the 1920s. Overall, though, Catalan nationalism has been more civic than primordial in orientation. For instance, while Castilian (Spain's official language) has never approached hegemonic status in the province and Catalan language is a core component of Catalan national identity, the language is one immigrants from elsewhere in Spain can and do readily learn (Laitin 1989: 299–301; Payne 1991: 479–82).

The basis of Catalan industry has been small-scale textiles and other consumer goods, funded by local agricultural production and primarily for the Spanish domestic (and colonial) market. Catalan industry has historically been sheltered by high Spanish protective tariffs and the region has long been comparatively prosperous, fostering accommodation with Spain (Payne 1971: 23–4). The industrial economy thus came to include a broader middle class than in the Basque case, with significant ties to other sectors. Catalan nationalism has hence been driven not so much by disputes over the nature of industrialization and class differentiation (as in the Basque Country), as by Catalan industrial elites' sense of exclusion from political decision-making, especially with regard to economic policies. While working class Catalans have agitated for independence, the bourgeoisie has been reasonably consistent in its demands for enhanced regional autonomy within a federal system (Díez Medrano 1995).

Political Catalanism took shape starting in the 1880s, centered around language and culture, and pioneered initially by newspaper editor Valentí Almirall, then by Enric Prat de la Riba, author of *La Nacionalitat Catalana* (1906) (Payne 1971: 19; Shabad and Gunther 1982: 446). The short-lived Centre Català, the first general association of Catalanists, formed in 1882. However, since Catalonia's economic interests were largely satisfied under the Spanish political system, it was not until after Spain lost the Spanish-American War (opposed by Catalans) in 1898 that a regionalist political movement made serious inroads (Payne 1971: 19–25). The Lliga Regionalista formed to contest parliamentary elections in 1901; it remained the dominant force in Catalan politics through 1923 despite a split early on between "bourgeois" and "radical" Catalanism. (Indeed, Catalanist organizations have been hampered ever since by their tendency continually to fracture, disappear and reconstitute themselves.) The Lliga sought enhanced autonomy and a more democratic constitution. Under pressure from the left, however, it rejected King Alfonso XIII's proposal for regional autonomy after the war, insisting autonomy must be established on the Catalans' own terms – what Payne calls "a classic example of the famed Catalan *totorresisme* (all-or-nothingism)" (Payne 1971: 27–9). Within weeks massive strikes began in Barcelona, followed by four years of violent, anarcho-syndicalist class struggle in Catalonia. Martial law was imposed, effectively undercutting Catalanism. The Lliga (apart from a more militant leftist group that split off in 1922) cooperated with the central government for the final years of the parliamentary system (1918–1923) and de-emphasized the cause of Catalan autonomy.

In 1923, General Miguel Primo de Rivera overthrew Spain's parliament and set up a military dictatorship. While he initially seemed to support Catalanism and enjoyed middle and upper class Catalans' support, his centralist, authoritarian rule was inimical to political Catalanism. Support for the movement expanded and shifted to the left under the radical leadership of Francesc Macià. In April 1931, on the day the monarchy collapsed, with overwhelming popular support for autonomy, Macià proclaimed the establishment of the Republic of Catalonia within Spain. Republicans in Madrid gave Catalanists control of their region. A Statute of Catalan Autonomy, providing for a fully-autonomous regional government (the Generalitat) and official status for the Catalan language, was then passed by the Spanish Republican parliament in 1932 (Laitin 1989: 301; Payne 1971: 39–40). This government remained troubled, however, by renewed strikes and insurrections, debates over the extent of devolution and specific policies, and splits in Catalan's governing coalition (particularly between the broad leftist Esquerra, supported by the lower classes, and the more middle class Lliga). Macià's successor, Lluís Companys, declared a Catalan state within Spain in October 1934 and Catalanist radicals planned a revolt to coincide with one by the Spanish Socialists that month. The Socialists made some inroads, but the Catalanists failed ignominiously. In response, Catalonia was returned to central rule (Edwards 1999: 667; Payne 1971: 40–2, 44).

During the Spanish civil war, Catalonia "exercised virtual *de facto* independence," though dominated by Spanish anarcho-syndicalists Confederacion Nacional del Trabajo/National Labor Confederation (CNT) rather than the Catalanist left. Central government control of Catalonia increased when the Republican capital moved to Barcelona in 1937 (Laitin 1989: 301–2; Payne 1971: 45–6). Franco ended the system of regional autonomy in 1939. His government's policies to suppress regional languages and cultures[4] were compounded by massive migration from less industrialized areas into Catalonia starting in the 1950s. The result was a political-linguistic project, with broad support at home and among the Catalan diaspora, that associated democracy and nationhood with official status for and free use of Catalan (Balcells 1996; Laitin 1989: 302–3; Payne 1971: 48–50; Shabad and Gunther 1982: 443).[5] Representatives of the Catalan government continued to meet as a (powerless) "Generalitat in exile," keeping the institutional precedent for Catalan autonomy alive.[6]

After Franco's death, regionalist demands echoing those of the 1930s resurfaced amid debates over democratization. Backed by massive popular demonstrations in the mid-1970s, the 11-party Council of Catalan Political Forces proposed a plan for Catalonian autonomy modeled on the 1932 statute and the Generalitat. The weaker, less democratic General Council of Catalonia established by Spain in February 1977 was thus poorly received locally (as was a similar initiative in the Basque Country) and abandoned after a matter of months. That September, a record million people demonstrated in Barcelona for a Catalan autonomy statute. The following month a provisional Generalitat was reestablished and the president in exile, Josep Tarradellas, was invited to return to lead it. The Generalitat did not have all the powers Catalanists sought, but it marked a symbolic victory and an important first step toward self-government (Edwards 1999: 666–9). Recognizing the "regional fact," President Adolfo Suárez granted Catalonia and 16 other regions substantial autonomy in 1978, without recognizing Catalan or Basque claims to nationhood (Edwards 1999: 666–9; Guibernau 2000: 61–2). Since that time Catalanists have continued (with some success) to seek further powers, including greater fiscal autonomy, a regional police force, full health services and representation in the European Union and other international bodies (Colomer 1998; *The Economist* 2000b: 13). Notably, Catalan nationalists have seen "Europe as an alternative campaigning ground to Madrid and an opportunity to further Catalan interests with another authority," and have used Europe as a context for building cross-regional ties (Edwards 1999: 675).

In Catalonia, as in the Basque Country, nationalist concerns have cornered the political agenda post-Franco. Catalan politics has been dominated since 1980 by Jordi Pujol and his Convergence Party, the dominant partner in the Convergence and Unity (CiU) coalition – CiU nationalism even came to be known in the 1980s as "Pujolism" (Ross 1996: 488–9, 498). While a declared Catalan nationalist, Pujol is also loyal to Spain and his Catalanist sympathies seem to be waning over time, despite calls from some members of his party for independence. The other party in the CiU, the Union or Unity party, specifically espouses the principle of subsidiarity. The CiU's chief opponent is the Socialist Party. All these parties want greater resources and powers transferred from Madrid to the regions. Shifting its support between leading parties in the central government has allowed the CiU to extract continuing concessions from the central state, most notably concerning taxes collected in, and retained by, the Catalan government[7] (*The Economist* 1998, 2000b: 13; Guibernau 1997: 30).

Catalonia has been held up as an example of successful devolution of power and is "thriving both economically and culturally" (Guibernau 1997: 30). Guibernau explains the success of the Catalan model: "Decentralisation in Catalonia, far from fostering uncompromising or extreme nationalism, has in fact opened channels for participation that have vastly improved both the Catalan economy and the quality of life in the region" (Guibernau 2000: 62). In contrast to Basque nationalism, Catalanism's premise of defending rights to cultural differentiation and participation in political decision-making has further helped the movement avoid violent and illiberal methods (Guibernau 1997: 30). Still, in both regions, "political regionalisation and state decentralisation have been the result of party strategies, competition, and bargaining within a loose institutional framework" (Colomer 1998: 40).

Spain's constitution proclaims the "indissoluble unity of the Spanish Nation," but also acknowledges that the country includes multiple nations and regions. It was this apparent contradiction that inspired the main nationalist parties in Catalonia, the Basque Country and Galicia to sign the Declaració de Barcelona (described above) in 1998, demanding that the historic regions be recognized as nations. All the same, whereas in 1932 Catalonia was defined as an autonomous region within the Spanish state, in the 1979 statute, it was labeled a "nationality" and "autonomous community," with an "inalienable right" to self-government (Colomer 1998; Edwards 1999: 672). Among the most important concessions granted Catalonia and the Basque Country were those related to language, especially implementing a policy of region-specific bilingualism. However, given the relatively high degree of internal heterogeneity in the two regions (over one-third are native Castilian speakers, transplanted from other parts of the country), implementation of the bilingual policy "has, in and of itself, significantly polarized Catalan and Basque politics and, in doing so, has made 'objective' linguistic differences in the two regions (especially in Catalonia) more salient politically than they were at the beginning of the post-Franco transition" (Shabad and Gunther 1982: 444–6).[8]

Overall, unlike the more exclusivist, primordially-defined Basque nationalism, "Catalonian nationalism manifests a predominantly civic character with a tradition of participating in Spanish politics" (Guibernau 2000: 58). However, Catalan demands for ever-greater autonomy, spurred by similar demands by other autonomous communities, have sustained tension between the regional and federal governments, posing a possible threat to Spanish democracy. The CiU acknowledges both Catalonian nationhood and the idea of Spanish unity, yet Catalan demands for recognition and self-determination have not been fully satisfied by current arrangements (Guibernau 2000: 62–3). Meeting or defusing these demands may require renegotiation of the regions' autonomy statutes and perhaps devolving additional powers to Catalonia. Still, secession seems unlikely to be demanded by a majority or ever conceded by the Spanish state.

### *Sikh nationalism in Punjab*

India is home to approximately 16 million Sikhs. They constitute a majority in Punjab (61 percent), but just under 2 percent of India's total population. Sikhs differ in religion from other ethnic groups in northern India, and the Punjabi language is closely identified with the community, though not exclusive to it. What is now referred to as Punjab has become smaller and more heavily Sikh since independence in 1947, not least since India lost almost two-thirds of the state to Pakistan at partition, then reorganized the remainder to include only Punjabi-speaking regions in 1966. Those who invoke "Khalistan" as a Punjabi Sikh homeland tend not to be specific about the incarnation of Punjab to which they refer (Oberoi 1987: 30). Its economy based on agriculture, Punjab is a prosperous state and the "granary" of India. The region is the birthplace of Sikhism and home to numerous historic Sikh shrines, even though the only Sikh empire there, in the early nineteenth century, was short-lived. Punjab has strategic significance, as well, since the region borders Pakistan and Kashmir. Sikhs have no history of antagonism with Hindus (and Sikhism derived from Hinduism in the late medieval period); relations with Muslims have been less placid. However, even as early as the late nineteenth century, competing religious revivals among Sikhs and Hindus made communal lines sharper and more antagonistic (Deol 2000). A key aim of Sikh reformists then (and now) was to retain control of religious practices and institutions. The Akali Dal, which subsequently became the primary nationalist organization and political vehicle for Punjabi Sikhs, formed in 1914 to take over Sikh shrines.

Under colonial rule, Punjabis were favorite military recruits and Sikhs were heavily over-represented in the armed forces, while Punjabi peasants enjoyed a protective patron-client relationship with British administrators (Tatla 1999: 16). All the same, Sikhs allied with Indian nationalists in non-violent protest against the British in the early twentieth century. Concerned with the escalating controversy, the colonial government instituted the Sikh Gurudwaras and Shrines Act of 1925, which conceded management and control of all Sikh religious institutions to the community – specifically, to the Akali-controlled Shiromani Gurudwara Prabahandak Committee (SGPC), certifying the political importance of the Akali Dal (Tatla 1999: 30–4; Telford 1992: 973–4). While the SGPC styled itself as representing all Punjabis politically rather than just Sikhs, after the 1925 act, "The primary political objective of the Akali Dal was to safeguard Sikh religious liberty by maintaining and promoting separately the political existence of the Sikhs and securing greater political leverage for Sikhs" (Deol 2000: 82).

As a dispersed group and minority in Punjab, and one with strong historical and cultural ties with Hindus, the Sikhs did not demand a separate state initially, but focused on questions of representation. Separate electorates for Sikhs were granted in 1921. In the anticolonial campaign (in which the Akali Dal urged participation), Sikhs were caught between Muhammad Ali Jinnah's vision of an Islamic state and the Congress Party's Hindu-dominated India. They first demanded an Azad Punjab (Free Punjab), not as a separate Sikh state, but a province in which no single community could dominate; the population would be 40 percent each Hindu and Muslim and 20 percent Sikh. Both British and Indian leaders rejected the plan. Then, in March 1946, declaring Sikhs a nation, the Akali Dal adopted a resolution calling for a Sikh state to protect Sikh economic, religious and cultural rights. Akali leaders gave up these demands only upon promises from Congress leaders that Sikhs would have special status in an independent India (Deol 2000: 82–3; Tatla 1999: 18–20). Partition and the internal migration it sparked left Sikhs concentrated in a more compact geographical area than before. Their claim on Punjab as homeland changed from an "imaginative vision into a realistic project" (Tatla 1999: 22).

Upon independence, India adopted a unitary constitutional structure, doing away with the colonial system of weighting representation for minorities and reservation of seats[9] and proscribing regional self-determination for fear of territorial disintegration. All major regional languages were granted constitutional status, though with Hindi and English as India's official languages. A massive reorganization of states in the 1950s and 1960s aligned territorial boundaries with major linguistic ones for all but Punjabi (deemed too similar to Hindi), Sindhi and Urdu (Deol 2000: 95). The Akali Dal started mobilizing in the early 1950s, then launched the Punjabi Suba Slogan Agitation of 1955, a campaign of political demonstrations and non-violent tactics in which 26,000 Sikhs were arrested, and a second campaign in 1962 (Deol 2000: 95–6). Its demands were initially (if somewhat ambiguously) framed in secular terms as safeguarding Punjabi language and culture (Telford 1992: 970). The central government eventually agreed to the reorganization of Punjab in recognition of Sikhs' efforts in the Indo-Pakistan War of 1965. With the September 1966 Punjab State Reorganization Bill, for the first time, Sikhs formed a slim majority of the population of Punjab. The Hindi-speaking south broke off to form the state of Haryana and the Hindi-speaking northern region merged with neighboring Himachal Pradesh.

The Akali Dal led coalition governments from 1967 on; Sikhs were too divided along caste and other lines for any one party to govern on its own. The need to sustain coalitions at both the state and federal levels helped keep Akali demands comparatively moderate and secular – but even so, three Akali coalition governments had been dismissed by the increasingly-interventionist center by 1980 (Tatla 1999: 22–4; Telford 1992: 971–3). The vulnerable position of party moderates, especially during Indira Gandhi's premiership, created space for more nationalistic Akalis, especially as socioeconomic changes in the state brought more Sikhs from lower classes into positions of leadership (Tatla 1999: 24–5). The Anandpur Sahib Resolution, drafted in October 1973 and widely endorsed, showed the shift among Akalis as the party tried to appeal to both a mass Sikh constituency and Sikh nationalists. As outlined in the resolution, the Akali Dal's core political demand is an "independent identity" for Sikhs – although not a sovereign Khalistan – allowing "full expression, satisfaction and growth" of their "national sentiments and aspirations" (quoted in Tatla 1999: 27; also Deol 2000: 101–2). The document offers seven specific objectives to reach this political goal, from the readjustment of Punjabi state boundaries to greater provincial autonomy and protections for Sikhs elsewhere in India.

Faced with the centralizing government of Indira Gandhi and deteriorating Hindu-Sikh relations, Akalis mobilized the Sikh peasantry in a non-violent campaign for Punjabi autonomy, including economic, cultural, constitutional and religious demands as per the Anandpur Sahib Resolution. The Dharam Yudh Morcha (Righteous Struggle) of 1981–1984 had the broad objective of "a radical renegotiation of powers for the centre and the states, and an explicit recognition of India as a multinational state" (Tatla 1999: 27). Still, the mainstream Akali leadership preferred negotiation to confrontation, if only to retain the support of key Sikh industrialists, businessmen, professionals and landowners who could not afford to cut themselves adrift from India (Major 1987: 46–8). The central government cracked down nonetheless on the rising movement: the Congress Party worked to foment disunity among Sikhs and took punitive and repressive measures against movement leaders, radicalizing the broader community in the process (Deol 2000: 103–4; Tatla 1999: 28; Telford 1992: 974–6).

The subregional and class dimensions of the conflict became more apparent over time. While Punjab was wealthy overall, the benefits of the green revolution spread unevenly. Furthermore, at the time of partition, Pakistan inherited the core industrial sector of the Punjab region and the state's industrial development has been limited since then. Small farmers have been marginalized and alienated by government measures to regulate distribution of agricultural inputs and products, while wealthier farmers seek better terms of trade. Educated rural youths find their chances of employment limited by the lack of a significant industrial base in Punjab as well as by an influx of cheap labor from other provinces. Uneven development has also aggravated environmental disorders, intensifying disputes over control of rivers, canals and hydroelectric power. The central government's bias toward industrialization, commercial growth and urban development conflicts with state governments' emphasis on agriculture. Over time, militant nationalism grew especially among students and youths from farming families in less prosperous areas (Leaf 1985; Major 1987: 49–51; Telford 1992: 969–85). Moreover, issues of religious authority and orthodoxy have arisen with urbanization and the commercialization of rural society, especially since the Akalis have made pragmatic alliances with Hindu political parties (Kohli 1997: 336; Tatla 1999: 30–4). As more orthodox groups came to challenge the Akalis, the central government exploited these divisions.[10] Aggravating these trends is the Hindu resurgence, which equates being Hindu with being Indian (Mahmood 1996: 244), as well as rising literacy rates and the availability of vernacular media (Deol 2000; Tatla 1999).

As Indira Gandhi and the Congress Party tried harder as of the 1970s to consolidate the party's grip on Punjab state politics, the Akali Dal edged closer to demanding a sovereign state (Kohli 1997: 336). The result was a series of massive demonstrations and other incidents of passive resistance, as well as increasingly-prevalent bank bombings, railroad station burnings, political assassinations and more (Deol 2000). The Akali Dal launched a mass non-cooperation campaign in June 1984, preventing the movement of food grain out of Punjab and stopping payment of land revenues and water rates to the government. In response, the government sealed Punjab's borders, imposed censorship and a curfew, and cordoned off the Golden Temple, where controversial Sikh leader Sant Jarnail Singh Bhindranwale had set up his headquarters. On 4 June, 2,000 army troops closed in on the temple; thousands of Sikh peasants converged upon

Amritsar in response. The military dispersed the crowds and launched a full-scale attack on the temple, also attacking 40 other gurudwaras allegedly sheltering Sikh activists. In the process, an estimated 5,000 civilians (including Bhindranwale) and 700 officers were killed, and the temple sustained substantial damage. Thousands more Sikhs, including all prominent Akali leaders, were arrested and many tortured or killed over the next several months; martial law and complete press censorship were declared in the state and the Golden Temple was occupied militarily. Sikhs at home and abroad were incensed (Deol 2000; Leaf 1985: 494). The Indian government justified its actions by saying the Akali Dal was communal, extremist and brutal; engaged in secessionist and anti-national activities; and involved criminals, smugglers and the like (Government of India 1984: 26).

On 31 October 1984, Indira Gandhi was assassinated by two Punjabi Sikh guards from her security force, presumably in retaliation for the attack on the Golden Temple. Anti-Sikh riots promptly broke out in several parts of India. As many as 10,000 Sikhs were killed and 50,000 displaced in Delhi, and a huge amount of Sikh property was looted or burned. Media and human rights organizations' reports implicated politicians and other authorities in the attacks. The Akali Dal and SGPC demanded an apology from Rajiv Gandhi's government and an official inquiry (which was denied), as well as relaxation of anti-terrorist measures. Secret negotiations produced the Rajiv-Longowal Accord of July 1985 – but the accord conceded little and was never implemented (Deol 2000). Splits within and strategic alliances among the Akali Dal and other Sikh organizations (see Major 1987: 49–51) and the flow of over 20,000 Sikh refugees into Punjab from other parts of the country (Deol 2000: 111) accompanied continued unrest. In May 1986, the central government again took control of Punjab (Tatla 1999: 29).

More militant Sikhs, especially village youths, mobilized and rapidly gained a political advantage over moderate Akalis, deriding as opportunistic the latter's attempts at compromise with the central government (Kohli 1997: 337). The strength of guerilla groups surged in 1987–1988, bolstered by arms from Pakistan and Afghanistan, and augmented by informal gangs of smugglers and criminals taking advantage of the unsettled situation. Civilians were squeezed between warring security forces and militants: civilian casualties accounted for nearly three-fourths of all killings, estimated at approximately 15,000 by 1992, and any who could abandoned their land and migrated to the cities. By the early 1990s, though, the guerilla movement (comprised of around 20 largely uncoordinated organizations) was increasingly struggling to sustain sufficient resources, recruits, ideological coherence and credibility among Sikhs (Deol 2000: 112–15; Kohli 1997: 337–8; Major 1987: 55–6; Telford 1992: 986).

Over time, the actions of the Indian state clearly helped to reshape Sikh identity and radicalize what otherwise may have been a far more benign initiative. First, the Congress Party's early acceptance of the principle of linguistic states helped fuse territoriality and Sikh ethnicity. When the new government then refused to carve out a Punjabi-speaking state, the issue became more incendiary. The struggle to attain a Punjabi state forged a nexus between Punjab and Sikh consciousness, exacerbated over time by the rise of Hindu nationalist parties (especially the Bharatiya Janata Party, BJP) and the dismantling of colonial-era safeguards for fair representation of minorities in favor of universal franchise and constitutional centralism (Oberoi 1987: 31–40; Tatla 1999: 34–9). Moreover, Indian leaders since Nehru have lacked the political will to grant meaningful concessions to opposition groups. Political institutions have deteriorated since the 1950s, especially as "personalistic leaders damaged the institutions that constrained their discretionary powers," while the weakening of the Congress Party since the 1970s has prompted special appeals to Hindu voters (Kohli 1997: 331–3). It was largely the uncompromising stance of the centralizing state – especially under Indira Gandhi, and particularly the 1984 attack on the Golden Temple – that turned demands for devolution to calls for sovereign statehood and left the population progressively more disenfranchised and radicalized (Tatla 1999: 34). In particular, Indira Gandhi's description of "the opposition as religious fanatics who advocated secession and separatism motivated by 'communalism' and 'regionalism'" became a "self-fulfilling prophecy" by magnifying extremists' case, discouraging moderates and tapping into underlying prejudices (Leaf 1985: 491–3).

At the same time, the global dimensions of the conflict are critical. Much of the support for an independent Sikh state of Khalistan has come not from local parties, but from Sikh expatriates. The Sikh diaspora comprises approximately two million Sikhs (of 18 million total), located primarily in England, Canada and the United States. Most had been rural peasants, many driven abroad by unfavorable land rights legislation in the early twentieth century. Expatriate Sikhs represent an increasingly prosperous community and have provided critical material and political resources since the 1960s (Deol 2000: 118–21; Tatla 1999: Chapter 4). While some diasporic Sikhs supported the idea of secession much earlier, after the events of 1984, the community offered vociferous support for the formation of an independent Khalistan (Deol 2000; Tatla 1999). Mahmood draws a parallel with Zionism, explaining:

> The power of the Khalistan idea is enhanced, not diminished, by the dispersion of Sikhs outside of Punjab and India. And this is expressed in monetary, political, and moral support for Khalistan from diasporan Sikhs despite the fact that many or most would not move to Khalistan if it were indeed created.
>
> (Mahmood 1996: 254)

In sum, widespread Sikh demands for an independent state rather than just greater autonomy under a reformed federalist India are a relatively new phenomenon. The actions of the central state have been key to the shift from communal self-awareness and religious revival, to linguistic ethnonationalism, to secessionism. A combination of India's decision to draw state boundaries along linguistic lines, economic transformation, unmet demands for greater devolution of power from the center to the state, and religious revivalism among Sikhs, compounded by a series of harsh government actions and mounting antagonism between Sikhs and Hindus, led to demands for a sovereign Sikh state of Khalistan by the 1980s. These demands were articulated perhaps even more stridently abroad, among the Sikh diaspora, than in India. However, by the mid-1990s, Sikh militancy had tapered off and politics had begun to normalize anew.

### *Kashmiri nationalism*

The state of Jammu and Kashmir is the largest in India, but sparsely populated, with about eight million people. It is bordered by Tibet to the northeast, the Chinese province of Sinkiang to the north, Turkistan to the northwest, Pakistan to the west and the Indian states of Himachal Pradesh and Punjab to the south. The Himalayas divide Jammu and Kashmir into three regions: Ladakh, the Kashmir Valley and Jammu. Around two-thirds of the population overall is Muslim, but the proportion varies by region: the Kashmir valley's population is overwhelmingly Muslim, mostly Sunni (and oriented toward Pakistan); Jammu's is about two-thirds Hindu (and oriented toward India); and over half the population of Ladakh (oriented toward Tibet) is Buddhist, with most of the remainder Shia Muslim. The Pakistan-administered Northern Areas contain just over half a million people, predominantly Shia Muslim, while Pakistan-controlled Azad (Free) Kashmir contains two million, predominantly Sunni Muslim (Schofield 2000: xv).[11]

As a Muslim-majority state contiguous to Pakistan, Jammu and Kashmir could have been expected to join Pakistan at partition. However, the British had given a Hindu maharaja domain over the state in 1846. Harboring "visions of independence" (Ganguly 1997: 8), he hesitated to choose between India and Pakistan as independence approached. Muslim opposition, percolating since the early 1930s, developed into a revolt in mid-1947; by late October, the overthrow of the maharaja seemed imminent. He sought military assistance from India in exchange for signing an instrument of accession, subject to later popular ratification. A plebiscite still has yet to be held, despite the demands of Pakistan, Kashmir and the UN. Pakistan aggressively challenged Kashmir's joining India. Full-scale fighting broke out between the two countries in November 1947 and has recurred since (Ganguly 1997: 6–13; Rahman 1996: 1–3). Despite periodic negotiations, no settlement has been reached. At present, 45 percent of the former princely state of Jammu and Kashmir is administered by India and 35 percent by Pakistan, part of it indirectly. China annexed Aksai Chin, comprising 20 percent of the original territory, in 1962 (Rahman 1996: 5–6; Schofield 2000: xiii–xiv).

Often described as "the unfinished business of partition" (Kumar 2002: 12), the Kashmir conflict is both between Kashmiris and the central state, and between India and Pakistan. It represents a self-determination or secessionist movement for Kashmiris based on ethnic nationalism (embodied in *Kashmiriyat*, a vague term for the confluence of Islamic, Hindu and uniquely Kashmiri cultural strains in the region) and increasingly, on religious nationalism; an irredentist movement premised on religious (Muslim) nationalism for Pakistan and Pakistan-controlled Kashmir; and a civil insurgency for India. The conflict has been heated and violent from the outset, though Kashmiris themselves were marginal to the Indo-Pakistani wars of 1965 and 1971 centering on control of the region.[12] Proposals to resolve the crisis have included partitioning the state on communal or regional lines (based on the "two nation" theory behind the division of Pakistan from India) or giving portions to Pakistan. India has refused both options (Ganguly 1997: 43–57; Rahman 1996: 4; Schofield 2000: xiv–xv). Initially, Kashmir was granted special constitutional status and considerable autonomy within India's federal system, as well as financial subsidies to speed economic development (Kohli 1997: 339). However, beginning in 1962–1965, the state's special status was curtailed as India sought to integrate it into the larger polity (Ganguly 1997: 43–57). Meanwhile, Pakistan treated Azad Kashmir as a formally separate, temporary protectorate, albeit curbing civil liberties and separatism, while the population gradually integrated with Pakistan's. The Northern Areas were more openly ruled from the center, with no elected government or administration (Kumar 2002: 13).

As Indira Gandhi worked to centralize her power, Kashmir pressed for a return to its pre-1952 status, under which India controlled only its defense, foreign affairs and communications. Instead, the Beg-Parasarathi Accord of 1975 granted only minor concessions. Meanwhile, Kashmiri "founding father" Sheikh Abdullah's government's undemocratic character and stringent security ordinances, plus the structure of the ruling National Conference (Kashmir's main non-Congress party) limited legal means for airing political grievances among increasingly well-educated, politicized and articulate Kashmiris. Several factors increased popular discontent, reflected particularly in the rise of Islamic radicalism in the valley. Young Kashmiris found their employment opportunities in new sectors limited. The spread of both madrassahs and video parlors worked to shift social mores and values. An influx of Muslim clergy and other migrants came from Assam, fleeing ethnic violence. Abdullah's introduction in March 1980 of a Resettlement Bill to facilitate the return of Kashmiri residents who had fled in 1947 antagonized Hindus and Sikhs residing on property that previously belonged to Muslims. President Zia-ul-Haq embarked upon an Islamization program in Pakistan that extended to supporting both Afghan mujahideen and young, disaffected Kashmiris (Ganguly 1997: 58–73, 78–9). At the same time, Indira Gandhi espoused pro-Hindu themes in the early 1980s to create a new national electoral coalition, boding ill for states like Kashmir with large non-Hindu populations (Kohli 1997: 339).

Sheikh Abdullah died in September 1982 after having designated his son, political neophyte Farooq Abdullah, as his successor as head of the National Conference and state government. Farooq's opposition and advocacy of Kashmiri autonomy antagonized Indira Gandhi. She replaced Kashmir's respected governor with one more tractable, then had him dismiss Farooq's government in July 1984. The unpopular regime that followed "convinced the vast majority of Kashmiris in the valley that the national government had a reckless disregard for constitutional procedures" (Ganguly 1997: 88). The alienation of Muslim Kashmiris, especially urban youths, increased when the politically-pressed Farooq formed a coalition with Congress for the 1987 state elections. This alliance – which won the elections amid charges of fraud – "had the profound impact of eliminating any major democratic outlet for Kashmiri Muslims who sought greater autonomy from Delhi" (Kohli 1997: 340). A number of Muslim organizations joined in the Pakistan-linked Muslim United Front (MUF), which organized among urban youths but was barred from contesting by a ban on religious parties (Ganguly 1997: 80–91; Kohli 1997: 338–40; Kumar 2002: 14–15). Meanwhile, the economic and security situation worsened. The ranks of the unemployed provided a recruiting ground for secessionist organizations which agitated with increasing success for Islamization (closure of bars and liquor stores, banning anti-Islamic books etc.), as well as for opposition parties that launched strikes and other protests against the central government. Rajiv Gandhi focused on expanding harsh anti-terrorist laws rather than improving governance to curb secessionist and pro-Pakistani organizations. While these measures may have limited militant activities somewhat, the government's high-handedness and disregard for local people's sentiments heightened popular resentment (Ganguly 1997: 80–91).

By the late 1980s, the defeat of the Soviets in Afghanistan; recent independence of six Muslim Central Asian republics; rise of ethnonational movements in Europe, Africa and elsewhere in Asia; and Hindu chauvinist rhetoric of the ascendant BJP encouraged a more assertive movement (Rahman 1996: 6). The coincidence of district lines with religious divisions in the state, geographical isolation of the valley that separated Kashmiri Islam from larger currents of Muslim politics in India, inadequacy of secular channels for political voice, and both material and tactical support from Pakistan channeled discontent specifically along ethnoreligious lines

(Ganguly 1997: 39–42). Overall, Ganguly concludes that "Kashmir represents both the mobilizational success and, simultaneously, the institutional failure of Indian democracy" (Ganguly 1997: 20–1). Furthermore, the lack of an indigenous capitalist class tied to India or non-local Indian capitalists' entry into the state (since non-Kashmir residents cannot own property there) meant relatively few in Kashmir had a strong economic stake in remaining part of India. A combination of patronage and repression suppressed agitation for a while, but ultimately, almost the entire population of the valley came to support secession (Tremblay 1996–1997: 476–9, 497).

The "patently rigged" 1987 elections – which "conveyed a message that the Kashmiris of the valley simply would not be allowed or trusted to freely exercise their franchise" – proved incendiary (Ganguly 1997: 92). A Kashmiri movement for democracy began in the valley, including mass demonstrations and affirmations of Kashmiriyat as the cohesive force holding together a multiethnic Kashmiri nation. By 1988, "a fundamentally qualitative change in the scope and extent of violence occurred . . . Violence and instability in the valley became endemic," even after the incumbent government was voted out of office in December 1989 (Ganguly 1997: 102). Still, Kashmiri activists were far from unanimous in their aims. Some wanted a plebiscite, to vote either to join Pakistan or for independence; some (Hindus and Sikhs of the Jammu region) considered themselves part of the Indian Union; and some (Buddhist Ladakhs and Shia Muslims of the Kargil area) did not support the movement (Ganguly 1997: 102–12; Schofield 2000: xv). A government crackdown left the valley in a "state of siege." By early 1990, tens of thousands of Hindus had fled to Jammu. The government passed the draconian Jammu and Kashmir Disturbed Areas Act in July 1990, giving security forces impunity even to kill, yet the violence continued. This period (beginning in February 1986) was also one of growing communal tension and violence elsewhere in India (Ganguly 1997: 93–112).

With the Soviet withdrawal from Afghanistan in 1989 and Pakistan's readiness to divert arms to Kashmir, thousands of recruits started to cross into Azad Kashmir and Pakistan's Northwest Frontier province starting in late 1989 for training. Among the earliest recruits were candidates who had been kept out of the 1987 elections, especially from the MUF. The bulk of the recruits, however, were young, unemployed college graduates. They blamed Indian rule for their limited prospects, despite the role of the corrupt state government in siphoning off federal development aid (Kumar 2002: 14–15). Most notable among "at least a dozen major insurgent groups of varying size and ideological orientation, as well as dozens more minor operations" (Ganguly 1996: 76) are the nominally secular, pro-independence Jammu and Kashmir Liberation Front (JKLF);[13] and the radical Islamic, pro-Pakistan, irredentist Hizb-ul-Mujahideen (HUM), Hizbollah, Harkat-ul-Ansar and Ikhwanul Muslimeen. Around 30 of these groups joined in the Kul-Jammat-e-Hurriyat-e-Kashmir (All Kashmir Freedom Front, Hurriyat), seeking a plebiscite on self-determination, an Islamic Kashmiri society, and unification with Pakistan. By 1993, the JKLF seemed to have lost military ascendancy to HUM, although it still claimed to have 85 percent of the people's political support: most Kashmiris preferred sovereignty to joining Pakistan. The JKLF and other groups were torn between working toward a non-violent political solution or pursuing militant action, as well as rift by personal disagreements and rivalries. Indian Muslims outside Kashmir have been reluctant to lend support to the Kashmiri Muslim cause since the state's withdrawal would encourage anti-Muslim sentiments in India and give the BJP a political advantage (Kohli 1997: 341; Schofield 2000: 174–5, 201–4; Tremblay 1996–1997: 472).

By the mid-1990s, the Kashmir valley was largely controlled by militant groups and "The more the democratic political process lost its meaning, the more a full-scale insurgency came to be unleashed" (Kohli 1997: 341). In the insurgency's first six years, over 15,000 militants, security personnel, hostages and bystanders died, and around 200,000 (mostly Hindu Kashmiris) were forced to flee their homes and businesses in the valley (Ganguly 1997: 1–2; Tremblay 1996–1997: 473). Nearly 400,000 Indian Army and paramilitary troops have been deployed in Kashmir and security-related activities have accounted for nearly 60 percent of the state's administrative expenses (Ganguly 1997: 1–2). Both sides have been accused of torture and extrajudicial killings. Amid the general lawlessness, education, health care and the overall quality of life have declined precipitously, while communal differences among Hindus in Jammu, Buddhists in Ladakh,[14] and Muslims in the valley have been sharpened (Rahman 1996: 147–8; Schofield 2000: 163–5, 169–74, 182–8). The central government has vacillated between periods of presidential rule and attempts to normalize politics in the state (coupling both with counterinsurgency initiatives). Many nationalist groups have refused to participate in elections or other forms of institutionalized politics, or have used these as a platform for expressing pro-Pakistani or other sentiments (Ganguly 1997: 119–27, 151–6; Schofield 2000: 165–8, 175–6, 192–6).

Pakistan denies having played so core a role as India claims in furthering militancy in Kashmir, but it has clearly played a part. It is estimated that Pakistan has provided training to several thousand Kashmiri militants, as well as serving as a staging ground, sanctuary and source of arms and resources, particularly for protégés of Pakistan's Jamaat-I-Islami party.[15] Also, large numbers of both Pakistani and Afghan fighters have joined Kashmiri militant groups, where they tend to be especially vicious in their tactics and to show little regard for the local population (Ganguly 1997: 125; Kohli 1997: 340–1; Kumar 2002: 16).[16] Attempts at negotiations between India and Pakistan have failed repeatedly, and both sides have tried to internationalize the issue, as through UN resolutions (Ganguly 1997: 119–27; Schofield 2000: 165). In the meantime, Atal Behari

Vajpayee's BJP-led coalition government, elected in March 1998, declared that all the former Jammu and Kashmir, including the parts held by Pakistan, belong to India. A series of nuclear tests by India in May 1998, then reciprocal tests by Pakistan later that month, unleashed an immediate, outraged response from the international community. Faced with sanctions, the two countries agreed to a moratorium on nuclear testing, promised to sign the Comprehensive Test Ban Treaty, and resumed formal talks. The result was the Lahore Declaration of February 1999 which, among other promises, committed India and Pakistan to intensify efforts to resolve the Kashmir issue (Kumar 2002: 17–19; Schofield 2000: 205–8).

The peace proved short-lived; within a few months India and Pakistan were again close to war. Pakistani-linked militants took over Indian-occupied defensive positions and India retaliated with aerial bombardments of Kargil in May 1999. These clashes were supplemented by a crackdown on political dissent in the Kashmir valley and curbs on the media both in India and Pakistan (which could not halt a "cyber-war" of propaganda from both sides), and were particularly worrisome given the nuclear threat. American intervention helped to curb the crisis, but Pakistani prime minister Nawaz Sharif was ousted for this diplomatic surrender and the violence had intensified anew by late 1999 (Kumar 2002: 17–19; Schofield 2000: xvi, 208–24). Musharraf of Pakistan and Vajpayee of India met at Agra in July 2001 to discuss an autonomy package for both India- and Pakistan-controlled areas. Pakistan wanted Kashmir formally recognized as the central issue of conflict between the two countries, which India was finally ready to grant. However, India demanded that Pakistan eschew support for violence in return, which Pakistan would not do. India declared both Jammu and the Kashmir valley "disturbed areas" and gave security forces free rein (Kumar 2002: 19–22). With the events of 11 September 2001, Pakistan became a key US ally in the war on terrorism. Pakistan broke its links with the Taliban and tried to curb Islamic extremism, including in Kashmir. Meanwhile, India tried again to move Kashmir toward democratic elections (Kumar 2002: 21–2).

However, normalcy will be hard to restore in Kashmir. Almost two decades of intense conflict have weakened all aspects of Kashmiri government and civil society, both political parties and secessionist groups are deeply fragmented, and criminal networks and the black market have flourished. Moreover, regional and ethnic tensions within the state are high, so any settlement will need to consider both autonomy for the state and devolution within it (Kumar 2002: 20–1). Azad Kashmiris have increasingly come to prefer independence, as well, rather than full integration into Pakistan; the Northern Areas, on the other hand, have offered less support for secession (Schofield 2000: 179–81). Any solution will require bilateral talks between India and Pakistan to end Pakistan's support for the insurgency and irredentist claim on Kashmir, together with internal reform and negotiations among insurgent groups to address underlying grievances (Ganguly 1997: 5). Ganguly offers several possible options to resolve the crisis: the current strategy of wearing down secessionists via force and repression over an extended period; altering the demographics of the state by offering incentives to encourage Hindus to move into the Kashmir valley; increasing military pressure to crush the insurgents (which would require somehow sealing the border with Pakistan); getting the US to pressure Pakistan to stop supporting the insurgents in exchange for concessions from India; conceding the Kashmir valley to Pakistan; shared sovereignty over the state between India and Pakistan; a plebiscite; making the Kashmir valley an Indian protectorate with autonomy in all areas but defense; or full independence for Jammu and Kashmir as it originally existed (Ganguly 1997: 131–50).

Actions of India and Pakistan have not only exacerbated the violence of the situation, but have created an untenable political climate. Viewing "every demand for local autonomy as potentially secessionist and virtually every indigenous leader as treasonous," Indira Gandhi left little space for moderation in Kashmir as in Punjab, weakened institutional channels and rendered the government ever more corrupt (Ganguly 1997: 84–5). Similarly, when Kashmir's state legislature asked the central government in 2000 to restore the autonomy the state used to enjoy – a move which might have undermined hard-line secessionists – the government refused and the violence intensified (Bienart 2002). The central government argues that "virtually all Indians consider Kashmir to be a part of India"; its secession could set a dangerous precedent and disrupt communal peace between Hindus and Muslims throughout India (Ganguly 1997: 128–30). Pakistan's official position is "that the people of Jammu and Kashmir should have the right of self-determination, and that the pledges given to them in this behalf should be fulfilled." At the same time, that the state "belongs with Pakistan ... is so self-evident that nothing else can override it – save, of course, the wishes of the people themselves" (Government of Pakistan 1968: 3). Schofield clarifies that Pakistan's encouragement of Kashmiri nationalism makes sense since, "it is clear that Pakistan has never accepted a definition of 'self-determination' to be anything other than a choice between India and Pakistan" (Schofield 2000: xvi).

The international context is critical to the Kashmir conflict even beyond the level of Pakistani intervention. The territory of Jammu and Kashmir is disputed by India, Pakistan and, to a lesser extent, China; the major players have sought international mediation or validation for their cause; and support for different factions has come from various quarters. American and European legislators and activists have listened to charges of human rights and other abuses and lodged complaints, but could do relatively little. Among other factors, the growth of western business interests in India left those governments less willing to provoke India, apart from some prodding regarding human rights violations in the early 1990s and later concern over Pakistan's alleged exporting of Islamist terrorism and both states' nuclear capabilities (Schofield 2000: 189–92). Overall, the contributions of the international community have been limited, despite appeals to the UN dating back to 1947. India in particular considers the issue a bilateral rather than multilateral one and has distanced itself from attempts at international mediation (Schofield 2000: xvi). Amid the global "war on terrorism," Kashmir is again in the global gaze, but probably not in a way Kashmiris would prefer: the state is described as a front in a transnational, terrorist war of religious zealots[17] rather than sympathetically as the struggle of an oppressed minority for human rights (Wirsing 2002).

Still today, the militancy-repression cycle in which Jammu and Kashmir has been locked since the late 1980s continues. Sumit Ganguly sums up the crux of the Kashmir conflict: the insurgency "demonstrates the dangers states face when political mobilization occurs against a backdrop of institutional decay. The failure of governments to accommodate rising political demands within an institutional context can culminate in political violence," perpetrated by militants as well as state forces. This tendency is particularly the case in multiethnic societies with limited channels for minorities to express discontent, and especially as literacy, education and media exposure increase with economic modernization (Ganguly 1996: 77). For India and Pakistan, the conflict over Kashmir is less a contest over strategic ground or resources as over competing visions of nationalism and state-building. For India, Kashmir is symbolic of secular nationalism. For Pakistan, Kashmir represents instead the failure of secular nationalism and the imperative of a Muslim homeland in the subcontinent, as well as the "incompleteness" of Pakistan. The conflict has always been international in aspect, too, given India and Pakistan's competing territorial claims; repeated appeals to the UN, the US and other third parties; the nuclear threat posed by the tensions between two nuclear powers; and its imbrication in wider Islamist terrorist networks.

## Ethnonationalism and globalization: what the cases suggest

We return to the question of the import of globalization to these conflicts. As described in the introductory chapter, we might expect two sorts of effects. The first involves limits to state sovereignty via transnational markets, institutions and the like. Clearly, though, the impact of these forces would depend on the state's level of integration into these institutions. The second is the magnification of attacks from subnational groups thanks to global allies. This threat mostly comes into play when local and non-local identities coincide (as through a religiously-based movement or diasporic nationalism). Even then, such support may be limited and transient. The issues at stake in these four cases are not born out of a backlash against globalization. Domestic contests and political opportunity structures are far more central to the movements' progress than international ones. However, the contemporary phase of globalization does carry implications for the viability of potential nation-states. For instance, Catalonia looks to the EU as providing a market, and Kashmir may reassess the costs and benefits of joining Pakistan based on similar economic and strategic considerations, given the extent of available supranational networks. Overall, then, while globalization has influenced these movements, they arise and thrive far less as a function of international trends or pressures than domestic ones.

While each clearly is distinctive, these cases suggest broader implications. The primordial identities at the root of ethnonationalist movements are far from outmoded, and still hold substantial sway even in this globalized era. States, too, retain primary authority in settling what are essentially political questions, even if global actors have a certain degree of influence. Notably, that external influence is not just an artifact of contemporary globalization processes, but has long been in play. The identities invoked by ethnonationalist movements are as fluid and overlapping as any; individuals have both transnational and local identities, which may be invoked at different times and for different purposes. Finally, the interest of non-local actors is likely to be inconsistent. The potency of diasporic identities tends to wax and wane over time, and conflicting interests may change the nature of other states' intervention. However, it is the confluence of these factors that really determines why certain groups' demands are less tractable than others.

### *The continuing salience of "primordial" identities*

Ethnic, regional and religious sentiments may be critical to political behavior, economic considerations notwithstanding, especially when local cultures, languages or religions appear to be under siege. All four cases demonstrate this tendency effectively. It was when Castilian was named Spain's official language – and especially when Franco moved to stamp out regional languages – that Basque and Catalan nationalism perked up to defend the community's cultural and linguistic heritage. Similarly, the rise of Hindu nationalism, first through the Congress Party's fishing for votes, then as manifested in the advance of the BJP, worked to throw religious differences into sharp relief in non-Hindu-dominated areas of India. Feeling marginalized by an Indian nation that seemed increasingly to be equated with a Hindu identity, Muslim Kashmiris and Sikh Punjabis were more prone to espouse secessionism. Bermeo generalizes (citing, among other cases, enforced monolingualism in Spain): "separatist movements are more often the stepchildren of threats than of concessions" (Bermeo 2002: 105).

At the same time, primordial identities, like all identities, wax and wane in conjunction with other affiliations. As the contrast between dynamics in the Basque Country and Catalonia makes clear, ethnic identities intersect with others – for instance, class affiliations – in contingent ways. Both the Basque Country and Catalonia are set off from the rest of Spain by linguistic differences; both were repressed culturally and otherwise under Franco's dictatorship; both have enjoyed substantial and ever-increasing autonomy as "historic nationalities" since devolution in 1978; and both have received significant immigration from other parts of Spain. However, Basque radical, anticapitalist separatism contrasts with more moderate, federalist Catalanism, largely on account of intraregional class dynamics (Díez Medrano 1995). These class dynamics have been shaped by long-term processes of economic development and play out in organizations catering to different constituencies and distinguishing themselves in terms of tactics, from the radical ETA to the more moderate PNV. In this case, neither the global context nor the pull of ethnic affinity in isolation does much to explain the varying subregional strands; the combination of the response of the state, intersection of identities, and developmental trajectory of the regions is far more critical.

### *The primacy of the domestic context*

While international sanction and support clearly inform the decisions of both states and movement activists in important ways, domestic political opportunity structures – determined by how states respond when faced with ethnonationalist demands – remain more important to the course of those movements. The international environment may come into play when a conflict is incendiary or otherwise disruptive beyond the local context, or when it spans state lines. However, state-level imperatives and actions remain definitive. Probably the clearest example of this balance is the Kashmir conflict. Given the known nuclear capabilities of both sides, plus contemporary global concern with curbing Islamist radicalism, international actors have a keen interest in resolving this regional dispute. However, while the UN, US, EU and other actors have been able to cajole India and Pakistan into holding talks – and have been the repository for complaints from all sides – they have not been able to force an agreement.

More specifically, how the state responds may present a critical juncture. In particular, Bermeo sums up from an international research team's examination of the relative merits of federalism and unitarism, "our authors were nearly unanimous in concluding that federal institutions promote successful accommodation," regardless of the level or age of democracy in the country (Bermeo 2002: 97–8). They find that the diffusion of power in federal systems encourages territorially-concentrated minorities:

> To engage in fewer acts of armed rebellion, to experience lower levels of economic and political discrimination, and to harbor lower levels of grievance concerning political, economic, and cultural policy ...

> Federal systems provide more layers of government and thus more settings for peaceful bargaining. They also give at least some regional elites a greater stake in existing political institutions.[18]
>
> (Bermeo 2002: 99)

Only some of this effect was due to the greater stability of federal than unitary regimes – and the former *are* more stable, probably at least partly due to federalist institutions' dampening effect on rebelliousness – or wealth of the state (and thus ability to quell economic grievances). Still, below a threshold level of gross national product, federalism carries less of an advantage over unitarism (Bermeo 2002: 101–2).

### *Transnational and local identities*

Not all ethnonationalisms encounter globalization alike; movements that can call upon a large and engaged diasporic population or that invoke transnational identities may find forces of globalization more useful than movements that truly are local in scope. Such broader identities may be available if the nation is defined in terms of traits not really specific to that territory (as is the case if Muslim or Christian identities are invoked), or if the nation is defined to include a diasporic population with continuing ties to the "motherland." Islam undercuts traditional understandings of ethnonationalism if only because the *ummah*, or technically-relevant community, is so broad (for instance, Gellner 1994). Indeed, Islamist supporters from outside Jammu and Kashmir have been critical to that conflict, whether by providing resources, offering examples and inspiration, or by volunteering as fighters themselves. The usefulness of those connections (together with domestic factors like the rise of Hindu nationalism) helps to explain why Islam rather than Kashmiriyat became increasingly more central to Kashmiri identity over time, although the majority of Kashmiri nationalists seem not to have lost their sense of the region as distinctive (hence, for instance, preferring independence to accession to Pakistan), while Muslims elsewhere in India hesitate to engage for fear of a backlash. Transnational connections have taken on a somewhat different slant in the case of Punjab. There, instead of the movement's realigning itself to take advantage of external opportunities, preferences among the Sikh diaspora differed from those of local nationalist groups. The relatively more vehement pro-secession stance of non-local Sikhs may have encouraged hardliners, but failed to redirect the movement overall.

### *The inconsistency of the global*

The global forces at play are mercurial. Shifts in global norms and priorities in particular may (de)legitimate ethnonationalist movements, provide or diminish inspiration, or shift political opportunity structures and available resources in important ways, even if global economic forces appear relatively insignificant to activists' calculations. For instance, the US's predilection to risk irking India by pressing for a resolution of the Kashmir conflict has varied with the strength of American business interests in the country. More broadly, while both Spain and India were previously vulnerable to international sanction on account of human rights abuses (most notably, repression under Franco in the former or Indira Gandhi in the latter), these issues are no longer so dominant internationally; business and security concerns have come to trump rights-based pressure. By the same token, international support for self-determination varies, as well. Apart from in the immediate post-World War II period and some windows thereafter, international norms have tended to favor maintaining the stability of juridical states. Even the availability of co-religionists' support for sectarian ethnonationalist claims may vacillate. Kashmir, for instance, cannot depend with certainty upon Pakistani support, since the latter is no longer so ready to support Muslim insurgents and risk aggravating the US.

## Conclusion

Under what circumstances or in what ways, then, does globalization matter to ethnonationalist movements? The Basque nationalist movement in Spain and the Kashmiri nationalist movement in India are less moderate and amenable to compromise than Catalan or Punjabi nationalist movements, which strive, on balance, more toward autonomy than independence. What accounts for that difference – especially when state-level political developments have been broadly comparable in the Basque Country and Catalonia, and in Punjab and Jammu and Kashmir? Globalization matters when a diasporic or otherwise-aligned population has resources and motivation to contribute, when international norms promote a particular trajectory, when other states are directly affected by the movement, or when geostrategic alliances require the settlement of distracting domestic disputes. These conditions and moments, though, are impermanent and have effect only as they concatenate with state- and local-level forces.

These cases suggest that states and sovereignty may increasingly find themselves counterbalanced by supranational institutions and global forces, but retain critical relevance. How the state responds to ethnonationalist unrest, and especially, what sorts of institutional outlets are available for protest, may significantly determine the timbre and course of the movement – how radical the demands expressed are, what sort of alliances form within or across regions and even with sympathizers abroad, and how palatable moderation seems to the contenders. Moreover, primordial ethnic and racial identities intersect with other dimensions – regional, class, ideological and more. Ultimately, though, despite the rhetoric and reality of economic globalization and expectations of shifts in the distribution of political power toward a supranational level, the basic processes of ethnonationalist contention remain much the same as ever, and both regional and state-level identities and processes retain core relevance.

## Notes

1 The conservative Navarre and Alava became Nationalist strongholds, while Vizcaya and Guipozcoa were controlled by PNV–leftist coalitions.
2 Only in the Basque Country did the constitutional referendum fail, and with a high abstention rate.
3 See Mees (2001: 810–11) for more on this comparison.
4 The public use of Catalan was forbidden and the state did what it could to proscribe even private use.
5 Catalanism is not premised upon ethnicity per se: "a Catalan is defined as 'a person who lives and works in Catalonia and wants to be Catalan' " (Guibernau 1997: 30).
6 Even during Franco's rule, Catalanists were able to rally broad support for autonomy. For instance, the clandestine Assembly of Catalonia, formed in 1971, united workers, students and representatives of the Church and intelligentsia to demand amnesty for political prisoners and exiles, civil liberties, a return to the provisions of the 1932 statute, and democracy – themes that remained central post-Franco (Edwards 1999: 667–8; Payne 1971: 48–50).
7 Since regional and national elections are held separately, voters can express distinct preferences for each.
8 In Catalonia, immigrant/native cleavages tend to parallel class lines (with immigrants disproportionately lower-class), and language policies may institutionalize forms of discrimination against immigrant minorities – even though Catalán, a Romance language like Castilian, is relatively easy for immigrants to learn. Euskera is less a prerequisite for high-status jobs than the more thriving Catalán (Shabad and Gunther 1982: 444–6).
9 Reservations were maintained for scheduled tribes and castes.
10 Most prominent was Congress leaders' support of Sant Jarnail Singh Bhindranwale, leader of an orthodox sect, as counterweight to the Akali Dal starting in 1979. Bhindranwale soon became an outspoken critic of Congress. He aimed to rejuvenate Sikhism by promoting orthodoxy and austere living. Within three years, he became one of the most popular of Sikh leaders, especially among the lower classes and frustrated youths (Telford 1992: 969–81).
11 The sectarian division between Shia and Sunni Muslims in Jammu and Kashmir is itself highly significant (Ramachandran 2003).
12 For instance, convinced of widespread dissatisfaction in Kashmir, Pakistan tried unsuccessfully several times to foment rebellion in the state in 1965 (Ganguly 1997: 43–57). Similarly, while India and Pakistan's 1971 war over East Pakistan (Bangladesh) confirmed India's dominance on the subcontinent and undermined Pakistan's irredentist claim on Kashmir, Kashmiris cooperated with Indian forces during the war (Ganguly 1997: 58–73; Kumar 2002: 14).
13 Its leadership is Muslim and the group has specifically attacked Hindus. The JKLF seeks unification of the parts of the state now controlled by India as well as Pakistan.
14 Ladakh has also campaigned for autonomy through the Ladakh Buddhist Association, founded in 1989. The Indian government had given eight communities in Ladakh scheduled tribe status by 1989, but the region remained restive (Rahman 1996: 147–8).
15 For instance, in 1993, Pakistani aid was estimated at over $3 million per month.

Suspended temporarily due to pressure from the US, funding resumed on a smaller scale in 1994.

16 For more on the international dimension and the extent of Pakistan's involvement, see Schofield (2000: 176–9).

17 Of particular note was an attack by Islamist extremists on the Indian parliament building in December 2001. 14 died in the attack. India responded with a massive troop buildup along its border with Pakistan until American and European diplomatic intervention defused the situation (Kumar 2002).

18 India is an outlier, though, among federal democracies, with an unusually high penchant for rebellion (Bermeo 2002: 100).

## References

Balcells, A. (1996) *Catalan Nationalism: Past and Present,* trans. J. Hall, ed. G. Walker, London: Macmillan.

Barrington, L. (1997) "'Nation' and 'Nationalism': The Misuse of Key Concepts in Political Science," *PS: Political Science and Politics,* December 1997: 712–16.

Ben-Ami, S. (1991) "Basque Nationalism between Archaism and Modernity," *Journal of Contemporary History,* 26: 493–521.

Bermeo, N. (2002) "The Import of Institutions," *Journal of Democracy,* 13/2: 96–110.

Bienart, P. (2002) "Free State," *New Republic,* 226/3: 6.

Calhoun, C. (1993) "Nationalism and Ethnicity," *Annual Review of Sociology,* 19: 211–39.

Colomer, J. M. (1998) "The Spanish 'State of Autonomies': Non-Institutional Federalism," *West European Politics,* 21/4: 40–52.

Deol, H. (2000) *Religion and Nationalism in India: The Case of the Punjab,* London: Routledge.

Díez Medrano, J. (1995) *Divided Nations: Class, Politics, and Nationalism in the Basque Country and Catalonia,* Ithaca: Cornell University Press.

Douglass, W. A. and Zulaika, J. (1990) "On the Interpretation of Terrorist Violence: ETA and the Basque Political Process," *Comparative Studies in Society and History,* 32/2: 238–57.

*Economist, The* (1998) "Loveless but Convenient," *The Economist,* 24 January, 51–2.

—— (2000a) "National Calm, Regional Turmoil," *The Economist,* 25 November, 55–8.

—— (2000b) "Robust Basques and Regional Catalans," *The Economist,* 25 November, 12–13.

Edwards, S. (1999) "'Reconstructing the Nation': The Process of Establishing Catalan Autonomy," *Parliamentary Affairs,* 52/4: 666–76.

Ganguly, S. (1996) "Explaining the Kashmir Insurgency: Political Mobilization and Institutional Decay," *International Security,* 21/2: 76–107.

—— (1997) *The Crisis in Kashmir: Portents of War, Hopes of Peace,* New York: Woodrow Wilson Center Press and Cambridge University Press.

Geertz, C. (1995) "Primordial and Civic Ties," in J. Hutchinson and A. D. Smith (eds) *Nationalism,* New York: Oxford University Press.

Gellner, E. (1994) *Conditions of Liberty: Civil Society and Its Rivals,* London: Penguin Books.

Government of India (1984) *White Paper on the Punjab Agitation, a Summary.*

Government of Pakistan (1968) *The Story of Kashmir: 1947–68.* Karachi: Department of Films and Communications, Original edition, 1965.

Guibernau, M. (1997) "Spain's Local Success," *New Statesman*: 30.

—— (2000) "Spain: Catalonia and the Basque Country," *Parliamentary Affairs*, 53/1: 55–68.

Kohli, A. (1997) "Can Democracies Accommodate Ethnic Nationalism? Rise and Decline of Self-Determination Movements in India," *Journal of Asian Studies*, 56/2: 325–44.

Kumar, R. (2002) "Untying the Kashmir Knot," *World Policy Journal*, 19/1: 11–24.

Laitin, D. D. (1989) "Linguistic Revival: Politics and Culture in Catalonia," *Comparative Studies in Society and History*, 31/2: 297–317.

Leaf, M. J. (1985) "The Punjab Crisis," *Asian Survey*, 25/5: 475–98.

Mahmood, C. K. (1996) *Fighting for Faith and Nation: Dialogues with Sikh Militants*, Philadelphia: University of Pennsylvania Press.

Major, A. (1987) "From Moderates to Secessionists: A Who's Who of the Punjab Crisis," *Pacific Affairs*, 60/1: 42–58.

Mees, L. (2001) "Between Votes and Bullets: Conflicting Ethnic Identities in the Basque Country," *Ethnic and Racial Studies*, 24/5: 798–827.

Oberoi, H. S. (1987) "From Punjab to 'Khalistan': Territoriality and Metacommentary," *Pacific Affairs*, 60/1: 26–41.

Payne, S. (1971) "Catalan and Basque Nationalism," *Journal of Contemporary History*, 6/1: 15–31, 35–51.

—— (1991) "Nationalism, Regionalism and Micronationalism in Spain," *Journal of Contemporary History*, 26: 479–91.

Rahman, M. (1996) *Divided Kashmir: Old Problems, New Opportunities for India, Pakistan, and the Kashmiri People*, Boulder: Lynne Rienner.

Ramachandran, S. (2003) "Kashmir: A Shi'ite Voice in the Wilderness," *Asia Times Online*, 25 July.

Ross, C. (1996) "Nationalism and Party Competition in the Basque Country and Catalonia," *West European Politics*, 19/3: 488–506.

Schofield, V. (2000) *Kashmir in Conflict: India, Pakistan and the Unfinished War*, New York: I. B. Taurus.

Shabad, G. and Gunther, R. (1982) "Language, Nationalism, and Political Conflict in Spain," *Comparative Politics*, 14/4: 443–77.

Tatla, D. S. (1999) *The Sikh Diaspora: The Search for Statehood*, London: UCL Press.

Telford, H. (1992) "The Political Economy of Punjab: Creating Space for Sikh Militancy," *Asian Survey*, 32/11: 969–87.

Tremblay, R. C. (1996–1997) "Nation, Identity and the Intervening Role of the State: A Study of the Secessionist Movement in Kashmir," *Pacific Affairs*, 69/4: 471–97.

Wirsing, R. (2002) "Kashmir in the Terrorist Shadow," *Asian Affairs*, 33/1: 70–8.

Woodworth, P. (2001) "Why Do They Kill? The Basque Conflict in Spain," *World Policy Journal*, 18/1: 1–12.

# 11 Globalization and fiscal decentralization

*Geoffrey Garrett and Jonathan Rodden*[1]

## Introduction

The international integration of markets and the decentralization of authority within nation-states are two defining trends of the contemporary era. A popular speculation is that globalization has caused a downward shift in the locus of governance by reducing the economic costs of smallness and allowing localities and regions with distinctive preferences to pursue their own political and economic strategies (Alesina and Spolaore 1997; Bolton and Roland 1997). This chapter analyzes these claims by examining the location of *fiscal* authority within states. Using a large cross-country data set composed of expenditure and revenue decentralization data for the 1980s and 1990s, it demonstrates a rather striking relationship – international market integration has actually been associated with fiscal centralization rather than decentralization.

There are several potential explanations, but we propose a straightforward argument for the globalization-fiscal centralization nexus that rests on perceptions of uncertainty and risk. First, macroeconomic conditions are perceived to be more volatile in more globally integrated countries (Rodrik 1998). Second, regional demands for insurance against asymmetric shocks increase with international market integration (following Persson and Tabellini 1996a, b). Thus, one should expect both more macroeconomic stabilization and more inter-regional risk sharing under globalization, and both objectives are better served via centralized fiscal arrangements.

It is important to note, however, that fiscal centralization does not imply the centralization of all authority – it may even be consistent with increased local discretion in choosing leaders, regulating the environment and economy, or spending centrally generated funds. For example, funds for regional assistance in the EU are generated centrally (via national VAT revenues) but administered at the subnational level. Similarly, Scottish devolution has entailed more Scottish self-governance without the decentralization of taxation away from London. We leave these issues to others and focus on fiscal decentralization.

Our measure of fiscal decentralization is simple: the subnational (combined state and local) share of total public sector expenditures. This measure has the advantage that it is available on a yearly basis for a large number of countries around the world. Furthermore, it has been used in previous studies that do not address globalization (e.g. Oates 1972; Panizza 1999), allowing us to replicate and extend their results. While it does not capture the decentralization of tax autonomy, it does provide a comparable measure of the share of total public sector resources that pass through the hands of subnational officials.[2] Table 11.1 provides an overview of countries for which yearly expenditure data have been available for most of the last two decades.[3] Averages for the period from 1982 to 1989 and for 1990 to 1997 are shown in the first two columns. This cut-off is useful because several countries underwent transitions to democracy in the late 1980s, and by all accounts, global economic integration has increased substantially after 1990. The countries displayed in Table 11.1 demonstrate a good deal of variation in vertical fiscal structure. They range from heavily decentralized Canada and the US, in which more than half of all government expenditure takes place at subnational levels, to countries like Paraguay or Thailand, where subnational governments undertake less than 10 percent of total expenditures.

For our purposes, the right-hand column in Table 11.1 is the most important. It shows that fiscal decentralization was by no means a universal phenomenon in the 1990s. Some countries – in fact nearly half of the sample – became more centralized. But on the other hand, some countries – most notably Brazil, Mexico, Peru and Spain – considerably decentralized expenditures between the 1980s and 1990s (by more than 10 percentage points of total expenditures). The question is whether and how these differences are related to the extent of international market integration in these countries.

The remainder of this chapter is divided into six sections. The second section begins with a general overview of the literature on fiscal decentralization and then elaborates arguments proposing a link between globalization and decentralization. We develop our alternative hypothesis that globalization should promote fiscal centralization in section three. Our empirical tests of these contending perspectives are presented in sections four (based on cross-section averages) and five (using time-series cross-sectional data). Section six discusses the results, draws out some broad lessons, and maps out an agenda for further research. The final section concludes.

## Globalization and decentralization: the conventional view

The key intuition of fiscal federalism theory is that the benefits of decentralization are positively correlated with the geographic variance in demands for publicly provided goods (Musgrave 1959; Oates 1972).

*Table 11.1* State and local share of total government expenditure

| | *1981–1989 average* | *1990–1997 average* | *Change* |
|---|---|---|---|
| Peru | 0.10 | 0.25 | 0.15 |
| Mexico | 0.12 | 0.26 | 0.14 |
| Spain | 0.23 | 0.36 | 0.13 |
| Brazil | 0.29 | 0.41 | 0.12 |
| Argentina | 0.35 | 0.44 | 0.09 |
| Bolivia | 0.14 | 0.21 | 0.07 |
| Guatemala | 0.04 | 0.10 | 0.05 |
| Nicaragua | 0.03 | 0.08 | 0.05 |
| United States | 0.48 | 0.53 | 0.05 |
| Israel | 0.10 | 0.14 | 0.04 |
| India | 0.46 | 0.49 | 0.03 |
| Luxembourg | 0.15 | 0.17 | 0.02 |
| France | 0.17 | 0.19 | 0.01 |
| Indonesia | 0.12 | 0.13 | 0.01 |
| Austria | 0.33 | 0.34 | 0.01 |
| Norway | 0.34 | 0.35 | 0.01 |
| Portugal | 0.08 | 0.09 | 0.01 |
| United Kingdom | 0.28 | 0.29 | 0.01 |
| Ireland | 0.28 | 0.29 | 0.01 |
| Bulgaria | 0.19 | 0.19 | 0.01 |
| Germany | 0.45 | 0.45 | 0.00 |
| Kenya | 0.05 | 0.04 | 0.00 |
| Thailand | 0.07 | 0.07 | −0.01 |
| Belgium | 0.12 | 0.12 | −0.01 |
| Philippines | 0.09 | 0.08 | −0.01 |
| Iceland | 0.24 | 0.23 | −0.01 |
| Denmark | 0.55 | 0.54 | −0.01 |
| Canada | 0.67 | 0.65 | −0.02 |
| Netherlands | 0.32 | 0.30 | −0.02 |
| Australia | 0.52 | 0.50 | −0.02 |
| New Zealand | 0.12 | 0.10 | −0.02 |
| Paraguay | 0.04 | 0.02 | −0.02 |
| Botswana | 0.06 | 0.03 | −0.03 |
| Sweden | 0.40 | 0.37 | −0.03 |
| Finland | 0.45 | 0.41 | −0.04 |
| South Africa | 0.26 | 0.22 | −0.04 |
| Switzerland | 0.59 | 0.55 | −0.04 |
| Malaysia | 0.19 | 0.15 | −0.04 |
| Italy | 0.30 | 0.23 | −0.07 |
| Nigeria | 0.54 | 0.46 | −0.07 |
| Romania | 0.20 | 0.11 | −0.09 |
| Zimbabwe | 0.21 | 0.12 | −0.09 |

Source: GFS.

Although the political process through which demands for decentralization are transformed into policy is not made explicit, this line of argument maintains that excessively centralized systems in large, heterogeneous countries will face overwhelming pressure to decentralize, lest they fall apart through secession or civil war.[4]

The new literature on globalization and decentralization provides a simple extension of this approach. Alesina and his collaborators examine a basic trade-off between the benefits of large jurisdictions and the costs of heterogeneity (Alesina and Spolaore 1997; Alesina and Wacziarg 1998). The benefits of size derive from scale economies in taxation, common defense, internal free trade and the decreasing per capita cost of non-rival public goods. But large size comes at a cost – the difficulty of satisfying a more diverse population.[5] As in the Musgrave-Oates formulation, sufficiently high levels of heterogeneity generate demands for decentralization or even secession. One of the original claims made in the new literature is that globalization reduces the costs of – and hence increases the supply of – decentralization. According to Alesina and Spolaore (1997: 1041):

> a breakup of nations is more costly if it implies more trade barriers and smaller markets. On the contrary, the benefits of large countries are less important if small countries can freely trade with each other. Concretely, this result suggests that regional political separatism should be associated with increasing economic integration.

But many countries might stop short of breaking up. Instead of seceding, regionally distinct groups with strong preferences might opt for a fiscal decentralization scheme. As Bolton and Roland (1997: 1057–8) contend:

> any benefits of decentralization that might be obtained in a world with several nations may also be achieved within a unified nation by replicating the administrative structure of the world with several nations and implementing a suitable degree of decentralization of authority among the regions.

In the globalization era not only citizens, but investors as well, might prefer decentralization. Weingast's (1995) "market preserving federalism" – directly applied to the context of globalization by McGillivray and Jensen (2000) – argues that fiscal decentralization, by forcing governments to compete for mobile capital, creates incentives for politicians to provide market-friendly policies. If these arguments are correct, and central governments are interested in pleasing investors, they face incentives to devolve fiscal authority to subnational governments.

## Globalization and incentives for fiscal centralization

We have no quarrel with important elements of the conventional wisdom about globalization and decentralization. Economic integration seems to increase the credibility of secession threats in countries with concentrated minority groups (e.g. Russia) or high levels of income inequality between regions (e.g. Italy). When there is sufficient will to hold the country together, it may well be possible to forestall secession by instituting a decentralization program that allows regions to pursue distinctive economic and political strategies (as in Belgium). Central governments might introduce local elections, set up regional parliaments, enhance the constitutional protections of subnational governments, or improve their representation in the central government (Scotland and Wales). The central government might loosen its regulation and oversight of subnational governments, transform conditional grants into block grants and allow local governments greater freedom over local schools and cultural institutions.

Such devolution need not translate, however, into a shift of fiscal resources into the hands of local governments. On the contrary, we believe that it is more likely for the relationship to go in precisely the opposite direction: globalization encourages the centralization of public expenditures (and, even more so, taxation), even if it simultaneously enhances the political autonomy and discretion of subnational officials.[6]

The conventional view has overlooked an important benefit of centralized fiscal arrangements. Larger fiscal units are more effective at risk-sharing – pooling economic resources to provide insurance for regions adversely affected by unexpected asymmetric economic shocks (Persson and Tabellini 1996a). Thus all regions – whether rich and poor, or dominated by the ethnic majority or a minority group – might benefit from fiscal centralization because they cannot predict *ex ante* which of them will be hit by negative shocks or when this will happen. Globalization is widely perceived not only by scholars but also by citizens to increase volatility and hence aggregate economic risk (Rodrik 1998; Scheve and Slaughter 2001); thus it also increases the aggregate social utility of automatic interregional tax-transfer insurance schemes. According to Atkeson and Bayoumi (1993: 91):

> Integrated capital markets are likely to produce large flows of capital across regions or national boundaries. However, they are unlikely to provide a substantial degree of insurance against regional economic fluctuations, except to the extent that capital income flows become more correlated across regions. This task will continue to be primarily the business of government.

More specifically, the pooling of risk via national insurance schemes can only be the business of the central government, which alone has the authority over tax rates and the geographical distribution of expenditures to make such schemes work. Among other factors, capital market imperfections prevent regional and local governments from being able to provide such insurance themselves (von Hagen 1998). In fact, subnational spending is often pro-cyclical – severely so in many developing countries (IADB 1997; Wibbels and Rodden forthcoming).

Regional specialization is another likely consequence of economic integration (Krugman 1991). As regions become more specialized, they become increasingly vulnerable to the vagaries of global markets, and hence have fewer incentives to "go it alone" by relying on themselves to provide insurance. Citizens in small, vulnerable export-oriented jurisdictions with relatively undiversified economies such as "export clusters" in the Brazilian and Indian states might not be enthusiastic about fiscal decentralization if it implies a smaller risk-sharing role for the central government.

There is considerable evidence that inter-regional risk-sharing and more permanent inter-regional fiscal redistribution are prominent features of several federations – including the US. Sachs and Sala-i-Martin's (1992) influential early study of the US may well have overestimated the magnitude of inter-state redistribution (see von Hagen 1998). Nonetheless numerous subsequent studies have found evidence of significant inter-regional insurance and redistribution in response to asymmetric shocks not only in the United States, but also in Canada, France, Germany and the UK.[7]

The logic of fiscal centralization for the purpose of inter-regional risk-sharing holds in countries where regional business cycles are not highly correlated. Thus this argument is most plausible in large, diverse countries. Even in smaller countries, however, if globalization increases aggregate risk, voters may demand increased provision of stabilization by the central government. The traditional fiscal federalism literature argues that fiscal stabilization can only be successful if firmly under the control of the central government. Except perhaps for very rare cases like the US states and Canadian provinces (even these are debatable), fiscal stabilization is not likely to be successful at lower levels of government.

Although risk-sharing and redistribution are distinct in theory, they blend together in practice. Persson and Tabellini (1996a, b) point out that under the realistic assumption that some regions have more favorable output distributions than others, nominal risk-sharing schemes will have long-term redistributive consequences. Indeed, many of the recent empirical studies designed to assess the short-term "insurance" quality of intergovernmental transfers find stronger evidence of outright long-term regional redistribution in response to asymmetric shocks (e.g. Kletzer and von Hagen 2000). That is, regions that suffer negative shocks are subsequently favored in the distribution of transfers and become more dependent on transfers in the long-term. Although not previously seen in such a light, this evidence is consistent with the literature on globalization and the compensation of "losers" from free trade. The compensation literature argues that globalization might lead to larger government because, in order to assemble a stable political coalition in favor of free trade, it may be necessary for those who benefit from free trade explicitly to "buy off" those who lose with a more extensive safety net or other redistributive transfers (Garrett 1998).

When protectionist barriers fall and capital constraints are lifted in a country, it is often not difficult to predict some of the winners and losers *ex ante.* Some of the losers are often regionally identifiable, and to the extent that the effected regions are represented in the central legislature or capable of undermining the regime's support coalition, it may be necessary to pay them off with increased transfers in order to obtain their political support for the move to freer trade. Other things equal, this would lead to a larger spending role for the central government vis-à-vis subnational governments.

Increased spending pressure on the central government might come not only from regions who fear volatility and the loss of jobs associated with globalization, but turning the logic of Alesina and Spolaore on its head, it might also result from the demands of ethnic minorities. To the extent that some large, diverse countries like Canada, India, Russia and Indonesia are able to stay together in spite of demands for secession, globalization might only increase the costs of staying together. Secession threats from a region with distinct preferences may not be credible in an autarchic world, but perhaps such threats gain credibility in a world of free trade. Consider the importance of potential trading partners in bolstering the credibility of exit threats made by Estonia, Quebec, the Slovak Republic or oil-rich Russian republics, or the importance of the European Union to Scottish and Basque independence movements.

These newly credible exit threats might be a useful bargaining chip in negotiations over the distribution of central government spending. To the extent that there are benefits to the rest of the country from keeping breakaway regions in the union (e.g. maintaining a larger risk-sharing pool), the rest of the country may be willing to send disproportionately large transfers to such regions to buy their cooperation (Fearon and Van Houten 1998). Knowing this, of course, such regions face incentives to amplify their threats. This is a familiar story in post-Soviet Russia (Treisman 1999) and modern India. Even if subnational governments end up gaining autonomy and spending more, this effect may be overwhelmed by the larger spending role of the central government. If the central government wishes to use public spending to "buy" the loyalty of voters in would-be breakaway regions, it might try to spend the money directly rather than through general-purpose transfers to regional governments. Alternatively, the central government may decide to beef up its spending on the military and internal security forces in order to quell the threat of regional violence. Either of these possibilities would lead to fiscal centralization.

In sum, our general point is that even if one accepts the Alesina-Spolaore and Bolton-Roland arguments about the effects of globalization on the breakup of nations, it is inappropriate to argue that fiscal decentralization within an existing country is a halfway house to secession. Indeed, we believe the opposite is likely to be true. In order to hold onto political power and perhaps even forestall secession, the national government may have to centralize fiscal policy so as to deliver benefits (in the form of risk-sharing and outright fiscal redistribution) to risk-averse groups, especially those in would-be secessionist localities.[8]

## Analysis of cross-section averages

This section examines the relationship between international market integration and the centralization of fiscal policy using data from a cross-section of countries around the world. We start out by conducting separate analysis on the two periods displayed in Table 11.1: 1981 to 1989, and 1990 to 1997. The cases are selected based on the availability of sufficient data on the dependent variable – logged subnational expenditure (and revenue) as a share of total public sector expenditure. These data are derived from the IMF's *Government Finance Statistics.* Higher values of the dependent variable denote more decentralization. We present results of separate models for expenditure and revenue decentralization.

The independent variables follow from the discussion above. First, to test arguments about size and heterogeneity, we include the natural logs of *area* (square kilometers) and average *population.* The basic model also includes the log *of GDP per capita* in inflation-adjusted US dollars, since Oates (1972) and Panizza (1999) find that wealthier countries demonstrate higher levels of decentralization.[9] Following Panizza (1999), we also include a measure of *ethnic fractionalization* as a proxy for preference heterogeneity.[10]

Next, we include averages of Gurr's 20-point measure of *democracy.*[11] According to Panizza (1999) and Alesina and Spolaore (1997), if geographically-dispersed heterogeneous preferences over public goods are taken as a given, a rent-seeking authoritarian government that can rule without consent might be more willing and able to suppress demands for decentralization than a democratically elected counterpart.[12]

We also include a simple dummy variable for political federalism.[13] Above all, federal systems are distinct from unitary systems in that they provide formal or *de facto* veto authority to regional politicians over all or some subset of federal policy decisions. In most cases this is accomplished through special constitutional protections and amendment procedures and an upper house that disproportionately represents the regions. All of these factors should allow subnational officials to bargain for larger shares of the public sector's resources. It is also possible that some of the variation in fiscal decentralization will be explained by urbanization rates if demands for local government services are higher in urban areas. Thus we include a variable that measures urban population as a share of the total.[14]

Next, we include two public finance variables calculated from the GFS. First, it is plausible that decentralization might be more advanced in countries with larger public sectors, so we include a control for the average overall scale of government spending as a portion of GDP. Finally, we consider the possibility that decentralization is little more than a thinly-veiled attempt by central governments to "offload" central government deficits onto state and local governments by increasing subnational expenditure responsibilities without a corresponding increase in revenues. This is a common complaint among critics of fiscal decentralization in a wide variety of contexts ranging from Latin America and Africa to the United States. In order to control for this in the cross-section regressions, we include the central government's average fiscal balance as a percentage of revenue.

The final group of variables addresses globalization using two simple measures. We use *trade/GDP* ratios to capture the international integration of national goods and services markets.[15] Second, *capital account openness* is a dummy variable from the IMF's annual Exchange Arrangements and Exchange Restrictions describing whether countries impose significant restrictions on capital account transactions (coded as "0") or not ("1" = open). This is a simple way to measure international capital mobility that is available for all IMF members on an annual basis.[16]

The results from the regressions on the first period (1981–1989) are presented in Table 11.2, and the results from the second period (1990–1997) are presented in Table 11.3. In each table, the first two columns use expenditure decentralization as the dependent variable, and the final two columns use revenue decentralization. For both cases, models are presented with and without the globalization variables.

The coefficients for the control variables are broadly consistent with previous studies, but with some exceptions. As expected, countries with larger *area* are significantly more decentralized. Note, however, that there is a rather high correlation between *area, population, trade/GDP* and the *federalism* dummy. Larger countries are more likely to have the constitutional trappings of federalism, and because of their larger internal markets, they are less dependent on trade than smaller countries. Note that the coefficient for *area* loses its statistical significance when the *trade* variable is included in the regressions for the earlier period. Moreover, federalism is positively associated with fiscal decentralization in all the models, but again, its statistical significance is sensitive to the inclusion of the *trade* and *area* variables. In more spare models, *federalism* and *area* are always highly significant.[17]

In addition, countries with higher *GDP per capita* are more decentralized, though in the models presented here, the positive coefficient does not quite attain statistical significance. In some stripped-down models

*Table 11.2* Between-effects decentralization models, 1981–1989

| | *Dependent variable* | | | | | | | |
|---|---|---|---|---|---|---|---|---|
| | *State and local expenditure as share of total government expenditure (average)* | | | | *State and local revenue as share of total government revenue (average)* | | | |
| | *Coef.* | *S.E.* | *Coef.* | *S.E.* | *Coef.* | *S.E.* | *Coef.* | *S.E.* |
| *Control variables* | | | | | | | | |
| Area (log) | 0.19 | 0.09** | 0.07 | 0.11 | 0.15 | 0.08* | 0.02 | 0.09 |
| Population (log) | 0.03 | 0.09 | −0.03 | 0.10 | 0.05 | 0.09 | −0.02 | 0.09 |
| GDP per capita (log) | 0.13 | 0.24 | 0.09 | 0.24 | 0.23 | 0.23 | 0.18 | 0.22 |
| Ethnic fractionalization | 0.003 | 0.004 | 0.004 | 0.005 | 0.003 | 0.004 | 0.004 | 0.004 |
| Urbanization | 0.001 | 0.01 | −0.001 | 0.01 | −0.002 | 0.01 | −0.004 | 0.01 |
| Democracy | 0.08 | 0.02*** | 0.07 | 0.02*** | 0.07 | 0.02*** | 0.06 | 0.02*** |
| Federalism | 0.38 | 0.28 | 0.53 | 0.28* | 0.33 | 0.26 | 0.45 | 0.25* |
| Total expenditure/GDP | 1.04 | 0.98 | 1.79 | 1.05* | 0.93 | 0.91 | 1.94 | 0.99* |
| Central balance/revenue | 0.44 | 0.47 | 0.83 | 0.50 | −0.18 | 0.45 | 0.26 | 0.46 |
| *Globalization variables* | | | | | | | | |
| Trade/GDP | | | −1.12 | 0.61* | | | −1.32 | 0.60** |
| Open capital accounts | | | 0.13 | 0.29 | | | 0.18 | 0.27 |
| Constant | −6.83 | 2.36 | −3.39 | 2.95 | −7.28 | 2.22 | −3.58 | 2.70 |
| R square | 0.69 | | 0.72 | | 0.67 | | 0.72 | |
| Observations | 42 | | 42 | | 43 | | 43 | |

Notes
***Significant at 0.01.
**Significant at 0.05.
*Significant at 0.10.

*Table 11.3* Between-effects decentralization models, 1990–1997

| | *Dependent variable* | | | | | | | |
|---|---|---|---|---|---|---|---|---|
| | *State and local expenditure as share of total government expenditure (average)* | | | | *State and local revenue as share of total government revenue (average)* | | | |
| | *Coef.* | *S.E.* | *Coef.* | *S.E.* | *Coef.* | *S.E.* | *Coef.* | *S.E.* |
| *Control variables* | | | | | | | | |
| Area (log) | 0.05 | 0.07 | 0.04 | 0.09 | 0.03 | 0.08 | 0.04 | 0.09 |
| Population (log) | −0.0001 | 0.07 | −0.01 | 0.08 | 0.0027 | 0.08 | 0.004 | 0.09 |
| GDP per capita (log) | 0.20 | 0.20 | 0.15 | 0.23 | 0.20 | 0.21 | 0.20 | 0.24 |
| Ethnic fractionalization | 0.002 | 0.004 | 0.002 | 0.005 | 0.004 | 0.004 | 0.003 | 0.005 |
| Urbanization | 0.01 | 0.01 | 0.01 | 0.01 | 0.01 | 0.01 | 0.01 | 0.01 |
| Democracy | −0.01 | 0.03 | −0.01 | 0.03 | −0.01 | 0.03 | −0.01 | 0.03 |
| Federalism | 0.75 | 0.21 | 0.77 | 0.23*** | 0.76 | 0.22*** | 0.75 | 0.24*** |
| Total expenditure/GDP | 1.59 | 1.08 | 1.74 | 1.28 | 1.78 | 1.13 | 1.63 | 1.33 |
| Central balance/revenue | −1.99 | 0.94 | −1.87 | 1.12* | −2.30 | 0.98** | −2.44 | 1.16** |
| *Globalization variables* | | | | | | | | |
| Trade/GDP | | | −1.10 | 0.44 | | | 0.11 | 0.45 |
| Open capital accounts | | | 0.10 | 0.22 | | | 0.08 | 0.23 |
| Constant | −5.67 | 1.77 | −5.01 | 2.61 | −5.52 | 1.84 | −5.67 | 2.70 |
| R square | 0.70 | | 0.70 | | 0.69 | | 0.69 | |
| Observations | 39 | | 39 | | 39 | | 39 | |

Notes
***Significant at 0.01.
**Significant at 0.05.
*Significant at 0.10.

resembling Panizza (1999) this variable is marginally significant. *Population* and *urbanization* have no effect on decentralization in any of the estimations.[18] Contrary to the findings of Panizza (1999), ethnic fractionalization was not significant in any of our estimations.[19] *Democracy* has the expected positive sign and is highly significant in the earlier period, but the result does not hold up in the later period. This is not surprising, given that after many successful transitions to democracy, the later period demonstrates less variation across countries.

It appears that countries with larger public sectors are also more decentralized, though the statistical significance of this coefficient is quite sensitive to model specification. Next, the coefficients for *central government balance* are difficult to interpret. Like globalization, the offloading argument is a dynamic one. Thus it is difficult to come up with clear predictions about cross-section averages, though the large negative coefficients in Table 11.3, which suggest that countries with larger central government deficits are more decentralized, may be consistent with the offloading hypothesis.

Next, we add the globalization variables. While the *openness* variable never approaches statistical significance, the *trade* variable is negative and significant in the 1980s in both the expenditure and revenue decentralization equations. Other things equal, greater dependence on international trade was associated with greater fiscal centralization. A 1 percent increase in trade as a share of GDP is associated with greater than a 1 percent decrease in the share of expenditures undertaken by (or revenues at the disposal of) subnational governments. These coefficients are even larger (around −1.5) and highly significant if other correlates of trade (country size and federalism) are dropped from the regressions. However, this cross-section relationship does not hold up in the 1990s. Even if the other correlates of *trade* are dropped, the coefficients, though negative, fall short of statistical significance.

Tests reveal that the main results discussed above are not driven by excessively influential cases. Additionally, since the dependent variable has a lower limit of zero and an upper limit of one, we also estimated all of the models presented in Tables 11.2 and 11.3 using Tobit, and the results were virtually identical.

In sum, the cross-section analysis finds reasonable support for the most important findings of Oates (1972) and Panizza (1999) that larger and wealthier countries tend to be more decentralized. Previous findings regarding ethnic fractionalization do not hold up but, as we have noted, the quality of the data is extremely low. Moreover, there is additional support in the cross-section data for Panizza's (1999) finding that more democratic countries tend to be more decentralized. In addition, federal countries are more decentralized. Above all, the cross-section results are inconsistent with the common wisdom that globalization favors fiscal decentralization. On the contrary, at least in the 1980s, trade dependence was associated with greater fiscal centralization.

## Pooled time-series analysis

Table 11.4 presents our analysis of spending and revenue decentralization using panel data, comprising observations for 57 countries for the period 1978–1997. The panel specification is important in this context because some of the independent variables of interest have changed considerably in the past 20 years. Most notably, many countries in our sample have democratized, expanded their trade with the rest of the world and opened their capital accounts. In any case, decentralization is a dynamic rather than static concept; thus the empirical specification presented in this section is a significant improvement over previous studies that, like the previous section, use cross-section averages or single-year observations. We have used a variety of different estimation techniques with largely similar results, and Table 11.4 reports the results of regressions using panel corrected standard errors, taking into account the unbalanced nature of our panels. We include lagged dependent variables and dummy variables for

*Table 11.4* Time-series cross-section decentralization models, 1981–1997

| | *Dependent variable* | | | |
|---|---|---|---|---|
| | *State and local expenditure as share of total government expenditure* | | *State and local revenue as share of total government revenue* | |
| | *Coef.* | *P.C.S.E.* | *Coef.* | *P.C.S.E.* |
| *Control variables* | | | | |
| Lagged dependent variable | 0.65 | 0.07*** | 0.68 | 0.07*** |
| Population (log) | 0.30 | 0.07*** | 0.27 | 0.07*** |
| GDP per capita (log) | 0.08 | 0.05* | 0.06 | 0.05 |
| Urbanization | −0.01 | 0.003*** | −0.004 | 0.003 |
| Democracy | −0.001 | 0.003 | −0.001 | 0.004 |
| Total expenditure/GDP | −0.23 | 0.15 | −0.25 | 0.11** |
| Lagged central balance/revenue | −0.08 | 0.09 | 0.23 | 0.06*** |
| Central balance/revenue | 0.18 | 0.10** | −0.31 | 0.05*** |
| *Globalization variables* | | | | |
| Trade/GDP | −0.20 | 0.08*** | −0.14 | 0.07** |
| Open capital accounts | −0.04 | 0.02** | −0.04 | 0.02** |
| Constant | −3.99 | 0.91 | | |
| R square | 0.98 | | 0.98 | |
| Countries | 57 | | 57 | |
| Observations | 540 | | 540 | |

Notes

***Significant at 0.01.

**Significant at 0.05.

*Significant at 0.10.

OLS with panel-corrected standard errors.

Fixed effects; coefficients for country dummies not reported.

all countries (fixed effects) to take into account over time and cross-national variations that should not be attributed to any of our independent variables.[20]

In general, the patterns of parameter estimates were very similar for both spending and revenue decentralization. For convenience, we therefore concentrate on the spending equation (the first column of Table 11.4), though we must compare both equations in order to interpret the relationship between decentralization and the central government's fiscal balance.

Let us begin with the basic control variables, noting that the time-invariant variables (area, ethnic fractionalization and federalism) are not included because of the inclusion of fixed country effects. As in the between effects regressions, we do not detect a very strong relationship between *GDP per capita* and decentralization over time within countries, though the coefficient is positive and at least in the expenditure equation, marginally significant. We find no effect of democratization within countries over time, though in an earlier version of this chapter using a smaller data set, we found evidence of a small positive impact of democratization on decentralization. We also obtain a positive and statistically significant coefficient using this sample of countries if the fixed effects are dropped and cross-section variation is allowed to influence the results.

The results also provide preliminary evidence that decentralization may be, in part, a strategic attempt by central governments to shift deficits onto subnational governments. Both the level and the lagged level of the central government's surplus (deficits are negative numbers) as a percent of revenue are included in the regressions. By including the lagged level, we attempt to control for long-term trends and isolate short-term dynamics. It is important to note that the coefficients for central government balance are statistically significant, but have the opposite sign in the expenditure and revenue equations. Controlling for the previous year's level, higher surplus levels (i.e. lower deficits) are associated with *higher* subnational expenditure and *lower* subnational revenue. Note that the models control for fluctuations in GDP and overall government expenditure. Other things equal, improvements in the central government's fiscal stance are associated with larger shares of total public sector expenditure taking place at the subnational level, but smaller shares of total public sector revenue flowing to state and local governments. Thus improvements in central government finances seem to be achieved, at least in part, on the backs of state and local governments. These results dovetail with frequent complaints of "offloading" or "unfunded mandates" around the world, but they are merely suggestive. Considerable further analysis is needed.

For present purposes, the most interesting parameter estimates concern the two globalization variables. Put simply, as countries became more exposed to trade and opened their capital accounts, their fiscal systems became more centralized. This is wholly inconsistent with the logic of the Alesina-Spolaore or Bolton-Roland arguments, in which decentralization is a compromise on the way to secession, made more likely by globalization because of the reduced costs of small size in open markets. Our results suggest that a ten percentage point increase in trade as a share of GDP (a typical year for Malaysia, or roughly the increase in Canada over the last five years) is associated with a 2 percent decrease in the share of total public sector expenditures undertaken at the subnational level. The *openness* coefficient suggests that removing all significant restrictions on capital account transactions is associated with a 4 percent decrease in the state and local share of total expenditures.

In order to check the robustness of these results, we have used a variety of additional estimation techniques. Similar results were obtained using AR1 correction rather than a lagged dependent variable. A model with a lagged dependent variable and no fixed effects yielded a similar result for trade, but the coefficients for "openness" fell below traditional levels of statistical significance. We also estimated the model in first differences, and estimated an "error correction" model using both first differences and lagged levels of the independent variables. We also included a panel of year dummies. These models yielded similar results for trade though again, the statistical significance of the coefficient for "openness" is sensitive to the model specification. In general, the coefficients are slightly larger and less sensitive in the expenditure equations. In every single equation, however, the signs for trade and openness are negative, and both are significant in most.[21]

## Discussion

It is commonly assumed that globalization has had two effects on political systems around the world. On the one hand, globalization has reduced the minimum efficient scale of politics, resulting in the proliferation of nations. On the other hand, globalization has also been associated – on the same logic – with fiscal decentralization within nations. We do not wish to debate the merits of the first proposition, but the empirical analysis above calls into question the globalization-decentralization nexus. We have discovered a modest but robust, significant relationship between trade integration and expenditure centralization.

One might respond that this finding is wholly consistent with the Alesina-Spolaore argument because globalization has facilitated secession and the creation of new sovereign states. If the impetus for secession were heterogeneity within old national boundaries, both new states and what remains of existing states would be more homogenous than the polyglots that preceded them. Given the increased homogeneity of preferences in all states after secession, there would be less reason to decentralize authority in any of them. This argument relies on asserting that globalization has been causally implicated in cataclysmic events such as the end of African colonialism in the 1960s and the breakup of the Soviet Union. No political boundaries, however, changed in any of the countries in our study during the period we analyze. Thus there must be another explanation for the fiscal centralization we observe.

We have argued that globalization, by increasing perceptions of aggregate and region-specific risk within countries, might actually undermine the credibility of regional exit threats and create powerful new demands for fiscal centralization. Decentralization of taxation increases economic competition among regions and, all else equal, this is likely to result in smaller government – and hence less cushioning of adverse economic shocks through fiscal policy. In more integrated economies, these shocks are perceived to be larger and less predictable, exacerbating the demands for governmental redistribution of wealth and risk. Regional governments know that centralized fiscal systems are likely to deliver the most stabilization and fiscal redistribution in favor of their citizens. Moreover, we have argued that the central government may get more involved in regional redistribution as a way of placating regions that stand to lose from trade integration.

Undoubtedly there are some regions for which globalization has raised the costs of fiscal centralization. The median voter in a relatively wealthy region is likely to prefer a more decentralized fiscal system than the median voter in a poor region (Bolton and Roland 1997), and the median voter in a persistently disadvantaged region will prefer less insurance than the median voter in a more productive, diversified region (Persson and Tabellini 1996b). Indeed, in accordance with the logic of Bolton and Roland (1997), the Italian North and the wealthy German states like Baden-Württemberg and Bavaria are growing increasingly weary of paying into centralized risk-sharing and redistribution schemes that benefit others. They prefer fiscal decentralization, and apparently are willing to push hard for it. It is unlikely, however, that they will win. As we have argued, the stakes have also been raised for the poorer, less diversified, or smaller and more vulnerable jurisdictions (e.g. Sicily, Saarland and Bremen) whose residents believe they have more to fear in a world of integrated markets.

Moreover, there is considerable support for our argument in the evolution of the European Union. In the 1985 deal to complete the internal market, the member states agreed to introduce a new system of development assistance to poorer regions of Europe. The 1992 Maastricht treaty that set the European Union on the course to the creation of the euro was accompanied by a large increase in this development assistance. The combination of 1992 and the euro render Europe the closest example we have of a completely open international market. But its creation generated risks, particularly for less well-off areas. As a result, the *central* EU budget was expanded considerably to pay for these fiscal transfers. Of course, the EU's budget is still only a tiny portion of European output. Our argument predicts that, in the future, demands for a larger EU fiscal authority will grow appreciably, especially from the most vulnerable.

Of course, the EU's budget has been the subject of considerable debate and acrimony among member governments in recent years, and strife over the renegotiation of intergovernmental fiscal contracts is growing in other countries ranging from Brazil, Argentina and India to Germany and Canada. The fault lines are the same – poor and vulnerable jurisdictions desire increased risk-sharing and redistribution while wealthy or well-positioned jurisdictions desire less. This fact is consistent with both the conventional wisdom about increased credibility of exit threats and our countervailing argument about increased perception of risk. But neither the existing literature nor our chapter provides a satisfactory positive theory of the conditions under which the wealthy or poor regions are likely to win these battles. The next steps in a positive theory of globalization and the vertical movement of fiscal authority are a more careful examination of the geographic distribution of risk and an assessment of the political institutions through which such battles are fought.

First, consider some simple demographic facts. Regional income disparities within countries around the world are often staggering, and in developing countries especially, regional inequality is on the rise (Shankar and Shah 2000). Poor regions almost always vastly outnumber the wealthy, and small rural jurisdictions are very frequently over-represented in legislatures (Samuels and Snyder 2000). In most developing countries, the lion's share of economic activity is concentrated in only one or two "urban giants" (Ades and Glaeser 1995; Henderson 2000). Unless the relatively wealthy (often urban) jurisdictions can threaten to bring down the regime through riots or credibly threaten to secede, there are few reasons to expect that vastly outnumbered wealthy regions can defeat the poor regions who prefer higher levels of risk-sharing and redistribution.

To better understand the conditions under which globalization leads to fiscal centralization or decentralization, it is necessary to examine more carefully the institutions through which regions are represented in the central government's decision-making process. For example, at one extreme, a country like Israel has no territorial aspect to representation and policymaking at all – it is a unitary system with one national electoral district and an integrated national party system. At the other extreme are Brazil and the European Union, federations in which small states are vastly over-represented in both chambers of the legislature, and political parties do little to create incentives for cross-jurisdiction cooperation. Fiscal policies in the latter type of system are more likely to be chosen through a process of regional intergovernmental bargaining than simple majority rule (Cremer and Palfrey 1999). Persson and Tabellini (1996a) hypothesize that this type of intergovernmental bargaining will lead to lower levels of centralized insurance than systems where risk-sharing schemes are chosen by majority rule with one-person-one-vote.

The European Union provides a good example of the importance of representation schemes in mediating battles over risk-sharing and redistribution. In contrast to other federations, the EU has not developed a full blown centralized risk-sharing scheme to rival other large federations (notwithstanding its innovations with respect to fiscal support for poorer regions). Under the current highly confederal configuration, however, the creation of such a system would require the consent of every state, including the wealthy states that are net contributors. It would be much more difficult for wealthy states to rebuff demands for greater risk-sharing and redistribution however, if, for example the European Parliament, using a simple majority decision rule, had exclusive authority over fiscal policy.

Future research might build from our findings, drawing on more refined institutional arguments to pinpoint the demographic and institutional conditions under which demands for more centralized risk-sharing overwhelm demands from wealthy states for greater fiscal decentralization. Such studies might try to improve on the blunt measure of fiscal decentralization used in this chapter. Detailed cross-national data for a large number of countries on the size, conditionality and distribution of intergovernmental transfers would be extremely helpful. Additionally, improved efforts should be made to conceptualize and measure political decentralization across countries.[22]

Our arguments about risk-sharing and redistribution may or may not be the driving force behind the observed relationship between trade integration and fiscal centralization. We have also addressed the argument that globalization leads to decentralization by enhancing the credibility of secession threats of ethnic and linguistic minorities. While this seems plausible, we point out that the price would-be secessionist regions demand to stay within the federation might result, if anything, in fiscal centralization. Of course our empirical results do not prove this conjecture. These arguments should only apply in countries with regionally concentrated groups with distinctive preferences who make secession threats that are taken seriously. In the vast majority of our cases, however, such groups either cannot easily be identified, or their exit threats would not be viewed as credible by the central government. The best way to examine arguments about exit threats and fiscal (de)centralization is to limit the analysis to a smaller group of countries where such concentrated groups exist and their threats are taken seriously (see, e.g. Fearon and Van Houten 1998).[23] Future work might use disaggregated regional fiscal, political and demographic data to examine the interaction of trade, exit threats and distributive politics in such countries.

## Conclusion

Along with several other chapters in this volume, this chapter departs from previous studies of globalization and shifting locations of governance by considering not only a binary choice between secession and staying together, but also the distinct possibility of (de)centralization within countries. It also contrasts the likely effects of globalization on political and fiscal authority. The conventional wisdom that globalization strengthens the credibility of regional autonomy movements and puts pressure on central governments to cede *policy* control and *political* autonomy to local officials is quite plausible, though Van Houten (2003) finds no evidence of this in his European sample. But this chapter has argued that globalization may also encourage regions that choose to stay within countries to push for fiscal arrangements that better mitigate market risk for citizens within their borders. Consistent with this argument, the data analyzed above suggest that increased trade integration is associated with mild fiscal centralization.

While this finding presents an interesting challenge to a common hypothesis, it is probably most useful as an invitation to further research. Future studies should continue to distinguish between globalization's effects on political and fiscal decentralization, and explore more carefully the varieties of each. This chapter also points toward several mediating factors that deserve more rigorous analysis, including the distribution of income and risk across jurisdictions, and the roles of constitutions, legislative rules and partisan incentives.

## Notes

1 This is an updated version of a paper originally published in M. Kahler and D. Lake (eds) (2003) *Governance in a Global Economy: Political Authority in Transition*, Princeton University Press, 87–109. Above all, we have updated and expanded the data set used to conduct the empirical analysis.

2 For a discussion of the costs and benefits of this and other measures of decentralization, see Rodden (2004).

3 All public finance data are taken from the IMF *Government Finance Statistics Yearbook*, various years. Most of the averages shown in Table 11.1 are for the entire period specified, but because of missing data, some of the averages reflect slightly shorter periods. Note that intergovernmental transfers are not removed from the numerator (total subnational expenditures). This would be inappropriate because the IMF's distinction between grants and own-source local taxation is quite misleading if used in cross-national analysis. It is necessary, however, to subtract grants from the denominator (combined central, state, and local expenditures) to avoid double-counting the grants in the expenditures of the central and subnational governments.

4 A newer literature revisits the relationship between heterogeneity and the normative case for decentralization from a political economy perspective that explicitly attempts to model government behavior. Inman and Rubinfeld (1997), Lockwood (2002) and Besley and Coate (2003) examine the costs of centralization from a distributive politics perspective that highlights the importance of legislative bargaining and legislative rules.

5 Bolton and Roland (1997) emphasize a related trade-off. In their model, the benefits of coordination and economies of scale are traded off against the benefits of setting tax rates and determining redistributive transfers locally in societies with heterogeneous income levels across regions.

6 Data limitations make it very difficult for us to test our argument directly on taxation. However, we would expect globalization to be associated not only with higher levels of fiscal centralization in general, but also with an increasing mismatch between more centralized taxation and more decentralized spending.
7 For literature reviews, see von Hagen (1998), Kletzer and von Hagen (2000) and Obstfeld and Peri (1998).
8 Of course these arguments are complicated by the fact that within countries, different regions are likely to have different preferences over levels of risk-sharing and redistribution according to their output distribution. These issues will be discussed in greater detail below.
9 All of the above are taken from the World Bank, *World Development Indicators*, 2000.
10 We use the standard "ethno-linguistic fractionalization" (ELF) index used by other authors, even though we are quite skeptical about this variable. Originally published in the *Atlas Narodov Mira* (1964), it is included in Taylor and Hudson (1972), and reflects the likelihood that two randomly drawn people will be from different ethnic groups. The variable is fraught with conceptual and measurement problems, and is very likely out of date (Laitin and Posner 2000). We include it in order to replicate Panizza (1999).
11 The source is the *Polity 98* data set.
12 Regional elites have also played important roles in the protests and negotiations that have led to democratic transitions. In new democracies, decentralization is often an attractive political strategy for reelection-seeking politicians who wish to build or consolidate local bases of support (O'Neill 2003).
13 This variable is taken from Rodden (2002). Cases are coded as federal if they feature constitutional protections for states and state-based representation in an upper chamber of the legislature.
14 The source is the World Bank, *World Development Indicators* 2000.
15 Ibid.
16 For these between-effects models, this variable captures the percent of years in which open = 1.
17 Note that federalism does not mean that states and provinces are less dependent on transfers from the central government. Our spending variable does not distinguish between expenditures funded by own-source revenue and those funded by transfers. Rodden (2002) shows that subnational units in federal and unitary systems display, on average, similar levels of reliance on transfers from higher-level governments.
18 We have also included another variable – defense expenditures as a share of total spending – but it did not effect the results presented here and did not approach statistical significance, so we do not include it.
19 There are several potential reasons for the divergence with the earlier finding. Panizza (1999) uses single-year observations, and of the three years considered, the coefficient for ethnic fractionalization was only significant for 1985. Moreover, the sample is somewhat different.
20 The presence of a lagged dependent variable can bias the fixed-effects estimator even if the error term is not correlated over time. But in panels where the time-series dimension is long (as is the case here), the bias is rather small.
21 When one or more of the control variables is dropped (including GDP per capita and total expenditures, neither of which ever attains statistical significance), the trade and openness variables are highly significant using either dependent variable and virtually all estimation techniques. We also obtain larger coefficients for trade and openness when using a larger data set of over 60 countries, but we do not include these additional countries here because the GFS only provides very limited, non-overlapping year coverage.

22 For a good start, see Henderson (2000). For an overview of other attempts, see Rodden (2004).

23 It is worth noting that when we estimate the model presented in Table 11.4 including only the cases from our data set in which secession threats seemed reasonably credible – Belgium, Canada, India, Indonesia, Italy, Spain and the UK – the "trade" coefficient was negative, similar in magnitude, and significant at the 10 percent level.

## References

Ades, A. and Glaeser, E. (1995) "Trade and Circuses: Explaining Urban Giants," *Quarterly Journal of Economics*, 110/1: 195–227.

Alesina, A. and Spolaore, E. (1997) "On the Number and Size of Nations," *Quarterly Journal of Economics*, 112/4: 1027–56.

Alesina, A. and Wacziarg, R. (1998) "Openness, Country Size and Government," *Journal of Public Economics*, 69/3: 305–21.

Arellano, M. and Bond, S. (1998) "Dynamic Panel Data Estimation," unpublished paper, Institute for Fiscal Studies, London.

Atkeson, A. and Bayoumi, T. (1993) "Private Capital Markets in a Currency Union," in P. Masson and M. Taylor (eds) *Policy Issues in the Operation of Currency Unions*, Cambridge: Cambridge University Press.

Bardhan, P. and Mookherjee, D. (2000) "Relative Capture of Local and Central Government: An Essay in the Political Economy of Decentralization," Dept. of Economics, University of California, Berkeley; Dept. of Economics, Boston University.

Besley, T. and Coate, S. (2003) "Centralized versus Decentralized Provision of Local Public Goods: A Political Economy Approach," *Journal of Public Economics*, 87/12: 2611–37.

Bolton, P. and Roland, G. (1997) "The Breakup of Nations: A Political Economy Analysis," *Quarterly Journal of Economics*, 112/4: 1057–90.

Cameron, D. (1978) "The Expansion of the Public Economy: A Comparative Analysis," *American Political Science Review*, 72: 1243–61.

Cremer, J. and Palfrey, T. (1999) "Political Confederation," *American Political Science Review*, 93: 69–93.

Dahl, R. and Tufte, E. (1973) *Size and Democracy*, Stanford: Stanford University Press.

Diaz-Cayeros, A. (2000) "Decentralization of Taxation and Expenditure: A Latin American Phenomenon?" Paper prepared for the Conference, "Decentralization in Latin America," University of Minnesota, 11–12 February 2000.

Fearon, J. and Van Houten, P. (1998) "The Politicization of Cultural and Economic Difference: A Return to the Theory of Regional Autonomy Movements," paper presented at the Annual Meeting of the American Political Science Association, Boston, USA.

Fornasari, F., Webb, S. and Zou, H. (1999) "The Macroeconomic Impact of Decentralized Spending Deficits: International Evidence," Latin American and Caribbean Sector, Poverty Reduction and Development Economic Research Group, World Bank: Washington, DC.

Garrett, G. (1998) "Global Markets and National Politics: Collision Course or Virtuous Circle?," *International Organization*, 52: 787–824.

Giddens, A. (2000) *Runaway World*, New York: Routledge.

Haggard, S. (1999) "The Politics of Decentralization in Latin America," unpublished paper. UCSD.

Henderson, V. (2000) "The Effects of Urban Concentration on Economic Growth," *NBER Working Paper* W7503.

Inman, R. and Rubinfeld, D. (1997) "The Political Economy of Federalism," in D. Mueller (ed.) *Perspectives on Public Choice*, Cambridge: Cambridge University Press.

Inter-American Development Bank (1997) "Fiscal Decisionmaking in Decentralized Democracies," in *Latin America After a Decade of Reforms, Economic and Social Progress in Latin America Report*, Washington, DC: Johns Hopkins.

Kletzer, K. and von Hagen, J. (2000) "Monetary Union and Fiscal Federalism," Working Paper B1, Zentrum fur Europaische Integrationsforschung, Bonn.

Krugman, P. (1991) *Geography and Trade*, Cambridge: MIT Press.

Laitin, D. and Posner, D. (2000) "The Implications of Constructivism for Constructing Ethnic Fractionalization Indices," *APSA-CP* 12, 1: 13–17.

Lockwood, B. (2002) "Distributive Politics and the Costs of Centralization," *Review of Economic Studies*, 69: 1–25.

McGillivray, F. and Jensen, N. (2000)"The Political Determinates of Foreign Direct Investment," paper presented at the annual meeting of the American Political Science Association, Washington, DC.

Musgrave, R. (1959) *The Theory of Public Finance: A Study in Public Economy*, New York: McGraw-Hill.

Oates, W. (1972) *Fiscal Federalism*, New York: Harcourt Brace Jovanovich.

Obstfeld, M. and Peri, G. (1998) "Regional Non-adjustment and Fiscal Policy," *Economic Policy*, 26: 205–59.

O'Neill, K. (2003) "Decentralization as an Electoral Strategy," *Comparative Political Studies* 36/9: 1068–91.

Panizza, U. (1999) "On the Determinants of Fiscal Centralization: Theory and Evidence," *Journal of Public Economics*, 74: 97–139.

Persson, T. and Tabellini, G. (1996a) "Federal Fiscal Constitutions: Risk Sharing and Redistribution," *Journal of Political Economy*, 104, 5: 979–1009.

—— (1996b) "Federal Fiscal Constitutions: Risk Sharing and Moral Hazard," *Econometrica*, 64/3: 623–46.

Rodden, J. (2002) "The Dilemma of Fiscal Federalism: Grants and Fiscal Performance Around the World," *American Journal of Political Science*, 46/2: 670–87.

—— (2004) "Comparative Federalism and Decentralization: On Meaning and Measurement," *Comparative Politics*, 36/4: 481–500.

Rodden, J. and Rose-Ackerman, S. (1997) "Does Federalism Preserve Markets?," *Virginia Law Review*, 83/7: 1521–72.

Rodrik, D. (1998) "Why Do More Open Economies Have Bigger Governments?," *Journal of Political Economy*, 106/5: 997–1032.

Sachs, J. and Sala-i-Martin, X. (1992) "Fiscal Federalism and Optimum Currency Areas," in M. Canzoneri, P. Masson and V. Grilli (eds) *Establishing a Central Bank: Issues in Europe and Lessons from the U.S.*, Cambridge: Cambridge University Press.

Samuels, D. and Snyder, R. (2000) "The Value of a Vote: Malapportionment in Comparative Perspective," *British Journal of Political Science*, 31/3: 651–71.

Scheve, K. and Slaughter, M. (2001) "What Determines Individual Trade-Policy Preferences?" *Journal of International Economics*, 54: 267–92.

Seabright, P. (1996) "Accountability and Decentralisation in Government: An Incomplete Contracts Model," *European Economic Review*, 40/1: 61–89.

Shankar, R. and Shah, A. (2000) "Bridging the Economic Divide within Nations: A Scorecard on the Performance of Regional Policies in Reducing Regional Income Disparities," unpublished paper, World Bank.

Taylor, C. and Hudson, M. (1972) *World Handbook of Political and Social Indicators*. New Haven: Yale University Press.

Treisman, D. (1999) "Fiscal Transfers and Fiscal Appeasement," in *After the Deluge: Regional Crises and Political Consolidation in Russia*, Ann Arbor: University of Michigan Press, Chapter 3.

Van Houten, P. (2003) "Globalization and Demands for Regional Autonomy in Europe," in M. Kahler and D. Lake (eds) *Governance in a Global Economy: Political Authority in Transition*, Princeton: Princeton University Press, 110–35.

von Hagen, J. (1998) "Fiscal Policy and Intranational Risk-Sharing," Working Paper B13, Zentrum für Europäische Integrationsforschung, Bonn.

Weingast, B. (1995) "The Economic Role of Political Institutions: Market-Preserving Federalism and Economic Development," *Journal of Law, Economics, and Organization*, 11: 1–31.

Wibbels, E. and Rodden, J. (forthcoming) "The Political Economy of Pro-cyclical Decentralised Finance," in P. Wierts (ed.) *Fiscal Policy Surveillance in Europe*, Cheltenham: Edward Elgar.

Yusuf, S. (2000) "Where the World is Heading Toward: Globalization, Localization, and the Pattern of Development," unpublished paper, World Bank.

# 12 Recentralizing while decentralizing

## How national governments re-appropriate forest resources

*Arun Agrawal and Jesse C. Ribot*

### Introduction

A prolonged period of institutional reforms has followed the fiscal crises of the developmental state in the 1980s, and the collapse of socialist economies since 1989. If one were to choose a single word to characterize the nature of institutional changes governments have instituted across many different sectors, that word would likely be "decentralization." More than 60 national governments in Africa, Asia and Latin America claim to have launched decentralization initiatives in policy arenas as diverse as development, environmental management, health care, welfare, education and credit provision (OECD 1997: 47). This chapter focuses on the environmental management sector via forestry cases and examines institutional changes four national governments have pursued: in Senegal, Uganda, Nepal and Indonesia. The chapter examines the role of different actors in pursuing such reforms, and shows how these reforms are incomplete in many ways. Our argument is based on a close examination of the mechanisms through which central governments attenuate the meaning of decentralization reforms even as they profess to practice them. We examine the pressures that lead central governments to yield reforms as policy concessions, and the political obstacles that the same governments use to reduce the exercise of meaningful local authority. The two main sources of pressures for reforms are international actors and local elite and decision-makers. Interested actors within central governments assist in realizing the pressures toward reforms, sometimes more willingly than others. The two main strategies central governments use to undermine the ability of local governments to make meaningful decisions are: by limiting the kinds of powers that are transferred and the domain in which such powers can be exercised; and by choosing local institutions that serve and answer to central interests.

Governments, donors, NGOs and theorists typically defend decentralization reforms on grounds of improved efficiency, equity, and responsiveness of bureaucracies to citizen demands (Blair 1998; Oates 1972; Tiebout 1956; Webster 1992). The underlying logic is that local institutions have better knowledge of local needs and, when endowed with powers, are more likely to respond to local aspirations. The belief in greater responsiveness is based on the assumption that local authorities have better access to information about their constituents and are more easily held accountable by local populations. Transfer of significant powers and "downward accountability" of local authorities are thus central to this formula (Agrawal and Ribot 1999; Ribot 1995a, 1996). Decentralization advocates also believe that the greater efficiency and equity along with local people's "ownership" of local decisions and projects will result in more effective local investments and management and ultimately in more socially and environmentally sustainable development.

But case studies of decentralization reforms suggest that the necessary institutional arrangements for the desired outcomes are rarely observed (Agrawal 2001; Agrawal and Ribot 1999; Larson and Ferroukhi 2003; Ribot 2002, 2003; Ribot and Larson 2004). Most decentralization reforms are either flawed in their design, or encounter strong resistance from a variety of political actors that erodes their effectiveness. We illustrate this observation by analyzing four different experiences of decentralization in the forestry sector. The cases we have selected are counted among the more innovative and visible of efforts to decentralize. Our objective is to examine comparatively the structure and outcomes of decentralization in these critical cases in relation to the justifications advanced for pursuing them, and show how calculations of political-economic gains affect decentralization processes. We document how central governments – ministries and frontline agents – often transfer insufficient and/or inappropriate powers, and make policy and implementation choices that serve to preserve their own interests and powers. Our comparative analysis suggests that fundamental aspects of decentralization, including discretionary powers and downwardly accountable representative authorities, are missing in practice.

This chapter is broadly empirical and comparative. It identifies common patterns and regularities across diverse cases from three continents. Our case discussion contributes to a more informed theoretical discussion of the reasons for the failure of decentralization initiatives. To motivate the presentation of our case studies, we first provide a working definition of decentralization, and outline the major justifications of decentralized decision-making. The second part of the chapter examines the main features of decentralization of forestry policy in the four cases, two each from Africa (Senegal and Uganda) and Asia (Nepal and Indonesia). In each case, we review articulated justifications of decentralization, the extent to which governments have actually decentralized decision-making and other powers regarding the environment and natural resources, the actors who have come to gain new powers, and some observable social and environmental outcomes. The ensuing section draws on the case evidence to examine the attenuation of decentralization initiatives and maintenance of centralized control. We conclude by focusing on key factors that would make decentralization reforms more effective.

## Definitions and justifications of decentralization

We define decentralization as any political act in which a central government formally cedes powers to actors and institutions at lower levels in a political-administrative and territorial hierarchy (see Mawhood 1983; Smith 1985). Devolving powers to lower levels involves the creation of a realm of decision-making in which a variety of lower-level actors can exercise a certain degree of autonomy (Booth 1995; Smoke 1993). *Deconcentration* (or administrative decentralization)[1] is said to occur when powers are devolved to appointees of the central government. In contrast, *political decentralization*[2] involves the transfer of power to actors or institutions that are accountable to the population in their jurisdiction. Typically, elections are seen as the mechanism that ensures this accountability.

We propose a definition of political decentralization that treats local accountability and discretionary powers centrally. If local authorities, whether appointed or elected, are made accountable to their superiors, the resulting reform can be termed *deconcentration*. This is because elections are often structured so as to make elected officials upwardly accountable. When powers are transferred to lower-level actors who are downwardly accountable, even when they are appointed, the reform is tantamount to *political decentralization*. Critical to understanding the process, then, is an empirical examination of the structures of accountability in which actors are located (see Agrawal and Ribot 1999).

The ability of accountable local authorities and governments to make and implement decisions is in some sense the defining feature of any effective decentralization. If local governments always must seek approval from superiors before undertaking an action, decentralization is meaningless. Discretionary authority for local governments is thus an integral part of any decentralization reform. If central governments grant local governments the rights to make and implement decisions but in practice withhold resources or otherwise check local ability to do so, then discretionary powers have not been effectively transferred. As the ensuing case analyses will show, central governments may use many different strategies to obstruct the real transfer of power.

Decentralized institutions are viewed as likely to perform better on the criteria of efficiency and equity for several reasons. Local authorities are presumed to have better time- and place-specific information which lead to better-targeted policies and lower transaction costs (Ostrom *et al.* 1993; World Bank 1997). Decentralization improves competition among jurisdictions and promotes greater political participation.[3] By channeling greater benefits to local authorities and local peoples, decentralization is believed to provide incentives for local populations to maintain and protect local resources. Bringing government decision-making closer to citizens, through decentralization, is widely believed to increase public-sector accountability and therefore effectiveness (Fox and Aranda 1996; World Bank 1997).

This implies that the purported benefits of decentralization are achieved through the establishment "of democratic mechanisms that allow local governments to discern the needs and preferences of their constituents, as well as provide a way for these constituents to hold local governments accountable to them" (Smoke 1999: 10). When these downwardly accountable local authorities also have discretionary powers – that is, a domain of local autonomy – over significant local matters, there is good reason to believe that the positive outcomes suggested by the previous theories will follow (Agrawal and Ribot 1999). We can infer, then, that if institutional arrangements include local authorities who represent and are accountable to the local population and who hold discretionary powers over public resources, then the decisions they make will likely lead to more efficient and equitable outcomes in comparison to the outcomes of decisions made by central authorities that are less representative or accountable.

Fundamentally, decentralization aims to achieve one of the central aspirations of just political governance – democratization, or the desire that humans should have a say in their own affairs.[4] In this sense, decentralization is a strategy of governance to facilitate transfers of power closer to those who are most affected by the exercise of power. In the rest of the chapter, we use "decentralization" as a shorthand for its political/democratic form.

## Case studies: decentralization in the forestry sector

A common narrative framework guides the following case descriptions of forest policy change so as to facilitate comparison. The exact presentation of the country case materials varies as a result of differences in timing and sequence of reforms, causal mechanisms, contextual factors and identity of actors. Typically, however, the history and context of decentralization sets the stage for a brief examination of its origins and justifications. We then describe the nature of reforms by identifying the local actors gaining powers and reviewing the kinds of powers they acquired. We describe the involvement of different international and local actors in the reform process. Each case discusses existing accountability mechanisms and provides available evidence about outcomes of reforms. The cases also describe the mechanisms through which the ability of local authorities to make decisions is undermined or limited. The process of reforms typically reveals central government priorities that differ significantly from the rhetorical claims defending the need for decentralization. Only rarely do the cases provide evidence for the emergence of downwardly accountable local decision-makers able effectively to exercise their powers.

We should add that the cases we have selected are not the only ones that could have helped make our point about limits on decentralization reforms and the mechanisms through which these limits are put in place. Studies in many other countries reveal similar findings.[5] Nor did we select the cases with a view to cherry-pick those that would best illustrate our argument. In significant measure, the selected cases are among the more important examples of decentralization in the developing world. Nepal, for example, is seen as a leader in initiating innovative decentralization reforms, after decades of experiments with different institutional arrangements. In the late 1990s and the early years of this century, Indonesia introduced among the most thoroughgoing decentralization of forest governance-related decision-making to the district level. Ironically, the level of decentralization is widely seen as being correlated with increased deforestation (Curran *et al.* 2004). Uganda's reform policy has been held up as a shining example by the international development community. And, finally, Senegal is considered a beacon of African democracy with one of the longer-standing decentralization processes – starting in the 1970s.

### *Senegal: decentralization to upwardly accountable local governments*

For much of the previous century, commercial access to Senegalese forests was mediated through concessions and permits directly handed out by the government ministries and agencies responsible for forests. Local authorities had no rights in these matters. Senegal's first forestry law to promote local "participation" was passed in 1993, aiming to integrate villagers into commercial forestry development, signaling a major change in past practices (RdS 1993, 1994). The 1993 law specified that "the rights to exploit forests and forest lands in the national domain belong to the State which can exercise them directly or grant them to third parties [concessions to private firms] or local collectives [elected local governments]" (RdS 1993: 1). This was a radical step forward. It gave elected rural councils the right to participate as concessionaires in forest exploitation and management.[6]

But, the conditions for participation gave rural councils little discretion. Rural councils could "participate" in the commercial exploitation of local forests if they agreed to implement imposed labors of forest management (a kind of participatory *corvée*). If they chose not to participate, they could or lose their forests to concessions (Ribot 1995a).[7] They had no right to choose to conserve their forests. Later in the decade, the government was forced to re-write the forestry laws to conform with the new 1996 decentralization laws. The 1998 new forestry law "intends first to transfer to local elected authorities power to manage forests" (RdS 1998: preamble). This progressive new law turned the situation around by decentralizing to the elected rural councils the right to stop production within their jurisdiction.

### *Actors involved in decentralization and their new powers*

The 1998 forestry code places the nation's non-reserve forests (called communal forests in this law) under the jurisdiction of the elected councils of regions and rural communities.[8] The enactment of this law followed significant demands from localities, and some pressure and financial assistance from international donors. Under the 1998 law, the rural councils of the rural communities (the most-local level of government) gained the rights to: develop management plans for the forests within their jurisdictions; determine whether or not commercial exploitation will take place within their jurisdictions; determine who can exploit commercial forest resources within their jurisdiction[9] – if they develop management plans (if they do not, the law is ambiguous as to whether the forest service can allocate or sell exploitation rights to others);[10] collect 70 percent of revenues from fines and the sale of products confiscated within their jurisdiction;[11] and add species to the protected species list.[12] The new code decentralizes significant authority by transferring commercial exploitation rights to the region or rural council,[13] and requiring approval of the president of the rural council before *any* exploitation can take place.

The new law gives the forest service and its agents the right to: determine whether a management plan or a work plan is valid within the specifications of the forest code; stop production if a plan does not conform to the forest code; allocate all production, storage and transport permits for commercial forest products; allocate professional licenses (*carte professionnelle d'exploitation forestier*) required for all commercial exploitation of wood or gum products; and give permission before rural councils or local producers can sell wood cut in forests under management plans and in non-managed forests.[14] In contradiction to the new rights specified for the rural councils, the forest service can auction off plots within the forests of local collectivities.[15] The minister responsible for forests[16] has the right to: set tax levels for all forest exploitation and to allocate access to the National Forestry Fund – which is fed by income from auctions and the sale of cutting plots.[17]

### *Powers devolved in practices*

By law local elected authorities now have the right to say no to commercial production. They also have significant rights to allocate access to productive opportunities. But, in practice, they exercise neither of these prerogatives. Despite the 1998 code, the minister and the forest service have retained almost all powers over commercial forestry decisions – they still decide how much production, where, when and by whom. Quota setting and allocation and the allocation of licenses and permits are the critical functions that determine who benefits from commercial extraction. These functions remain with the minister and the forest service.[18]

The 1998 law required the forest service to make a transition within three years (before 20 February 2001), from a quota fixed by the forest service and minister in consultation with commercial merchants, to a quota based on the estimated potential of each rural community forest based on an inventory done for the rural community's management plan (RdS 1998: arts.L76, R66). The law states that after the initial three-year period commercial production in non-managed areas [those areas not under a management plan in an area where the president of the rural council has signed] is illegal "except in exceptional and limited cases" (RdS 1998: art.L77). These exceptional cases, however, remain the rule. Only several forests are under management plans, and all of these are within areas covered by international donor projects. In addition, the code states that in all cases where exploitation of the sale of forest products takes place in non-managed areas, preference is to be given to the local populations (RdS 1998: art.L78). In current practice, the vast majority of rural communities – almost all of which have non-managed forests – still have no say.[19]

In practice, the forest service and Ministry determine a national charcoal production quota, where production will be permitted, when, and who has production rights. The quota is set at roughly half of urban demand, leaving a gap for the allocation of unofficial quotas that is later filled in by allocations made by the minister and by the forest service. For these actors, the difference between the quota and consumption represents a significant patronage resource. The official quota is divvied up among commercial cooperatives and firms by the minister with the council of the forest service and these commercial actors. Representatives of the rural councils, including the regional council presidents or their representatives are present in the official quota-fixing meeting, but they have no influence over its outcome. Their presence is consultative.[20] The regional council representatives are then asked to go back to the region and to call a meeting of rural council presidents and to "announce" the quota and its allocation – by cooperative, firm and by rural community.[21] Despite widespread local opposition to commercial production, the rural council presidents all sign off and permit production to begin. This procedure is the inverse of the bottom-up process outlined in the 1998 law.

### *Accountability and outcomes*

Legally, the rural council presidents could refuse to allow for production in their jurisdictions. But none have done so despite that the rural populations are widely against production in their zone (Ribot 1995b; Ribot 2000; Thiaw 2002; Thiaw and Ribot 2003). Interviews with rural council presidents revealed that they all feel compelled to sign off when the forest service asks them to. They are members of their political party, elected on party slates.[22] They appear to be accountable to the forest service and their political party, rather than the people who elected them. When asked why he did not exercise the rights he had under the new law, one rural council president explained: "The law is the state, the Forest Service is the state – what can we do?" Another gave an almost identical response. Yet another council president told us that he did not want to sign. He refused to sign for three weeks. Then, they "made me understand that it is better to sign." He refused to explain this statement. The president of another rural community explained that he has never been consulted concerning the fixing of the charcoal quota, its distribution within his commune or who could have permits. He said he just signed the papers because "I knew I had no choice."[23]

Forest service agents felt very ambivalent about local management. The regional forest inspector in Tambacounda explained: "The legislation says that the Rural Council can refuse charcoal producers. But, charcoal is a national good. It is a strategic resource that is important for the government. There will be marches in Dakar if there are shortages."[24] It is easy to explain – through history of practice and through the politics of patronage, payoffs and profit – why the system is functioning as it is (Ribot 1998). Clearly there are vested interests in political and material gains and losses at every level of forest management and exploitation. It is harder to understand how local elected rural councilors, forest service agents and officials, international donors and their project personnel all tolerate or fall into line with the party in power. By not screaming foul every day, they are all supporting the ruling party's interest in denying the gaping inconsistencies between law and practice. These obvious contradictions indicate a strong unspoken upward accountability.

The forest service agents, who retain most powers over forest use and management, are upwardly accountable to the regional and national forest services. The only mechanisms that would make them accountable to the rural councils or rural populations is the required signature before production.

### *Uganda: decentralized powers, disappearing territorial jurisdiction*[25]

Uganda is widely cited as a model of decentralization in Africa (Bazaara 2002b; Saito 2000). During Uganda's civil war (1981–1986), the National Resistance Movement (NRM) set up a system of elected local governments called "Resistance Councils" (RCs). In 1987, after the NRM (now the ruling, and only, party) won the civil war, the Ugandan legislature gave the RCs official status as local governments (RoU 1987). The 1993 Local Governments (Resistance Councils) Statute,[26] the centrepiece of Uganda's decentralization reforms, aimed "to increase local democratic control and participation in decision making, and to mobilize support for development which is relevant to local needs" (RoU 1993).[27] In addition, the Ugandan constitution states that the decentralization of government functions and powers will be a guiding principle for the state, with the express purpose of ensuring people's participation and democratic control in decision-making (Muhereza 2001: 3). It is evident that local pressures for reform, especially during and after the civil war, played a significant role in the establishment of new local administrative political bodies, and in the transfer of new powers of environmental governance.

Uganda has a number of large forest areas and forests play an important role in local economies. Following donor (mainly USAID) pressures, large areas of forests were transformed into national parks in 1991. Several of the new national parks are quite well known: Mt. Elgon, Kibale, Mgahinga and Bwindi Impenetrable Forest National Park are examples. They serve as nature conservation reserves in which commercial logging is forbidden. In 1995, the Local Governments (Resistance Councils) Instrument of 1995 was amended so that all forest reserves with an area of more than 100 hectares, mines, minerals and water resources were defined as central government resources.[28] The amendment effectively centralized the management of all forest reserves.[29]

### *Nature of powers devolved*

In 1998 the Forest Reserves (Declaration) Order divided forests into Central Forest Reserves (CFRs), the control of which was retained by the central government and Local Forest Reserves (LFRs) whose control was passed to local governments.[30] The powers of local governments are limited to management and control functions in Local Forest Reserves.[31] All CFRs are "protected" areas in which commercial activities are not permitted. In buffer zones around CFR, where commercial activities are permitted, the private sector, civil society organizations and local governments can enter into co-management agreements at the discretion of the Forest Department.

The districts have powers to issue licenses for cutting, taking, working or removal of forest produce from open land that is not a central forest reserve. In addition, they can, with the approval of the minister, convert lands occupied by a community as a village forest. Village forests are controlled by people appointed by the local authorities, and the authority also has the right to make rules for using, protecting, and managing the forests within its jurisdiction (Muhereza 2001: 18). Revenues from these forests are part of the funds of local authorities, and are supposed to be used for community welfare. These powers were a result of the 1964 Forest Act. But all unallocated privileges, rights, title, interest or easements in forest reserves, embodiments of absolute ownership, are vested in the central state.

About 70 percent of Uganda's forested area falls outside of parks and reserves (personal communications, Bill Fischer, DFID, 2001). Much of this area is private forests (Muhereza 2001: 20). But non-gazetted and non-titled lands, for the most part, are effectively in the "public domain." The Draft National Forestry and Tree Planting Bill (2002) has recognized this problem and permitted the creation of private natural or plantation forests in accordance with the 1998 Land Act.

### *Mechanisms that limit local authority over forests*

The translation of the different pieces of legislation into practice opens up spaces for centralized control even in the context of rhetorical claims about decentralization. The case of Masindi District[32] illustrates the point. Following the differentiation of the forest estate into central and local forest reserves in 1995, and a subsequent re-centralization of all forests designated as Central Forest Reserves, local authorities in Masindi became apprehensive about the loss of revenues from licenses, fees, fines and other royalties generated from central reserves. Their apprehensions were not unfounded. The 1997 Local Government Act transferred management functions over local forest reserves to the district and sub-county councils (Muhereza 2003: 6). The 1998 Forest Reserves Order further restricted their functions by reducing local government territorial jurisdiction.

The Order affected the management of 17 forests in Masindi that were re-classified as central forest reserves.[33] By May 2000, only two of the local forest reserves – Kirebe (49 hectares) and Masindi Port (18 hectares) – remained under district council jurisdiction. Six other local reserves were returned to the Kingdom of Bunyoro-Kitara in May 2000. In 2001, the Kingdom also gained the Masindi Port eucalyptus plantation, leaving only the Kirebe Forest to the Masindi District Council.[34] One new village forest was established in 1999 in Alimugonza village with the help of a USAID-funded conservation and development project. In 2002, the forest still did not have clear rules of use and management and was being governed in an ad hoc fashion (Muhereza 2001: 17–19).

As the Masindi case illustrates, decentralization initiatives in Uganda have granted local government significant forest use and management powers, but often left them with virtually no forests. Centralization of some forests, privatization of others, commercial concessions over yet others, and slowness in the passage of rules to manage local forests has severely curtailed the territorial jurisdiction over which local authorities can exercise their decentralized power.[35]

### *Accountability and outcomes*

Muhereza (2003: 11) also points out that many of the meaningful powers in commercial forestry were privatized or given to customary authorities – reducing the scope for public accountability. In the Bunyoro Kitara Kingdom, the king appointed loyal elders to a "Cultural Trust" to manage the kingdom's forests. Since the Trust was accountable to the King, people living around the forests in question found their needs routinely ignored. Forest villagers expressed resentment in many ways, even going as far as burning trees in protest against greater limits on access to the forests (see also Bazaara 2002a: 20).

The revenues of local authorities have increased to a significant extent in some parts of the country as they have gained rights over revenues from fees for reserves and commercial activities. The revenues of sub-counties have increased less since many sub-county councilors are not aware that they can gain a share of the revenues (Muhereza 2003: 21–2). But it is commercial groups who have gained significant power through privatization. Some of them have even been able to influence forest management policies in specific localities (Muhereza 2003). It must also be noted that even when the laws and the forest service do not give local councils clear rights, decentralization reforms have emboldened local governments to contest policy. Bazaara (2002a: 15) describes local governments as being "locked in conflicts with the central government over who should wield the power to issue permits and what proportions of the resources generated from fees and taxes should go to local government." Overall however, the discretionary powers of local governments remain low. Changes on paper have not been matched by on-the-ground realities, and subsequent legislation has often served to undermine the extent of territorial control that local governments can exercise.[36]

### *Nepal: subsistence as the rationale for community forestry*

The kingdom of Nepal nationalized all Nepali forests in 1957 in a centralizing effort to control actions and outcomes related to forests. This assertion of control was cemented through a series of measures between 1961 and 1970 when the state tried to curtail even the use rights of rural residents. In the absence of effective monitoring and enforcement systems, however, the new laws had perverse effects. They undermined existing local systems of management and led to widespread deforestation as people came to view forests as state property.[37] The overwhelming evidence of deforestation showed that the existing policy needed rethinking.

Today Nepal is often seen as a leader among developing countries in setting conservation goals and priorities, and creating progressive programs and legislation related to resource management and conservation (Heinen and Kattel 1992). New steps toward decentralization of forest control began in the late 1970s. The precursors of current community forestry legislation were the Panchayat Forest Rules of 1978 and the Community Forestry program of 1980.[38] The limited conservation objectives of these initiatives were revised when the government realized that deforestation was approaching epidemic proportions. The pace of reforms accelerated with the widespread movement for democratization, and the restoration of democracy after 1990. The current framework for community forestry legislation is represented by the Master Plan for the Forestry Sector in 1989, the Forest Act in 1993 and new Forest Regulations of 1995. Under the impact of these new pieces of legislation, the area of forests managed by local user groups and the number of these groups has increased exponentially. International donor NGOs and the funds they have made available for the pursuit of decentralized forestry in Nepal have been crucial to the new reforms. Thus, the creation of decentralization reforms in forestry policy was a result in Nepal both of local pressures, some interest among central government actors, and substantial groundwork and aid by international donors.

*Nature of powers devolved*

The major objectives of the new legislation are to provide forests to willing community groups, especially in the hill areas, and establish and promote community plantations in open and degraded areas. The overall goal of decentralization of forestry policy is to:

1 reduce deforestation;
2 provide greater benefits to local users and managers;
3 reduce costs of administration;
4 enhance participation by common Nepali villagers in the process of forest management.

The creation of local authorities to manage forests takes place with a significant involvement of the forest department. Community user group members are identified by the district forest officers. These user groups then prepare their own constitutions that govern day-to-day functioning and management. Following the demarcation of a forested area that can be handed over to a community, a five-year operational plan is prepared for the forest. User groups frequently play a direct role in preparing and implementing the plan.[39] The district forest officer can hand over any part of a national forest to a user group in the form of a community forest, entitling it to develop, conserve, use and manage the forest, and to sell and distribute forest products by independently fixing the price in the market. User groups can thus legally use their forests for subsistence, cultivating non-timber forest products, growing trees and harvesting forest products for commercial processing and sale. Users are not permitted to clear the forest for agricultural purposes. But control over commercial profits from sale of timber products is already a major departure from forestry policies around the world.

Executive committees of ten to 15 members are elected by the general membership of the Forest Panchayat Committees. They undertake most of the everyday tasks associated with the management of the community forest. These tasks include protection of the forest (either directly or by a guard the user groups appoints), allocation of both commercial and subsistence benefits from the forest, steps to improve the condition of vegetation cover, and sanctioning rule breakers. Rural residents in many areas have begun to generate substantial benefits from their community forests, including cash revenues. Revenues are not taxed, but user groups are required to spend 25 percent of all cash income on collective development activities.[40]

### *Accountability and outcomes*

The main mechanism of accountability of local decision-makers to users is the election process through which committees are constituted. Elections are highly politicized. Many of the panchayat elections have been characterized by political polarization and infighting among community-level decision-makers.

By 1999, the new legislation had led to the formation of 8,500 community forest user groups comprising nearly a million households. These user groups were managing more than 6,200 sq kms of forests. This is about 10 percent of the total forest area of Nepal. Unofficial estimates of these numbers are even higher. New user groups are being formed at the rate of nearly 2000 a year and they are now active in 74 out of 75 districts of Nepal. In some areas of Nepal hills, a slow reversal of earlier deforestation can also be witnessed (Mahapatra 2000; Varughese 2000).

Community-level decision-makers are able to use all the products from their forests, buy and sell in markets, manage how the forest is to be used, and finally, change everyday rules for managing forests. In the Middle Himalaya in Nepal, where the community forestry program is the most widespread, rural households have begun to rely on forests to a greater extent for their livelihoods. But a potential problem is the question of succession. At present most groups, mainly because they have been formed relatively recently, have the same leaders that were selected at the time of their creation. As the groups grow older, issues of who will lead the group, and how transitions will occur will become increasingly important.

### *Mechanisms limiting local authority*

Although there has been widespread appreciation of the Nepalese effort to decentralize control over forests through its community forestry program, some significant problems have emerged since the late 1990s. The program has been implemented mostly in the middle hills of Nepal. The lower plains in the Terai region, which contain more valuable timber trees, have few forest panchayat committees, and the government seems not to have any intentions of extending the spatial scope of community forestry legislation.

An important development in Nepal community forestry is the emergence of a nationwide federation of community user groups (FECOFUN or Federation of Community Forestry Users of Nepal), that seeks to lobby the government on behalf of its members, and to disseminate information about community forestry more widely (Britt 2000). It has already led active protests against government signals that users' rights to commercial profits from forests may not be available in the Terai region of Nepal (because Terai forests are commercially more valuable). Indeed, efforts by the government to limit commercial use of community forest products to only the hill regions of Nepal signify the limits of the willingness of forest departments to devolve control. They also demonstrate that, in the absence of influence at the national level, the ability of local user and manager groups can be limited quite easily. The presence of strong commercial interest in the valuable timber trees in the Terai have helped limit the extension of community forestry. Government hopes of foreign exchange and revenues from large timber harvesting companies operating in the region have meant that claims of communities to these same forests have found little attention among government officials.

### *Indonesia: the limits of regional autonomy*[41]

Decentralization of forestry policy in Indonesia has taken place in the context of a history of highly centralized commercial exploitation of forest resources, widespread demands for regional autonomy by various provinces and the presence of many different actors competing for revenues from timber-rich forests. Recent legislation for decentralization is embodied in two main acts concerning regional governance and sharing of funds. Both these laws have come into force in the last two years and are beginning to have a profound impact on how different actors use and attempt to appropriate benefits from forests. These laws, in no small measure, have been enacted as a result of perceived demands from regional and provincial actors interested in greater control over revenues from forests.

#### *Main actors*

The main actors involved in decentralization are the central government and its agencies, regional governments and legislative bodies, and NGOs and media organizations. Decentralization of decision-making powers over forests has sought to include district-level municipalities rather than provincial governments as important partners because many provinces have made secessionist demands, and districts are seen as less likely to have separatist aspirations. Local capacity at the district level is limited.

Most of the decision-making authority for forests has been transferred to the districts rather than the provinces, based on the justification that district governments are closer to the people. Hence they are seen as better placed to make decisions and provide public services that would be in accordance with citizens' needs and aspirations. District leaders, *bupatis*, instead of reporting to provincial governments, are now elected by and accountable to local legislative assemblies, which have become more powerful. Changes have also occurred at the village level, with the creation of the Village Representative Body.

### *Nature of powers transferred*

Some of the dynamics of reforms are easy to understand. The local bodies that have been empowered are uncertain about the permanence of their powers in light of the long history of centralized government. This is in part because of conflicting interpretations of the law. For example, it is not clear who actually has authority over which forests: article 7 of the 1998 Regional Governance law suggests that authority remains with the central government, while article 10 states that regions are authorized to manage natural resources within their territories. The Ministry of Forests has argued that local governments do not have the expertise or capacity to manage the country's forests. Clarifications outlined by the implementing regulation (no. 25/2000) have only set out the responsibilities of the provincial and central governments, the implicit assumption being that authorities beyond those mentioned in the regulation belong to district governments.

One of the most controversial powers handed over to district governments was the right to authorize small-scale (100-hectare) logging licenses. The response by many local governments was to offer a proliferation of such licenses, even in areas where it was prohibited to do so, such as in the designated areas of large concessionaires. Protests by concessionaires led the Ministry of Forestry to repeal their earlier decision.

Indeed, many of these issues are still in the process of being clarified as provinces resist the stripping of their powers, central ministries contest the extent to which district authorities are autonomous, and district officials enter the process of transition toward a more decentralized political decision-making.

The new decentralization laws have also expanded the regulatory functions and political powers of district authorities, and also enabled them to raise taxes to meet budgetary and development needs. Scores of district governments have come together to form an association called the APKASI[42] to share information, improve communications and strengthen their position through the process of regional autonomy. For their part, provincial governments have also created a new organization called the APPSI with similar objectives at the provincial level. These associations take up various administrative issues in addition to forestry.

### *Outcomes*

Sharing of revenues from natural resources has proved a highly contentious issue, especially in resource-rich regions with oil, gas and forests. In contrast to the earlier revenue-sharing formula where the center retained 30 percent of revenues and 70 percent went to the provinces, the current legislation provides for 64 percent of revenues for the districts (with 32 percent for the producing district and the remaining 32 percent for other districts and towns in the province), 20 percent for the center, and only 16 percent for the provinces. Disputes also surround the allocation of the lucrative reforestation funds. Districts have complained about the amount they are allocated, the calculation of specific allocations and delays in receiving their share of payments.

Decentralization reforms, in addition to producing disputes over revenue-raising and allocation, have also generated new timber regimes at the district level. Districts have used their new authority to authorize small-scale concession permits and timber extraction and utilization rights, to charge taxes on goods transiting through their territory and on forest enterprises, and to attract new investment. The net result of contradictory laws and decrees is that each actor defends its position based on a different law. For example, despite the revocation of the power of district governments to issue 100–hectare permits, some district governments have continued to issue them. Since the *bupatis* at the district level are no longer located in a hierarchy below provincial governors, lobbying by large concessionaires at the provincial level to limit the issuance of these permits has failed. These permits generate significant revenues, sometimes in the range of millions of dollars. In the race to gain as much revenue as possible in this uncertain period, it seems the goal of environmental conservation or forest protection is fast sliding into oblivion.

District authorities have little interest in forest conservation in comparison to their interest in expanding their income sources and increasing the level of funds to which they have access. They favor logging and deforestation even when illegal: these activities still provide employment and generate second order growth. With legal rights to hand out logging concessions, they prefer enacting their preferences over the diffuse influence of conservation NGOs or conservation-minded officials. Protected areas represent a foregone opportunity for raising revenues. Since decentralization has for the most part helped local populations generate greater revenues through exploitation rather than conservation, it is difficult to see how it will lead to better protection. Conservation through decentralization to the districts faces major challenges: illegal logging, reclassification of land and conversion to agriculture (Resosudarmo 2004: 112).

The experience of decentralization as it has occurred until now suggests that additional monitoring capacity and regulatory agencies will be needed to convert the potentially higher protection capacity of local governments into greater protection. Decentralization has increased some tangible economic benefits to local communities, but only because of the mining of natural resources. Greater access of local groups to forests, higher revenues to district governments, and more authority to exercise decision-making powers have been achieved without adequate controls over what happens to forests and without any incentive structures that might encourage longer-term sustainable use and management patterns.

It is evident that decentralization in Indonesia has happened without sufficient upward or downward accountability. It is not surprising that district authorities feel neither the pressure to protect forests in accordance with guidelines laid down by higher authorities, nor to incorporate local preferences into their decisions, except those that encourage earning revenues from forest resources that have been off-limits to locals for decades.

## Discussion: compromised decentralization reforms

The case analyses above show that the configuration of actors, powers and accountability relations that may constitute an effective decentralization reform in the forestry sector is hard to find in practice (also see Agrawal and Ribot 1999; Larson and Ribot 2004; Ribot 1999). The cases suggest that the political dynamics related to policy reforms play a crucial debilitating role in the divergence between the rhetorical claims for decentralization, the pressures from international donors and local actors in favor of meaningful reforms, and the institutional changes that actually take place. Consider briefly the principal dynamics we have outlined. In Senegal, the 1998 decentralized forestry code enables local councils to determine whether or not commercial production takes place and to determine who can exploit the forests. But, the central government (the party, ministry responsible for the environment, and the forest service) forces councils to continue commercial production even against the expressed will of those who elected them.[43] Further, despite contrary provisions in the new code, production quotas are still set and allocated by central authorities who use them to reward supporters of the new ruling party. Local councilors appear primarily accountable to their political and administrative superiors.

In Uganda, changes in central government and the civil war led to significant initial steps toward decentralization of authority. But the center reasserted control by severely curtailing the territorial jurisdiction of local authorities. With only insignificant areas of forests over which to exercise their newly gained powers and governance functions, local governments remain disenfranchised – what is given by one law is taken back through another. Some local councils earned revenues at the beginning, but the gains were short-lived.

In Nepal, the government decentralized a variety of powers over forests in the Middle Himalayas, both as a result of local needs, and donor funds made available by a variety of international agencies. Forests play a critical role in the subsistence of villagers. But the government remains unwilling to decentralize control over *terai* forests that contain commercially valuable timber. The presence of international corporate timber interests that were willing to provide lucrative revenues to the national government reduces the likelihood of transfer of control over commercial revenues. Additionally, the continuing Maoist insurgency that is spreading through much of rural Nepal undermines any possibility of central willingness to pursue reforms that will strengthen localities. Decentralization in Nepal has remained incomplete in terms of the resources of local governments and the areas of forests they control.

In Indonesia, the national state undertook decentralization reforms in the context of increasing demands for regional autonomy from the provinces. To undercut the ability of the provinces to raise revenues from sale of valuable timber resources, it created thoroughgoing legal instruments that empower district-level authorities. It has installed mechanisms of accountability that further weaken provincial executive authority by making district executive authorities horizontally accountable to legislative assemblies at the same level rather than upwardly accountable to provincial authorities or downwardly accountable to their constituents. The multiple, competing, and sometimes violently conflicting claims over forests in the entire country, eviscerate the ability of any authority to protect timber. The politics of national cohesion has undermined any environmental public goods that new decentralization policies supposedly produce.

It is clear, then, that in many of the cases, the underlying reasons for the initiation and implementation of decentralization reforms are quite different from the explicitly stated objectives of reforms, and a result there is a vast gulf between the articulated policy and enacted practice of decentralization. While the ostensible reason to pursue decentralization lies in greater efficiency, more thoroughgoing equity, and more democratic local participation, it is political-economic calculations and pressures that actually prompt – and thus shape – reforms (Agrawal *et al.* 1999). In Indonesia and Uganda, decentralization was forced onto the agenda because of demands from powerful provincial actors who sought a share in decision-making or in revenues that could be generated from sale of forest timber. But the very strength of these actors, coupled with their unreliability in being a part of political designs of central political actors, meant that the reforms were designed in such a way as to undermine provincial secessionist movements and political leaders.

In Senegal and Nepal donor pressures played an important role in the initiation of decentralization reforms. Interestingly, thus, globalization of ideas and resources, as represented in the common agenda of a number of international donors, has a strong bearing on the global pursuit of decentralization. Although donors have been influential in getting the idea of decentralization placed on national agendas, they have been far less effective in ensuring adequate implementation of transfer of powers because of a lack of capacity for (or perhaps even interest in) close supervision of the reform process as it is enacted. Certainly, most central governments do not want to subject themselves to such supervision. In both Indonesia and Nepal, central governments wanted to use decentralization as a means to promote industrialization based on forest products at least as much as they wanted to empower local governments. The fact that donors were willing to support and subsidize decentralization helped place the issue on the agenda and facilitated some initial steps toward reform. But ultimately, the corporate-industrial pressures for a share in the gains to be made from cutting forests have proved to be significant enough to prevent local decision-makers from gaining meaningful control over forests. Such differences between intent and practice account in significant part for the divergence between the positive rhetoric that defends the creation of decentralization reforms and the negative experiences one encounters on the ground.

On the one hand, the four cases above illustrate the reasons central governments are pressured toward reforms: demands from localities (Uganda); resources that international donors make available (Indonesia, Nepal); desire to undercut the power of competing factions at provincial or other levels (Indonesia, Senegal). On the other hand, the cases also highlight the specific mechanisms that central governments use to limit the scope of reforms and ensure that outcomes of reforms will not threaten existing political authority.

It is worth considering these specific mechanisms in greater detail because they are so commonly involved in the undermining of decentralization reforms. They can be grouped into two structural types. The first concerns the kinds of powers that local actors gain and the constraints on these powers; the second concerns the type of local actors who gain powers, and the accountability relations within which they are located (Ribot 2003; Ribot and Oyono 2004).

### *Powers and constraints*

Among the most important limits on local authority is the lack of control that local decision-makers have over raising or spending significant levels of resources, or deciding about the fate of high-valued resources. That is, few local governments have the right to allocate revenue-rich commercial rights to exploit forests; more often, they gain the power to allocate commercially irrelevant use rights for products such as fodder and firewood. Where they have rights to a share in timber revenues, gaining access to the local share, which usually passes through centrally controlled funds, is typically cumbersome. Central governments seldom give up control over the allocation of lucrative opportunities, even when central expertise is unnecessary for such allocation (Bazaara 2003; Fairhead and Leach 1996). Transfers of revenues from parks and natural resources fees sometimes seem to be an exception to the rule that central governments are averse to giving up control over commercial revenues. But it should be kept in mind that these fees usually represent a small fraction of resource profits, even if they comprise significant amounts of income for poorly funded local governments. And, in practice, we often find that central governments fail to return the local share in its entirety, or do so after significant time lags (Larson 2002).

One reason central governments resist local fiscal autonomy is simply that such steps are also a loss of political control. But in some of our cases, the unwillingness of central governments to permit local autonomy is related to existing threats to national integrity. Secessionist demands in Indonesia, and the Maoist insurgency in Nepal mean that central government political actors are all the more unwilling to give up control over revenues to local actors. The joint pressures from international donors in favor of greater efficiency through decentralization, and local actors interested in greater ability to use resources as they see fit tend to be vitiated on the rock of central-level unwillingness to make meaningful concessions when such concessions also simultaneously threaten the territorial integrity of the state.

Decentralizations are also constrained by the lack of information provided to local governments about the new reforms. This compromises their ability to make demands on the central government and also their capacity to manage resources effectively. In Nicaragua, for example, where logging contracts are managed by the state Forestry Institute, municipal councils are often unaware of the number and extent of logging operations operating in their jurisdictions. But municipal governments may also be unaware of their rights and responsibilities – a problem compounded by the lack of legal clarity. Indeed, if municipal governments are sometimes unaware of their rights, the same is even truer for local populations. In Senegal, few villagers even know that local leaders can make decisions over forests (Ribot 2004). Such lack of information makes a mockery of accountability even where local leaders are democratically elected.

The problem of lack of resources at the local level is compounded by the extent to which local governments typically get saddled with new responsibilities and tasks – the odium of management. The devolution of management responsibilities without corresponding funds to carry them out is common (Larson 2002; Ribot 1995). Unfunded mandates and failure to turn over mandated funds means that management tasks, instead of helping increase the discretionary powers of local governments, reduce their ability to undertake even those tasks that they had been carrying out prior to decentralization.

Central governments limit the scope of powers they transfer by instituting new patterns and systems of oversight, such that local authorities need permissions and clearances before their decisions can be implemented. Local powers over forest resources are often so highly circumscribed by supervision, or pre-determined through management planning requirements, that they hardly remain a "power." Instead of establishing a field of local discretion, central guidelines create new controls over implementation.

Spatial limitations on the jurisdiction of local authorities are another major way in which the effects of decentralization reforms are contained. All natural resources are located in space. By controlling the amount of space or territory over which local authorities can exercise even extensive powers, and effectively, it becomes possible to control the extent of decentralization. This is exactly what a number of governments have done in the cases we have described. While local authorities may, as in Uganda, have great powers over forests in the "local domain," the local domain may not contain much forest. In Nepal this domain is limited to the less-lucrative forests of the middle hills and in Indonesia to 100-hectare concessions (over which several local authorities may have a claim). Control over the remaining territory is usually retained by the central government. In other words, in those cases where local governments can exercise real powers, we find that their powers apply only to very small areas of forests or to low-valued products from forests.

Finally, central governments limit the ability of local authorities to exercise power by either creating ambiguity in their reforms, or by exploiting ambiguities inherent in all policy measures. Lack of legal clarity or a requirement that the local authority should coordinate its decisions with higher level officials make it easy for central departments and ministries to maintain control and ignore local government input. Legal ambiguities also make it very difficult for a local government to act because it may be taken to task for having undertaken an illegal action (Larson 2002).

On a case-by-case basis, the limitations on local powers that we describe may be seen as deviations or aberrations. But their presence across the different cases, and the similar effects they have on local governments suggests that the story is not quite simple. Rather than representing technical failures of adjustment in newly developed decentralization frameworks, they seem to be intentional mechanisms to serve the interests of those who are already in control.

### *Actors and accountability*

Another set of limitations on the effectiveness of decentralization reforms can be attributed to the nature of local authorities that come to exercise decentralized powers, and, in particular, their accountability relations. In the name of decentralization, powers are transferred to representative local governments, local administrative bodies of the central state, elected or appointed single-sector or single-purpose authorities or committees,

NGOs, customary authorities or private organizations or individuals. But if the fruits of decentralization depend on the extent to which these local bodies are accountable, competitive, participatory or well-informed, then surely the identity of the local authority makes a significant difference. Customary authorities, NGOs, appointed officials and private organizations are not elected and may not be particularly accountable. Certain groups may encourage participation, but more often they do not. Some are no better informed than central governments about locality-specific information. There is no reason to suppose that such local authorities, when they gain powers to make decisions, will perform well. But most importantly, the degree to which the empowerment of any of these local actors constitutes decentralization depends on the degree to which they are accountable to local populations.

In all of the case studies presented here, some management authority has been transferred to elected local bodies, although this is not the case in many other countries. This may, in fact, be one of the reasons that these four cases count among and stand out as examples of democratic decentralization, even if we find that the practice of decentralization does not meet its promise. However, one important problem our cases reveal is that although an electoral process can establish a degree of accountability, the depth of accountability relations depends on the type of elections and the extent to which they are competitive and regular. In Indonesia and Senegal local government officials are not elected as individuals but by party slate. In Uganda as well, local government candidates are selected by higher-level party leaders. Hence, elected leaders are at least as – if not more – upwardly accountable to these officials as they are downwardly accountable to local constituents. With the dissolution of democracy in Nepal, the local-level electoral process has been severely compromised. In addition, even where other accountability mechanisms exist, such as the resistance councils in Uganda, they do not work in practice if marginalized groups are unable to take advantage of them.

In any event, given the newness of the decentralization reforms we have discussed, and the frequent lack of familiarity of local populations with the electoral process, a full sense of accountability will emerge only as elections become institutionalized. The rough "two-changes-of-power rule" may apply as well to local elections – if so, there is little reason to suppose that, at this point in time, elections constitute a meaningful accountability mechanism. As the case studies show, other mechanisms of accountability that might supplement electoral ones – such as ombudsmen, active media reporting and effective judiciaries – are typically absent from the contexts we have described.

Again, central actors attempt to institute accountability mechanisms that channel effort and information toward superiors rather than downward toward constituents. The creation of downward accountability mechanisms is not just a way to generate greater participation through the practice of decentralization reforms – when effective, it also permits local decision-makers to create an autonomous power base. By being responsive to local demands, new decision-makers can become far more powerful than if they are beholden to their superiors for their position and revenues. Central governments recognize this all too well – it is not a coincidence, therefore, that decentralization reforms are accompanied by arrangements to create accountability patterns that keep upper level officials and politicians closely tied to local action.

## Conclusion

A large number of national governments claim to have initiated decentralization reforms, often under pressure from domestic local actors or international donors. In this sense, the occurrence of decentralization reforms in the arena of renewable resources as discussed in this chapter, illustrates the two-sided stresses that national governments face. International actors seek to increase the decision-making powers of local actors in the belief that devolution of powers will improve efficiency, generate greater equity and enhance participation. Local actors are themselves interested in greater autonomy and control over revenues because they can then deploy resources in the directions they wish without interference from superiors. Even if some central actors are sympathetic to such pressures, they also attempt to balance them against very real secessionist threats that can threaten the territorial integrity of a nation-state.

Therefore, at the same time as governments have claimed to initiate reforms, they have also tried to attenuate the reforms by transferring insufficient decision-making powers, and choosing inappropriate local institutional arrangements. Choices over powers and institutional arrangements are the basis of central government actions that compromise the process of decentralization in practice. Our comparative analysis, based on close attention to the complex ways in which decentralization reforms have unfolded in four important countries, reveals the combinations of mechanisms that various interested actors use to undermine decentralization reforms. The analysis shows that the political context of decentralization cannot be ignored. Our study also raises doubts about the underlying intentions of central government officials and politicians when they claim to decentralize and simultaneously create institutions that slow the pace of decentralization. Such double-faced policies reflect both a lack of faith in the capacities of the very people who are supposed to be empowered by decentralization reforms, and a clear desire to retain political control at the central level in the face of global pressures to decentralize that stem from international agencies, and local demands for greater control over revenues and decision-making authority.

There may be some grain of truth in arguments about lack of local capacity, absence of technical expertise to govern forests, and low levels of financial aptitude at the local level. But these arguments also seem to be more than a little self-serving. After all, the "science" of forestry in practice is often not so much science as much as a complex collection of bureaucratic procedures that can confuse the most capable of silvicultural experts. In any case, technical experts can be hired or consulted, if necessary, were local government to have access to sufficient financial resources. And finally, the record of central governments in managing finances or forests is scarcely one that elicits admiration. We conclude therefore that the calculus of interests and competition for power and revenues plays a much more compelling role in explaining the seeming paradox that central actors initiate decentralization reforms but simultaneously seek to hobble their effectiveness.

But the case descriptions above also show that the central state is not a monolithic actor. While some elements within the state pursue decentralization policies, others find their interests better served by resistance to decentralization. Indeed, the politics inherent in decentralization reforms means that alliances among different political actors can be formed across administrative levels of the state, and that actors at the same level – central, provincial, or local – are not necessarily united by a common set of interests (Agrawal *et al.* 1999). In this sense our comparative study of four cases illustrates the need for more careful attention to the many rivalries that set different groups within the state apart from each other. The literature on decentralization can gain important insights from institutional ethnographies of the decentralizing state. It is also important to note that resistance to decentralization comes from outside the government as well (see Ribot 2004; Ribot and Oyono 2004). NGOs and donors, by steering away from local government and emphasizing private and "civil society" institutions, can encourage institutional choices that compromise the establishment of the local democratic institutions that are the basis of effective decentralization.

To sum up, our comparative case analysis demonstrates that the experiments in decentralization of forest-related decision-making have not yet taken root, let alone borne fruit. Central governments, regardless of official rhetoric, policy and legislation, erect imaginative obstacles in the path of decentralized institutions and choices. However, decentralization reforms may be made more comprehensive by attending to four important issues. The first step obviously is to enhance the *awareness* of the ways in which specific arguments and mechanisms are used to compromise democratic decentralization, and to recognize that the real reasons behind those arguments and mechanisms are not the ones being stated.

Second, *downwardly accountable institutions* at various levels of governance can play an important role in meaningful decentralization. Mechanisms of accountability go beyond the electoral process. Multiple accountability mechanisms – providing information and enabling sanction – can be applied. At a minimum, they should include *information sharing* across governmental levels and with the general population, and *civic education* of local peoples and authorities so that people know what they can demand – what they can hold local authorities accountable for – and so local authorities know what they can offer.

Third, accountable local officials should possess *discretionary powers* that offer a secure domain of autonomous decision-making, and funding that allows these decisions to be implemented. Those powers, and the limits to them, should not be seen as simple technocratic or scientific judgments, but rather recognized as political decisions. Hence, a *broadly participatory political-institutional process* should be constructed through which such decisions could be debated.

Finally, in order to overcome central government resistance, *broad coalitions* that bring together a diversity of interest groups from different sectors of society and government could provide an effective institutional forum for the promotion of democratic decentralization. Such coalitions are needed to counter-balance the centralizing tendencies of national governments, and as such might serve as important political allies for the long-term development of a real, democratic decentralization. Whether such coalitions can actually emerge in practice depends in no small measure on the ability of international/global and local/regional actors to come together in their common desire for greater autonomy in favor of constituent units of the nation-state.

## Notes

1 "Bureaucratic decentralization" is another name for deconcentration. See Rolla (1998). Adamolekun (1991) points out that deconcentration often takes place in the name of decentralization. The two need not however be confused.

2 Political decentralization is also called *democratic decentralization* by some authors. See Manor (1999) and Blair (1998). When governments cede powers to non-state bodies such as private individuals or corporations, the process can be termed *privatization*, and we do not consider it decentralization. When, under governmental supervision, powers and specific responsibilities are allocated to public corporations or any other special authorities outside of the regular political-administrative structure, it is called *delegation*. See Ostrom *et al.* (1993).

3 See Breton (1996), Tiebout (1956) and Oates (1972). Webster (1992) is only one of the later figures to argue that decentralization can be seen as a means by which the state can be more responsive, more adaptable, to regional and local needs than is the case with a concentration of administrative powers.

4 Agrawal *et al.* (1999). Several authors (Nzouankeu 1994; Souza 1996) discuss the relationship between decentralization and democracy.

5 See Ribot and Larson (2004) for cases from Mongolia, China, Brazil, India, Indonesia, Bolivia, Cameroon, South Africa and Nicaragua. Also see Mapedza and Mandondo (2002) on Zimbabwe, Bazaara (2003) and Muhereza (2003) on Uganda, and Vallejo (2003) on Honduras. See Agrawal (2004) for a review of the extent to which decentralization reforms have led to an increase (typically limited increases) in local powers to govern forests in 52 developing countries.

6 The 1993 code was designed to make forest management more "participatory" through the inclusion of local governments as *possible* recipients of forest use

permits. RdS, "Projet de Decret Portant Code Forestier (Partie Reglementaire)" (Ministere de l'Environnement et de la Protection de la Nature, 1994), p.1.

7 The state practiced a double standard in that the rural councils were obligated to manage forests following detailed management plans while the commercial concessionaires did not have to conduct follow-up work. Further, the councils could not sell to anyone other than the commercial concessionaires who held professional licenses. See Ribot (1995a).

8 Regional and rural councils govern these local levels, with the rural community being the most-local unit.

9 They can engage individuals or any legally recognized group to exploit forests. Individuals, cooperatives, corporations and interest groups recognized by the government can apply to rural councils for permission to work in commercial forestry.

10 RdS (1998). Art.R29 allows the forest service to allocate the third parties. It is not clear in what cases this right applies.

11 The fiscal incentives here are perverse. Rural Councils have no right to tax the resource. Local councils can only profit from the control of illegal legal activities – which will give it an incentive to have illegal activities in its jurisdiction. If the council cleans up illegalities, it loses its income.

12 RdS (1998). Code Forestier, Loi No. 98/03 du 8 Janvier 1998, Décret No. 98/164 du 20 Février 1998. Ministère de l'Environnement et de la Protection de la Nature, Direction des Eaux, Forêts, Chasse et de la Conservation des Sols. Articles L7,L8,L10–17,L74,L77; and R63,R66. Also see Article R29 which contradicts some of these new powers.

13 There is no discussion of how the relevant level is determined, however, the only two levels mentioned in the code are the region and the rural community.

14 After an initial three-year period from the enactment of the forestry code, commercial production in non-managed areas is illegal "except in exceptional and limited cases" which can be authorized by the director of the Forest Service. RdS (1998: art.L77). At present these exceptional instances represent the vast majority of cases (personal communications with forest service agents and projects in Senegal).

15 This disposition is ambiguous. It is not clear from the code whether they need permission from the PCR to do so. See (RdS 1998: Art. R29).

16 The ministry has changed names several times.

17 Access to the National Forestry Fund will be defined by ministerial decree (RdS 1998: art.L6).

18 Observations based on field research and numerous interviews of foresters, rural councilors and rural council presidents, ministry of environment agents, forestry merchants, woodfuel wholesalers and donors in Senegal during 2002–2004.

19 Interviews with rural councilors in 2003.

20 Personal communication with a participant in last November's meeting. This participant, who wishes to be anonymous, mentioned that several merchants objected to the distribution of quotas, but were ignored.

21 Personal communications with the deputy to the President of the Regional Council of Tambacounda, and interviews with rural council presidents in the Tambacounda Region, November 2003.

22 Senegal's rural councils who receive most of the newly transferred powers are elected. These elections, however, do not make the council's representative accountable to local populations. Candidates for rural councils can only be presented for election by nationally registered political parties. The role of political parties in local government needs more in-depth examination. See Cowan (1958: 221). This is not a new phenomenon. A villager (in Koumpen-

toum, June 1994) explained: "the Councilors are chosen by Deputies in the National Assembly. Deputies choose people based on those who support them in their elections ... The Councils are chosen by the parties" (Ribot 2000). Hesseling (n.d.: 17) writes, based on her research in Senegal in 1983, that councils "are at times nothing more than sections of the Socialist Party [the party in power at the time]." Indeed, in 1994, the ruling Socialist Party dominated over 300 of Senegal's 317 rural councils. Elections in Senegal are structured to create upwardly accountable rural councils.

23 Personal communication, November 2003.

24 Personal communication, M. Faye, November 2003.

25 The research for this case was conducted and written up by Frank Muhereza (2003).

26 The Local Government (Resistance Councils) Statute, 1993, *Uganda Gazette* No. 55 Vol. LXXXVI, 31 December 1993.

27 Bazaara (2002a) explains this decentralization as the result of attempts to resolve regional conflicts and pressure from the World Bank, IMF and other programs.

28 Correspondence from Mr E. D. Olet, Commissioner for Forestry, to all district forest officers, 26 April 1995, Statutory Instrument 1995, No. 2; The Forest Reserves (Declaration) Order of 1998 (Statutory Instrument No. 63), Statutory Instruments Supplement No. 23 of 11 September 1998.

29 Local Governments (Resistance Councils) Amendment of Second Schedule (No. 2) Instrument of 1995.

30 Statutory Instrument No. 63 of 1998 revoked the Forest Reserves (Declaration) Order of 1968 or Statutory Instrument No. 176 of 1968.

31 Section 5(i) of the 1964 Forest Act.

32 Although many of the dynamics found in this district are reported elsewhere, generalizations are always subject to caution and qualification. We present the information from this case to show how it is possible to manipulate decentralization-related legislation.

33 The Forest Department provided for some revenue sharing and forest uses with local populations under a pilot scheme for comanagement. In Masindi, collaborative forest management is occurring in some communities around the Budongo Central Forest Reserve.

34 Ironically, the National Forest Authority (which replaced the Forest Department in 1998) reduced their staff in 2000, crippling their ability to manage forest resources effectively (Muhereza 2003: 7).

35 A similar story unfolded in Mali where the government gave new powers to local authorities but almost no territorial jurisdiction over which to exercise the newly granted powers (Ribot 1999).

36 Muhereza (2003: 33) points out that not all outcomes may be attributable uniquely to decentralization policies since many other socioeconomic changes are also ongoing in Uganda.

37 Arnold and Campbell (1986: 440–4).

38 Literally, a panchayat in rural south Asia refers to a decision-making collective or council of five persons. Many government regulations for rural organization building seek to empower such informally existing bodies, or to create them *de novo*. The actual membership of the council, usually an odd number, can comprise up to nine persons.

39 As with any policy of this kind, the manner of implementation of the law is sometimes more arbitrary and less participatory than it is at other times. A 1995 study of 419 "chairpersons" of forest committees uncovered that "most of them did not know if they were members of a forest committee, or what they were expected to do" (Britt 2000: 22).

40 There is an initiative currently under consideration to tax the revenue that user groups obtain under this program; see Mahapatra (2000: 7–8).
41 Based on Resosudarmo (2004).
42 APKASI is the Assosiasi Pemerintah Kabupaten Seluruh Indonesia (or, the Association of Regency Governments of Indonesia); APPSI is the Assosiasi Pemerintah Provinsi Indonesia (or, Association of Provincial Governments of Indonesia).
43 Senegal's previous "participatory" code produced an image of local inclusion under a system that effectively allowed the forest service to mobilize local labor in a kind of "participatory *corvée*" (Ribot 1995a).

## References

Adamolekun, L. (1991) "Promoting African Decentralization," *Public Administration and Development*, 22: 285–6.

Agrawal, A. (2001) "The Decentralizing State: The Nature and Origins of Changing Environmental Policies in Africa and Latin America," paper presented at the annual meeting of the American Political Science Association, 30 August to 2 September 2001.

—— (2004) *Decentralization of Resource Policies in the Developing World, 1980–2005*, book manuscript presented at the CHAOS-Cambridge University Press seminar series at University of Washington, Seattle, 8–9 May.

Agrawal, A., Britt, C. and Kanel, K. (1999) *Decentralization in Nepal: A Comparative Perspective*, San Francisco: ICS Press.

Agrawal A. and Ribot, J. C. (1999) "Accountability in Decentralization: A Framework with South Asian and West African Cases," *The Journal of Developing Areas*, 33/Summer: 473–502.

Arnold, J. and Campbell, G. (1986) "Collective Management of Hill Forests in Nepal: The Community Forestry Development Project," in *Proceedings of the Conference on Common Property Resource Management*, Washington, DC: National Research Council, National Academy Press, 425–54.

Bazaara, N. (2002a) "Ugandan Decentralisation and the Promise of Popular Participation in Environmental Management: *Byoya bya Nswa* (Form Without Substance)?," working paper draft, Decentralization, Accountability and the Environment Research Program, Institutions and Governance Program, World Resources Institute, January 2002.

—— (2002b) "Actors, Powers, and Environmental Accountability in Uganda's Decentralization," paper presented at the World Resources Institute's Workshop on Decentralization and the Environment, Bellagio, Italy, 18–22 February, 2002.

—— (2003) "Decentralization, Politics, and Environment in Uganda," *Environmental Governance in Africa Working Paper*, No. 7, Washington, DC: World Resources Institute.

Blair, H. (1998) "Spreading Power to the Periphery: An Assessment of Democratic Local Governance," *Program and Operations Assessment Report*, No. 21, Washington DC: USAID.

Booth, P. (1995) "Decentralization and Land-Use Planning in France: A 15-Year Review," *Policy and Politics*, 26/1: 89–105.

Brannstrom, C. (2004) "Decentralizing Water Resources Management in Brazil," *European Journal of Development Research*, 16/1: 214–34.

Breton, A. (1996) *Competitive Governments*, Cambridge: Cambridge University Press.

Britt, C. (2000) "Forestry and Forest Policies," working paper, Bloomington: Indiana University, Workshop in Political Theory and Policy Analysis.

Cowan, L. G. (1958) *Local Government in West Africa*, New York: Columbia University Press.

Curran, L. M., Trigg, S. N., McDonald, A. K., Astiani, D., Hardiono, Y. M., Siregar, P., Caniago, I. and Kasischke, E. (2004) "Lowland Forest Loss in Protected Areas in Indonesian Borneo," *Science*, 303/February: 1000–3.

Fairhead, J. and Leach, M. (1996) *Misreading the African Landscape: Society and Ecology in a Forest-Savanna Mosaic*, Cambridge: Cambridge University Press.

Fox, J. and Aranda, J. (1996) *Decentralization and Rural Development in Mexico: Community Participation in Oaxaca's Municipal Funds Program*, San Diego: Center for U.S.-Mexican Studies, University of California.

Heinen, J. and Kattel, B. (1992) "A Review of Conservation Legislation in Nepal: Past Progress and Future Needs," *Environmental Management*, 16: 723–33.

Larson, A. (2002) "Natural Resources and Decentralization in Nicaragua: Are Local Governments Up to the Job?," *World Development*, 30/1: 17–31.

—— (2004) "Formal Decentralization and the Imperative of Decentralization 'From Below': A Case Study of Natural Resource Management in Nicaragua," *European Journal of Development Research*, 16/1: 55–70.

Larson, A. and Ferroukhi, L. (2003) "Conclusiones," in L. Ferroukhi (ed.) *Gestion Forestal Municipal en America Latina*, Bogor, Indonesia: CIFOR/IDRC.

Larson, A. M. and Ribot, J. C. (2004) "Democratic Decentralization through a Natural Resource Lens: Countering Central Resistance, Fostering Local Demand," *European Journal of Development Research*, 16/1: 1–25.

Mahapatra, R. (2000) "Community Forest Management: The Nepalese Experience," *Down to Earth*, 8/9: 1–10.

Manor, J. (1999) *The Political Economy of Democratic Decentralization*, Washington, DC: The World Bank.

—— (2004) "User Committees: A Potentially Damaging Second Wave of Decentralization?," *European Journal of Development Research*, 16/1: 192–213.

Mapedza, E. and Mandondo, A. (2002) "Co-Management in the Mafungautsi State Forest Area of Zimbabwe – What Stake for Local Communities?," *Environmental Governance in Africa Working Paper #5*, Washington, DC: World Resources Institute.

Mawhood, P. (1983) *Local Government in the Third World*, Chichester: John Wiley.

Mearns, R. (2002) "The Consequences of Post-Socialist Transition and Decentralisation for Rural Livelihoods and Pasture Land Management in Mongolia," paper presented at the World Resources Institute Workshop on Decentralization and the Environment, Bellagio, Italy, 18–22 February.

—— (2004) "Decentralization, Rural Livelihoods, and Pasture-land Management in Post-Socialist Mongolia," *European Journal of Development Research*, 16/1: 133–52.

Muhereza, F. (2001) "Environmental Decentralization and the Management of Community Forests in Pakanyi Subcounty, Masindi District," draft report for the Programme on Decentralization and the Environment, WRI and Centre for Basic Research, Kampala, February.

—— (2003) "Commerce, Kings and Local Government in Uganda: Decentralizing Natural Resources to Consolidate the Central State," *Environmental Governance in Africa Working Paper Series #8*, Washington, DC: World Resources Institute.

Ntsebeza, L. (2002) "Decentralization and Natural Resource Management in Rural

South Africa: Problems and Prospects," paper submitted to the Conference on Decentralization and the Environment, Bellagio, Italy, 18–22 February 2002.

—— (2004) "Democratic Decentralization and Traditional Authority: Dilemmas of Land Administration in Rural Africa," *European Journal of Development Research*, 16/1: 71–89.

Nzouankeu, J. M. (1994) "Decentralization and Democracy in Africa," *International Review of Administrative Sciences*, 60: 214–15.

Oates, W. (1972) *Fiscal Federalism*, New York: Harcourt Brace Jovanovich.

OECD (Organization for Economic Cooperation and Development) (1997) *Evaluation of Programs Promoting Participatory Development and Good Governance: Synthesis Report*, OECD.

Ostrom, E., Schroeder, L. and Wynne, S. (1993) *Institutional Incentives and Sustainable Development: Infrastructure Policies in Perspective*, Boulder, CO: Westview.

RdS (République du Sénégal) (1993) Code Forestier, Loi No. 93-06 du 4 Fevrier 1993, Dakar, Senegal: Ministère du Développement Rural et de l'Hydraulique.

—— (1994) Projet de Décret Portant Code Forestier (Partie Reglementaire), Dakar, Senegal: Ministère du Développement Rural et de l'Hydraulique.

—— (1998) Code Forestier, Loi No. 98/03 du 8 Janvier 1998, Décret No. 98/164 du 20 Février 1998. Ministere de l'Environnement et de la Protection de la Nature, Direction des Eaux, Forêts, Chasse et de la Conservation des Sols.

Resosudarmo, I. and Pradnja, A. (2004) "Closer to People and Trees: Will Decentralisation Work for the People and the Forests of Indonesia?" *The European Journal of Development Research*, 16/1: 110–32.

Ribot, J. C. (1995a) "From Exclusion to Participation: Turning Senegal's Forestry Policy Around," *World Development*, 23/9: 1587–99.

—— (1995b) *Local Forest Control in Burkina Faso, Mali, Niger, Senegal and Gambia: A Review and Critique of New Participatory Policies*, Africa Region, World Bank.

—— (1996) "Participation without Representation: Chiefs, Councils and Forestry Law in the West African Sahel," *Cultural Survival Quarterly*, 20/1: 40–4.

—— (1998) "Theorizing Access: Forest Profits along Senegal's Charcoal Commodity Chain," *Development and Change*, 29: 307–41.

—— (1999) "Decentralization, Participation and Accountability in Sahelian Forestry: Legal Instruments of Political-Administrative Control," *Africa*, 69/1: 23–65.

—— (2000) "Rebellion, Representation and Enfranchisement in the Forest Villages of Makacoulibantang, Eastern Senegal," in C. Zerner (ed.) *People, Plants and Justice: The Politics of Nature Conservation*, New York: Columbia University Press.

—— (2002) *Democratic Decentralization of Natural Resources: Institutionalizing Popular Participation*, Washington, DC: World Resources Institute.

—— (2003) "Democratic Decentralization of Natural Resources: Institutional Choice and Discretionary Power Transfers in Sub-Saharan Africa," *Public Administration and Development*, 23/1: 53–65.

—— (2004) *Democratic Decentralization of Natural Resources: Encountering and Countering Resistance*, Washington, DC: World Resources Institute.

Ribot, J. C. and Larson, A. (eds) (2004) "Democratic Decentralization through a Natural Resource Lens: Experiences from Africa, Asia and Latin America," Special Issue, *European Journal of Development Research*, 16/1.

Ribot, J. C. and Oyono, P. R. (2004) "Resisting Democratic Decentralization in Africa: Some State and Elite Strategies for Holding onto Power," in C. Wisner, B. Toulmin and R. Chitiba (eds) *Toward a New Map of Africa*, London: Earthscan Press.

Rolla, G. (1998) "Autonomy: A Guiding Criterion for Decentralizing Public Administration," *International Review of Administrative Sciences*, 64: 27–39.

RoU (Republic of Uganda) (1987) *Commission of Inquiry into Local Government*, Republic of Uganda.

—— (1993) "The Local Government (Resistance Councils) Statute, 1993," *Uganda Gazette*, LXXXVI (55): December 31.

Saito, F. (2000) "Decentralisation in Uganda: Challenges for the 21st Century," paper presented at the workshop on Uganda, Institute of Commonwealth Studies, 7 April. Paper delivered at the Seminar Series, Centre for Basic Research, 25 May, University of London.

Secaira, E., Lehnhoff, A., Dix, A. and Rojas, O. (2001) *Delegating Protected Area Management to an NGO: The Case of Guatemala's Sierra de las Minas Biosphere Reserve*, Washington, DC: Biodiversity Support Program.

Smith, B. C. (1985) *Decentralization: The Territorial Dimension of the State*, London: George Allen.

Smoke, P. (1993) "Local Government Fiscal Reform in Developing Countries: Lessons from Kenya," *World Development*, 21/6: 901–23.

—— (1999) "Understanding Decentralization in Asia: An Overview of Key Issues and Challenges," *Regional Development Dialogue*, 20/2: 1–20.

Souza, C. (1996) "Redemocratization and Decentralization in Brazil: The Strength of Member States," *Development and Change*, 27/July: 529–55.

Thiaw, S. (2002) "Populations, Pouvoirs Locaux et Ressources Forestieres: Analyse comparative des cas des Communautés Rurales de Maka et Pata (Sénégal)," draft Report to World Resources Institute. Mimeo.

Thiaw, S. and Ribot, J. C. (2003) "Insiders Out: Forest Access through Villager Chiefs in Senegal," paper presented at the International Conference on Competing Jurisdictions: Settling Land Claims in Africa, Vrije Universiteit, Amsterdam, 24–27 September 2003.

Tiebout, C. (1956) "A Pure Theory of Local Expenditures," *Journal of Political Economy*, 64: 416–24.

Utting, P. (1998) "Biodiversity Protection and Action Research in Costa Rica," *UNRISD News*, 19: 1–4.

Vallejo, M. (2003) "Gestión Forestal Municipal: Una Nueva Alternativa para Honduras," in L. Ferroukhi (ed.) *La Gestion Forestal Municipal en America Latina*, Bogor, Indonesia: CIFOR/IDRC, 57–88.

Varughese, G. (2000) "Population and Forest Dynamics in the Hills of Nepal: Institutional Remedies by Rural Communities," in C. Gibson, M. A. McKean and E. Ostrom (eds) *People and Forests: Communities, Institutions, and Governance*, Cambridge: MIT Press, 193–227.

Webster, N. (1992) "Panchayati Raj in West Bengal: Popular Participation for the People or the Party?," *Development and Change*, 23/4: 129–63.

World Bank, The (1988) *World Development Report 1987–88*, New York: Oxford University Press.

—— (1997) *World Development Report 1997: The State in a Changing World*, Oxford: Oxford University Press.

Xu, J. (2002) "Decentralization and Accountability in Forest Management: A Trend and its Policies on 'Natural Forest Protection' and 'Upland Conversion'," paper presented at the World Resources Institute's Workshop on Decentralization and the Environment, Bellagio, Italy, 18–22 February, 2002.

# Index of authors

# Subject index

*For Product Safety Concerns and Information please contact our EU representative GPSR@taylorandfrancis.com Taylor & Francis Verlag GmbH, Kaufingerstraße 24, 80331 München, Germany*

T - #0078 - 160425 - C0 - 234/156/21 - PB - 9780415512749 - Gloss Lamination